Nijinsky's *Faune* Restored

Nijinsky's *Faune* Restored

A STUDY OF

VASLAV NIJINSKY'S 1915 DANCE SCORE

L'Après-midi d'un Faune

and

HIS DANCE NOTATION SYSTEM

Revealed, Translated into Labanotation and Annotated

by

ANN HUTCHINSON GUEST

and

CLAUDIA JESCHKE

The Noverre Press

First published in 1991

This edition published in 2010 by
The Noverre Press
Southwold House
Isington Road
Binsted
Hampshire
GU34 4PH

Copyright © 2010 by Ann Hutchinson Guest and Claudia Jeschke.

ISBN 978-1-906830-16-8

Cover Photo: Vaslav Nijinsky as the faun in the 1912 photograph by Baron Adolf de Meyer.

Photographs of the 1912 production of L'APRES-MIDI D'UN FAUNE by Baron Adolf de Meyer, reproduced by Richard Benson, courtesy of the Eakins Press Foundation. © the Eakins Press Foundation.
Photographs by Karl Struss (nos. 21, 22 in text) courtesy of the Amon Carter Museum, Fort Worth, Texas; all other Karl Struss photographs courtesy of The Collection of John and Susan Edwards Harvith.
Valentine Hugo Gross - Five sketches of Nijinsky 1912, © DACS 1990.
Vaslav Nijinsky notation excerpts by permission of the Estate of Vaslav Nijinsky. Reference British Library Manuscript: Add 47215 f.4.
Music score (E.1426.F.) by permission of Société des Editions Jobert, Paris.

All rights reserved. Permission for public performance must be obtained in writing from Ann Hutchinson Guest, Language of Dance Centre, 17 Holland Park, London W11 3TD, England and royalties paid to the Vaslav and Romola Nijinsky Foundation, 4925 North 43rd Street, Phoenix, Arizona 85018, U.S.A.

This book and all the research which

preceded it are lovingly dedicated to the

memory of

Vaslav Fomich Nijinsky

without whose belief in and dedication to dance notation

we would never have come to know this enchanting definitive

version of his first choreographic work -

L'Après-midi d'un Faune

CONTENTS

Introduction to the Series ix

Foreword xi

Acknowledgements xiii

Introduction to Nijinsky's *Faune* 1

Historical Background 3

Nijinsky's Production Notes 13

Study and Performance Notes
    Introduction to the Overall Style 17
    Details on Movement Style and Usage 21
    Casting 32
    Description of the Dance 33

Labanotation Glossary 47

Introduction to the Labanotation Score 55

Photographs and Sketches of Nijinsky's *Faune* 57

The Choreographic Score of Nijinsky's *L'Après-midi d'un Faune* 71

An Explanation of Vaslav Nijinsky's System of Dance Notation 141

Appendix A - Chronology of Nijinsky's Performances in the Rôle of *Faune* 177

Appendix B - Chronology of Nijinsky's Notation Experience 179

Appendix C - Nijinsky's Word Notes 180

Appendix D - Teaching Notes 182

Appendix E - Transcription - Adjustments Made 192

Appendix F - Bibliography
    Nijinsky's *Faune* 195
    Nijinsky's Notation System 197

Index 198

INTRODUCTION TO THE SERIES

The *Language of Dance Series* aims to expand the literature of dance through publication of key works that cover a range of dance styles and dance periods.

A language is spoken, written and read. Those intimately involved in the study and performance of dance will have experienced the language of dance in its "spoken" form, i.e., when it is danced. During the years spent in mastering dance, the component parts are discovered and become part of one's dance language. Through its written form these component parts, the 'building blocks' common to all forms of dance become clear, as well as how these blocks are used. The study of the Language of Dance incorporates these basic elements and the way they are put together to produce choreographic sentences. How the movement sequences are performed, the manner of "uttering" them, rests on the individual's interpretation.

Through careful selection of appropriate movement description, these gems of dance heritage have been translated into Labanotation, the highly developed method of analyzing and recording movement.

In the *Language of Dance Series* understanding of the material is enriched through study and performance notes which provide an aid in exploring the movement sequences and bringing the choreography to life. Whenever possible there is included historical background to place the work in context, and additional information of value to researchers and dance scholars.

Dr. Ann Hutchinson Guest, Editor

REHEARSING WITH LES GRANDS BALLETS CANADIENS

(Courtesy of *The Globe and Mail*, Toronto, Canada)

Claudia Jeschke and Ann Hutchinson Guest confer over a detail in the dance score.

Ann Hutchinson Guest demonstrates to Pedro Barrios how the faun holds and relates to the nymph's dress.

(Courtesy of *The Globe and Mail*, Toronto, Canada)

FOREWORD

The image of Nijinsky which surfaces most often in the mind of today's devotees of the ballet is of a rose-costumed figure soaring from view in a leap from which no descent seems imaginable. Except to a tiny handful of very ancient survivors, this mental picture is no longer a direct memory but has been handed down, mostly by the written word. Nijinsky the dancer belongs, rightly, to legend, but this book raises a curtain on another aspect of this remarkable artist, an aspect in which the mind and the intellect are supreme.

Nijinsky's contribution to the development of choreography has been assessed by numerous biographers and historians, but all have lacked access to the sole primary source - his own written record of his first work and the sole ballet of his to survive, *L'Après-midi d'un Faune*. Written very shortly after its creation in the system of notation which he himself developed, this precious manuscript has lain in the British Library for forty years, the donation of his widow. Until recently it was little more than a curiosity for no one was able to read it. It awaited its Champollion, and only now, thanks to the persevering efforts of the authors of this book, can it at last be read. It is difficult to overstate the importance of their discovery, for not only has it revealed in clearest detail the choreography of *Faune* as Nijinsky himself conceived it, but it also offers the most direct and compelling evidence of the innovative nature of his dance composition, so revolutionary in its time that one can understand the shock waves it created.

Until now *Faune* has been handed down by memory, a procedure rendered necessary in the absence of the choreographer himself or any available notated record. One has frequently heard of dancers who claim perfect recall of ballets in which they have danced, and one is entitled to ask, "How perfect is perfect?" Everyone knows how memory can at times play false, how an event can appear different when seen from another viewpoint or by other eyes, and so it must be with remembering a ballet; indeed even more so when so much depends on accuracy of the movement and its dynamics. A memory-based version of an old ballet can therefore only approximate the original or later version to which the particular reconstruction relates, and in the case of *Faune* such versions are no less than third-hand. With Nijinsky's score now translated, the extent of the loss of accuracy can be ascertained, and by comparing it with film and video recordings made at various times we can see how much of the original subtlety of the movement and the individual characterisation have been lost or watered down, and how far the choreography has diverged from the clear reflection of Debussy's languorously evocative music which Nijinsky so successfully achieved.

The notated score of Nijinsky's choreography for *Faune* forms only the core of the study which is presented in this book. Recounted in an early chapter is the story of the decipherment itself, an exercise in detection which must excite the imagination of all who are intrigued by the solving of mysteries. This achievement has resulted not only in the ability to read Nijinsky's score but also the revelation of his own system of notation, which can be recognised beyond dispute as an extraordinary intellectual achievement. The collection of photographs of the ballet included in this book, which complements the score by recapturing the period flavor of the early performances under Nijinsky's direction, forms an exceptionally

FOREWORD

comprehensive iconographical record for its time. Although many of these were taken in the studio, all faithfully reproduce actual moments from the choreography, as reference to the score makes abundantly clear.

In sum this work is not a dry academic exposition, but a work which should interest and inform at many different levels. It is, above all, a comprehensive practical record on which scholarship of impressive scope sits lightly. With working notes on such aspects as style and casting, and a word description for those less versed in notation it enables the ballet not only to be studied in hitherto unattainable depth but also to be staged with a very high degree of authenticity. It remains to be seen whether respect for Nijinsky's original conception will seal the fate of the corrupted versions with which we have been accustomed for so long.

Ivor Guest

ACKNOWLEDGEMENTS

This book has been the result of much individual help during the whole process from the first tentative research to the final production. It would be difficult to pinpoint the sequence or the degree in which various people and institutions gave us help, so we shall list them under the specific activities.

Background Research: Research on Nijinsky's ballet *L'Après-midi d'un Faune* involved background history, reviews, bibliography, chronology of performances and photographic evidence. We wish to thank Madeleine Nichols and Dorothy Lourdou of the Library of the Performing Arts in New York City for access to photographs and videos. Martine Kahane at the Bibliothèque de l'Opéra was most helpful in a similar way. Francesca Franchi searched the Covent Garden Archives on our behalf. The British Library music department gave assistance regarding the possible existence of another version of Debussy's score. Jane Pritchard, curator of the Rambert Archive, provided a copy of the 1931 film of *Faune* for us to study. Jean-Michel Nectoux at the Musée d'Orsay, archivists of London Festival Ballet, American Ballet Theater, and the Joffrey Ballet all responded with information on performances of *Faune*. Joan Acocella alerted us to the existence of the Karl Struss 1916 photographs of *Faune* and was most helpful in assisting us in obtaining copies of the ones appropriate to illustrate the score. Claire de Robilant most generously searched through her archives for reviews and dates of South American performances and translated several pieces from Spanish and Portuguese. Nesta MacDonald gave us access to her research files on Diaghilev reviews and the benefit of her extensive knowledge of the period. Susan Baker, who was researching *Faune* herself at the time for her degree project at Middlesex Polytechnic shared clippings and other information.

For sparing time for personal interviews we extend thanks to William Chappell, Tamara Finch, Dame Alicia Markova, Lady Menuhin (Diana Gould) and Elizabeth Schooling.

In gathering materials in connection with the deciphering of Nijinsky's system we are grateful to Irina Nijinska who was able to give us additional materials from her mother's archives. In relation to Nijinsky's later notation ideas (1917-18) we are indebted to Noa Eshkol for so generously providing us with the research she and members of the Movement Notation Centre in Tel Aviv had undertaken some years before. The Russian text in Nijinsky's score was translated by Jan Jirousek with additional assistance from Irina Kirillova. Thanks are also due to Gaby Vetterman who helped to collect the dates for the chronology of Nijinsky's performances in *Faune*.

Transcription: The Labanotation score has undergone several stages. The first literal transcription from Nijinsky's notation needed translating into our more familiar 'tongue'. Our desire to keep as much as possible the flavor of Nijinsky's description proved problematic. Having been obviously too close to the score and to the movement we welcomed outside readers. Professor Rhonda Ryman at Waterloo University, whose students learned the ballet with and through the score, provided many helpful comments. One of this group, Elizabeth Kettle, followed through by overseeing a production of the work, writing a diary of the reconstruction process which raised many pertinent questions. The most stringent testing of the score took place in New York City where members of the Juilliard Dance Ensemble under the direction of Dr Jill Beck, learned their parts solely from the Labanotation score. Her comments and those from the dancers pointed clearly to where the score needed to be more detailed. Through such trial by very different groups the score was tested and strengthened.

Performance: Bringing the ballet to life has also undergone stages both in clarification of the details of movement coordinations and the best way to teach the sequences. We must express great thanks to Dame Merle Park, director of the Royal Ballet School, London, for providing the opportunity to work with William Glassman's third year repertory class in the first piecing together of the ballet. The opportunity given by Beppe Menegatti to mount the ballet in Naples for the special Nijinsky centenary program was a valuable experience. Our thanks go also to Colin McIntyre, director of Les Grands Ballets Canadiens, for deciding to include the ballet in the company's second Diaghilev program. The experience of working with the Juilliard Dance Ensemble gave additional confidence in knowing that the score could come to life so faithfully and successfully and in revealing the wealth of motivation and concepts to be gleaned from the movement contexts and relationships.

Support for the Project: The deciphering of Nijinsky's notation system and the transcription of his score into Labanotation was made possible through a grant from the National Endowment for the Humanities and additional funding from the L. J. Skaggs and Mary C. Skaggs Foundation in the U.S.A. As we were not able to promise success from the start we are particularly grateful for their support. A generous contribution from Lincoln Kirstein made it possible to include photographs as valuable visual images in the capturing of the style. We are grateful to the Eakins Press, New York City, to the Amon Carter Museum, Fort Worth, Texas, and to John and Susan Edwards Harvith for permission to reproduce the photographs without fee. Our thanks go to Kyra and Tamara Nijinsky for permission to use excerpts from Nijinsky's score to illustrate the explanations of his notation system and to the British Library Rare Manuscripts Department for assistance in procuring a clear copy of his score.

Presentation: Clarity in expression, particularly for the verbal description of the choreography, was carefully scrutinized by Juli Nunlist for whose valuable suggestions we are most grateful. Ray Cook provided welcome guidance in the early stages of the score as well as his eagle proofreading eye in spotting inconsistencies in the final draft.

Production: The whole project as well as the preparation of this book would have taken four times as long were it not for the devoted work of the staff at the Language of Dance Centre: Edna Geer, Nancy Harlock, Rob van Haarst, Régine Charrière, Zoe Hill and in particular, Jane Whitear Dulieu. Not to be overlooked is my patient and supportive husband, Ivor Guest, whose excellent dance library was much used and who helped in numerous other ways. We hope this book will be enjoyed by all as much as we have enjoyed working on it.

* * * * * * * *

The autography for the Labanotation score has been produced by Jane Whitear Dulieu on CALABAN, the Computer Aided Labanotation system developed by Andy Adamson at Birmingham University, UK.

INTRODUCTION TO NIJINSKY'S *FAUNE*

The lack of a definitive recording of Nijinsky's ballet *L'Après-midi d'un Faune* during the seven decades and more since its premiere in 1912 resulted in a range of versions being handed down from memory. Some attempted a faithful recreation of the original, others obviously took liberties in the casting and range of movement: witness the Paolo Bortoluzzi version with twelve supporting nymphs performing *grands jetés en tournant*. If memory is the sole source then we must be grateful to it for allowing us some idea of the ballet. But what survived in memory, the structure? The story line? The style? (bolstered usually by Adolf de Meyer's photographs?) Acquaintance with the choreography as Nijinsky himself recorded it (hereafter called Nijinsky's *Faune*) reveals startling and disturbing differences in both structure and style. The memory-based versions should no longer be labelled as choreography by Nijinsky, but as choreography **after** Nijinsky - and in many cases **long** after.

We now have a definitive version of *Faune*, Nijinsky's version as he himself recorded it in his own dance notation system, which has proved to be highly efficient in capturing the many specific details in the choreography. The question that arises is how close his written score is to the 1912 choreography. Did he remember the choreography exactly? Did he make changes, intentionally introducing new ideas? The chief source of evidence that he did not intentionally make changes is the collection of photographs by de Meyer, Bert and Struss. De Meyer and Bert photographed the ballet soon after its first presentation; Struss' collection was taken in 1916 in the U.S.A. Most of the poses captured on film were found in Nijinsky's score, a few were not. Were these latter posed especially for the camera? Or had Nijinsky forgotten them? One such pose is of the six attending nymphs in two groups of three. The placement of limbs and heads is very different from a moment in the score when two groups of three nymphs take a pose. In the score the six nymphs appear to have become inattentive and have wandered off, away from the chief nymph. As though reminded that they have a task to perform, they retrace their steps and sink into a pose with heads bowed, a pose which suggests a sense of shame and hence is referred to in rehearsals as the 'apology'. Immediately afterward they return to center stage to attend the chief nymph who has been waiting for them. In the photograph of the two trios each nymph has a different pose. No suggestion of an apology is conveyed; the arrangement appears to be simply an architectural design. Did Nijinsky decide to give this pose more meaning? Where, indeed, in the choreography did the pose in that photograph occur? In some memory-based versions it appears on music passages other than that indicated in the score. Apart from the key events which are easy to relate directly to the music score, other moments could not be musically pinned down; thus with no guide the reconstructors working from memory had a hard time knowing when certain actions took place.

Nijinsky made clear when specific actions occured by adding word notes in his score adjacent to movements appropriate to such actions. It is possible that Nijinsky could have forgotten exactly how many steps the nymphs or the faun took at certain moments. In measure 44 N1 and N2 have more steps than are needed to travel toward stage left; N4 has a greater distance to travel and could have used more steps. Through careful rehearsing the dancers learn to travel appropriately and the desired result is achieved without changing what Nijinsky wrote. On measure 92 N2 has four fast steps to enter and eight equally fast steps to exit. The same holds true for N6's entrance and exit on 93. Why this discrepancy in number of steps?

Does each move urgently toward the faun, covering ground, and then hold back on exiting, taking smaller steps because of a desire to linger? Such an explanation fits the expression provided by the head, torso and arms.

Reassurance that Nijinsky recorded his 1912 choreography is reinforced by the discovery of a previously unpublished de Meyer photograph. In one moment in the score a seemingly unlikely crossing of arms for four nymphs holding hands was proved to be correct. Regarding the pictures with poses not found in the *Faune* score, the full face pose of the faun holding the grapes is taken to be a study of Nijinsky and not an audience view of the faun. In his score Nijinsky has the faun only looking at the grapes; he does not "devour" them, or "drink the juice", as stated by his sister Bronislava in her *Early Memoirs*, and as followed in some productions. If the grapes were drunk, why did de Meyer not catch this moment, rather than the less dramatic moment of the faun's simply looking at them?

Having considered the question of choreographic content and found considerable evidence which points to the conclusion that the score very closely expresses the 1912 choreography, we must turn to the question of style in the ballet's performance. The memory-based versions contain many sharp, almost aggressive movements, gestures which 'hit' the air. The nymphs 'freeze', there is a noticeable lack of femininity in their poses and movements. The ballet clearly features stylized movements but should the gestures be so harsh?

Let us take first the question of sharpness, suddenness. There are many quick movements, particularly for the feet, but for none of them has Nijinsky added a strong accent sign, such as would appear in his music-based notation system. Arm, head and torso movements are written with quarter- or half-notes (crotchets or minims). The slower notes allow some movement duration to take place and also indicate the moment of arrival on the beat. Once a position is reached it is usually held. In a few instances Nijinsky wrote sustained arm gestures covering several beats, a duration not seen in memory-based versions. Absence in his score of both suddenness and strong dynamics suggests that the sharpness and force of memory-based versions are not Nijinsky's ideas.[1]

A study of the de Meyer photographs reveals flatness for the hands and upper body but absence of tension. The hands of the nymphs are feminine: they are not rigid; arm muscles are not tense but show a normal balance between tension and relaxation. No sense of strain is evident in the photographs. In the course of the ballet moments of heightened animation result from the movement context and the dynamics of the music; the ballet is by no means all on one level. Proof of this conclusion lies in the subtle change in dynamics when the attending nymphs hold their heads in a normal way, (when they are 'off duty') and when they hold their heads in the 'alert' position (when they are 'on duty' serving the chief nymph) - for the latter the back of the neck is lengthened, with a resulting minor upward shift of the crown of the head and a very slight lowering of the chin. This head position is clearly seen in the photographs. Combining the stylistic details evident in the photographs with the features derived from the carefully indicated timing in the score, one arrives at a softer, more flowing style of performance than that seen in memory-based versions.

---

[1] See the quote on page 18 from the *New York Times*, October 1916.

HISTORICAL BACKGROUND

As a dancer Vaslav Nijinsky established a reputation which was to become an enduring legend. His wide popular acclaim succeeded in restoring the position of the male dancer after years of its decline in Western Europe. He was also recognized as an innovative choreographer who in the span of a few years established an important break with the classical genre and developed new possibilities seen today as the basis of modernism in dance.

Nijinsky choreographed only four ballets, all of which left their mark in the minds of those who saw them and on the world of dance. Of these, only his first creation, *L'Après-midi d'un Faune*, has survived through being handed down by memory. His larger, more extensive work, *Le Sacre du Printemps*, in which he himself did not dance, can now be seen through the reconstruction resulting from years of painstaking research by Millicent Hodson and Kenneth Archer.

Although in terms of duration and the number of dancers employed *Faune* was conceived on a smaller scale, it was the work with which Nijinsky was identified most of all. Ironically, while it was to be the only one of his ballets to survive in memory-based versions, the choreography which he so painstakingly recorded in his own system of notation lay unread in the British Library until it was deciphered by the present authors.

The score of *Faune* survives as an authentic record of Nijinsky's creative genius, a primary research source which illustrates the use of his system of notation and movement analysis, documents *Faune*'s original movement sequences and offers insight into his concept of theatrical dance composition. Not only is the score the most reliable point of departure for reconstruction, but its study also reveals Nijinsky's personal approach to dance, an approach unique both in its complexity and in its relationship to his art.

I.   NIJINSKY'S EARLY CAREER

In 1898 at the age of eight Vaslav Nijinsky entered the ballet school of the Imperial Theatres in St. Petersburg. The school's curriculum reflected traditional classical dancing; dancers and choreographers from Italy, France and Denmark imported their knowledge of ballet technique and style to the classroom and, in addition to creating new works, produced established ballets for the company of the Maryinsky. Although at the turn of the century ballet was in a decline in Western Europe, with the Tsar's support it flourished in Russia.

Nijinsky was not entirely inexperienced as a performer when he entered the ballet school. At four, Vaslav, born in 1890 in Kiev, and his elder brother Stanislav, born in 1886 in Tiflis, had begun to receive instruction in ballet from their father, dancer Thomas Lavrientievitch Nijinsky, and they appeared on stage in short dance numbers. Their mother, Eleonora Nicolaevna Bereda, was also a dancer, and the youngest member of the Nijinsky performing brood, Bronislava, born in Minsk in 1891, entered the ballet school of the Maryinsky in 1900, two years after her brother.

As was the custom, Nijinsky participated in school performances and also appeared occasionally as an extra in the Maryinsky productions. Obviously gifted, he had been offered membership in the Maryinsky Company while still a pupil, but his mother vetoed the proposal. When he finished his schooling on 20 May 1907, he became a regular member of the company.

In the Maryinsky company Nijinsky made an immediate impression on choreographer Mikhail Fokine. For example, he created the rôle of the Slave of Armide in Fokine's *Le Pavillon d'Armide* during his first year. While visiting a rehearsal of this same ballet in 1908, impresario Serge Diaghilev became so taken with the dancing and the person of Vaslav Nijinsky that he made him his protégé, and, one year later, the star of his new touring company, the Ballets Russes.

During the 1909 debut season of the 'Ballets Russes de Serge de Diaghilev' at the Théâtre du Châtelet in Paris, Nijinsky appeared in four major and most successful Fokine ballets: *Le Pavillon d'Armide* and *Le Festin* were premiered on 19 May and *Les Sylphides* (formerly entitled *Chopiniana*) and *Cléopâtre* were first presented on 4 June. The company was received with extraordinary enthusiasm and Nijinsky was an overnight sensation. He established his status as the star of the company during the next two seasons in further Fokine rôles: as the Golden Slave in *Schéhérazade*, premiered in Paris on 4 June 1910; in *Spectre de la Rose*, premiered on 19 April 1911, and in *Petrouchka*, given for the first time on 13 June 1911.

Choreographer

In 1912 Nijinsky choreographed his first ballet, *L'Après-midi d'un Faune*. According to his sister Bronislava, he had begun to deliberate the project as early as 1910 during an extended holiday with herself and Bakst in Carlsbad, and afterwards, with Diaghilev and Bakst in Venice and Paris. Bronislava also reports Nijinsky's comments on his choreographic ideas:

"I want to move away from the classical Greece that Fokine likes to use. Instead, I want to use the archaic Greece that is less known and, so far, little used in the theatre. However, this is only to be the source of my inspiration. I want to render it my own way. Any sweetly sentimental line in the form or in the movement will be excluded. More may even be borrowed from Assyria than Greece. I have already started to work on it in my own mind..."[1]

Back in St. Petersburg in December 1910, Nijinsky explored the rôles of the faun and the chief nymph with his sister, and *Faune*'s general theme was sketched; it was to be an evocation of archaic Greece to the music of Debussy's *Prélude à l'Après-midi d'un Faune*. Bronislava summarised her impressions of this period in her diary:

"I see that Vaslav has found something new and monumental in choreographic art, and is uncovering a field entirely unknown up to now in either Dance or Theatre. I cannot yet define these new paths and discoveries, but I know and feel that they are there. Not long ago Fokine freed himself from the old classical school and the captivity of Petipa's choreography, and now Vaslav is freeing himself from the captivity of Fokine's choreography so that, again, we enter a new phase in our Art. ...."[2]

---

[1] Nijinska, Bronislva, *Early Memoirs*, p. 315, New York, 1981.

[2] Ibid., p. 327.

In the spring of 1912 the ballet went into production: Nijinsky cast himself as the faun, his sister Bronislava as the joyful (fourth) nymph and Lydia Nelidova as the chief (fifth) nymph. After 120 rehearsals *Faune* was premiered on 29 May 1912 in Paris at the Théâtre du Châtelet.

The performance caused a storm of controversy. Heated discussion revolved around the sexually overt final movements of the faun and his symbolic union with a nymph's veil at the close of the ballet. (Nijinsky appears subsequently to have modified this controversial ending.) What was truly daring about the work went unobserved in the tumult of unbridled emotional reaction: its fresh dramatization of the 'faun and nymphs' motif transcended the bucolic and suggested a playful attic romp; Nijinsky's novel way of interrelating movement and music produced short movement phrases culminating in frieze-like tableaux that contrasted with Debussy's fluid music; above all, Nijinsky's choreographic concept departed from traditional theatrical precepts of scenic representation and audience response.

Maturity

The period which began with the choreography of *Faune* might be classified as Nijinsky's 'coming of age' on several levels. He continued to choreograph, and premiered two new ballets in 1913: *Jeux*, on 15 May, and, even more provocative than *Faune* in its reduction of form, *Le Sacre du Printemps*, on 28 May, both at the Théâtre des Champs Elysées in Paris.

On 10 September of the same year in Buenos Aires he married the young socialite Romola de Pulszky during the company's tour in South America. Afraid of crossing the ocean, Diaghilev had refused to accompany the tour. Romola, an aristocrat and daughter of the famous Hungarian actress, Emilia Markus, had become enamored of Nijinsky, whom she had first seen dance in Budapest. She had proceeded to follow the company's tours at her own expense as a private pupil of the company's balletmaster Enrico Cecchetti, and it was during the Atlantic crossing that she became engaged to Nijinsky. She ultimately danced one of the nymphs in the *Faune* performances during this South American tour.

When Diaghilev, furious at losing control over Nijinsky, discharged the newlyweds toward the close of 1913, Nijinsky found himself unemployed and entirely on his own as an artist for the first time in his life. He set about establishing his own ballet company in collaboration with his sister and her husband. The 'Saison Nijinsky' was premiered at London's Palace Theatre on 2 March 1914 for an eight-week season, but Nijinsky contracted influenza and the management cancelled the rest of the engagement.

Soon after his daughter Kyra was born on 19 June 1914 in Vienna, Nijinsky visited Romola's family in Budapest. With the outbreak of World War I, as a Russian national he was considered to be an enemy alien and was put under house arrest. He filled his time by working on his notation system, and in August/September 1915 he wrote the final draft of the score of *L'Après-midi d'un Faune*. It is interesting to note that the Hungarian police suspected his notations to be a secret code.

Decline

The troubling final chapter of Nijinsky's professional life included a long, ill-fated American tour with the Ballets Russes in 1916-17. When he arrived in New York City in the spring of 1916 to join the company, he at first refused to dance in *Faune*, regarding it as no longer representing his initial choreography. After additional rehearsals had taken place, however, he finally reappeared in the ballet in October. His last ballet, *Till Eulenspiegel*, was premiered on 23 October 1916 at the Manhattan Opera House, New York City. On 26 September 1917 he finished the tour with a performance in Buenos Aires; it was to be the last time he appeared on stage. Returning to Europe, he took up residence in St. Moritz, Switzerland, where he began writing his diary and continued to work on notation ideas, documenting the results in four copybooks. Nijinsky himself referred to this period of his life as a very significant and productive one. In a letter in 1918 to Reynaldo Hahn, he wrote:

"I work, I compose new dances and I am perfecting the system of dance notation, which I have invented in these last years. I am very happy to have found this notation, which for centuries has been searched for, because I believe, and I am sure, my dear friend, you will agree, that this notation is indispensable for the development of the art of the dance. It is a simple and logical means to note down movements. In a word, this system will provide the same service for the artists of the dance that musical notes give to musicians.[3]

On 19 January 1919 Nijinsky announced a recital for the benefit of the Red Cross in the ballroom of the Suvretta Hotel in St. Moritz. The spectators were filled with growing alarm as he danced his 'marriage with God'. After this event he underwent psychiatric examination. The diagnosis was schizophrenia.

II. NIJINSKY'S MOVEMENT NOTATION

It is rare for a prominent choreographer to become fluent in notation and to record a complete ballet. Choreographers have frequently recorded their works in some form of *aide-memoire* - for example, Bournonville - but Nijinsky had only one predecessor who recorded his choreography in a more detailed, sophisticated system: Saint-Léon. Both men were too busy with their professional careers to promote or make full use of their systems. As we have seen, Nijinsky was only able to give notation his full attention while away from dance during World War I and living in Switzerland in 1917-18.

The notebooks he filled in 1917-18 are not, however, directly relevant to his work on *Faune* a few years earlier in 1915. In the *Faune* score, the positions of body parts are recorded on a five-line grid; only three lines are employed in the notebooks of three years later. Furthermore, the system used in the notebooks appears to be concerned with another manner of conceiving and portraying directional movement, possibly akin to the geometric, graphic concepts seen later in other systems. The notebooks also disclose an obsession with the circle that increased as his illness progressed.

---

[3] Hahn, Reynaldo, *Expositions des Ballets Russes*, in Le Figaro, p. 5, 6th April 1939.

The method of notation used by Nijinsky in his score of *Faune* has similarities to the Stepanov system which he had learnt at ballet school. Vladimir Ivanovitch Stepanov's system, which had been adopted into the curricula of the Imperial Schools in St. Petersburg and Moscow, was built on an anatomical movement analysis and used adapted music notes to indicate movements. The method had been adequate for recording the ballet repertoire of the period, but Nijinsky modified and elaborated it according to his unprecedented scoring needs. Although his system remains close to Stepanov's concept, Nijinsky's notation could not be deciphered by following Stepanov's rules and usages. There is no evidence that Nijinsky produced an explanation of the 1915 version of his system. Thus, the contents of his score of *Faune* were inaccessible and Nijinsky's own documentation of the movements of his first ballet was considered lost to posterity. After his death Romola gave the score of *Faune* to the British Library. It was to be 74 years before this score, written in 1915, was to 'come to life' in a theatrical performance.

III. DECIPHERING NIJINSKY'S *FAUNE*

How did this circumstance come about? Although Romola claimed that Nijinsky had taught her his notation system, she was obviously unfamiliar with it and sought help from others in order to prepare the notation notebooks for publication and to read the *Faune* score for stage production. She handed Madame Nicolaeva Legat the task of organising the contents of the notebooks, providing her with a French translation of Nijinsky's original Russian notes. When Madame Legat gave a lecture on Nijinsky's system for the British Dance and Movement Notation Society in 1956, she was at a loss to explain the notation's practical application, never having used the system herself. When she asked for help, Ann Hutchinson Guest, who was present, offered her assistance. In becoming acquainted with the material, Ann soon realised that Nijinsky had been working with at least two concepts simultaneously. With Romola's permission she obtained a copy of the *Faune* score. Applying the contents of the notebooks to the score proved fruitless and she virtually reached a dead end. Having been advised that Marie Rambert "knew the ballet well", Ann sought her aid. Rambert's memory was visual: she knew if the movement was 'right' when she saw it, but could not describe the positions or sequence of events. She failed to tell Ann, and others later concerned with this research who sought her aid, that there existed a silent black-and-white film made in 1931 when Leon Woizikowski mounted the ballet for her company. During the next two decades Ann returned to the project again and again trying to find another point of view, another approach to the way in which Nijinsky might have analyzed movement in general and, specifically, the movements in *Faune*.

Hearing of Noa Eshkol's work in movement notation in the early 1970s, Romola enlisted her help and provided her with copies of all four of Nijinsky's original notebooks. After arranging to have the Russian text translated into English, Noa and her colleagues spent nearly two years trying to make sense of the notes. They also arrived at the conclusion that Nijinsky seemed to be working on two different versions. Certainly no functioning system emerged, let alone one which could be helpful in deciphering the code he used in the *Faune* score.

In 1974 Romola met Claudia Jeschke, who was then working on dance notation systems for her doctoral thesis and wanted to include Nijinsky's system. At the time Romola was unwilling to supply her with any information. In 1976, however, she invited Claudia to attend rehearsals of *Faune* at the Paris Opéra. Romola and Léonide Massine were attempting to remember the choreography using Baron Adolf de Meyer's 1912 photographs as a source. Since, in Romola's opinion, Massine "was doing everything wrong", she urgently wanted Claudia to read the *Faune* score in order to save Nijinsky's work. She made a copy of the *Faune* score as well as of the French translation of the notebooks available to Claudia, who soon came up against the same stumbling blocks as had Ann Hutchinson Guest and Noa Eshkol. It was at this stage, in 1984, that, Noa having bowed out, Ann and Claudia, hearing of each other's work, decided to join forces. They applied for a grant from the National Endowment for the Humanities in Washington D.C. When the grant finally came through in 1987 they were able to speed up the process of deciphering the system. A grant from the L. J. Skaggs and Mary C. Skaggs Foundation contributed to completion of the project.

The 'Rosetta Stone' Materials

The key to the movement content of the score, inaccessible for nearly three-quarters of a century, was found through examination of additional Nijinsky notation materials deposited by Romola at the library of the Paris Opéra. These documents, which employed the same five-line grid that he used to score *Faune*, were transcriptions of Cecchetti classroom exercises and reproductions of the poses in figure groupings from Luca Della Robbia's celebrated Cantoria. Nijinsky had come across pictures of these latter in the catalogue of Kunstanstalt Gerber in Cologne. Since the Cecchetti exercises remain familiar, their notation provided a first breakthrough in deciphering Nijinsky's system. After photographs of the *bas relief* tablets of the Cantoria had been obtained, those corresponding to Nijinsky's notation were identified. These proved to be a useful source of substantiation as they provided naturalistic poses not included in the ballet vocabulary. His notation materials also included the starting positions and the first opening movement of a group dance entitled *Sarabande*, probably part of *Les Ballets Inachevés*, which Nijinsky planned to choreograph to music by Johann Sebastian Bach.

Revival of Nijinsky's *Faune*

Nijinsky had notated *Faune* in great detail. Only in a few areas were usages unclear. The clues to the solution of these particular notation problems were revealed in the photographs of the ballet taken by Baron Adolf de Meyer soon after its premiere. Photos of later performances (by Karl Struss, for example) were also studied. The many verbal instructions that Nijinsky had written into the score, indicating exactly when certain actions were to take place, were translated into English and proved to be of invaluable help in making sense of the gestures. He had also included five floor plans in the score to indicate the precise spatial relationships of the dancers to the performing area and to each other. The fact that he had outlined three further plans and the absence of the rest of the plans needed for the ballet indicated that the score was never completely finished.

Extensive background research was added to the essential task of reading and interpreting the score. To understand the ballet's history and reconstruct its style, the researchers studied books, personal reminiscences, reviews in Europe, the United States and South America and also undertook personal interviews.

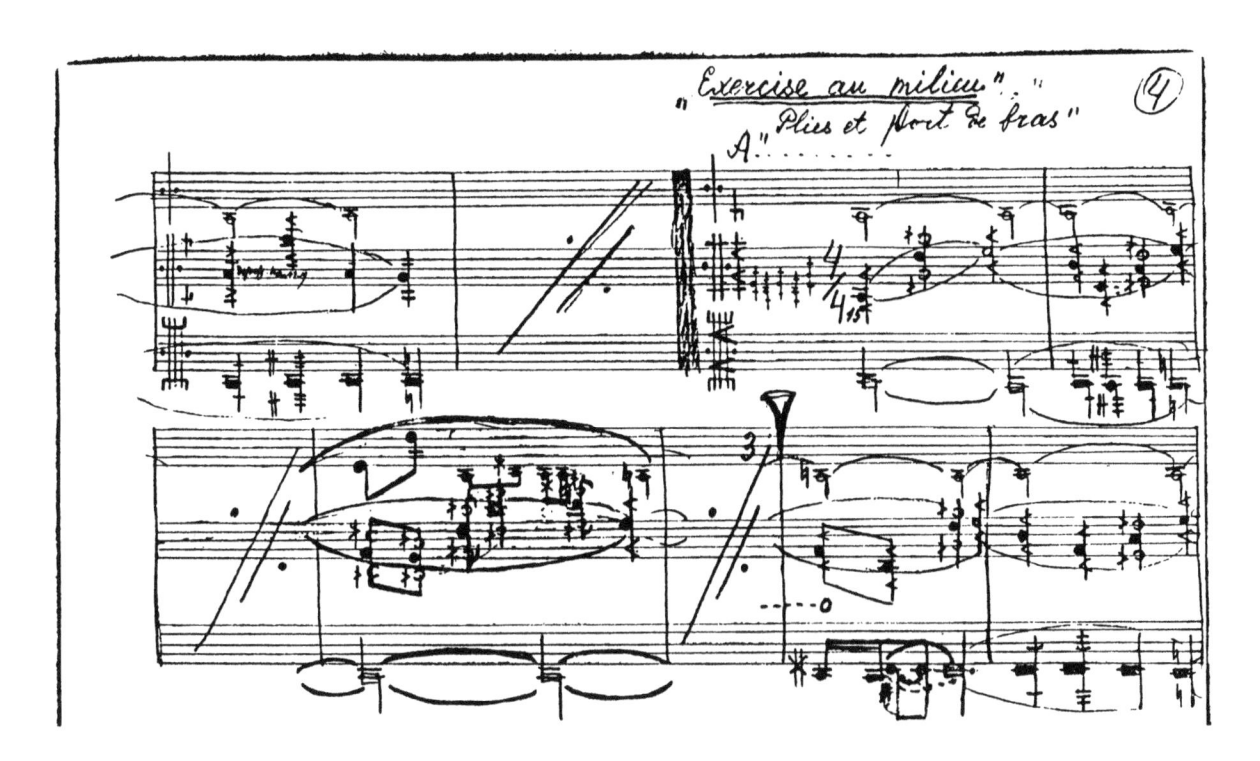

Example of Nijinsky's notation of Cecchetti classical ballet technique

A section of the opening position of *Sarabande*.
The floor plan is drawn from the audience point of view.

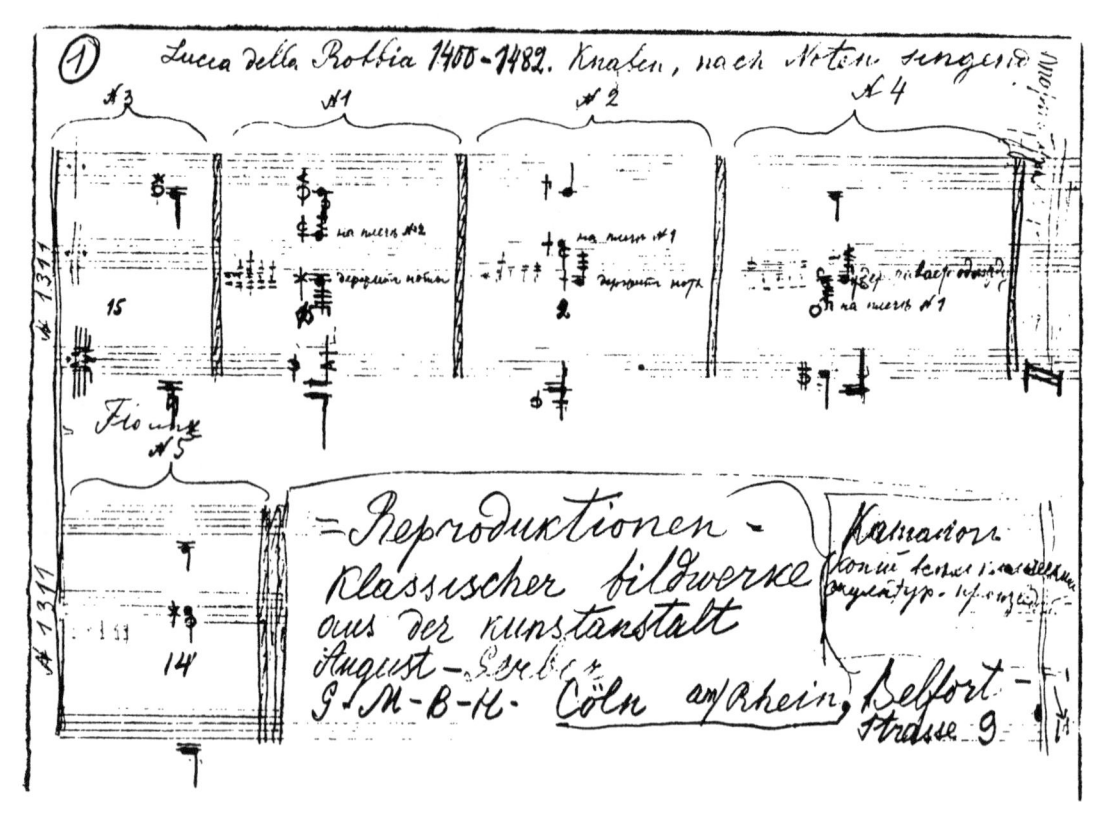

Nijinsky's notations of the individual poses of group no. 1311 from the Luca Della Robbia Cantoria, the position of each individual being clearly marked.

Productions of the Ballet

It is interesting to note that the materials and information needed to decipher Nijinsky's score of *Faune* were actually available during all those years; Romola merely failed to set about the task in an organised way by informing those concerned of all the sources. Nevertheless, after this long period of scattered efforts, Nijinsky's notation system was finally decoded and his score of *Faune* transcribed, symbol by symbol, into Labanotation. The first working score was finished in spring 1988, and with Dame Merle Park's permission the choreography was tried out on students in William Glassman's repertory class at the Royal Ballet School in London. This showing gave an impression of the ballet's sequence and general appearance. Ray Cook provided the initial checking of the Labanotation score. Classroom reading of this score was undertaken at the College of the Royal Academy of Dancing in London and by Professor Rhonda Ryman's students at Waterloo University in Canada. In the process of reconstructing the movements from the Labanotation symbols, improvements were suggested where the score lacked sufficient detail. An even more stringent test took place at the Juilliard School in New York. Muriel Topaz, director of the Dance Division, saw this ballet as an excellent dance heritage experience as well as the chance for practical application of their notation knowledge. Under the supervision of Dr Jill Beck the dancers learned their parts solely from the Labanotation score. Subsequent coaching by Ann Hutchinson Guest brought the work up to performance level. Experience in teaching the work to professionals was gained in Naples for the Nijinsky Centenary Program devised by producer Beppe Menegatti and produced at the Teatro San Carlo on 11 April 1989. In Montréal Les Grands Ballets Canadiens featured the work in their second Diaghilev program, the premiere being on 27 October 1989. The ballet is now part of their repertory. The successful performance by the Juilliard Dance Ensemble in New York, 8 December 1989, revealed the degree to which the dramatic inner tension is an important part of this gentler, more subtle version of the ballet.

The process of reconstructing Nijinsky's notation system and the close study of his *Faune* score reveal a previously unappreciated side of Nijinsky's nature: he possessed remarkable analytic and conceptual skills, both as a dance theorist and a choreographer. Building on this work other avenues of study may be opened up, such as consideration of his specific approach to notation and of the choreographic choices he made on the levels of dramaturgy, movement style and musical interpretation. Indications of all these aspects are at long last accessible through availability of the contents of Nijinsky's score.

* * * * * * * * * *

Of particular interest to researchers and students of Nijinsky's *Faune* is the issue of the international journal CHOREOGRAPHY AND DANCE entitled "A Revival of Nijinsky's Original *L'Après-midi d'un Faune*" (Volume 1 Part 3, 1991). This issue, edited by Dr. Jill Beck, centers on the Juilliard Dance Ensemble production of Nijinsky's ballet. It contains revealing articles on the original research undertaken by Ann Hutchinson Guest and Claudia Jeschke; the experience of dancer Rebecca Stenn, in mastering the choreography from the Labanotation score and finding the inner meaning; Jill Beck's article "Techniques and Perspectives on Reviving Nijinsky's *Faune*" which examines in depth the process involved in such a revival and the rewards of direct contact with the movement through the notated score, and dance critic Sally Sommer's reflections on seeing the performance.

Nijinsky's listing of the cast for the first performance of *Faune*. The following is a transcription of his own spelling; for identification of the dancers see page 177.

Dancers: 1912, Paris   Nymphs: Klementovich, Maikerskaya, Kapazinskaya, B. Nizinskaja, - Nelidova
N. Baranovich, Cherepanova.

Faun: Nijinsky.

The curtain rapidly pulled and lowefed.

NIJINSKY'S PRODUCTION NOTES

At the beginning of his score Nijinsky dedicated the score to his wife and added detailed production notes, including specific statements concerning the set and props. These are presented here, translated from the Russian. Additional details established by the reconstructors from experience are added at the end.

Translation of Nijinsky's Wording concerning the Set, etc.

I dedicate this piece to Romola
Afternoon of a Faun
Score conceived by Vaslav Nijinsky
Notated: August - September 1915, Budapest[1]

Afternoon of a Faun

The scenery consists of a backdrop, practicable[2], curtains and mats. Depicted on the backdrop is a parched, Greek summer landscape. To be seen from the perspective of the audience is a stream, and to the left a hillock, which can be created with the help of the practicable.

The backdrop with practicable should be placed upstage. Should there be no apron, it should be placed far upstage so that an artificial apron is created.

At the beginning a frame-like curtain, decorated with Greek ornaments should hang downstage[3].

The floor is to be covered with the mats, from forestage to backdrop. That section of the mat which covers the apron is to be painted black, the rest (and this has priority) painted green. It is essential for choreographic reasons to effect this[4].

The dancers and the set should be lit from forestage with a strong sunlight. The lighting behind the practicable should be so constructed that no shadow falls on the backdrop, neither from the dancers nor from the practicable. Dimly lit from the sides so that the figures do not seem like out of a relief. The aim is for everything to be almost flat, more like a low-relief.

---

[1] It is possible that these are the dates of making the neat pencil copy of the score. In view of Nijinsky's meticulous analysis of the movements, writing down the ballet must have required many months.

[2] Moveable set.

[3] This is now never included.

[4] This is usually omitted.

Properties

A gilded basket, with three clusters of grapes, and a single-rowed panpipe.

Costumes

The nymphs wear a light, transparent frock, effected in Andrassin/Persian silk of the finest quality. One of the nymphs wears a golden chemise, knee-length (from strong cloth); the others wear clothing of silver with dark blue, etc. The headpiece with (colored) patches are green-matt gold.

The faun's costume consists of tights (tricot) painted with dark/colored patches against a light background, creating the impression of a glazed skin. The headpiece is gilded green-matt gold. Horns of the same material; placed on the head is a wreath evoking something ibex-, ram-like. The footwear consists of sandals of the same gold tone as the other gilded accessories.

The faun plays the panpipes and enjoys the grapes.

The nymphs go bathing. One of the nymphs is undressing. The nymphs catch sight of the faun and scatter. The faun intercepts the half-undressed nymph. The nymphs return and help her. The faun remains alone with a frock which one of the nymphs lost. The nymphs return repeatedly, sporadically in groups or alone, to jeer the faun[5].

The faun carries the frock carefully to his bed on the hillock. He carries the frock there, has fun with it and lays it beside him.

Dancers: 1912, Paris[6]

Nymphs: Klementovich, Maikerskaya, Kapazinskaya
         B. Nizinskaja, - Nelidova
         N. Baranovich, Cherepanova.
Faun: Nijinsky.

The curtain rapidly pulled and lowered[7].

---

[5] This description does not tally with the events as recorded in the score. The nymphs do not 'scatter' as his words suggest, only one of them, the 'Joyful Nymph' is frightened and runs off. Later N1 and N2 decide to depart quickly [53] but during the group entrance in [71-73], the pose and gradual exiting in [77-79] the nymphs are fairly slow-moving and appear relaxed.

[6] Nijinsky's spelling; for identification see page 177.

[7] In the score he writes that the curtain is lowered slowly.

Wording for the Stage Set

Translation of Nijinsky's notes, as written next to his opening floor plan:

1. Black carpet (floor cloth) artificial apron (forestage)
2. Dancing space, floor cloth same as on the apron
3. Stage scenery, (moveable) stairs and plateau, (little mountain)
4. Background (cloth), landscape in summer
5. a) - Painted screen (little mountain, young forest)
6. b) - Basket of grapes

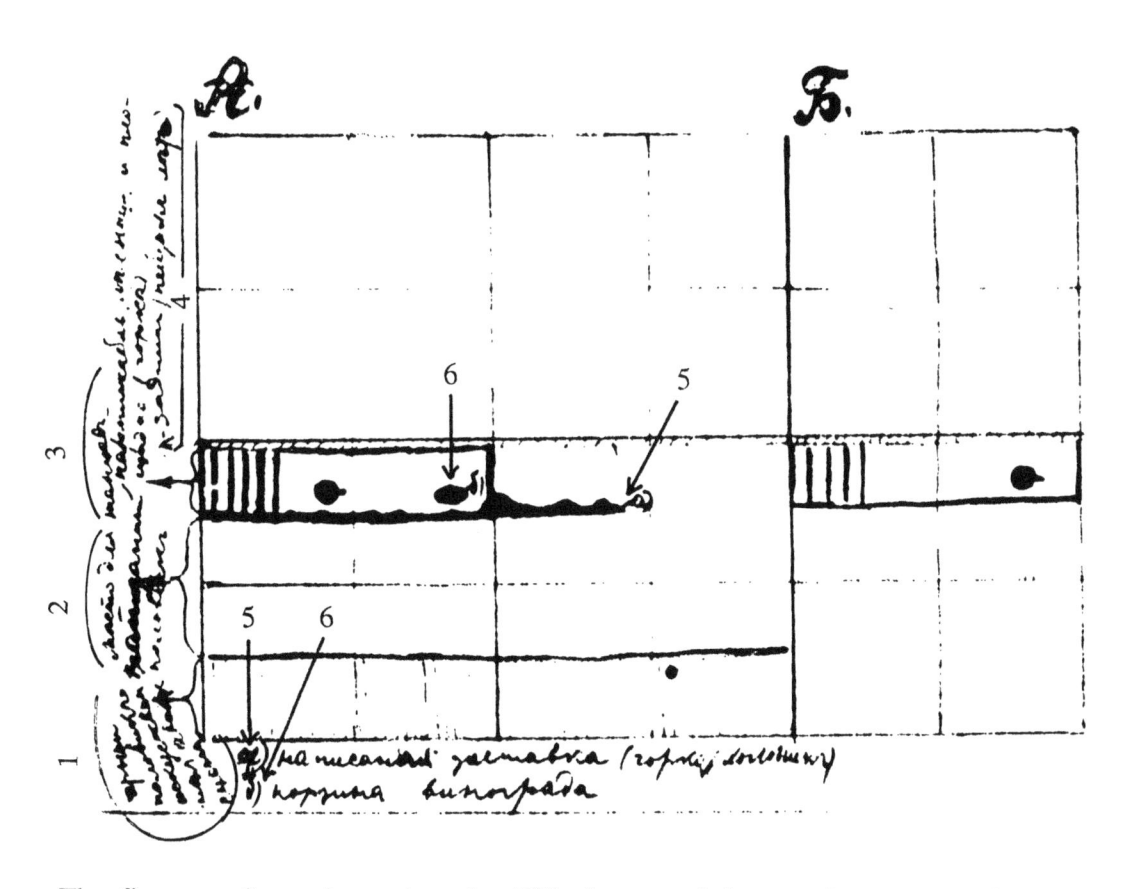

The first two floor plans given by Nijinsky are of the opening scene and measure 16. The Russian letters 'A' and 'B' at the top also appear at the appropriate places in the movement score.

Additional 1989 Production Notes

The Stage Area

Following Nijinsky's indications, the dance area is 8ft. deep and 40ft. (11m.) wide.

Aerial View of Rock and Dance Area

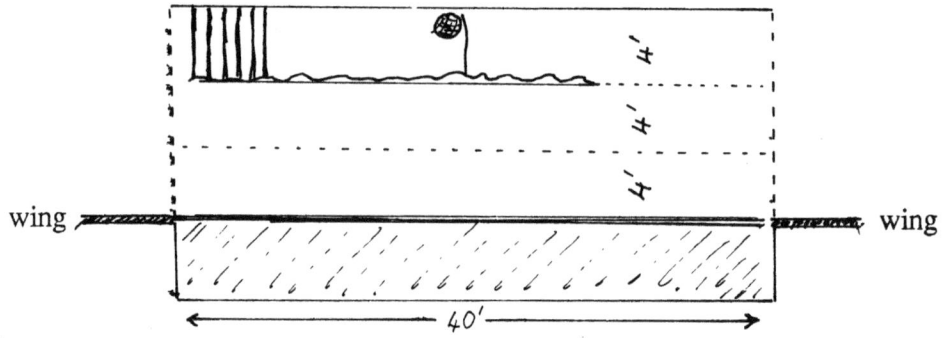

The Set

The rock on which the faun lies is 4ft. high near the steps, and slopes upward to 4ft. 9ins. It is 3ft. wide and 10ft. long. There are six steps, the top step being the rock itself. Each step is 10ins. wide and 8ins. high.

Front Elevation of Rock

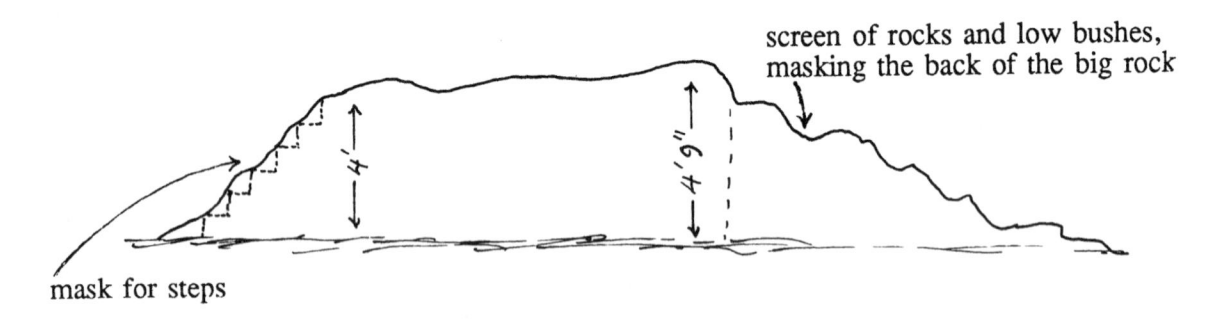

The rock slopes slightly upward toward stage left. The surface is padded canvas with the edge curved to look like rock. The steps are also rounded at the edges to look less angular, more like uneven rock. They must be regular in the center for the dancer to gauge the steps. The sides of the steps can have 'moss' growing to soften the edges.

Props

1 long flute (not Pipes of Pan) (drawn as: ⎯⎯ , as on first page of the Labanotation score).
1 gilded basket (size unknown) (drawn on floor plan as: ⊛).
3 bunches of grapes (different colors are suggested; they need to show up against backcloth).

STUDY AND PERFORMANCE NOTES

Introduction to Overall Style

Nijinsky's ballet *L'Après-midi d'un Faune* has long been noted for its two-dimensional use of the stage space as well as of body direction and body shape. The lines of progression, the pathways, are always parallel to the footlights. The dancers' front (direction of the feet) and the facing direction for the head are, with only two exceptions, toward either stage left or stage right. Half-turns used to face the opposite direction occur swiftly so that the illusion of flatness is maintained. The chest faces toward the audience, with an occasional facing away from the audience. Thus the effect is of flatness, and yet the dancers' bodies are three-dimensional; we see from the 1912 photographs taken by Baron Adolf de Meyer that perfect flatness is not always achieved, particularly by the faun. The effort to achieve full audience-facing for the chest while feet and hips remain toward stage right or left can produce a tension, an unnatural stiffness unsuited to the ballet. While the pelvis should not rotate toward the audience, as this would destroy the twist within the body (the effect of a divided front), some slight - but minimal - 'give' in the pelvic alignment is usually necessary in order to achieve the impression of a full ¼ twist in the upper body without strain. This body position requires an inner relaxation which allows maximum upper body twist with ease and freedom. The torso is alert but not tense. The arm gestures follow (i.e., are placed on) the line between stage right and stage left, being focused mainly toward or away from the directions into which the performers are traveling. Body-related gestures can be seen in several passages, e.g., the pose for the six nymphs in measure 41 and the pose for the five nymphs in measure 76. Most of the arm gestures concerned with handling the veils are body-related.

Style of Gestures

Because this is such a famous ballet about which so much has been written, a concept of its correct style has become established over the years. The word 'angular' is commonly used. It is true that in the ballet many positions involve bent arms, the angle at the elbow often being 90°, sometimes less, sometimes more. These angles can be registered with stiffness to stress the angularity; equally, the same positions can be held but with a normal relaxed softness, a quality evident in the de Meyer photographs. As Lydia Sokolova wrote:

> " *In order to preserve the patterns of the frieze, you had to keep your hands and arms flat in profile: to do this it was necessary to relax the hand and arm, for if you forced or tightened the gesture, the wrist fell back and the straight line from elbow to fingers was lost.*"[1]

In de Meyer's pictures the nymphs are feminine, not puppet-like, not static statues. How then did the present-day performance style using stiff, angular gestures creep in? The answer may well be the influence of reports at the time *Faune* was first produced. Critics and audiences

---

[1] Sokolova, Lydia, *Dancing for Diaghilev*, pp. 40-41, ed. by Richard Buckle, London 1960.

were accustomed to the soft, curved, flowing arms used in classical ballet and in choreography such as Fokine's *Les Sylphides*. In comparison, the arm movements in *Faune* looked angular and the poses were held. In recent decades truly angular movements have predominated in jazz dance and contemporary choreography. It is therefore conceivable that, in recreating the ballet solely from memory, individuals have been influenced by reviews and eye-witness accounts of the first performances and have applied a present-day concept of angularity to their revivals of *Faune*.

However, changes in style in the ballet began early on, as is revealed in the following excerpts from the *New York Times*, 1916. On April 8 we read:

Nijinsky's Objections to Diaghileff's Way of Performing His Ballet "Faun" Leads to Its Withdrawal

Nijinsky stated: "......*the ballet, 'The Afternoon of a Faun', should not be given as the organization (The Ballet Russe) is now presenting it. That ballet is entirely my own creation, and it is not being done as I arranged it. I have nothing to say against the work of Mr. Massine, but the choreographic details of the various rôles are not being performed as I devised them. I therefore insisted strongly to the organization that it was not fair to me to use my name as its author and continue to perform the work in a way that did not meet my ideas.*"

On October 25 the *New York Times* reports:

Nijinsky in Rôle of Faun
First Appearance Here of Creator of 'L'Après-midi d'un Faune' Ballet

"*Waslav Nijinsky appeared as the faun in 'L'Après-midi d'un Faune' with the Diaghileff Ballet Russe for the first time in America at the Manhattan Opera House last night.......As Mr. Nijinsky performed the principal rôle, it seemed hard to remember why so much unfavourable comment had been caused last season, leading to professional interest in the presentation on the part of the police.*

The curious poses of the nymphs, which seemed to make ancient Greek bas-relief live again, had their old appeal. It was noticeable, however, that the queer, jerky timing of their movements which had been apparent last season was less conspicuous last night. Whether this was due to the fact that Mr. Nijinsky desired the movements to be smoother, it was nevertheless, a noticeable different effect and one which to many would probably seem to lack all of the piquancy that was formerly present."

Clearly Nijinsky's version of his ballet is in a gentler, more subtle style.

Style of Walking

Another question of style concerns the manner of walking. The choreography requires a sense of grounding, a relationship to gravity familiar to the natural deities, creatures of woods, brooks and rocks that are being depicted. Early reports on the ballet refer to the faun walking heel first and this has now become exaggerated, particularly for each step during his last slow walk back to the rock. In his notation score Nijinsky did not add the detail of initial heel contact for the walking steps, although his system is quite capable of including such a description. One comes, therefore, to the conclusion that, since the manner of walking in classical ballet was (and still is) with the toe first contacting the floor before weight is transferred onto the foot, people saw as an important departure the fact that Nijinsky employed a natural walk, a stepping progression, in which the initial heel contact with the floor changes at once to the whole foot taking weight. The significant difference lies in the angle of flexion at the ankle; in an ordinary walk this angle is not stressed and there is little lifting of the front part of the foot as it approaches the place where the weight is to be transferred. The ball of the foot and the toes are placed on the floor immediately after heel contact. In the exaggerated 'heel-first' walk used in contemporary, memory-based productions, the front of the foot is significantly raised and putting it down is delayed enough to make this exaggeration a deliberate feature. It should be noted that in fast steps the natural heel-first placement is barely perceptible and should not be stressed. For the swifter runs the heel does not touch the ground, as is natural and automatic when speed is increased.

In the Labanotation score Nijinsky's detailed descriptions of the walking sequences have been included. At speed these specifics cannot always be fully executed but, if they are borne in mind, they will influence the performance. For faster steps, the progression traveling across the floor must be the main focus, rather than foot articulations.

Expression

Expression in performing the ballet should come from within and result from the movement context. There should be no overt facial expressions. Interviews with earlier generations of dancers indicate that none was ever taught; thus this is an important aspect in performing the ballet. Sokolova again gives an insight:

"*Nijinsky as the Faun was thrilling. Although his movements were absolutely restrained, they were virile and powerful....*"[2]

However the de Meyer and Struss photographs show a few moments involving facial expression for the faun and also for the fourth nymph when she runs away frightened. Details recorded by Nijinsky indicate that many movements appear to be the result of distinct thought patterns and these should be reflected in the body, in the head movements and in the accompanying arm gestures. In his system Nijinsky did not indicate looking at a person, though from the turn of the head and line of vision one can conclude that the dancer's gaze is probably directed toward another performer, particularly when it seems evident from the context.

The Music

Debussy's *Prélude à l'Après-midi d'un Faune* is familiar to most people and evokes images of sustained, flowing movement. The fact that Nijinsky chose simple, sparse actions, punctuated by linear poses means that Debussy's flowing sound must be experienced inwardly by the dancers, and dance and music must relate through a sustained inner dynamic (an alert

---

[2] Sokolova, Lydia, *Dancing for Diaghilev*, p. 41, ed. by Richard Buckle, London, 1960.

attention) on the part of the performers. Sokolova is also revealing on this aspect of the ballet:
"The dancers had to be musical as well as rhythmical and it was necessary to relax and hear the music as a whole: it had to trickle through your consciousness, and the sensation approached the divine. One walked and moved quite gently in a rhythm that crossed over the beats given by the conductor....For every lift of the hand or head there was a corresponding sound in the score. It was most ingeniously thought out."[3]

In the learning process relating the choreography to the music is not easy. The changes in meter from 6/8 to 9/8, 12/8, 3/4, 4/4 etc., make counting difficult. The very flow of the sounds often hides the basic beat, a beat which the dancers seek to follow. In addition there is much *rubato* throughout the piece and each conductor has his own feeling regarding pace and the handling of *accelerando* and *ritardando* passages. Research revealed that former performers had been taught the ballet without counts; others of more recent years inform us that all sequences were carefully counted. In either case the dancers must get to know the music intimately and learn to place the movement phrases on the music through a movement sense rather than through any mechanical metronomical counting. (See **Appendix D, Music Recording**, p. 191)

Timing of Steps

For many phrases in which no marked pulse is discernible a certain number of steps must fit smoothly into a particular melodic span. In contrast, on measure 44 when the meter changes to a clear 4/4 and the music becomes full and more strident, the basic beat can clearly be heard. Because Nijinsky wrote the timing of each step and gesture in such careful detail in his music-note system, one feels a compulsion in studying his score to produce great accuracy in timing. Practical necessity may dictate that some form of counting be used at first, but the aim should be a movement relationship to the music through a sense of 'spacing in time', a sense of proportioning the parts of the step or movement sequence so that its inner timing remains intact when the whole is placed correctly on the music phrase. In memory-based versions there is no indication of stepping between the main beats; in contrast Nijinsky occasionally indicates such off-beat progressions which the dancer then fits to the music once the steps and the notes are familiar.

Timing of Arm Gestures

Through his choice of music-note values Nijinsky indicates slower or faster movements. In his score arm gestures are never written as being sudden, i.e., with a sixteenth note. They may occur on the first beat of the measure as in the passages in 3/4, but there is no indication of staccato movement, of any suddenness with a sharp stop. For example, the arm gestures of the six nymphs, performed in canon (measure 32), move smoothly up to the position stated with a slight anticipation so that the arrival is clearly on the beat. (Note that unit timing is used in the Labanotation score for these gestures.) After the six nymphs cross behind N5, they lower their arms slowly. For this slow lowering Nijinsky spelled out the stages (positions) through which the arms should pass, thus describing sustained, fluent movement.

---

[3] Sokolova, Lydia, *Dancing for Diaghilev*, p. 40, ed. by Richard Buckle, London, 1960.

Relationship between Faun and Nymphs

The relationship between the nymphs and the faun needs to be considered and clearly established. Much has been heard over the years about the nymphs being afraid of the faun; to what extent is this true? A different relationship emerges from Nijinsky's own notation of his choreography. One does not get the impression that nymphs and faun encounter each other for the first time; it seems more likely that the nymphs are aware of the faun's existence and know he may be on his favorite rock. To them he is part of the scenery of the glade where they come to bathe. They may not know what mood he will be in, whether stand-offish or playful, thus there is an element of uncertainty. In mythology faun and nymphs are descended from the same mother; they are closely related, being by nature creatures of springs, brooks and grottos. Thus Nijinsky's choreography logically presents a look at an event in an ordinary day in the lives of these mythical creatures. Nymphs and faun have retained their natural sensuality unspoiled by civilization and its accompanying moral judgements concerning the senses and sexuality. It is interesting to note that mythology describes and depicts Faun, Pan and Satyr as closely related beings, all three representing a sensual life: Pan's flute relates to music, his head circlet signifies dance; Faun as shepherd has a natural affinity to what can be called a simple, primitive life; and the Satyr, sporting his miniature horse's ears and tail, is related directly to Dionysus. Nijinsky's *Faune* appears more as an illustration of sensual behavior, a view into natural, playful situations, rather than as a presentation of dramatized sexuality between male and female. In its balance between the rôles of faun and nymphs the choreography is simple, and in this very simplicity lies its strength. A powerful inner dynamic emerges from the movement understatement. It has been commented that this version reveals psychological overtones long since lost. In the memory-based versions that have been handed down, changes have occurred in the movement patterns: sharp, staccato head movements for the faun, gestures which 'slap' the air, an exaggerated use of energy - all of which change the meaning of the movements. Elements of fear and anger have entered and become exaggerated. Nijinsky's notated choreography suggests less strident gestures, a less emotion-laden relationship.

Details on Movement Style and Usage

In the following notes reference is made, when appropriate, to where the item first appears in the score.

1. THE HEAD

Inclining the Head

In his score of *Faune* Nijinsky gives two degrees for forward inclination of the head. Where these indications appear in the score a comparison with the available photographs of the same movement in the ballet produced the following decisions: what he wrote as a slight forward tilt, as in Ex. 1a, is performed as a lengthening of the back of the neck which produces a slight rising of the crown and a very slight lowering of the chin. In this position the head is very slightly off the normal vertical line but the eye-line is still in the normal forward direction, Ex. 1b. The end result should be a slight rise in energy without stiffness. This head position suggests awareness, alertness and involvement. In the score the position of 1b is abbreviated to the special sign of 1c (F, meas. 14). The sign of 1c does not exist in Labanotation and is used here to represent this specific head position. The term 'alert' head is used in the verbal description to emphasize the expression of this arched position. A helpful way to achieve the alert head position is to lie flat on the ground, supine, and lengthen the neck to get the base of the skull on the floor. This action lengthens and straightens the neck without any tension or active pulling in of the chin. For the faun there are moments of intensity when lengthening of the neck is more pronounced, a more active and energised motion. At such times this detail is written as a greater degree of neck lengthening with a rise in energy.

The second degree of forward inclination for the head is a normal forward high tilt, 1d (F, meas. 7). In most cases the eyes are lowered as usual to the degree that the head inclines. The contexts suggest that such head lowering may express shyness, contrition or thoughtfulness, rather than occurring just for the purpose of design.

1d

Head Inclination Combined with a Turn

With rare exceptions, the head of each performer is turned to right or left at all times. In most instances the rotational state is written as an 'attached sign' added to the direction symbol; this is true also for the alert head position, 1e.

1e

While it is turned, the head may incline forward, backward, and occasionally into the forward or backward diagonal (bringing the ear near one shoulder).

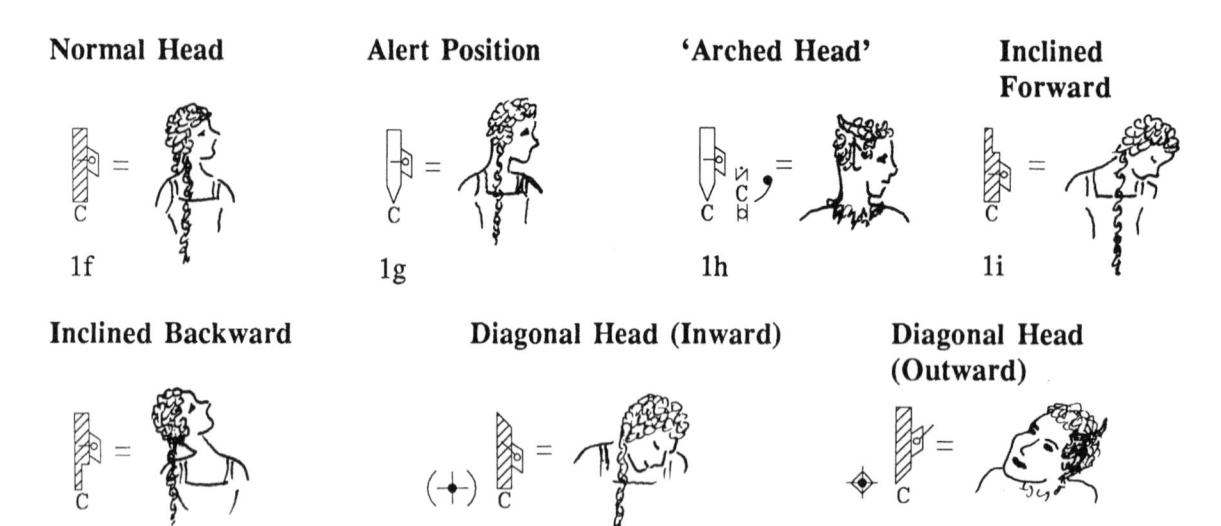

Normal Head　　**Alert Position**　　**'Arched Head'**　　**Inclined Forward**

1f　　1g　　1h　　1i

Inclined Backward　　**Diagonal Head (Inward)**　　**Diagonal Head (Outward)**

1j　　1k　　1l

2. THE BODY

Twist of the Chest

The degree of chest twist given by Nijinsky varies from 45°, Ex. 2a, to 67½°, Ex. 2b, or 90°, Ex. 2c. To augment the 67½° Nijinsky added forward and backward shoulder indications. In Labanotation such shoulder movements, Ex. 2d, produce isolated actions which do not involve or displace the rib cage. To take one shoulder forward and the other backward produces a tautness in the shoulder area, a tension that is not at all evident in the de Meyer photographs of the nymphs or the faun. Therefore his description is taken to mean an augmented twist in which the upper extremity of the torso, the shoulder line, is carried farther so that the shoulders do appear to be 'forward and backward'. This twist has been written in Labanotation as one of the chest-plus-waist, Ex. 2e. In teaching these movements the instruction used is "Allow the shoulder line to be carried around" rather than "Make the shoulder line arrive at this degree of twist".

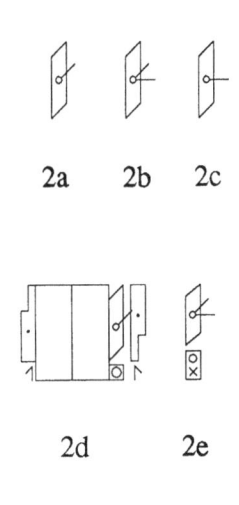

While practice will make the twisted positions required in the ballet easier to achieve and perform, it is important that strain be avoided. The photographs reveal that the front of the chest is not always exactly flat to the audience (this is particularly true of the faun); however, the audience has the impression of flatness because the appropriate expression of the movement has been achieved. In Labanotation such a chest twist could be described as the front surface of the chest facing the audience, Ex. 2f. With this description a space hold can be given to show that the chest remains facing the same direction when the performer changes front, as in swiveling to the opposite direction, Ex. 2g. However, direction for chest facing was not the description chosen because the meaning of the movement is not that of the front of the chest addressing the audience, but that of the flattened two-dimensionality of the torso's stance resulting from this upper torso twist. (See also **Labanotation Glossary - Body Twists; Change of Direction**, p. 51).

Torso Contraction

Nijinsky spelled out very clearly the torso contractions over the back diagonal surface used by the faun and the chief nymph. His description combined a forward tilt for the pelvis with a diagonally backward folding for the chest. Ex. 2h shows the Labanotation equivalent for the right diagonal back contraction. This contraction is maintained during the walking sequences in the duet and during the faun's slow walk back to the rock. This particular use of the torso is important for required style and expression; its indication in the score is too easily overlooked. It is also difficult for many dancers to remember this detail and to give it full value.

3. THE ARMS

Frequently Used Positions

In the **Description of the Dance** the verbal explanations of the sequences do not attempt to cover all the details given in the notation; they are intended to serve as a guide to those less familiar with reading Labanotation. For ease in reference some special terms and indications are used in the word notes. The following analysis of the positions also provides insight into the range of Nijinsky's use of arm designs in this ballet.

As an aid in describing and differentiating the individual angled arm positions the following particular signs and names are used:

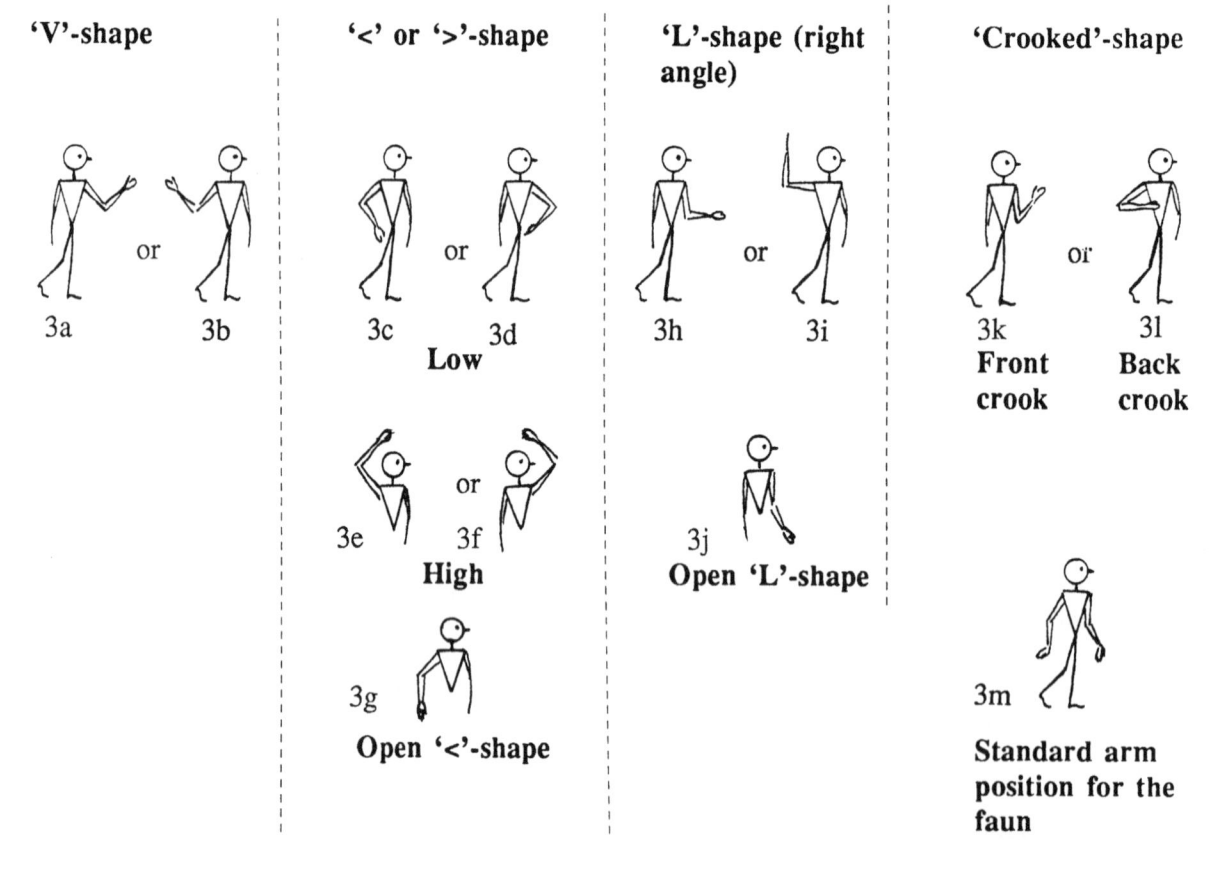

'V'-shape

3a   or   3b

'<' or '>'-shape

3c   or   3d
Low

3e   or   3f
High

3g
Open '<'-shape

'L'-shape (right angle)

3h   or   3i

3j
Open 'L'-shape

'Crooked'-shape

3k   or   3l
Front crook   **Back crook**

3m
Standard arm position for the faun

The 'V'-shape may be 3a or 3b. The '<'-shape may be low, as in 3c and 3d, or high as in 3e and 3f. The open '<' angle of 3g occurs only in the backward direction. The 'L'-shape (right angle) may be down, as in 3h, or up as in 3i. It may also be more open as in 3j. The 'crooked' position may have the elbow down or backward, as in 3k and 3l. In almost all these positions the palms face toward or away from the audience. Ex. 3m shows the standard arm position for the faun; there is no comparable standard position for the nymphs.

4. SYSTEMS OF REFERENCE FOR ARM, HEAD AND CHEST DIRECTIONS

For the translation of Nijinsky's score, decisions had to be made as to which directional description, i.e., which key, would convey most appropriately and clearly the desired movement. Decisions as to which system of reference should be used were determined by the emphasis of the movement and by what is being expressed.

Nijinsky's description of direction was totally body-related, i.e., using ✛, the Body Cross of Axes system of reference. In Labanotation other choices exist; the fact that the composition of *Faune* is so predominantly two-dimensional - being based on the line between stage right and stage left (directions 4 and 12 in Nijinsky's system) - suggests that all arm gestures as well as head and chest inclinations should relate directly to this line, i.e., forward being where the base, the feet, is facing. Such directional description is called Stance in Labanotation. In this score the Stance Key: ◆ is used for gestures in line with the direction of travel and also for gestures directed toward the faun. These are usually open gestures, away from the body.

In the Standard Key: ✛, arm direction relates to the front of the chest, the shoulder line. In several instances gestures of the nymphs relate to themselves, as when the hand is near the shoulder, or when the veils are being handled; for these gestures the Standard Key is more appropriate than the Stance Key. Head inclinations are judged from where the head is facing, that direction being 'forward'. In a few instances where torso tilts are involved, direction for the arms is taken from the Body Key.

The arm positions given in the previous section are now amalgamated and illustrated using both ✛ and ◆ systems of reference.

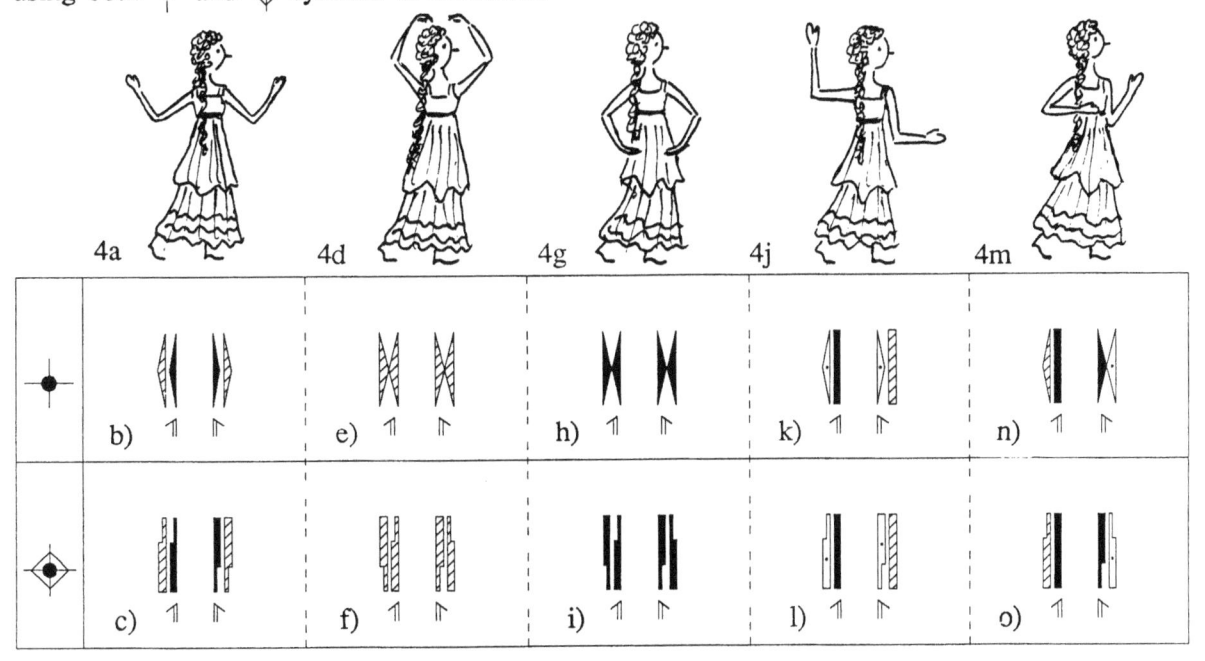

From the above one can see clearly that positions which are physically symmetrical are visually seen as such in the direction symbols when the ✛ key is used, as in Exs. 4b, 4e and

4h. In contrast the ✦ key relates arm directions to the established Front and thus is suitable when the focus or attention should be directed there.

In the few instances when the head is directed backward, away from the established Front, as in 4p, it is more difficult to relate arm and head directions to the Stance Key; hence ✦ is used for the whole position, as in 4q. In 4r the Stance Key is stated and ✦ is used for the head, as its forward tilt is away from the Stance Front (N5, meas. 38; N4, meas. 48, etc.).

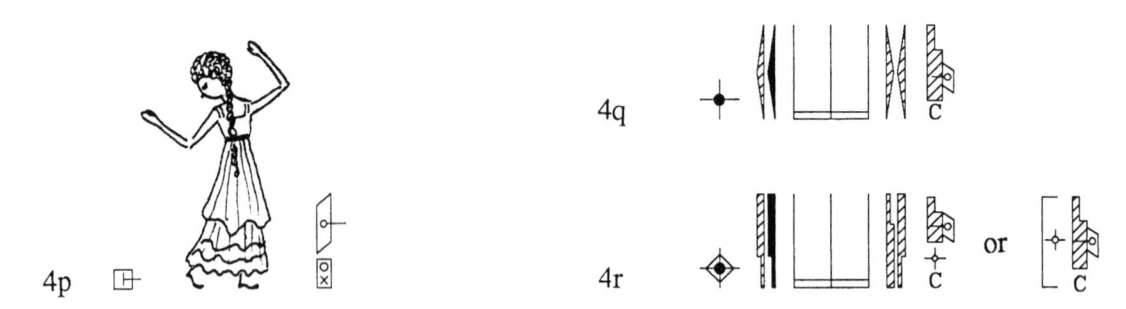

Directional Description for Arms

In **Description of the Dance**, the word notes given for arm directions refer to the Standard Key (i.e., direction from the shoulder line), this being the easier description to render verbally, even when the Stance Key may be used in the score. When reference for arms is more easily described as toward the stage directions of 4 and 12, the verbal description makes use of these numbers.

5. HAND POSITIONS

Palm Facing

Palm facing directions are usually included even though they are the standard palm facing understood in Labanotation, i.e., facing 'in'.

Flat Hands

When the nymphs' arms are 'open', i.e., away from the body, or crossing the chest, the hands are usually flat. When they are down, close to the body, the hands are usually curved. When they are raised, near the head, the hands are sometimes flat, sometimes curved.

When the hands are flat they are not stiff, but held with a relaxed firmness, the fingers and thumb being laterally closed, but not pressed tightly together, i.e., comfortably together as in 5a (F, meas. 7; N6 etc., meas. 76). It is important to give the hands energy and expression without making them stiff and thus drawing unnecessary attention to them. In a few instances the hands of N5 are energised (meas. 62, 67, 69) as indicated by addition of the sign ⌒. Examples given here for the right hand apply equally to the left.

The standard hand position is with the hand flat, fingers close together and with a gentle quality, not tense or stiff. There are several places where the nymphs' hands are curved.

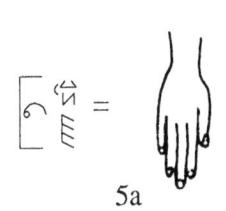

5a

The faun's flat hand position usually includes an abducted wrist, as in 5b. As a male he uses slightly more energy than the nymphs but the position does not become hard.

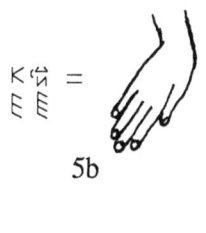

5b

The flat hand position of 5a is always used when the wrist abduction of 5c or 5d occurs.

5c or 5d

Hands Spread

The one instance of lateral opening of hand and fingers (fingers spread 'sideward' in Nijinsky's terms) occurs when N4 encounters the faun and separates her fingers in fright as she runs away (N4, meas. 48), Ex. 5e.

5e

Angled Thumb

The 'angled thumb' position occurs in moments of increased intensity for both N5 and the faun.

In the 'angled thumb' position the hand is flat, the thumb is extended sideward (90° abduction) as in 5f, and there is accompanying wrist abduction. This position is used by N5 (the chief nymph) when 'repulsing' the faun, Ex. 5g (meas. 62, 67, 69). This hand position is used by the faun in many contexts, e.g., meas. 7, 17, etc.

5f

5g

Wrist Fold

In a wrist fold, 5h, the degree of bend is 45°. The indication of 5i, a 30° fold in the 6/6 scale, should, for this score, be read as 5j, the indication of 45° on the 8/8 scale (N2, N3, meas. 25). This degree of wrist fold applies to other directions as well.

5h 5i 5j (45°)

Hands Curved

When their arms are down the nymphs' hands are usually curved. This curve, described as a two-degree hand fold, 5k (N1, N2, N3, meas. 21), involves folding the base joint of the four fingers as well as the other finger joints. The thumb is not included in this folding, but remains relaxed and unobtrusive.

Combined Wrist Fold and Curved Hand

Occasionally the line of a raised curved arm is further softened by both wrist and hand being curved, as in 5l. In these positions the hands are held more naturally, the palms facing toward the shoulders, 5m (N4, meas. 25).

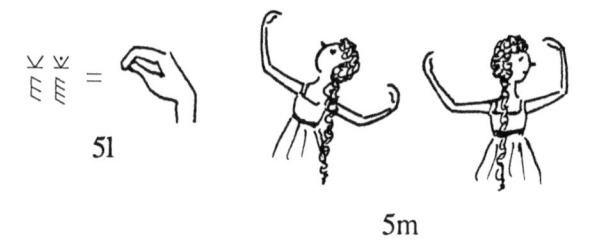

'Linked' Hands

This same curved hand and wrist are used in Nijinsky's notation when he indicates the contact between the nymphs' hands. The photographs show a loose linking, hands and wrists curved, fingertips touching, as in 5n (N2, N3, meas. 21; N6, N7, meas. 28, etc). This position is called 'linked' hands.

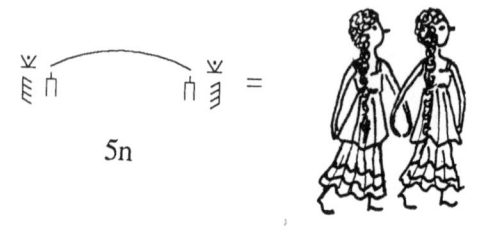

'Holding Hands'

Nijinsky used words in measure 77 to state that N3 holds N7's hand. In his notation Nijinsky wrote a greater degree of folding by including a direction as well as folding for the fingers, 5o, to indicate grasping another person's hand or wrist, as when N2 grasps N6's wrist, measure 78. In the Labanotation score the standard indication for a grasping contact suffices, 5p.

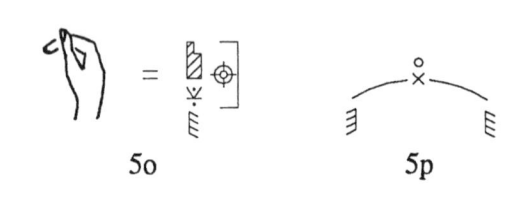

6. WALKING STEPS

Throughout the Labanotation score Nijinsky's specific analysis for the different walking steps is given near the simpler version demanded by the tempo of the music. While at speed not all his details can be clearly 'enunciated', knowing what he described helps the reader produce the right style (see **Score**, p. 77, style of walk for N1, N2, N3, meas. 24). All walks should be smooth. When distance must be covered an even, free-flowing progression can be achieved by carrying the weight forward and skimming the foot along just off the floor before weight is taken. This forward displacement of the center of weight results in the weight leading into each step. Because there is to be no rise and fall (as indicated in the bracket, the horizontal level is maintained) no *tombé* action results from this leading with the weight.

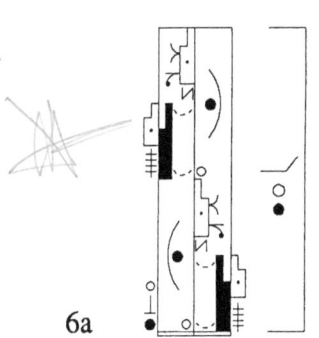

6a

7. PROPS

Holding the Flute

Nijinsky's detailed description of holding the flute, 7a, given in the starting position, is simplified elsewhere to the abbreviation of 7b (F, meas. 10). Direction for the flute is judged from where it is held, the free end being the end opposite the mouthpiece.

7a   7b

Holding the Grapes

The two bunches of grapes in the golden basket are handled in a normal manner. They are numbered 1 and 2 in the score, 7c and 7d (F, meas. 16-18). (Nijinsky gave word notes for picking up the grapes and putting them down.)

7c   7d

8. THE VEILS AND THE DRESS

In the score the word 'veil' is used for the first two parts of N5's clothing. The two veils are identified by curved oblongs to help indicate how they are handled. The first veil to be discarded is shown as dotted, the second as striped, 8a (N6, N3, meas. 44; N5, meas. 54). The dress, the last part to be discarded, is left blank. On the floor plan the veils are also shown as dotted and striped but are drawn smaller, 8b (N5 floor plan, meas. 33). The veil is drawn slightly to the side of two pins when carried by two dancers, 8c (N6, N7, floor plan, meas. 45) and across the pin representing the performer when carried by one dancer, 8d (N3, floor plan, meas. 45).

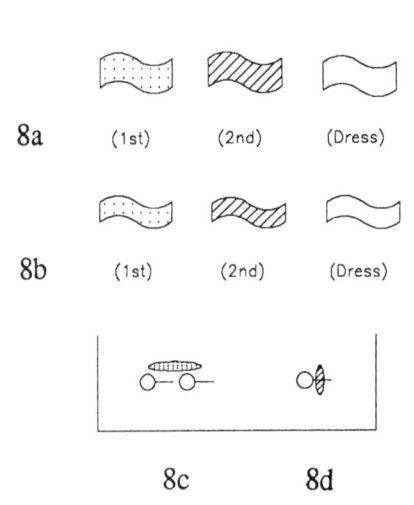

8a   (1st)   (2nd)   (Dress)

8b   (1st)   (2nd)   (Dress)

8c   8d

In the order of under-garment to top garment the dress and the veils of N5 are worn as follows:

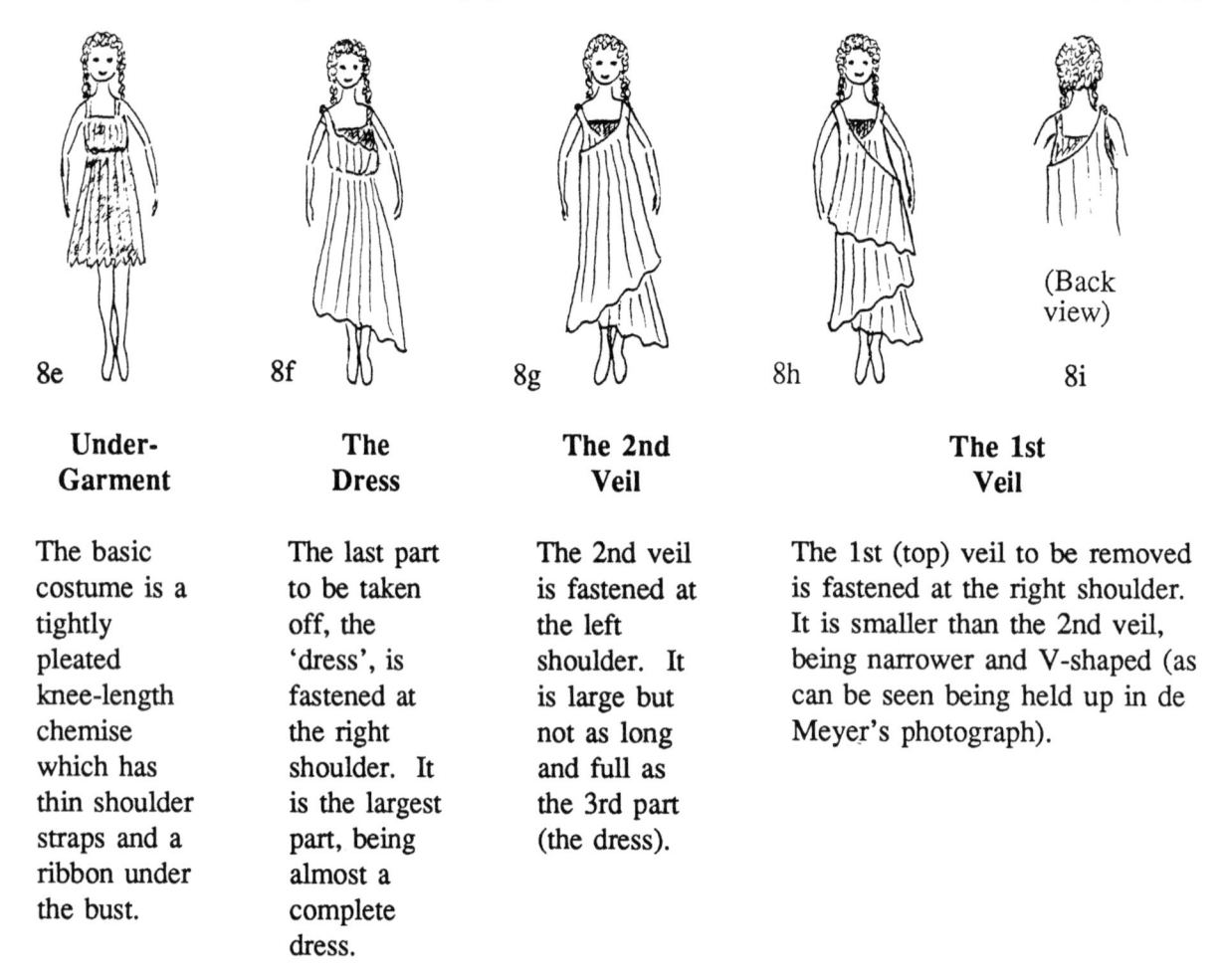

8e	8f	8g	8h	8i
Under-Garment	**The Dress**	**The 2nd Veil**	**The 1st Veil**	(Back view)
The basic costume is a tightly pleated knee-length chemise which has thin shoulder straps and a ribbon under the bust.	The last part to be taken off, the 'dress', is fastened at the right shoulder. It is the largest part, being almost a complete dress.	The 2nd veil is fastened at the left shoulder. It is large but not as long and full as the 3rd part (the dress).	The 1st (top) veil to be removed is fastened at the right shoulder. It is smaller than the 2nd veil, being narrower and V-shaped (as can be seen being held up in de Meyer's photograph).	

When the garments are stretched out their approximate size is as follows: Veil No. 1 - 30" wide, 62" long, Veil No. 2 - 34" wide, 62" long, the Dress - 42" wide, 72" long.

The upper corners of each veil (marked ⟨ and ⟩ in the score) have either tiny velcro circles with which to fasten them together or tapes tied with a slip knot which comes free with one slight pull.

Handling of the Veils

Measure 31: after undoing the corners of the top veil N5 transfers the front edge to her right hand by slipping her thumb under the edge of the material from behind, 8j, thereby making a fold at the upper edge of the veil, 8k, the cloth being between thumb and base of index finger. Once done, the hand is held in the stylized manner indicated. While this is being done, the other end of the veil drops down, the nymph can then place her left hand near the right in a symmetrical manner, thumb under the fold in the material, a little distance from the right, marked (a) in Ex. 81. The left hand then slides along the top almost to the end of the left side of the veil, marked (b).

DETAILS ON MOVEMENT STYLE AND USAGE

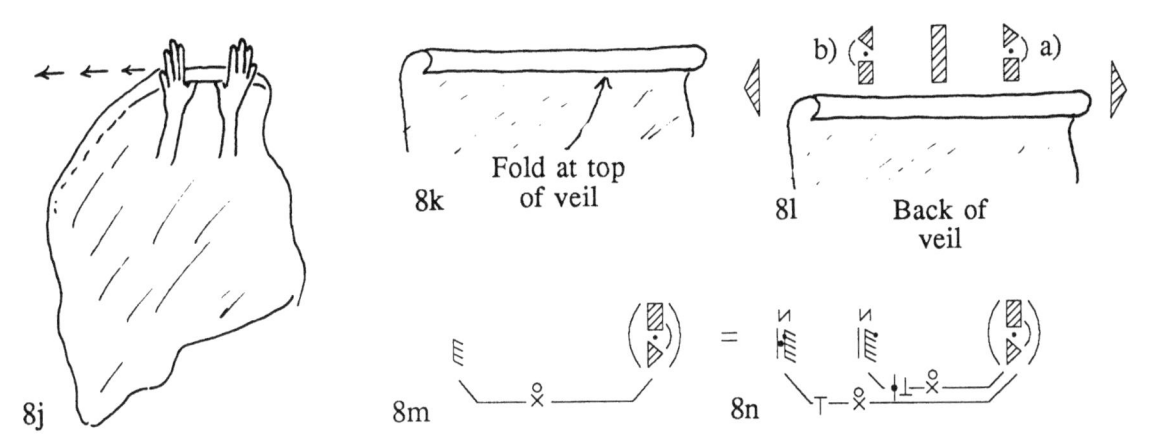

Ex. 8m is the abbreviation used in the score for the hand grasping the fold at the top of the veil, spelled out in 8n. For the second veil, this right-hand instruction is changed to the left hand.

Picking up the veils

When the attending nymphs pick up the veils the sign for ad lib. is used for the arm gesture to indicate that some freedom may be needed to accomplish the end result, 8o. The ad lib. sign is bowed to the following arm indication (N6, N3, meas. 44).

Holding the veil against the body

During the duet N5 holds the dress by pressing it against her body (pressure backward), the hands being flat (N5, meas. 54). Thus, while the hands are supporting the dress, it is the dress that contacts the body. At the end of measures 61, 66, 68, 71, 72 and 73, as N5 changes sides in placement of her arms, she must switch hands rapidly so that the dress does not fall.

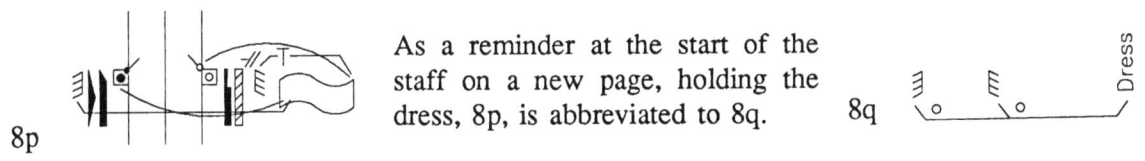

As a reminder at the start of the staff on a new page, holding the dress, 8p, is abbreviated to 8q.

9. INCLUSION OF NIJINSKY'S WORD INSTRUCTIONS

Important moments in the ballet were described by Nijinsky in words. These have been included in the Labanotation score even though much of the action is evident from the notation. They are given in three forms: wording in quotes is Nijinsky's (see start of **Score**); wording in parentheses has been added to make the score easier to read (see **Score**, meas. 22); statements **in quotes** between parentheses are modifications of Nijinsky's wording (see **Score**, meas. 21). Nijinsky referred to the chief nymph's clothing as 'part of the dress' or 'tunic'. Here and in the Labanotation score the word 'veils' is used to refer to the first two smaller drapes which the nymph discards, and 'dress' to refer to the part of her clothing she retains until her exit.

10. REHEARSAL AIDS

Placement of the appropriate section of music on the same page as the dance score was deemed an essential aid in overcoming any initial difficulty encountered in establishing the correct correlation between movement and music. In the early stages rehearsals are also much aided by using a music tape with voice-over counting the measure numbers. In this way it is easy to keep track of both music and movement. Later the voice-over tape is replaced with a standard orchestral tape for 'polishing' and run-through rehearsals.

Casting

The Faun

Inevitably there is a tendency to cast the faun in the image of Nijinsky. It is more important, however, that the dancer have the quality, the presence, the inner dynamic tension to be believable in the part: he must be able to dominate the scene and to express the changes in mood throughout events as they unfold during the ballet. A sinuous feeling in the body for the animal characteristics of the faun is important, as well as the acting ability to find motivations behind the movements and thus to give meaningful expression to the actions.

The Chief Nymph (N5)

In the original production the chief nymph, Nelidova, was taller than Nijinsky. She was not pretty but had a commanding mien. N5 should be of good height and must have a clear sense of importance, of dignity and of maturity, in contrast to the supporting nymphs.

The Supporting Nymphs

There should not be too much disparity in height among the supporting nymphs, though some differences will provide interest. The outer nymphs (N1 and N4) are usually shorter than the inner nymphs (N6 and N3). As N4 appears younger, being shorter is logical. Heights are most noticeable during the section where all six wait as N5 sheds the first two veils. At one point or another each of the supporting nymphs has something of importance to do, some responsibility in leading the group, picking up the veils, etc.

First Nymph (N1)	She is the first to lead in and should have an air of self-assurance as well as a musical sense, i.e., awareness of timing. She usually leads her group in the crossings. Later she stands ready to catch the dress.
Second Nymph (N2)	She is a central figure in her group. Later in the ballet N2 has a solo entrance when the faun is alone and she runs in to see what he is doing.

Third Nymph (N3)	She leads in the traveling toward stage right. She also picks up the second veil and leads N6 and N7 as they depart.
The 'Joyful' Nymph (N4)	Originally danced by Bronislava Nijinska, who was shorter than the other nymphs, this dancer should be smaller and appear more youthful, more impressionable, with the bubbling inner impatience of the young. Startled by her sudden encounter with the faun she runs off.
Sixth Nymph (N6)	On her first entrance she comes in alone and then must lead N7 into place for the bathing ritual of the leading nymph. N6 picks up the first veil that N5 discards and carries it off. She also leads the group that comes to try to retrieve N5's dress and 'chastises' the faun when he is found standing close to the dress. A little later she has a solo entrance running in to see what the faun is doing, pausing a moment before exiting swiftly.
Seventh Nymph (N7)	She also enters alone (after N6). She must blend with the group and have a good sense of spacing. She leads the second set in chastising the faun.

Note: the last entrances of the nymphs [82, 92 and 93] can be performed by others of the cast than those listed. Some dancers fall more naturally into certain movement patterns, hence may be better suited to these particular individual sequences. However, N4 exits stage left and therefore does not come in again.

Description of the Dance

The following description of the dance contains interpretive conclusions which the authors believe stem from the choreographic structure. They are offered here as an aid in bringing the dance to life. Note the inclusion of Nijinsky's identifications of 4 for stage right and 12 for stage left. Measure numbers are indicated in square brackets.

* * * * * * * * * * * *

[1-10] As the curtain opens the faun is seen lounging on his rock, leaning on his left elbow, his right hand holding a flute close to his lips. For a short time he is motionless; then he stirs [3] and, taking a breath as though playing the flute, raises the flute as he tilts his head back. This position is suspended for a brief time before, as though with another thought in mind, he lowers the flute [5] and sits up, moving the flute slightly away from his lips. Perhaps aware that someone might be coming (a very slight but visible 'listening' head motion is appropriate here) he prepares to turn and look by transferring the flute to his left hand before

twisting to the right [7] to look toward 4, his head inclining forward, both arms opened sideward in a 'V'-shape. His right hand, in gesturing toward 4, takes the position so familiar from the photographs by Baron Adolf de Meyer[1], the position in which the four fingers are flat and held together, the thumb abducted sideward and the wrist abducted toward the little finger side, the 'angled-thumb' position.[2] At this point the faun is still looking toward 4, the direction from which the nymphs usually come, which suggests that he anticipates they might appear soon. As though satisfied that no one is there yet, he returns to facing 12 [9], moves the flute to his right hand [10] and resumes his lying position, as at the opening.

[11-31] Once more there is stillness and, on the repeat of the music theme, he again raises the flute to play it [13], after which he again sits up [14]; but now he draws in his left leg to transfer weight forward into a crouch on his left foot [15]. Once more he turns his head to 4, perhaps still curious about the nymphs, before focusing again toward 12. Seeing the basket of grapes, he takes two crouching steps (R, L) toward it. Putting down the flute [16] he leans forward, extending his left arm to take a bunch of grapes and, during a *crescendo* in the music [17], he lifts them up regarding them at eye-level, his right arm bent in front of him with angled-thumb. In preparation for the repeat of the *crescendo* in the music, the faun puts down the first bunch of grapes [end of 17] and raises another bunch in the same manner.[3] These grapes are then put down before he leans forward and, placing one hand after the other on the floor [19], raises his head before extending his right leg backward on the ball of the foot, the left leg still in a crouch. After a cat-like stretch in which he arches his head and upper spine backward, he twists to the right [20] as he moves his left hand across to the right to put weight on it, and at the same time picks up the flute in his right hand; all these actions lead into a smooth swiveling around to end facing 4. With his right leg normally extended, his left leg bent, he sinks back onto his left elbow into the same position as that of the opening, but this time because he is facing 4, his chest is twisted toward the audience. He remains in this position with the flute at his lips for nine measures [21-30], moving again only on measure 31 when the leading nymph starts unveiling.

[21-23] Three nymphs (N1, N2, N3) enter half-way through measure 21. They walk close together traveling fairly leisurely, yet purposefully, toward 12, each in a slightly different position. The first nymph (N1), the leader, holds her left arm in a V-shape directed toward the way they are traveling, as though pointing the way they should go. The second nymph (N2) has her head inclined forward and her left hand is holding the tunic of N1. These two features give the impression that N2 is shy, perhaps uncertain. Her right arm is behind her, the hand linked with the left hand of the third nymph (N3), their wrists bent, fingertips touching with the palms facing each other[4]. On their fifth step [22] N3 looks back to where they came from and,

---

[1] See **Photographs**, p. 58

[2] See **Details on Movement Style and Usage**, Ex. 5f, p. 27

[3] Nijinsky's word notes make it clear that the faun only looks at the grapes. Smelling them, or appearing to devour them, drink the juice, etc., are not indicated in either movement or words.

[4] See **Details on Movement Style and Usage**, Ex. 5n, p. 28

leaning in that direction, raises her right arm into a V, gesturing toward 4. Her head is 'alert'[5], the eyes looking into the direction of 4, and her steps are now with slightly bent legs.

[23] All three nymphs stop after seven steps as though N3's backward leaning drew them to a halt. N2 raises her head and looks toward 4, as does N1; perhaps they are looking to see why N3 is behaving differently. N3 then comes upright, turning her head to look at the others, who then turn their heads to look again toward 12. All lower their arms with 'hands curved'[6] [23] before continuing to walk toward 12. At the end of the phrase they all turn to face 4. This subtle interplay during their entrance establishes the nymphs as individuals who, while there to serve the chief nymph (N5), are still young beings with thoughts of their own and, as is seen later, momentary lapses of attention. In his notated choreography Nijinsky clearly does not present them as a uniform, stylized frieze, placed on stage for decorative purposes. It is the subtle detail which Nijinsky provides in his score which changes our idea of the rôle of these attendant nymphs.

[24-26] The 'joyful' nymph (N4) now enters and soon reveals why she received that name. She comes in [24] with fast steps in triplet timing, the knees soft, then slows down before pausing in a small high 4th position, knees slightly flexed, head bowed and palms close together in front of her. This momentary position suggests praying but is more likely her way of calling for attention. It is also the preparation for a light-hearted, high-spirited upward spring on the spot, the right lower leg kicking backward, the arms raised in sideward V-shaped gestures, the right higher than the left, the head flung backward. Immediately after landing she turns to walk [25] with fast steps toward 4, holding her tunic at front and back with rounded arms, hands and wrists curved. As N4 travels toward 4, N1, N2, and N3 follow her, also taking fast steps, their left arms in a high raised <-shape, the curved hand and wrist being over the shoulder. On the fifth step they pause, inclining head and upper body toward 4, perhaps in a gesture relating to N4, for she quickly turns back toward them, taking swift steps toward 12, but leaning and looking back toward 4, her arms up and rounded in an open V-shape gesture. As she comes to rest, she slowly lowers her arms, the right arm ending in a sideward V gesturing back toward 4.[7] The impression given by her swift to and fro traveling is of excitement that the chief nymph is about to arrive, almost as if N4 is a neophyte, and anxious about her rôle. As N4 advances toward 12 the other three nymphs back up with swift high steps, lowering their left arms at the end of the phrase, the hands curved in toward the body. This flurry of activity is followed significantly by a whole measure of stillness [26] in anticipation of the entrance of the chief nymph. This stillness heightens the tension, thus giving additional importance to N5's arrival.

[27-30] As though aware of her more exalted status, N5 enters [27] with nine high steps, the foot being extended (pointed) in preparation for each step. Each step occurs on the 'and' of each beat in the music. As she enters her right arm is curved backward, her hand

---

[5] See Labanotation Glossary, Ex. 6a, p. 52; Details on Movement Style and Usage, Exs. 1a-c), p.21

[6] 'Hands curved' refers to the position of Ex. 5k in Details on Movement Style and Usage, p. 28

[7] It is important that N4 ends far enough away from the other nymphs to allow room for N6 and N7 to slip into place and thus produce symmetrical spacing for the nymphs on either side of N5.

holding her tunic; the left arm gestures forward in a V-shape toward 12, the direction of travel. Right after N5's ninth step the sixth nymph (N6) enters [28] and at that moment N5 takes a single step forward, lowering her right arm. N6 enters with five steps off the beat on the 'and' count. Her head is inclined forward (is she apologetic for being late?), her left arm in a low V toward 12, her right arm in >-shape toward 4. Pausing after the last step, she raises her head and looks back at the seventh nymph (N7) who enters in the same manner [second half of 28]. As N7 enters, N5 takes another single step forward lowering her left arm. Linking hands, N6 and N7 both walk slowly with a pause between each step [29], moving past N4 and arriving in place between N5 and N4, N5 having turned her head to watch them. These four steps with pauses between for N6 and N7 are evenly spaced, but are not placed on the music as the music seems at first to demand; a delay of one beat is needed between each gesture-step. On their last step [30] they adjust into place. N4, who has lowered her arm as they passed her, takes two soft steps in place, adjusting her position if need be so that she is in line with the others. These steps for N4 need to be performed quite deliberately and in the same rhythm as those of N6 and N7, to make it clear that they are intended and not a mistake on the part of the dancer. As they arrive in place N6 and N7 lower their arms. All nymphs now have the alert head position which suggests that they are aware they are now on duty. Stillness follows; the scene is set for the chief nymph (N5) to prepare for bathing; the attending nymphs are ready, anticipating the part they are expected to play in the ritual.

[31-32] Raising her hands to her right shoulder [31], her head inclined so that she is looking at her shoulder, N5 loosens the ends of the first veil[8]. Transferring the front upper-right side of the veil to her right hand, she allows the other end to slip free, dropping behind her body; then, stepping up into a high parallel 5th position (usually a very small parallel 4th), right foot front, still facing 12 but with chest and face toward the audience, she brings her arms in front of her, then opens them out as she smooths the top of the veil[9]. This she does by first placing her right thumb under the material near the top, grasping the resulting fold between thumb and fingers (thumb in front and fingers behind the fold, palm facing forward toward the audience); then, as she opens her arms out, she slips her left hand along the material, smoothing the top as she does so. In this handling of the top of the veil it is important that the hands are held in a stylized way, fingers together and flat, thumbs straight, the veil grasped between the thumb and the base of the fingers. The veil need not be held taut: it is shown with a dip in the de Meyer photograph[10]. As she takes this pose she looks straight ahead in the direction of the audience - a rare view of her full face (profile view being the rule). As she loosens the ends of the veil [31] the faun lowers his flute and sits up, apparently aware that now something interesting is happening. He turns his head to the left to look at N5 [32].

[32-33] The music has changed to 3/4 and on each beat [32] the attendant nymphs raise their arms one after the other in canon, those nearest N5 raising their arms first. Each turns her head toward the next nymph as her arms move (as though relaying a message?), and

---

[8] Undoing these smoothly and with simple elegance requires practice. The action can too easily become fidgety. The exact technique depends on how the veils are tied at the shoulder.

[9] Details of the notation for handling the veil are given in the **Details on Movement Style and Usage**, p. 29-31

[10] In the de Meyer picture N5's face is in profile; such a position is clearly not indicated in Nijinsky's score.

then with unison movement [33] each set of three nymphs crosses behind N5 moving to the other side with fluent, gliding steps. This traveling is performed with the weight forward, the center of weight leading and the knees slightly bent to achieve a free-flowing covering of space; N4, N6, and N7 pass behind the others with their backs to the audience. While they cross the nymphs form a cover for N5, thus shielding her from the gaze of the faun, as she drops the first veil, allowing it to fall slightly to her right. The six crossing steps for the nymphs should be off the beat, on the 'and' count. Before this precise timing can be achieved it is important that they cross completely to the other side and are not late in turning[11].

[34-38] Having passed one another, the nymphs turn to face in again toward N5 [34]. As they softly lower their arms, N5, having turned to face the other direction (toward 4), unfastens the second veil, loosening the ends at her left shoulder. Thus begins a repeat to the other side of the whole sequence of loosening the veil, holding it up, and of the nymphs raising their arms in canon before crossing behind N5 [34, 35, 36]. As the nymphs start to raise their arms in canon [35], the faun rises into a crouch on his right leg, his head in the alert position, still looking at N5. He then takes a crouching step forward [36] and puts the flute down before rising slowly [37, 38], his left arm coming to an open-angled backward <-shape, his right arm down but in view, both with angled wrists. This is standard arm position when he is walking. As the faun rises, the nymphs conclude their crossing and turn to face the opposite direction, slowly lowering their arms. N1, N2 and N3 adjust their weight onto the right foot, changing the upper body to face front, the head alert, looking toward 4 [38, count 1].

[38] At this point N5 performs a sequence of steps which appears to be part of a familiar bathing ritual. During this brief passage N5 must be careful not to step on the two veils which are now lying on the ground to either side of her: she must move at the start slightly downstage so as to be in front of the veils when, a little later on, two nymphs come to pick them up. With two bright, 'prancing' steps, knees slightly lifted, as though she is stepping into a pool of water, her head inclined back toward 12, her left arm in an open <, her right in V toward 4, both wrists angled, she advances slightly downstage facing 4. Turning quickly to face 12, her arms now in a low and a high 'L'-shape, she performs light 'feathering steps' in place, i.e., going through the foot as though paddling [38] before stepping out of the water with two high backward steps. She ends with her weight transferred forward, head inclined, looking toward 4, her right arm in a V-gesture in that direction.

[39-43] Immediately following N5's brief solo, perhaps because the chief nymph has been busy with her 'bathing', focusing on herself, N4's attention appears to lapse, for, as though feeling frisky [39], she takes two quick light steps into a small high 4th position, left foot front (R, L, pause). She repeats this twice traveling toward 4, her arms up in fairly open <-, >- shapes. In this manner she wanders away from the chief nymph whom she is supposed to be attending. She stops in a high 4th position and looks back at the other nymphs [40], who catch N4's mood and copy her light, springy traveling steps. N6 and N7 travel toward N4, while N1, N2 and N3 travel in the opposite direction toward 12. During these steps, which take the nymphs out toward the wings, their heads are held normally upright. In the meantime [39, 40] the faun has taken three steps toward the end of the rock and then turned to face 12 in

---

[11] Use on-beat walks if the dancers cannot produce this timing clearly.

preparation for climbing down. He pauses before starting to step slowly backward down the six stairs [42, 43]. His arms remain in the same standard position.

[41-43] As though suddenly remembering that they are there as attendants to the chief nymph, all six nymphs retrace their paths, taking three quick backward high steps [41] to end sinking into a pose on count 2. These three steps and the sinking are uneven in timing. Now close together, each set of three nymphs forms the same picture, the inside hands of the outer girls touching behind the center girl, their outer arms in a V; all are facing 4 except the center girls, who face 12 and whose arms are in a narrower V, closer to the body. As they sink on the supporting leg all incline their heads forward (as though a bit ashamed of having been inattentive?). During this sequence N5's head has turned toward 4. As though observing the nymphs' 'apology', N5 lowers her right arm and takes a step forward toward 12, her head upright but still looking toward 4 (perhaps as though recognizing their apology and indicating that their services are now needed) [42]. As she takes the step, the six nymphs rise into a high parallel 5th position and, heads now alert, they link hands and walk purposefully toward N5 with four high lifted steps [42]. These steps should be off the beat, however, attaining this timing is difficult and on-beat steps may be used at first. The nymphs let go hands and slowly lower their arms while N5 remains still [43], the only other action being that of the faun concluding his backward walk down the last steps.

[44-47] At this point the music swells, the meter changes to 4/4 and a sense of purpose is felt. Now comes the section of greatest activity in the ballet, all participants being involved. A focal point is the picking up of the two veils. N6 steps forward and kneels [44] as she leans forward to pick up the first veil, scooping it up first with her right hand, then with her left. As she rises, she allows it to slide down to her elbows (as stated in Nijinsky's words). Although this movement of picking up the veil must be swift, it should not look hurried: the veils are a revered part of the ritual. During this action N7 waits at her side. N6 then takes three steps toward 12, traveling slightly upstage in order to pass behind N3. N7 joins N6, following behind her toward 12. As they both turn to face 4, N7 takes one end of the veil on her left arm, the position of her arms now being identical with that of N6, who frees her right arm. Perhaps having observed N6 picking up the first veil, N3, still facing 4, leans over two counts later to pick up the second veil. She then leads the way toward 4. N7 and N6 soon follow her so that all three are walking in line. The carrying of the veils has the air of a familiar ritual. Looking back toward N5 they walk [45] with six smooth, swift steps (the meter is now 3/4), pausing on the last step [end of 45] to raise their heads upright and look in the direction they are going. Then, again with an alert head, they look back toward N5 [46] and, making a small dip on the supporting leg while raising the left lower leg slightly backward, they raise their right arms at the same time into a high >, their left arms being backward in an open V. This departing gesture leads at once into their exiting walk [47][12].

[44-46] As the music becomes more intense [the start of 44], N5 turns to face 4, taking a pose with her left arm in a low 'crooked'-shape, her right in a low V, both wrists angled. On count 3 she steps backward and, still facing 4, takes a pose with her back to the

---

[12] Because Nijinsky gives N3 one step less in [46], it gives the others time to close in to her, but puts her on the opposite foot for the exit walk. Nijinsky showed all three nymphs veering upstage on [45] as they carry the veils. In practice there seems to be no need for such veering.

audience, her right arm in a rounded >-shape toward 12, the wrist and hand curved and near the shoulder, her left arm out toward 4, slightly bent, the wrist angled, her head inclined forward. After holding this pose she swivels around to face 12, taking this same pose to the other side, her back again to the audience [45]. Again she pauses and then steps back repeating the first pose to the other side, her right arm in a low backward crooked-shape, her left in a low forward V, both wrists angled. Two forward off-beat steps follow [46] on the first of which she lowers her arms.

[44-47] Measure 44 is a change for N1 and N2 and also for N4. As if knowing that they have no immediate duties, the first two nymphs wander off toward 12, taking three steps and a pause, three times. Starting with an alert head, they incline their heads forward on the third step, return them to alert and then incline them backward on the sixth step, return to alert and then on the ninth step incline them forward again. During these steps they must travel comparatively little so that N4 can catch up with them [end of 45]. On [44] N4 starts toward 12, and, passing upstage of N3, N6 and N7, she follows N1 and N2 with steps in the same timing, but starting on the right foot and taking an extra step at the end. Her head, however, remains quiet. She then turns quickly to face 4 [45]. N1 and N2 make a similar turn a moment sooner. As they turn they take hands,[13] N4 taking N2's hand while N1 and N2 take hands; N1 holds her tunic with her left hand. All then walk evenly on the beat toward 4 as N4, looking back toward them, leads them [46]. After four steps, perhaps because they see the faun, N1 and N2 stop [47], N2 letting go of N4's hand. They watch N4 as she continues walking, still looking back at N1 and N2 as though wondering why they are not following.

[44-49] The faun, having come down the steps [end of 43], still facing 12, takes two diagonal steps (to move downstage of the rock) and then continues with eight even steps toward 12 [44, 45]. He turns to face 4 and, seeing N4, follows her, moving slightly downstage [46, 47] until he has passed her. Just before [48] he swivels around to face her. Because N4 has been looking back at N2 she does not see him until she is close to him. Startled, she turns quickly away from him and, looking back at him, arms up with fingers spread, she leans toward 4 as she runs away from him with light springy steps[14], exiting at 12 [48-49].

[48-55] The faun watches N4 depart [48-49] and then follows after her with seven even steps [49, 50]. N1 and N2 realize they should be assisting N5 and so walk past her [49] into position at her right side, turning to face her[15]. A quiet moment ensues [50] as the music leads into a return of the unveiling theme and N5 begins to loosen the last part of her dress in the same manner as she did the first veil [51], spreading it out in front of her before dropping it [52]. As she begins to loosen the dress her action catches the faun's attention, for on his last step toward 12 he turns his head to the right, observing N5. As N5 is about to drop the dress,

---

[13] Nijinsky's words here state "holding hand".

[14] For this light springy run Nijinsky wrote that her torso leans forward on each landing support, coming upright in between while in the air, a rather fast coordination not easy to achieve, but suggestive of a panting reflex in breathing.

[15] There is a question as to whether N1 and N2 see the faun here and are focused on him; perhaps this is the reason N1 fails to catch the dress when the faun turns and steps toward them. Or it could be they are watching N5 and only look at the faun when he makes his abrupt movement.

N1, who is near her, bends forward with arms out ready to catch it [52], but at this same moment the faun turns abruptly to face 4, and takes a step toward the nymphs. Startled, N1 misses the dress, looks quickly at N2 as if giving her a signal, for they both turn toward 4, raise their arms, left arm in a low V, right in a high >-angled position, and, looking back toward 12, exit with fast, slightly low steps [53]. As they start to depart [53] N5 looks at them and then, turning to face 4, feeling undressed, she places her left arm across her chest and then her right across her hips. Looking down at the dress she then lowers into a kneel, bends forward and, as she begins to pick it up, raises her head to look toward 4 where the nymphs exited [54]. With the dress now in her hands, she places her right arm across her chest and with head inclined forward as she begins to rise, places her left arm across her lower torso. While N5 is thus engrossed in picking up the dress, the faun has traveled toward 4. Passing N5, who does not see him, he turns quickly to face her, taking a step directly toward her[16]. Holding the dress against her body, N5 moves toward 4 with four fast low steps, being stopped on the fourth by encountering the faun [55]. She freezes in her tracks; thus, with N5 and the faun face to face, both standing perfectly still, the duet begins.

[55-63] For two measures [55, 56] total stillness creates dramatic tension. What is the relationship between them? What will she do? What will the faun do? He is not a complete stranger, yet he is unpredictable. He stands tall, regarding her, his neck tautly lengthened, his chin slightly in. Slowly N5 sinks toward the floor, her head gradually inclining forward [57]. She lowers with dignity, not submissiveness. Again there is stillness [58, 59]. Lifting her head and slowly inclining it backward, she rises to normal standing [60] and then leans backward away from the faun [61]. During this time she is still covering her body with the dress. Spurred now into action, the faun makes three 'pawing' movements in place, lifting the lower leg slightly backward like an impatient horse, stepping on high half-toe while moving enough upstage to be able to pass behind the nymph. In reaction to his sudden display of energy, N5 turns away from him to face 12 [start of 62] and, leaning away from him but with her head upright, looking at him, she thrusts her right arm backward toward him, her thumb abducted and pointing downward, as though to repel him (or show displeasure at such antics?). Before extending her right arm she must place her left hand where her right hand was holding the dress to prevent it from slipping down. The faun's pawing steps, left, right, and right again, end with weight in place on the left foot. Both arms then extend in front of him, the left higher than the right, the right on the center line of the body, both with angled thumbs [62]. This upward movement of the arms lifts him into two high forward steps which serve as a preparation for a swift run forward into a big *croisé* leap toward 12. He passes behind N5 just before taking off so that this goat-like leap can be seen. During the leap he turns his head to look back at her, swinging his right arm down and out into a V toward her, thumb still angled; his left arm lowers toward 12, the hand now flat, wrist abducted. During this leap the right leg is carried forward, the left is bent backward, with ankle flexed[17]. Pausing after landing from the leap (a deepening of the landing here gives an animal-like quality), he takes three more

---

[16] Rhythmically it is significant that the faun's step toward N5 is on the 16th note (semi-quaver) just before measure 55, a last moment, abrupt step, which stresses the act of confrontation. N5's arresting step toward him occurs a moment later [55, count 1].

[17] As the scenery depicts a brook between centre stage and stage left, it has been suggested that he is leaping over the brook at this point. A nice idea, but not a realistic one, since he does not leap over it again, and he and N5 subsequently travel to and fro between stage left and stage right. It is more likely that he is showing off in a moment of exuberance, of high spirits.

steps toward 12 before whipping around to face N5 again, arms down, hands in the standard low position, wrists angled [start of 63]. As the faun passes her [62], N5 turns her head toward him, inclining it forward, and at the same time closes her right arm across her hips to hold the lower part of the dress. Perhaps thinking that he is going off, she follows him toward 4 with three quick steps, stopping abruptly with a low forward step as he turns to face her.

[63-70] The next passage of music, marked *"très expressif"*, accompanies two more measures of stillness [63, 64]. The nymph breaks this stillness by slowly rising. The backward inclination of her head at the end of this rise leads into a repeat of the previous torso tilt away from the faun [65, 66]. As the music becomes more animated the faun rises swiftly into a 4th position on high half-toe, arms extended forward as before, the right higher than the left, both hands with angled thumbs [67]. As before N5 whips around, stepping and leaning away from him, again looking at him as she extends her left arm backward toward him as though saying "No!" [67]. Once more she must swiftly take hold of the dress with her right hand before releasing her left hand to gesture toward the faun[18]. Holding quite still [during 67], both then walk toward 4 [68], the nymph taking four low steps, the faun walking in a 'tall' dominating manner with six high, extended steps, passing behind and beyond her[19]. As he passes her she stops, turning her head to watch him. The faun lowers his arms, his hands now in standard carriage as he takes another step toward 4 and then swiftly turns to face N5 once more. Immediately he rises again into a high 4th position, arms extended (as at the start of 67), and again she turns and leans away from him, repelling him with her right arm [69]. As before, they remain motionless until they repeat the same number of steps traveling toward 12 [70], the faun passing behind N5 and again turning suddenly to face her.

[71-73] The unison style of walk which now follows suggests some degree of harmony between them. Each has the torso contracted (shortened) over the left back diagonal body direction, the back arching so that the left shoulder comes closer to the left hip. (Note that this contracted torso position is always on that back diagonal surface which is closest to the audience. As they change direction the body contraction and arms also change to the other side). The faun's arms are crooked, close to the body, his left (downstage) arm higher than the upstage arm, both thumbs remaining angled during the traveling. The nymph holds the dress against her body as before, her left arm being higher, the right lower. Traveling toward 4, each takes swift low steps in which, on each step, the knees remain close together. Less distance than before is covered with these steps [71]. As they travel she is in front looking back at the faun, her head inclined toward her 'back' shoulder, giving an expression perhaps of self-protection. His head is also inclined over his 'back' shoulder but turned into the direction of travel, giving a more aggressive expression. After four steps she stops and the faun passes beyond her before both turn at the same time to face the other way. Both then travel toward 12 (a symmetrical repeat of the previous phrase), N5 again looking back at the faun [72][20].

---

[18] Nijinsky has written these actions of faun and nymph as being completely simultaneous. A split second delay on the part of the nymph can be psychologically more effective.

[19] For both faun and nymph all these walking patterns start with the downstage foot.

[20] While traveling they need to work their way slightly more to stage left so that later the third dress is not dropped center stage.

Note that for each change of direction she changes her arms in holding the dress, the right one being higher as she travels toward 12, the left higher as she travels toward 4.[21] Their restless traveling to and fro is interrupted by the arrival of the attendant nymphs. First N6 and N2 enter from 4 [71], their left arms sharply angled, elbows downward, while the right arms are held backward, in a low >. After four steps they stop, lower their left arms and raise their right so that the hand is curved and near the shoulder, at the same time turning their heads to look toward 4, anticipating the arrival of the next nymph. N1 enters in the same manner [72], and similarly, while raising her right arm, hand near shoulder, turns her head toward 4 where N7 and N3 are about to enter. These last two having arrived in a similar manner [73], all five nymphs lower their arms, hands curved, and with alert heads look at N5.

[73-75] The faun and N5 travel once more with swift, low steps toward 4 [73], but now only three steps, the momentum diminishing. N5 pauses on count 2 and her right hand replaces her left in holding the dress against her chest, thus freeing her left arm to gesture toward the faun. As she takes an additional low step forward toward 4, sinking to her left knee, she leans away from the faun but, looking back at him, allows the faun to link his right elbow around her left. At this point her right arm opens into a sideward V, the dress dropping to the floor. The faun has turned away (toward 12) but leans toward her, looking at her as he links his right elbow from above around her left. His left arm is now raised in a high <-angled position toward 12. This is the only moment in the ballet where there is physical contact between the faun and the chief nymph. It is at this moment that the attending nymphs pause and lower their arms as they witness the elbow-linking [end of 73]. As the nymphs start walking slowly toward the couple [74 count 1], the faun raises his head and sees them. N5 also turns her head and sees them. She quickly looks back at the faun, slips her arm out of his and reaches down to pick up the dress. Clearly she is no longer interested in any further close encounter with the faun. As she slips her arm away the faun straightens up, lowers his left arm and places his right hand near his head, the base of the thumb touching high on his forehead, the hand being in the angled thumb position directed toward the nymphs. Nijinsky refers to this position as "Pointing with his thumb like a horn". It is actually his hand which points away from his forehead. Since he maintains this position long after N5 has exited, it is clearly directed to the other nymphs who continue to walk slowly toward him [74, 75], their arms still down at their sides, hands curved. N5, having picked up the dress, rises [75] and drapes it across her body, her right arm across her chest, but, although she keeps her arms close to her body as though still holding the dress, she lets it drop and exits with low steps, head erect [76]. As she picks up the dress and rises, the faun, while still looking back toward 4, takes four slow steps toward 12, away from the other nymphs[22]. As N5 begins to exit, the five nymphs stop walking and stand close together in line, N6 and N2 turning to face 4. All have the left arms down, the right arms across the chest, hands near the shoulder, except N1, whose arms are in the opposite position. All look at the faun (toward 12) except N2, who looks toward 4.

---

[21] N5 must manipulate the dress so that a) it is sufficiently spread to cover her body without having one end trail on the floor, thus posing the danger of catching her foot in it, and b) it is not so bunched up that she appears to be holding the washing!

[22] For stage spacing it is important that the size of these steps be appropriate to allow him comfortably to return to the dress later on.

[76-78] After holding this pose briefly [during 76], the nymphs begin to turn away and leave. First N3 and N7 turn toward 4 [77]. N3, who leads, is looking back toward 12 and holding N7's hand; N7 leans back toward 12, her head inclined back (perhaps with disdainful disapproval?). They exit with quick steps, knees slightly bent. N1 follows two counts later, also looking back toward the faun but with her head inclined forward, her right hand close to the shoulder, palm facing in, her left arm out toward 12 in a low V. The last nymphs to leave are N2 and N6. N2 takes two steps away from the faun; N6 pauses and takes only one step [78, count 2]. With her left hand N2 grasps N6's left wrist, as though pulling her toward 4, urging her to leave. N6, her back to the audience, is looking toward the faun, her right arm gesturing toward him as though still curious as to what he will do. Both nymphs then exit, [79] with quick, springy steps on high half-toe with soft knees. As they start to exit the faun, who has remained still since [76], drops his right hand from his forehead and turns quickly to face 4. He remains still as he watches the last two nymphs depart.

[79-86] The opening theme of the music returns, now in 4/4 [79]. The faun continues to remain still, then, drawn to the dress, he takes two steps forward toward it, moving toward 4 [80]. Fascinated, he pauses, and then with another step arrives next to the dress [81]. Two gentle pawing steps in place suggest his remembering the excited feeling before his one big leap; they also suggest 'marking the ground' in the manner of an animal establishing territorial rights [82][23]. Perhaps seeing the nymphs coming, he takes a firm step forward, past the dress, his gaze now in their direction. He then pauses and it is at this point that four nymphs, N6, N7, N3 and N1, return to tease/taunt him. Led by N6, they enter holding hands with arms crossed, i.e., the left arm is across the body holding the right hand of the nymph behind. This tight, protective formation includes the detail of N6 looking back at the others as they come in, her free right arm held with the hand close to the shoulder. The last nymph, N3, holding N7's left hand with her left hand, gives an impression of reluctance as she leans away toward 4, her head also inclined backward. All travel quickly toward the faun, then, as they stop, N6 turns her head to look at him. All release hands as the faun turns quickly away from them to face 12 [end of 82]. Almost aggressively, the first two nymphs (N1, N6) take a low step forward [83], twisting the body so that the back of the chest is toward the audience, their arms gesturing toward the faun, the right in a low V, the left more backward in a low L-shape. As they start toward him the faun takes a step away from them, his head turned to look at N6. She and N1 in unison continue to advance toward him. Next, with their chests turned to face toward the audience, they perform rapid arm gestures with which they express their teasing[24]. The intensity of the music suggests intensity on the part of the nymphs, but how 'angry' are they? He has disturbed the chief nymph's bathing ritual, and they seem intent on communicating that this disturbance is not acceptable. Also it is probably evident to them that they cannot retrieve the dress. The question arises as to how vehement this chastisement is, to what degree does it express "Shame on you!" or "How dare you!"? After these arm gestures the first two nymphs turn quickly to face 4, rising into a high 4th position, right arms in a high

---

[23] The two steps in place can be used to travel if he is not close enough to the dress. It is important that the last step be beyond the dress so that he will be next to it when he kneels.

[24] In Nijinsky's version these chastising gestures include rotation of the upper arm. Because the arms are bent, this rotary action changes the directional placement of the lower arms and produces rounder, more three-dimensional gestures. These are less severe than the sagittal, scissor-like gestures of the lower arms seen in memory-based versions of the ballet.

>, left arms bent and gesturing backward toward the faun, both arms with rounded wrists and hands. With steps on high half-toe in triplet rhythm [84], followed by four slower steps, N6 and N1 travel toward 4, veering slightly upstage in order to pass behind N7 and N3 who now, in their turn, are advancing toward the faun with the same 'chastising' movement phrase as that performed by N6 in [83]. As N7 and N3 travel away from the faun [85] they move into line with N6 and N1. All then lower their arms and, as they link hands, their heads incline forward toward 4, except that of the leader, N1, whose head is turned and inclined toward 12. Just before they start to exit all incline their heads backward except N1, who, as leader, has her head upright looking back toward 12, her right arm in a low V gesturing toward the way they are going. The last nymph, N7, has her free arm in an open backward V toward the faun. All exit with six triplet steps [86][25] (or as many triplet steps as are needed).

[84-92] As the first two nymphs turn away after gesticulating toward him [84], the faun, still facing 12, lowers onto his left knee close to the dress, his arms open in a low V, his torso contracted over the right back diagonal, his head turned and inclined forward toward 4. The focus of his attention is on the dress; he disregards the nymphs. He remains there until the nymphs exit, at which point he concentrates on the dress, slowly inclining his head to the left to look down at it, and changing his arm gestures to relate more directly to it, his right arm sharply angled backward, his left in an open angle closer to the floor, the hand being in front of his right knee; both thumbs are angled [86]. In this position his fingertips point toward the dress as though his energy is 'pouring' through his hands to it. Remaining there, the faun slowly lifts his head [87], turning it to look back toward 4 (where N5 had exited; is he perhaps thinking of her?). After a pause he returns to looking down at the dress, his head inclined again over his left shoulder [88]. He then leans forward, reaching his hands down to pick up the dress by the hem, allowing most of it to hang down. Rising into a low 4th position [89] and straightening up his torso, he then contracts it over the right, backward, surface as he slips the dress onto his arms so that it hangs over his elbows, his arms now being bent with the lower arms directed inward. With a swift turn to face 4, his torso contracting over the backward left side, he takes a step forward in preparation for the highly animated passage which follows. With arms now more separated, the right (upstage) arm higher than the left, he performs six swift, slightly low steps toward 4, his head inclined into that direction [90]. Stopping abruptly, he quickly swivels around and, head still inclined forward, torso contracted on the other side, left arm now higher than the right, he throws his head backward as he opens his mouth wide and, as Nijinsky stated, "laughs like an animal"[26]. This running pattern and the laugh are repeated to the other side as the faun travels slightly upstage [91]. As though to repeat the sequence a third time, he takes three steps toward 4 [92], but seeing N2 enter he turns swiftly and travels toward 12, with a total of seven steps moving again slightly upstage.

[92] N2 enters [92] advancing swiftly toward the faun, her left arm in a low V toward him, her right arm in an L-shape parallel to the floor. She pauses briefly, then, as if changing her mind, perhaps because the faun is moving away, she steps back into a high 4th position

---

[25] Nijinsky gave no rotational state for N1's head here, thus it would face the audience, which seems out of character. It is likely that she either continues to look backward, or looks into the direction where they are all exiting.

[26] For this laugh the mouth should open wide; a lateral stretch of the muscles as well as the vertical opening.

and swivels quickly to face 4, bringing her arms in closer to her body and then opening them up, the right in a high >, the left in a low V position toward the faun as she starts to travel rapidly away from him. As she departs her head is upright, looking back toward the faun [92 end].

[93] Having ignored N2, the faun continues toward 12 with the last three steps of this path [93]. Stopping abruptly on the last one and straightening up from his contracted torso position, he turns his head to 4 to look at N6, who has just entered. During his last three steps N6 enters, running in swiftly in the same manner as N2. However, perhaps because the faun is looking at her, N6 quickly turns away from him to face 4, but continues to look back at him (her back toward the audience). She pauses briefly, head upright, her right arm gesturing backward toward the faun. As she rises on her right leg, her left leg gestures toward 4 while her torso inclines slightly backward toward the faun. Inclining her body away from the faun, she then travels to 4, her arms now in the same positions as that of N2 on her exit, but N6 still has her back toward the audience. As she exits she looks back at the faun, appearing to wish to linger, perhaps still curious as to what the faun will do [93 end].

[94-101] Alone again, the faun turns quickly to face 4, holding still as though uncertain as to whether more nymphs might appear [94]. Perhaps realising that they have all gone, he sinks into his own world, concentrating on the dress as he starts to walk slowly toward his rock, his torso again in the contracted position, his head inclined forward over his right shoulder [95]. He takes four slow steps with somewhat bent legs, the knees fairly close together, but not as exaggeratedly as when he and the chief nymph were 'parading' to and fro during the duet. As he takes the fourth step, which is lower with knees close, his head returns to the arched neck position. Standing still, he slowly raises his arms higher (the dress still over his elbows) as he turns his head to the left, inclining it over his left shoulder. Turning his head to the right he starts to walk again toward 4, with his head much inclined over his right shoulder [97]. As though in another world, deeply absorbed in the dress, he continues his slow walk back to the rock taking a total of twelve steps [97, 98, 99][27]. At the end of this sequence when he is near the steps, he turns to face 12. At this point he adjusts the dress[28]. With arms reversed and lowered, his head now inclined over his left shoulder, the faun slowly mounts the steps [100, 101]. At the end of this measure he is at the top on his right foot. All this time he has maintained the diagonal torso contraction, always on the side which is toward the audience.

[102-106] His body returns to normal carriage; he begins to sink on his right leg while raising his left knee before stepping forward on the left and lowering first to his right knee, then to his left [102]. Holding the dress now only with his left hand, he slips his right hand along the dress as his right arm begins to extend backward low, rotated outward toward 4. This gesture is like a last wisp of remembrance of the departed nymphs. Coming upright and

---

[27] The 'other world' mood will be sustained if each step is on a slightly bent leg and each has a careful preparatory gesture near the ground with a bent leg. The foot is placed on the ground as though on a cloud, as with a cushioning effect.

[28] Nijinsky's instructions are: "The dress lies on the elbow joints and the palms hold it more at the edge." This is the moment for the faun to slip his left hand closer to the end of the dress; it will then be better placed for his smelling it and later for his laying it down. The right elbow may be bent more tightly to grasp the dress so that the left hand can be slipped toward the end.

placing his right foot next to his left knee, he returns his attention to the dress, inclining his head forward to look at it, his right arm bending so that the hand comes close to the side of the chest [102 end]. With his left hand he raises the dress close to his face [103] and "smells" it (Nijinsky's wording), his head inclined right diagonally backward, his torso contracted, his right arm crooked in front of his body with angled thumb. After a brief pause he lowers the dress, his head coming upright. He draws his right elbow backward, hand again close to his chest [104] as he inclines his head forward, turning it to the right in the direction of the audience. This movement suggests that he is concerned with the free end of the dress and is contemplating what he will do. Moving his right hand in front of the dress he gathers the lower part of it in toward him [105], laying the end down near his right side. As he kneels forward on his right knee, he leans forward and extends his left arm forward (thus guiding the upper end of the dress). He then comes partially upright, torso contracted as he brings his left foot near to his right knee. Then, kneeling forward on his left knee, the instep on the floor, he inclines his torso forward. His right arm, having unfolded backward as it slipped along guiding the free end of the dress, now returns to the crooked arm position with angled thumb [106]. His left arm lets go of the dress and takes weight as he lowers his body, his right leg extending backward onto the ball of the foot.

[107-110] With weight on his right foot and left hand and his upper body no longer twisted, he slowly extends his left leg backward to join the right, taking weight on the ball of the foot [107]. He then places his right hand on the floor in line with the right side of his waist, the hand turned in as he puts weight on it. His body is now at a forward angle, feet-to-shoulders, his chest rounded forward, his head inclined forward toward the floor. He sustains this body position for a moment, then his arms bend as he sinks slowly down to the floor until he is lying prone, feet no longer tucked under [end 107]. Lifting his head and pushing away from the floor with both hands, he arches his upper spine backward before again sinking slowly to the floor. As he sinks, his upper body is turned slightly to the right so that he rests on the left front diagonal surface of his chest, his right shoulder being slightly raised as a result [109][29]. Slowly he extends his right arm backward alongside his body until the hand is on the thigh. His last movement is that of relaxing, resting his forehead on the floor, his right arm dropping to the floor [110][30].

This ending is much simpler than those of memory-based versions. Nijinsky wrote only an outline for these last measures; this outline has been followed with the addition of only a few linking movements. With sustainment of the appropriate dramatic tension such a simple ending can be far more expressive than the overtly sexually suggestive versions seen in recent decades.

---

[29] It is important that in [109] the left elbow be dropped out of sight to avoid a 'grasshopper leg' elbow.

[30] Some performers choose to add the detail of the arm extending backward with tension, the conclusion being a sudden relaxation of arm and hand.

LABANOTATION GLOSSARY

Many items listed here are standard Labanotation usage; they are pointed out only as an aid in reading. All items marked with an asterisk (*) are special usages adopted for this score. The first time each item is used is indicated in parentheses.

1. MUSIC AND SCORING

Indication of Meter

Change of meter is shown just before it comes into effect, to serve as a warning of the change. In this placement it does not conflict with indications placed immediately after the bar line (meas. 22).

1a

Because of the frequent change in meter, the current meter is placed at the start of each new page as a reminder. Such reminder indications are placed in parentheses (meas. 15).

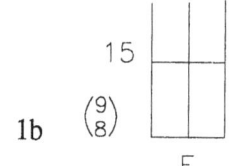

1b

Measure Numbers

On recto pages measure numbers are written in brackets to indicate they are not new measures, but the lateral continuation of the score. Use of these numbers provides a practical ready reference for reading recto pages (meas. 29).

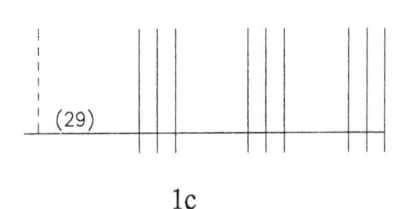

1c

Entrances and Exits*

Placement of the entrance and exit signs below and above the extended lines allows more room for other signs (front signs, measure and count numbers, etc.) (meas. 21: entrance, meas. 47: exit). Note use of the offstage area signs.

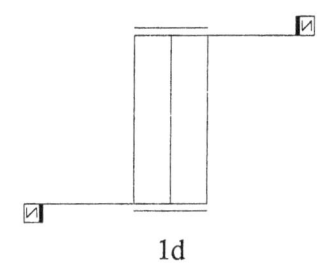

1d

Meeting Line*

Because the meeting line indicating "pass N4, N6, N7 on your right" cannot show the exact moment when each nymph is passed, a dotted line is extended from either side of the meeting line (N1, N2, N3, meas. 33).

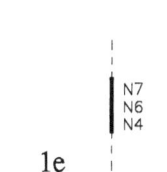

1e

Floor Plans

Small numbers in brackets refer to the number of steps taken (floor plan, 21-22).

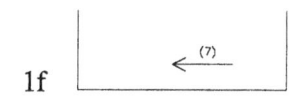

1f

Retracing a path is shown as in 1g (N4, meas. 25). Ex. 1h shows turning the corner and stepping in the opposite direction (F, meas. 62). When lines which were facing each other cross, as 1i (Nymphs, meas. 33) the slight spatial adjustment needed is not stated in the movement score.

A single arrowhead is used for one person, two arrowheads mean two people traveling, while the wedge arrowhead indicates several traveling.

Holding hands is indicated on floor plans by thin curved lines with a dot representing the hands (meas. 41).

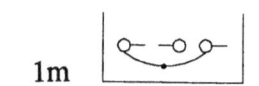

2. SUPPORTS, STEPS

Leg Rotation

Legs are parallel throughout (F, starting position).

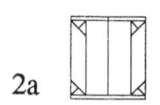

Style of Walk

For faun and nymphs all middle level steps are initiated by a brief contact on the ¼ heel (N1, meas. 21). (See **Style of Walking**, p. 18; **Style of Walking Sequences**, p. 182).

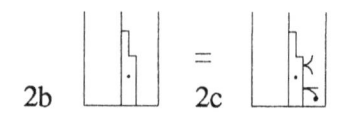

Indication of slightly bent legs while walking means relaxed, soft knees, i.e., with very little bend, 2d (N4, meas. 24). A greater degree (ˣ) indicates a shallow *demi-plié* level (N3, meas. 22; N1, N2, N3, meas. 33).

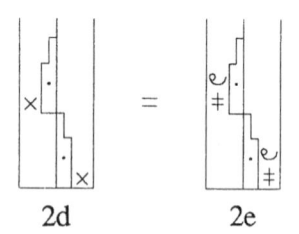

Resultant Contact

In walking, for each resulting ball of foot contact the gesturing leg is bent (N1, meas. 21, count 7). The level of the step (the support) dictates the degree of flexion for the leg performing the resultant touch. For a low step, as in 2h, the gesturing leg is more bent (N5, meas. 68).

Instep on the Floor*

The symbol for 'nail of toe' used in the leg gesture column indicates that the foot is stretched, and the instep touching the floor (F, meas. 107).

Amalgamated Turn

The swift open turns from one foot to the other have been simplified in the notation as Nijinsky gave no emphasis on exact performance. In Ex. 2k the right foot remains where it is, taking weight during the turn while the left leg results in a touching gesture (N1, N2, N3, end of meas. 23).

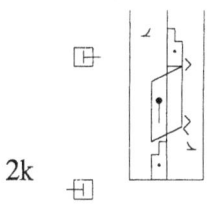

However, to avoid ending with an in-turned leg on the new support, it is practical to achieve most of the turn on the already supporting leg so that placement of the foot for the new support is more easily controlled. In 2l the right leg turns out during the first ¼ turn. As weight is transferred to the right foot a ¼ 'blind turn' occurs resulting in the right leg ending parallel.

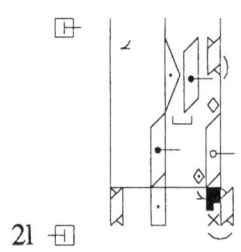

Deviation in Step Direction

Veering slightly toward the diagonal is shown by modification of the step direction, as in 2m (N4, meas. 44; F, meas. 47).

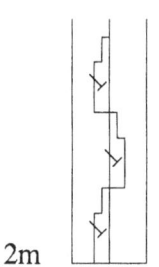

3. ARMS

Intermediate Directions*

A direction symbol preceded by a dot refers to a point between the stated direction and the nearest lower neighbouring direction in the same plane, Exs. 3a-g). In other words, the direction is slightly lower (22½°) than the stated direction without the dot. For 3g see F, meas. 7.

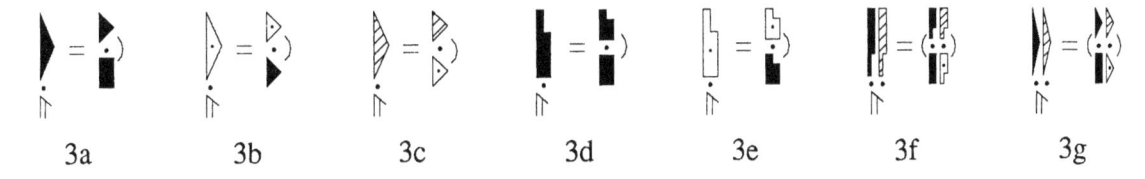

Minor Shift*

A very small shift forward is written as 3h.

The flute is shifted forward as it comes horizontal, 3i (F, meas. 5).

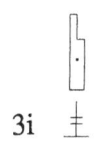

Stretching

3j, the motion of 'stretching' (no exact ending state) (F, meas. 107).

3k, the motion of 'bending' (no exact ending state) (F, meas. 107).

Timing of Folding*

For indications such as ⊻, ⊻, duration lines have not been included, 31. Timing for these movements is not sudden, but coincides with the timing for the arm movement as a whole (N1, N2, N3, meas. 23). Note: F, meas. 7 is an exception because of the slow movement.

31

'Angled Thumb' Position

The 'angled thumb' position used by the faun first occurs on meas. 7. The wrist is abducted, the hand is flat with the fingers together, the thumb abducted 90°.

3m

The base joint of the thumb touches the forehead (F, meas. 74).

3n

Linked Hands

When the nymphs have their hands 'linked' the palms of the two dancers face one another, and the fingertips touch. This is achieved by crossing the wrists, (N2, N3, meas. 21).

3o

Rotation*

A rotation symbol attached to a whole arm sign refers to a rotation of the upper arm, 3p (N2, N3, meas. 21). When such rotation is an action on its own, it is written with the upper arm symbol, (F, meas. 9).

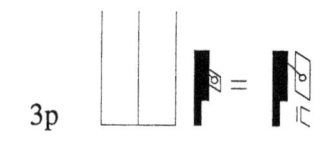

3p

A twist of the lower arm occurs when the faun places his hands on the floor, 3q (F, meas. 19). It is also used in connection with picking up a veil, 3r (N6, meas. 44).

3q   3r

Wrist Abduction

An angled wrist indication, 3s, is a folding (abduction) toward the little finger, (F, meas. 7).

3s

The wrist is occasionally angled diagonally backward, 3t (F meas. 70, 86).

3t

4. TORSO

Column for Augmented Chest

The right third column is understood to be for the augmented chest when indicating twists and folding, i.e., no presign is stated (F, meas. 1). Tilts of the chest and of the torso are written in the left third column; the appropriate presign being used for clarity (F, meas. 1).

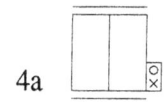

4a

Body Twists; Change of Direction*

During the half-swivel turns a space hold sign is used in the third right column in connection with the previous twist indication. The result of the space hold is that the chest should continue to face the same direction, usually the audience. A small vertical bow shows that the new rotational state is the destinational result of the space hold (N1, N2, N3, meas. 23). See also **Twist of the Chest**, p. 23. Description in terms of chest facing is not used in this score except when shown in parentheses as a reminder that the back is toward the audience, see **Orientation**, p. 52.

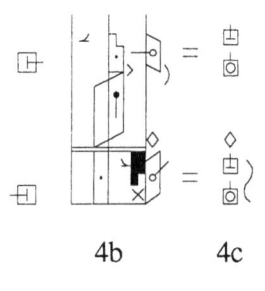

4b 4c

Torso Contraction

The indication for contracting the torso over one of the back diagonal surfaces, as in 4d, is the Labanotation equivalent of the movement as described by Nijinsky, 4e (F, N5, meas. 70). The sign for 'disappear', 4f, is used to cancel this torso contraction, or the sign for 'neither flexed nor bent', 4g, is used when appropriate.

4d 4e

4f 4g

Direction from Body Part (DBP)

Ex. 4h states that direction is judged from the right side of the waist (F, meas. 107).

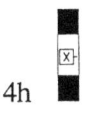

4h

5. HEAD

Minor Tilt - The 'Alert' Head Position*

The convention of the special sign of 5a is used for the lengthening of the back of the neck together with a very slight pulling in of the chin, the eyes remaining forward. An attached head rotation can be added as in 5c. See **Details on Movement Style and Usage**, p. 21 for fuller explanation.

5a 5b 5c

In a forward somersault for the head the forward rotation occurs on the Atlas joint, the chin moving in to the base of the neck (F, meas. 109).

Looking

The face sign, in combination with a Front sign, means that the performer actively looks into that stage direction, 5e (N4, meas. 25). The face sign, combined with an indication of a person, means that the performer is actively looking at the person stated, 5f (N5, looking at N6, N7, meas. 29).

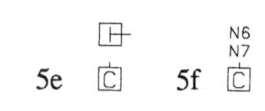

Note that a small Front sign in parentheses does **not** mean active looking, 5g (F, start. posn.). See also **Orientation** below.

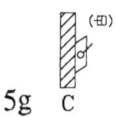

In 5h, N5 has her face directed to the audience, an unusual feature which occurs only when opening the veil or the dress (N5, meas. 31).

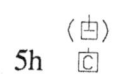

The eyes (not the full face) look into the stated direction, 5i, (F, meas. 7). When such orientation is toward a person without actively looking at her (i.e., the person is in the peripheral vision) the indication of that person is placed in parentheses, 5j (N5, meas. 38).

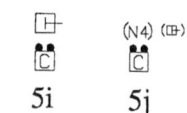

Awareness

The right side of the head (ear) is aware of the side of the room (as if listening) (F, meas. 6).

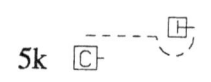

Sign for Mouth

The flute is near the mouth (F, starting position).

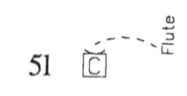

Three-dimensional extension of the mouth, i.e., 'mouth open wide' (F, meas. 90).

Sign for Forehead

The forehead is the 'forward high' part of the head (F, meas. 74; meas. 110).

6. ORIENTATION*

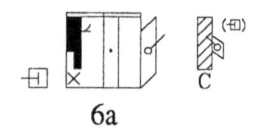

A very small Front sign placed in parentheses is used alongside the head indication as an aid in determining quickly into which stage direction the head is facing. Without this clue three sources of information have to be checked: the performer's Front, direction and degree of chest rotation, and direction and degree of head rotation. Note that this special indication does not contain the instruction that the head should actively look into the stated stage direction (N1, meas. 21).

On a few occasions the performer's front is towards upstage, i.e., her back is to the audience. As a reading aid a Front sign with the front of the chest symbol is placed in parentheses on the left-hand side of the staff to indicate the room direction into which the front of the chest is facing (N6, N7, N4, meas. 32).

6b

7. VALIDITY*

The rule used in this score is automatic cancellation. When the result of a previous movement is to be retained a hold sign is used, this must be specifically cancelled by ⊙ , ∧ or another movement of the same kind.

Head

To simplify keeping track of the validity of head tilts and rotations, attached rotations are used with the appropriate head direction. Repetition of the head direction may be needed when a change of rotation occurs, as in 7a, or repetition of the same attached rotation may be required when a head direction changes, as in 7b (N1, meas. 22; F, meas. 3).

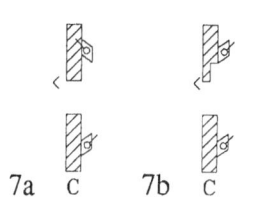

7a c   7b c

The special 'alert' position for the head is understood to cancel a head tilt and vice versa (F, meas. 14-15).

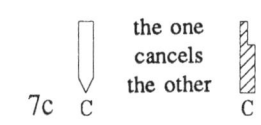

the one cancels the other

7c c   c

Hand, Fingers

A new arm direction cancels previous flexing, stretching, and/or abducting of the wrist, hand or fingers. Hold signs are used if such hand and/or wrist positions are to be retained. They are then cancelled by another indication for that part, or by ⊙ or ∧ .

The angled thumb position in meas. 7 is cancelled in meas. 9 by ∧. In meas. 17 the hand position is cancelled by the forward low arm movement which follows, 7d.

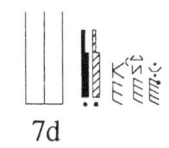

7d

8. CENTER OF WEIGHT

Ex. 8a shows the center of weight shifted forward (N1, N2, N3, meas. 32) in anticipation of the free flow traveling led by the center of weight, 8b (N1, N2, N3, meas. 33).

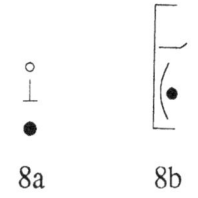

8a   8b

9. DYNAMICS

      9a   9b   9c   9d   9e   9f

The above examples indicate the various dynamic signs used throughout the score: 9a shows the sign for press (F, meas. 14); 9b indicates free flow (as in continuous walking) (N1, N2, N3, meas. 33); 9c is the sign for strong (N5, meas. 62); 9d indicates emphasis (used for lengthening the neck) (F, meas. 52) and 9e is a strong accent (used for the head and mouth when the faun "laughs like an animal") (F, meas. 90).

These signs relate to the individual body parts but when placed in an addition bracket, 9f, they relate to the whole movement (F, meas. 48).

10. AUTOGRAPHY

In 10a and b), the dots refer to the directions (N6, meas. 29; N1, meas. 43).

          10a   10b

In 10c the dot refers to the degree of flexion (N1, N7, meas. 82).

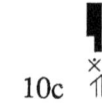

          10c

11. KEYS

The Stance Key ◆ is used for gestures relating to the direction of travel on the basic direction faced (the Front).

The Standard Key ✢ is used for gestures relating to the performer's body, as in handling the veils. See **Details on Movement Style and Usage**, p. 25, **Appendix D, Teaching Notes** p. 188 and the chart on pp. 189-190 for more detailed discussion on use of these keys.

INTRODUCTION TO THE LABANOTATION SCORE

The Photographs

Those photographs which link directly with Nijinsky's choreography of *Faune* have been selected for reproduction here, and are arranged in sequence with identification of the moment in the ballet in which they appear. They give an immediate image of the dance and illustrate the quality of the gestures caught at that moment. The visual impression of the line of the torso and head as well as placement of the limbs is a valuable aid in capturing a sense of the style of the work.

Labanotation Usages

It is most important that the **Labanotation Glossary**, pp. 47-54, be carefully studied before the score is read.

Position Reminders

Because there are so many changes in the direction and degree of upper body and head rotations, position reminders have been added. On each new page the previous concluding position is stated below the staff. Such reminder notes allow the reader to start at any point in the score, obviating the need to leaf back to find the placement of limbs, torso and head. When a turn has just occured the reminder gives enough information to get into the next movement phrase.

Interpreting the Score

While in certain respects *Faune* is a simple score, it is not easy to learn. Bringing the sequences to life requires a deep understanding of the choreographic devices used, the basic 'material', and the intent of the movement. The detailed **Study and Performance Notes**, pp. 17-46, which include the positions of the head, hands and arms, should be studied first. Reference should also be made to **Appendix D - Teaching Notes**, pp. 182-191.

It is possible to revive the ballet faithfully by following the score and at the same time to imbue it with personal expression and a deep understanding of the defined choreography.

The Costumes

Only outline costume sketches have been included; drawings of the veils give an indication of their size (see **Details on Movement Style and Usage**, p. 30). Much can be determined from published books containing de Meyer's photographs. In his preliminary notes Nijinsky himself gives a description (see **Nijinsky's Production Notes** p. 14).

It is important that the dancers have simple versions of the dresses to work with early on during rehearsals. The faun should wear his sandals during rehearsals to become familiar with them, particularly when he is on the rock or walking up and down the stairs. Simple versions of the two veils and of the part of the chief nymph's overdress must be on hand from the start to allow the dancers to practice their handling.

Practising Walks and Arm Positions

To get a sense early on of the style of this ballet, before starting in on the score itself, it is advisable to practise the various walking patterns and the appropriate stance in holding the head and torso, while at the same time using one or other typical position for the arms. The natural placement of the feet and the many different types of walking must be understood physically, as must the forward carriage of the weight, which helps to produce smooth, gliding steps. Changes from one arm position to another should also be practised. For additional recommendations on learning the ballet see **Appendix D - Teaching Notes,** pp. 182-191.

At first the constant twist in the body and head may prove tiring; the dancers must learn how to relax until these configurations begin to feel natural.

Style of Walks - Nijinsky's Literal Description

Nijinsky's method of writing walking (transference of weight) was more complicated than that used in Labanotation. Nijinsky's description was translated into what actually happens at the speed which the music demands. However, to give the reader an idea of what Nijinsky had in mind, and provide an understanding of his concept of a particular walk, the details which he specifically stated are written in Labanotation adjacent to the pertinent walking phrase.

Wording in the Labanotation Score

Words in quotes are a literal or appropriate translation of the wording Nijinsky included in his score. Words in parentheses are instructions added by the translators. Statements **in quotes** between parentheses are modifications of Nijinsky's wording.

PHOTOGRAPHS

and

SKETCHES

OF

NIJINSKY'S *FAUNE*

In the following photographs important moments in the ballet are identified. Except where otherwise stated, these photographs were taken by Baron Adolf de Meyer in 1912, soon after the first performances.

The line drawings, sketched during performances in 1912, are by Valentine Gross Hugo © DACS 1990.

58 NIJINSKY'S *FAUNE* RESTORED

1.

F, meas. 1
The opening pose.

2.

F, meas. 3
Lifting the flute
as he plays.

3.

F, meas. 7
The moment of looking back toward
where the nymphs will enter.

4.

F, meas. 17
Looking at the grapes.
(He does not eat them.)

PHOTOGRAPHS OF NIJINSKY'S *FAUNE* 59

5.

N4, meas. 24
(In Nijinsky's score her
arms are not so high.)

6.

N4, meas. 24
Landing from the spring.
(In the score her right
arm is higher.)

7.

N3, N2, N1, meas. 25
Position for the first three nymphs
as they follow N4 toward stage right.

8.

N5, meas. 31
Starting to undo
the first veil.

9.

N5, meas. 31
Holding up the first veil.
(Her face should be looking
straight ahead to the audience.)

10.

F, meas. 31
Sitting up as he
becomes aware of N5.

11.

Nymphs, meas. 33
(L to R: N4, N7, N6, N5, N3, N2, N1)
(The picture is not quite correct as N5 should still be holding
the veil when the other nymphs arrive at this position.)

12.

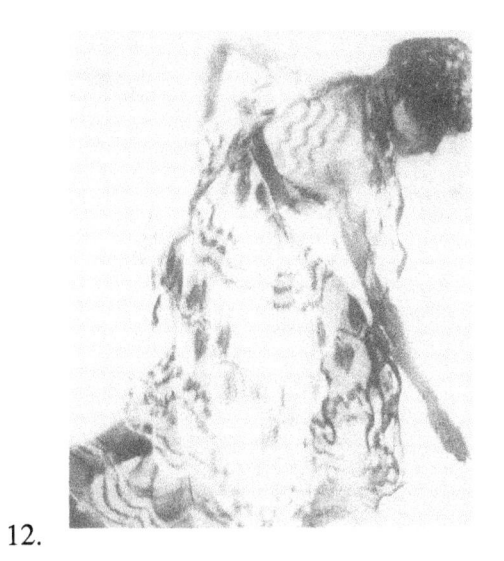

N6, meas. 44
Picking up the first veil.

13.

N3, meas. 44
Picking up the second veil.

14.

N5, meas. 44, ct. 3
(During these movements N5
should still be wearing the dress.)

62   NIJINSKY'S *FAUNE* RESTORED

15.

F, N4, meas. 48
The joyful nymph is surprised by the faun.

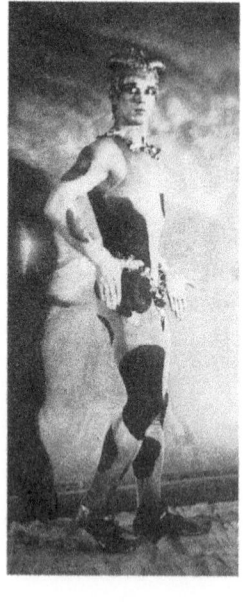

16.

F, meas. 51
His attention is
caught by N5.

Struss, 1916 (Harvith Collection)

17.

N1, (and also N2) meas. 53
Their exit after the dress
has been dropped.

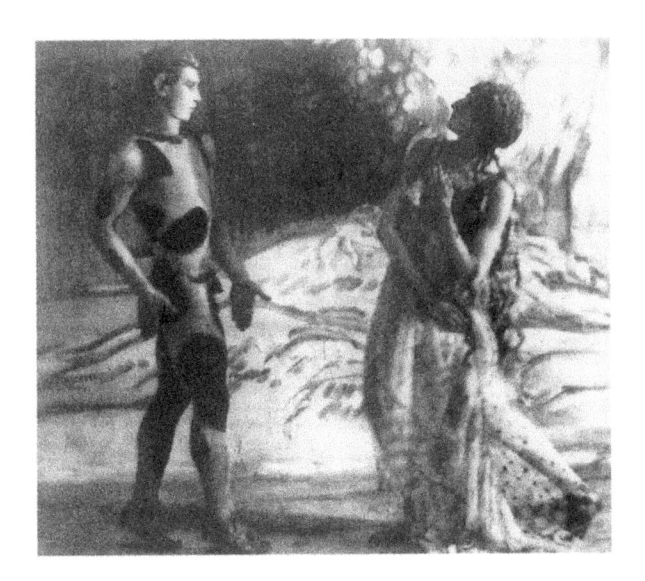

18.   F, N5, meas. 55
The moment of encounter.

19.

F, N5, meas. 62
The culmination of N5's
sinking and rising.

Struss, 1916 (Harvith Collection)

20.

F, N5, meas. 67
(Her costume is incorrect,
she should be in her chemise,
holding her dress.)

21.   N5, meas. 69
(The costume here is correct.)

22.   F, N5, meas. 73
The moment of linking elbows
(The costume here is correct.)

Struss, 1916 (Amon Carter Museum)

Struss, 1916 (Amon Carter Museum)

23.

Meas. 73
(L to R: N3, N7, N1, N2, N6; N5 with F)
The moment of N5 and F linking elbows,
the five nymphs having entered.

Comoedia Illustré, June 1912

24.

Struss, 1916 (Harvith Collection)

N5, F, meas. 74
After slipping her arm out of his,
she reaches for her dress.

25.

N5, meas. 75
Her arm position
as she exits.
(Her right arm should
be the upper one.)

26.

Meas. 76
(L to R: N3, N7, N1, N2, N6; N5 with F)
This picture is correct for the five nymphs.
However in the score N5 has already departed and the
faun has walked away as the nymphs approach him.
(This composite picture was probably for the camera.)

27.

F, meas. 76
Pointing with his thumb like a horn as he walks away from the nymphs.

28.

N3, N7, meas. 77
The first two nymphs leaving after having witnessed the elbow link.

29.

N1, meas. 77
Arm position as she leaves.

30.

N2, N6; F, meas. 78
The last two nymphs leaving.

31.

Nymphs, meas. 82
(L to R: N3, N7, N1, N6)
Four nymphs enter to
chastise the faun.
(The arms of N1 should be
crossed, as those of N7.)

32.

N6, meas. 83, ct. 1
Her step and arm position
as she begins to advance.

33.

Nymphs and faun, meas. 84
(L to R: N1, N6, N3, N7, F)
The second two nymphs chastising the
faun, the first two having drawn aside.

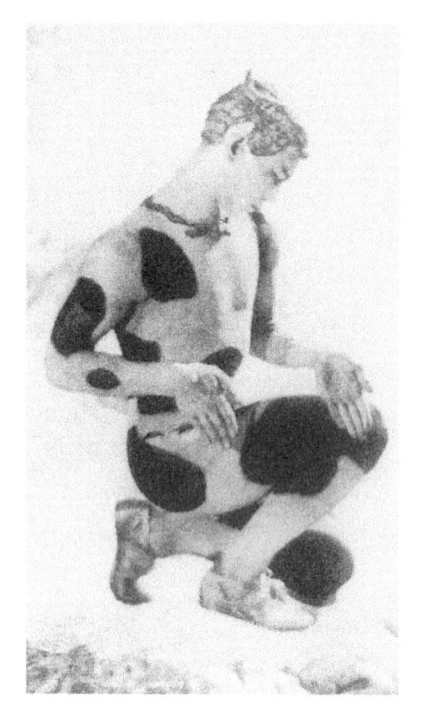

34.

F, meas. 86
About to pick up the dress.

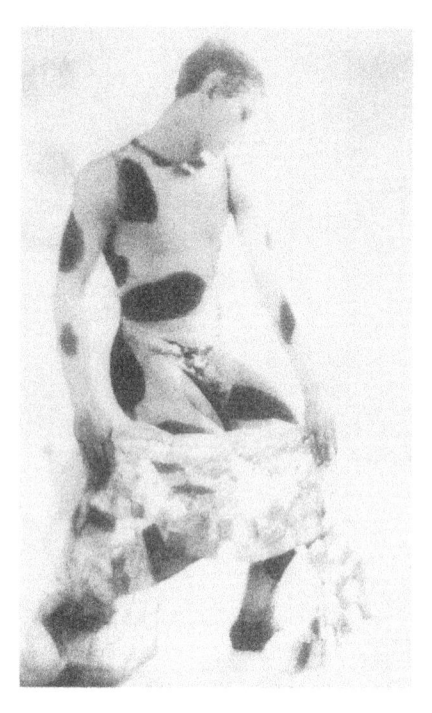

35.

F, meas. 89
Picking up the dress.

36.

F, meas. 90
Running with the
dress over his arms.

37.

F, meas. 90
"Laughing like an animal."

38.

N2, F, meas. 92
N2 retreating after her brief encounter with the faun.

39.

N6, F, meas. 93
N6 leaving after her brief encounter with the faun.

40.

F, meas. 103
The moment before lifting up the dress to smell it.

41.

F, meas. 106
Laying down the dress.
(In the score he has the other
knee forward at this moment.)

42.

F, meas. 110
The final repose.
(In the score the faun's right arm is
alongside his body, resting on the ground.)

THE CHOREOGRAPHIC SCORE

OF

NIJINSKY'S

L'APRES-MIDI D'UN FAUNE

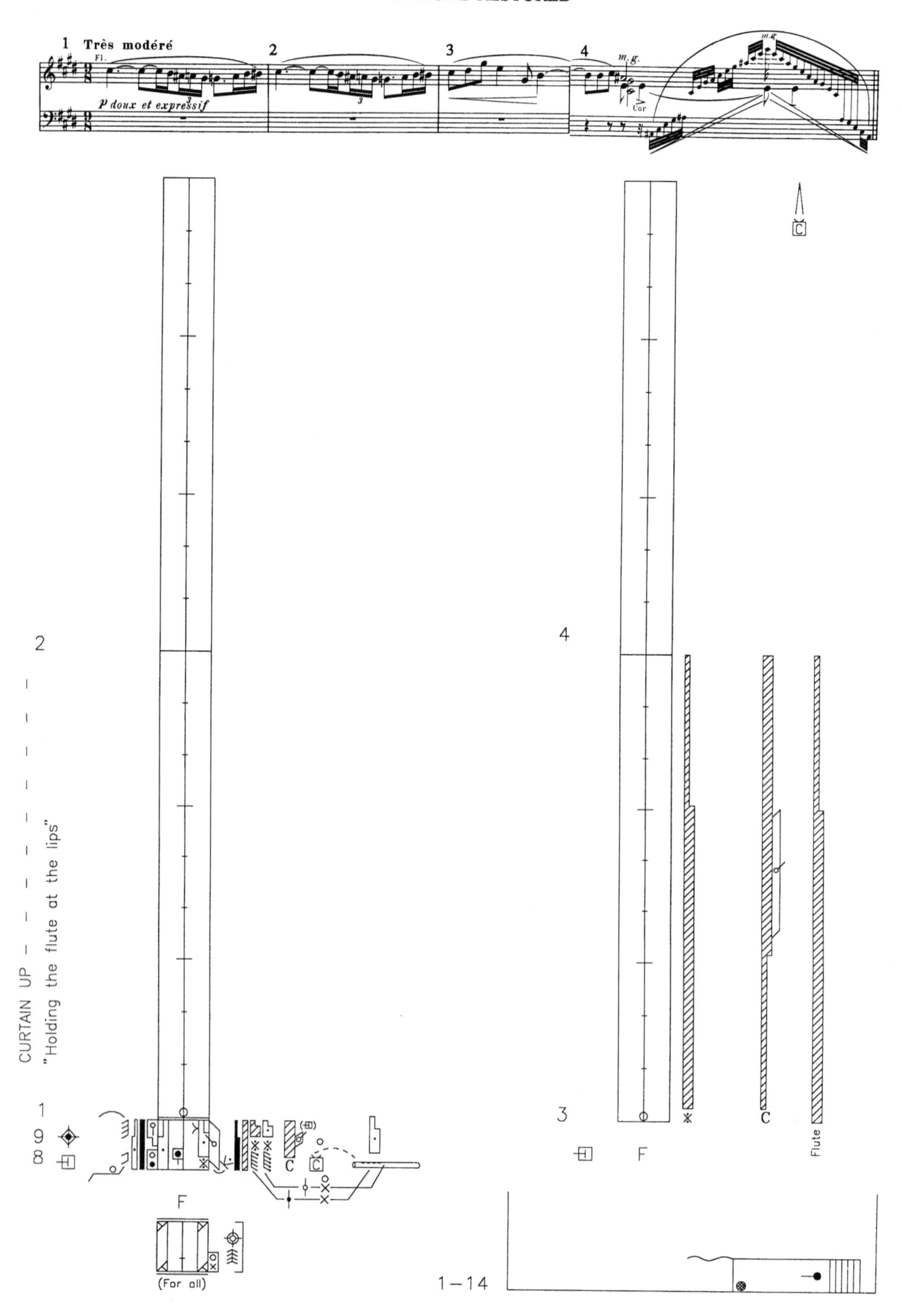

NIJINSKY'S *FAUNE* RESTORED

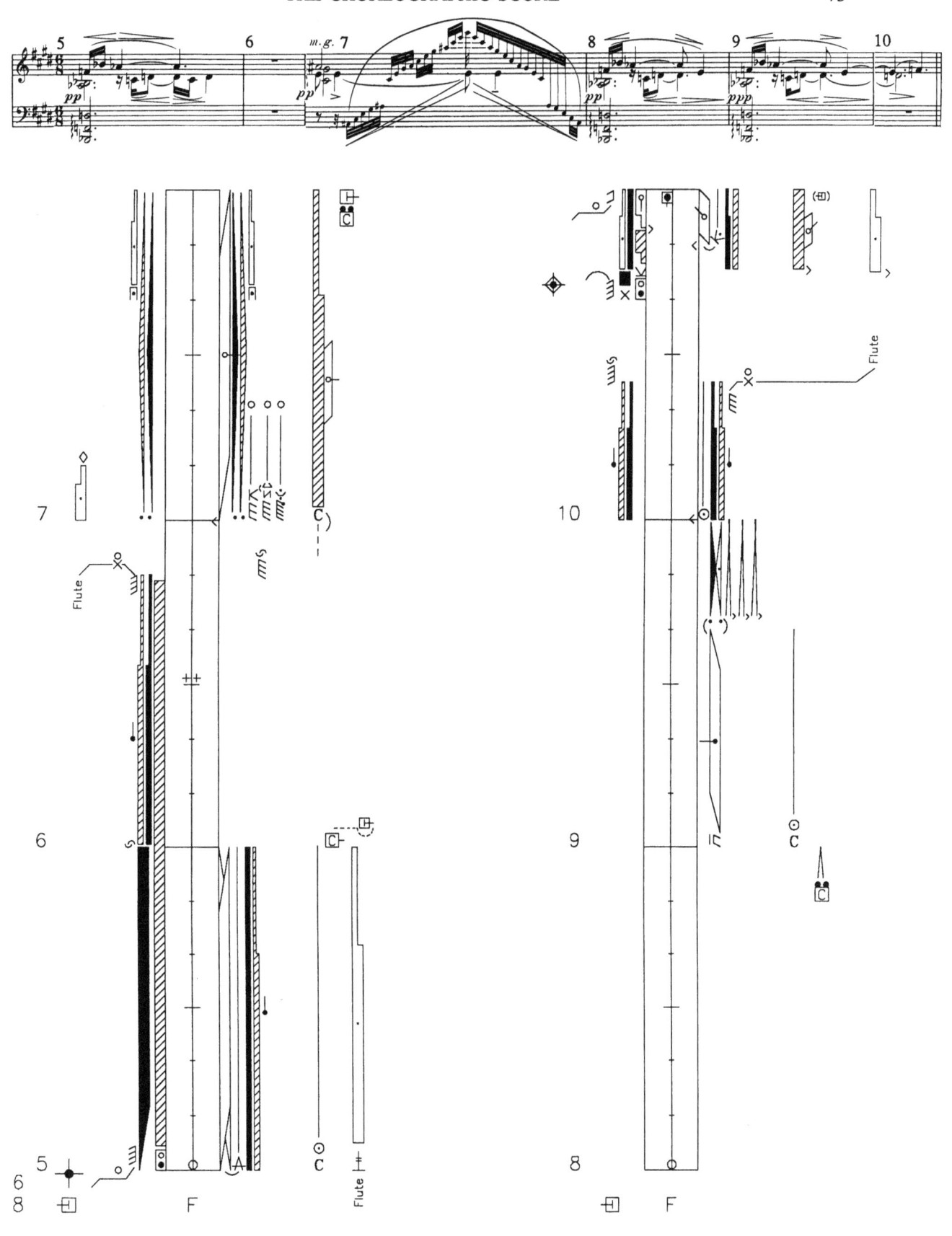

THE CHOREOGRAPHIC SCORE

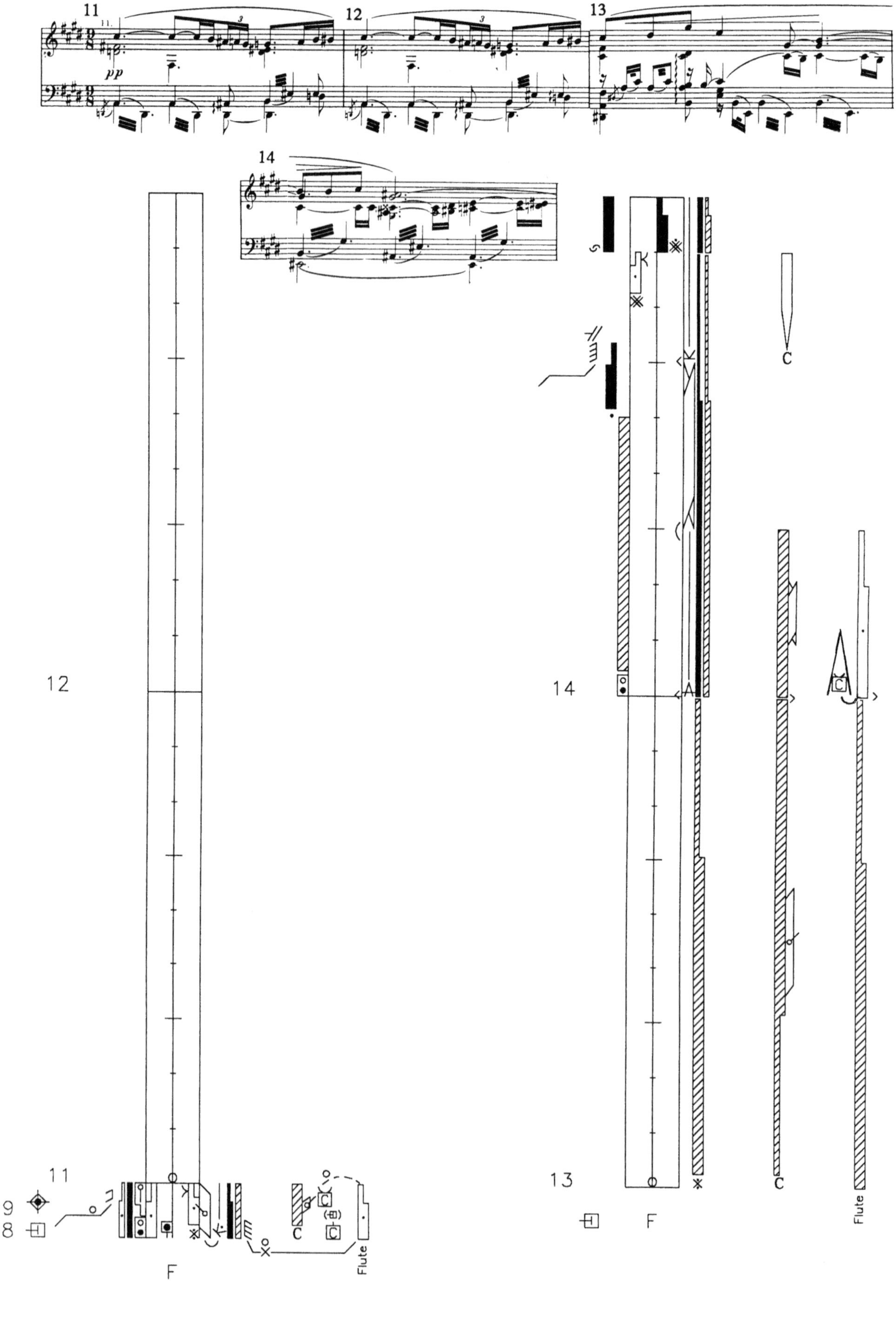

11
12
13
14
pp
C
12
14
13
11
F
Flute

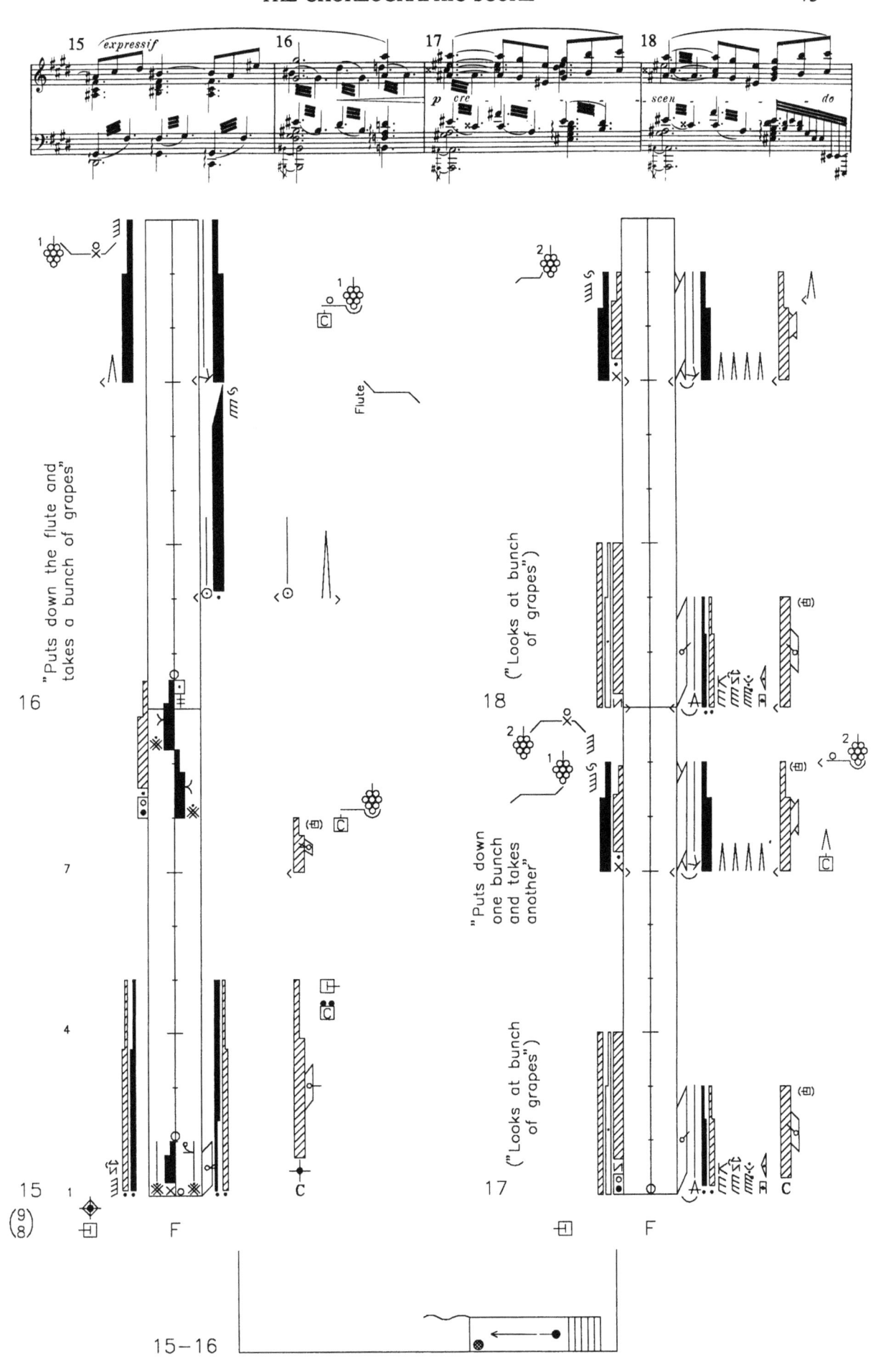

THE CHOREOGRAPHIC SCORE

"Puts down the flute and takes a bunch of grapes"

("Looks at bunch of grapes")

"Puts down one bunch and takes another"

("Looks at bunch of grapes")

15–16

76 NIJINSKY'S *FAUNE* RESTORED

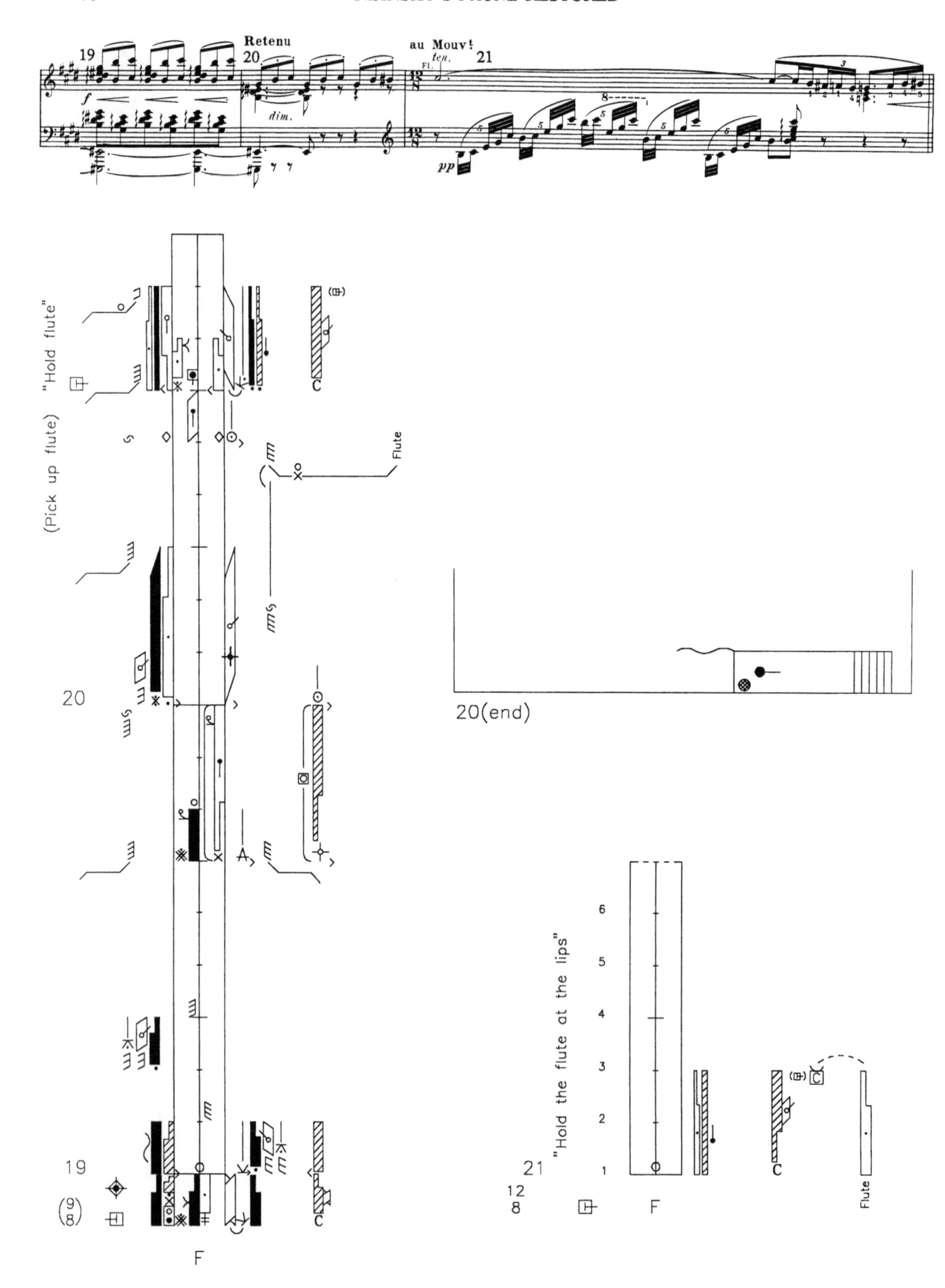

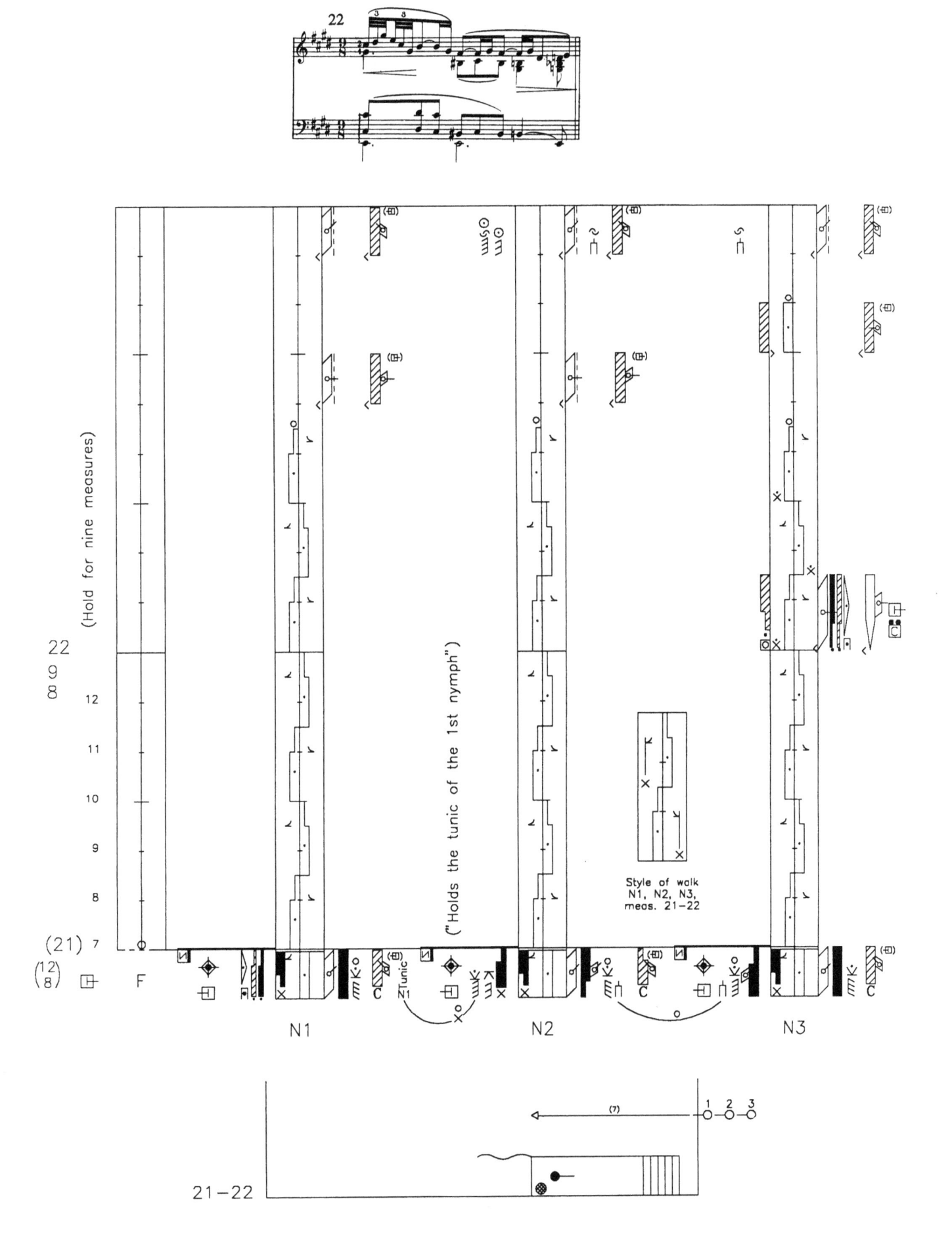

THE CHOREOGRAPHIC SCORE 77

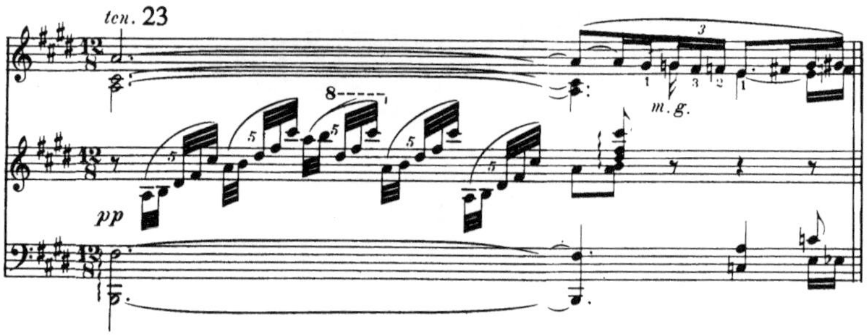
ten. 23
pp
m.g.

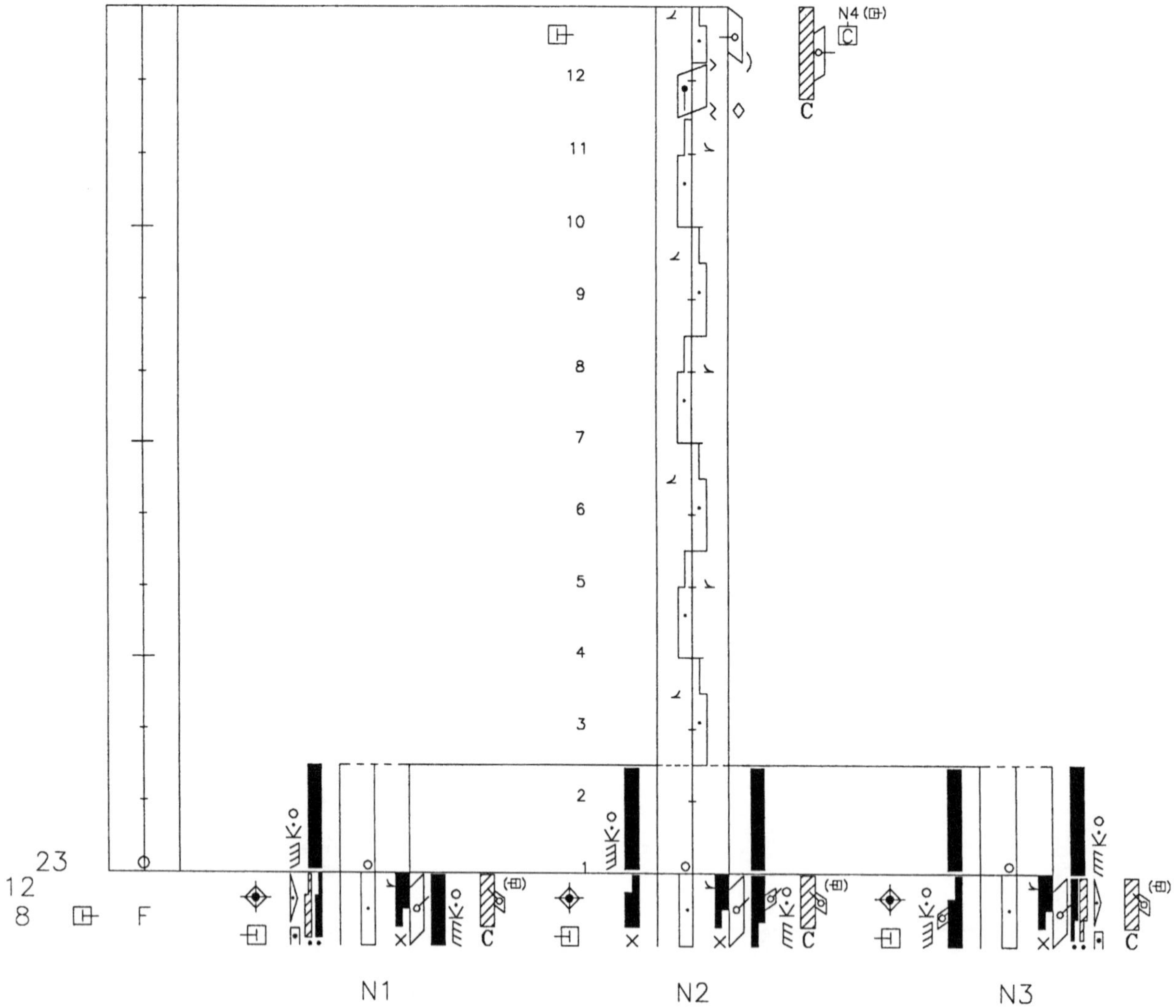
N4
C
12
11
10
9
8
7
6
5
4
3
2
1
23
12
8
F
N1
N2
N3

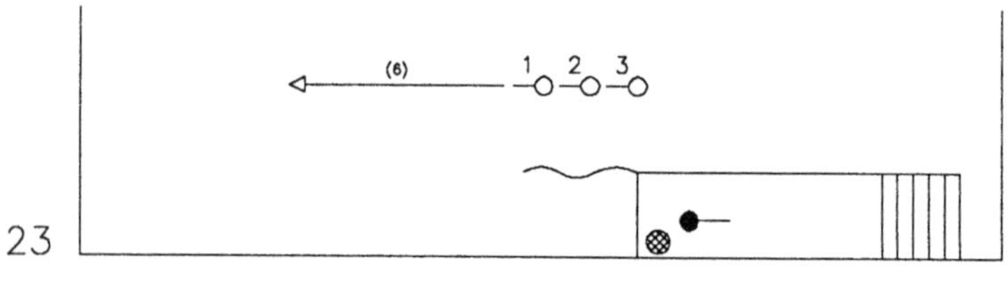
(6)
1 2 3
23

THE CHOREOGRAPHIC SCORE

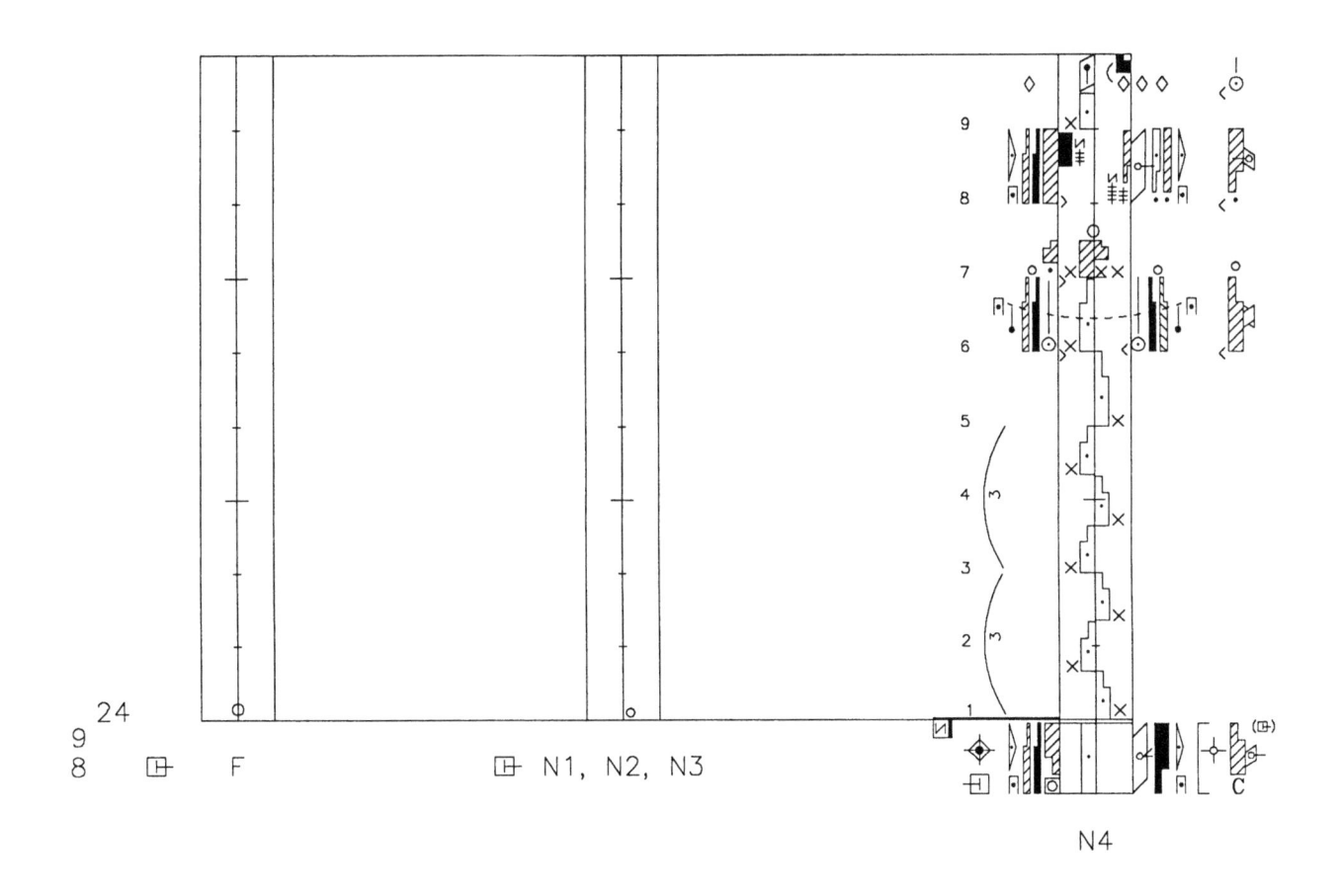

24
9/8 ⊞ F   ⊞ N1, N2, N3

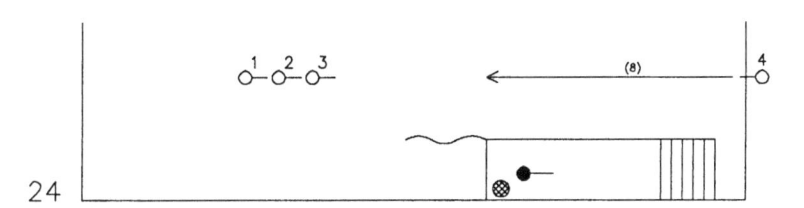

N4

24

80 NIJINSKY'S *FAUNE* RESTORED

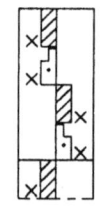

Style of walk
N4, meas. 25

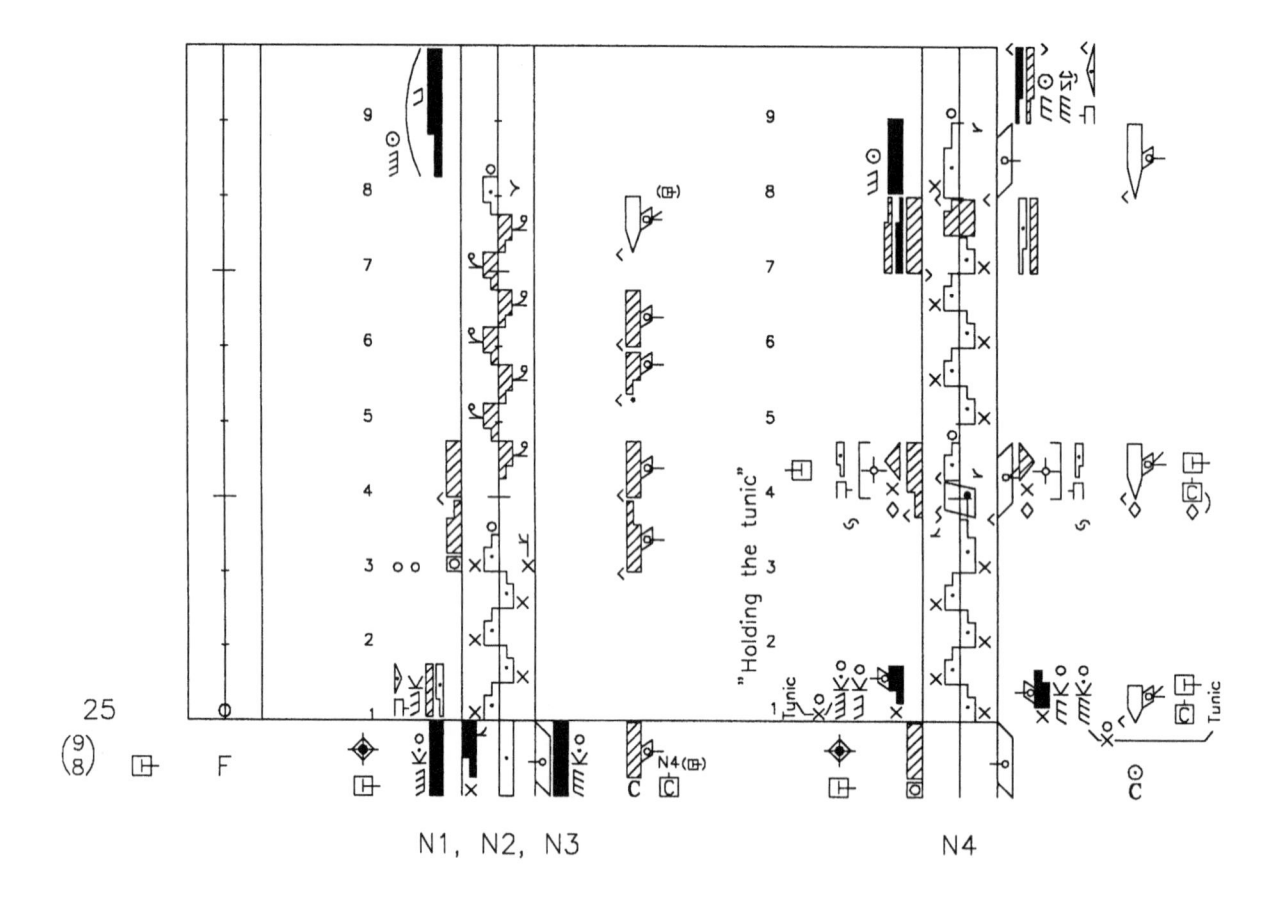

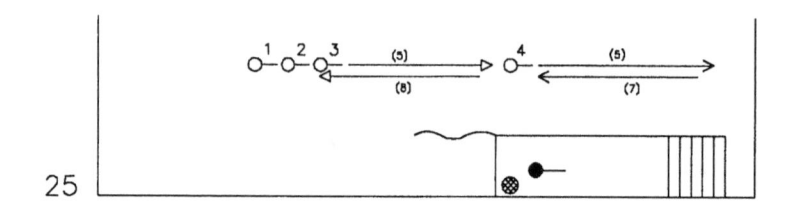

N1, N2, N3   N4

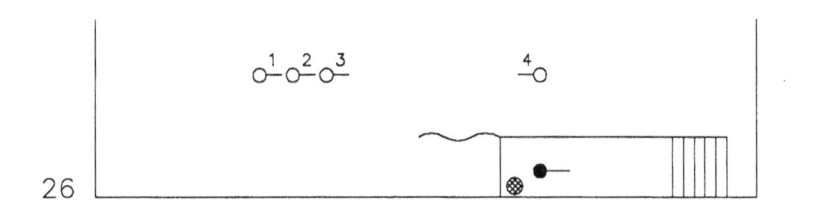

THE CHOREOGRAPHIC SCORE 81

82 NIJINSKY'S *FAUNE* RESTORED

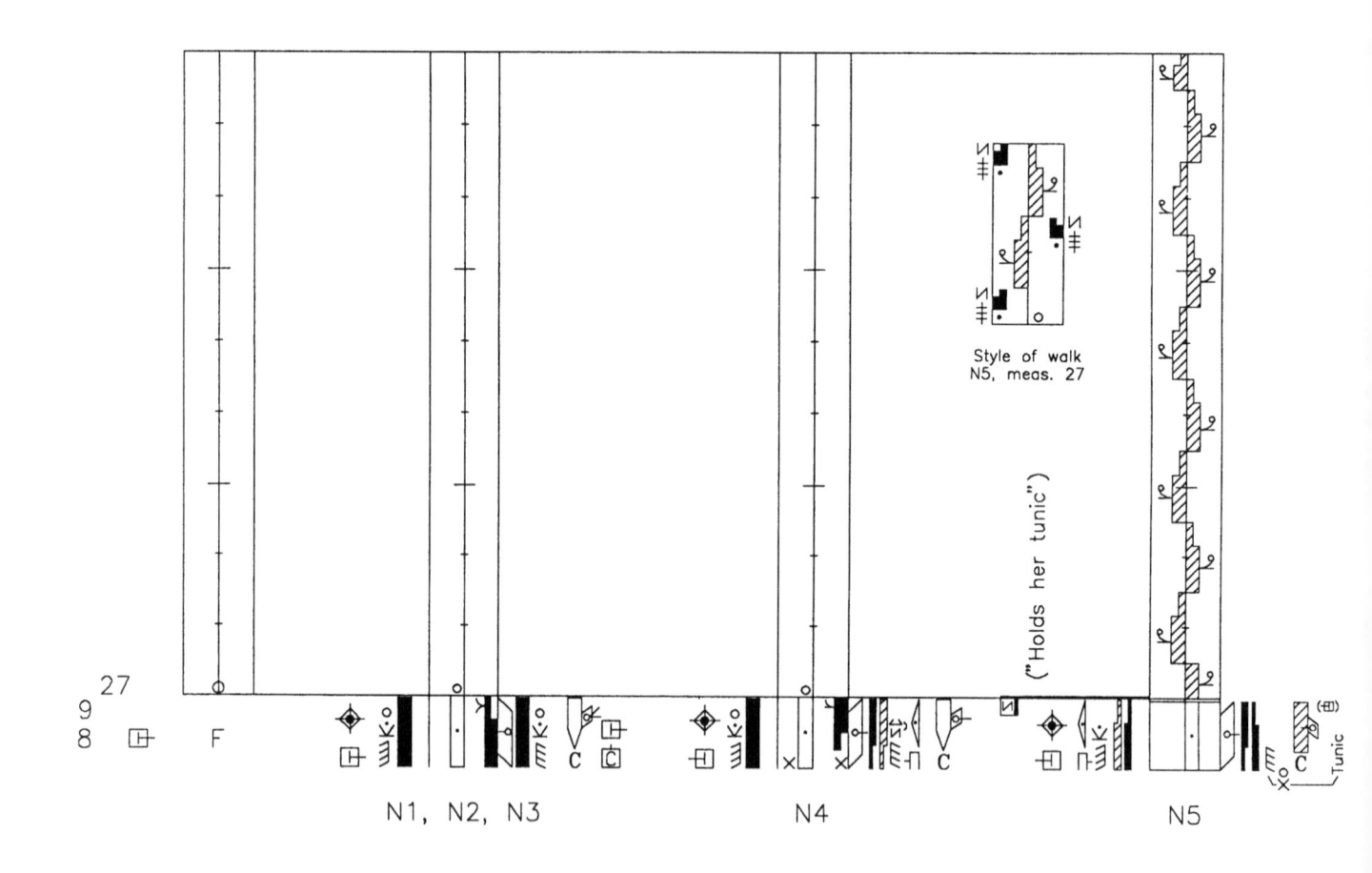

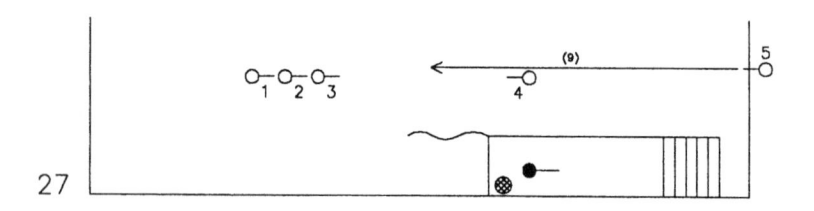

THE CHOREOGRAPHIC SCORE

83

N7

Style of walk
N6, N7, meas. 28

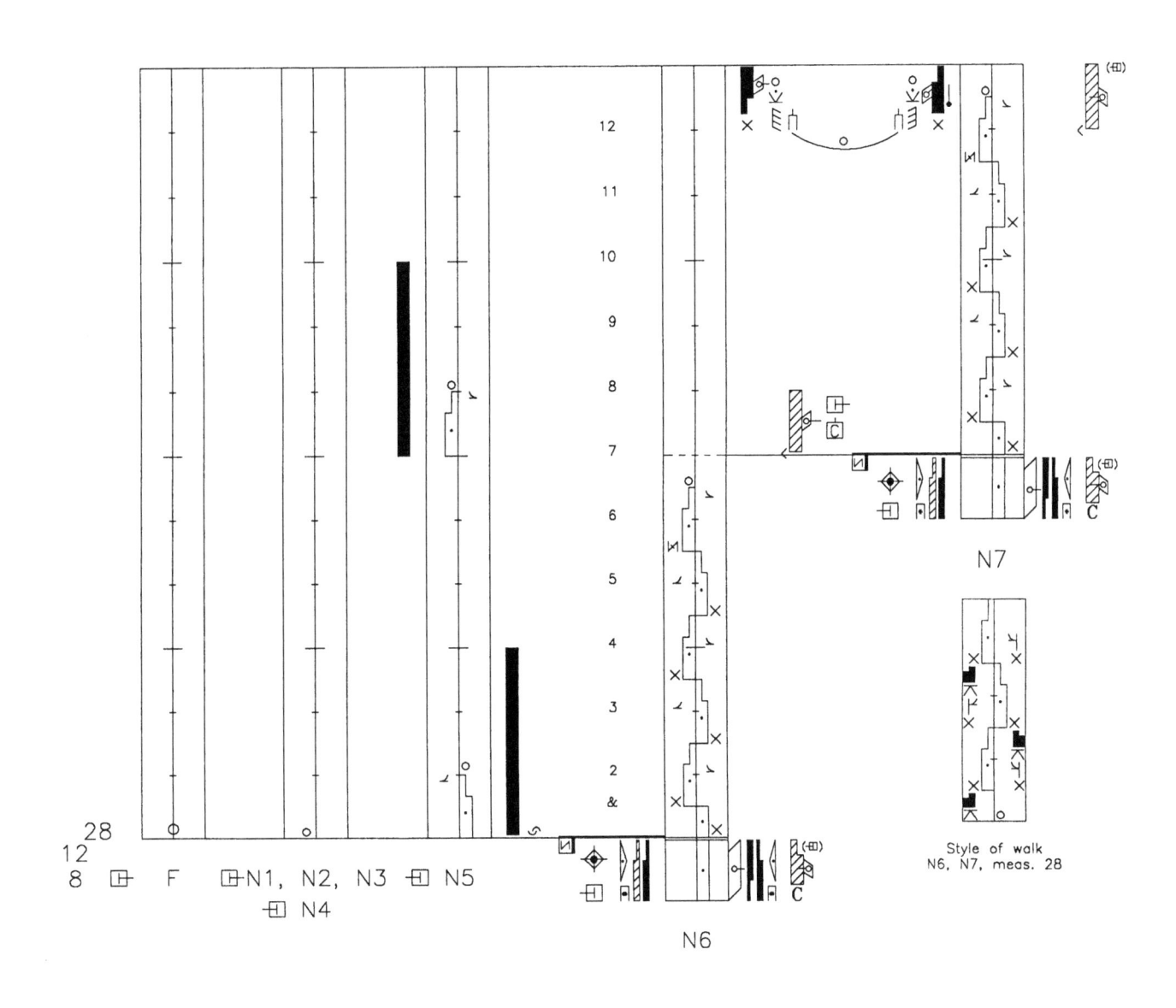

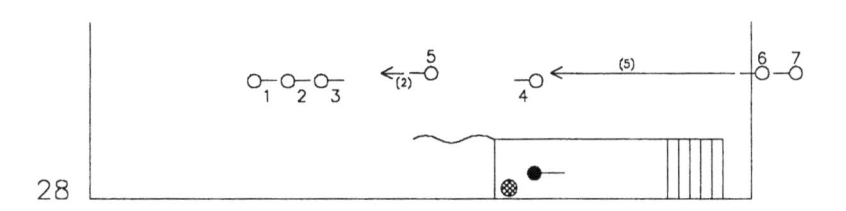

N6

N5

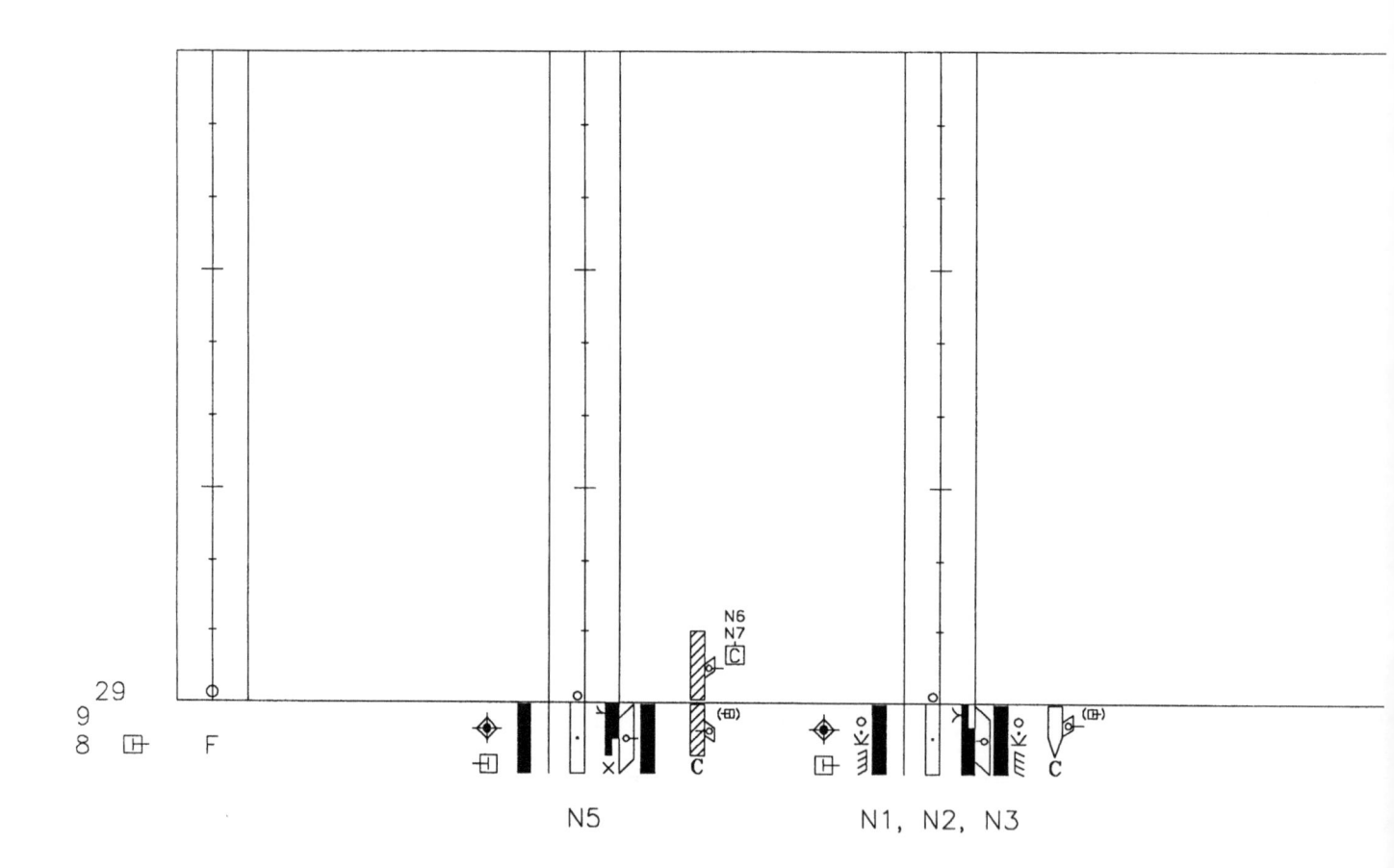

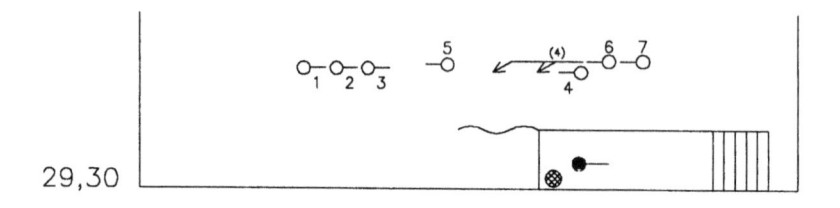

N1, N2, N3

29,30

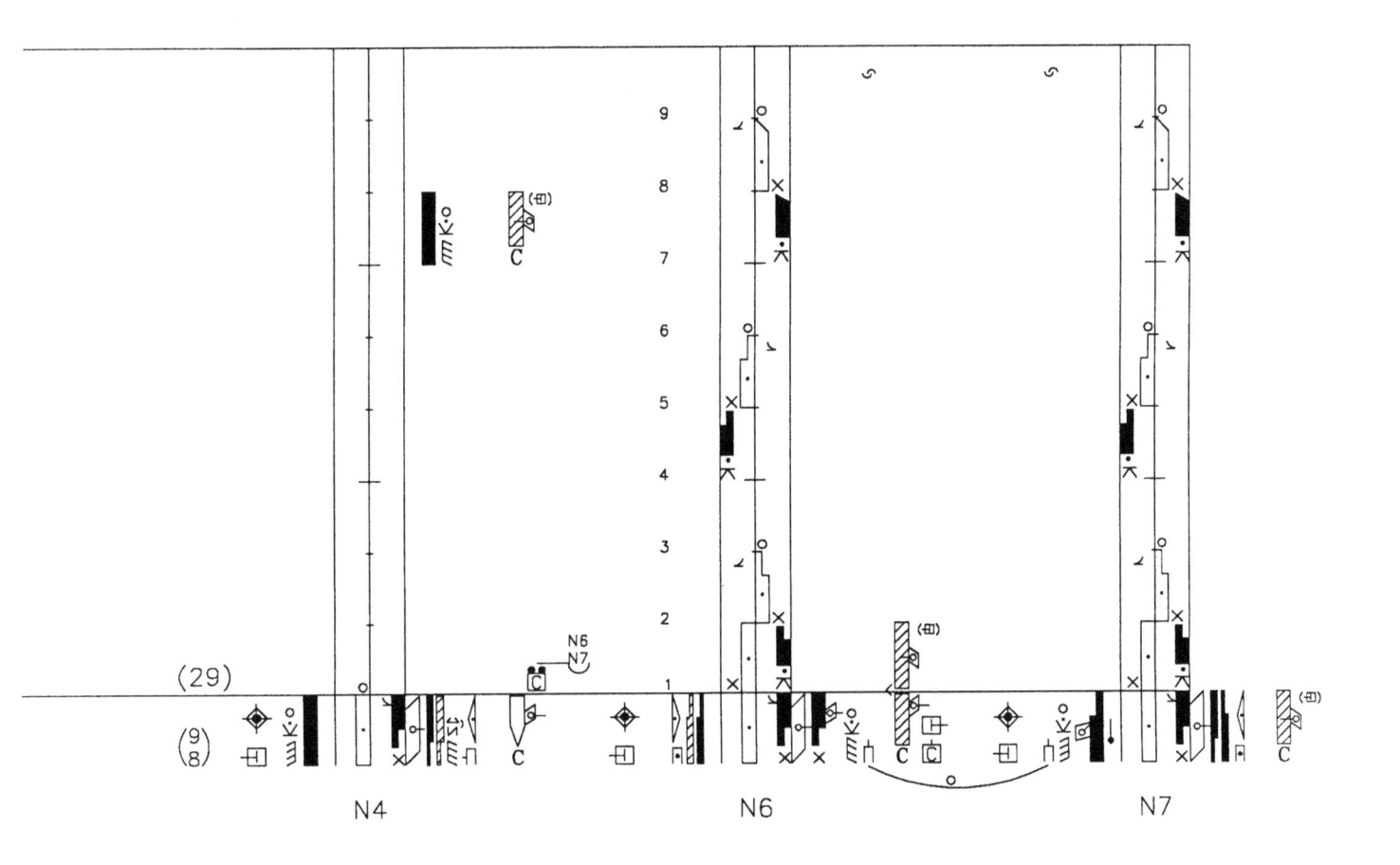

THE CHOREOGRAPHIC SCORE

86 NIJINSKY'S *FAUNE* RESTORED

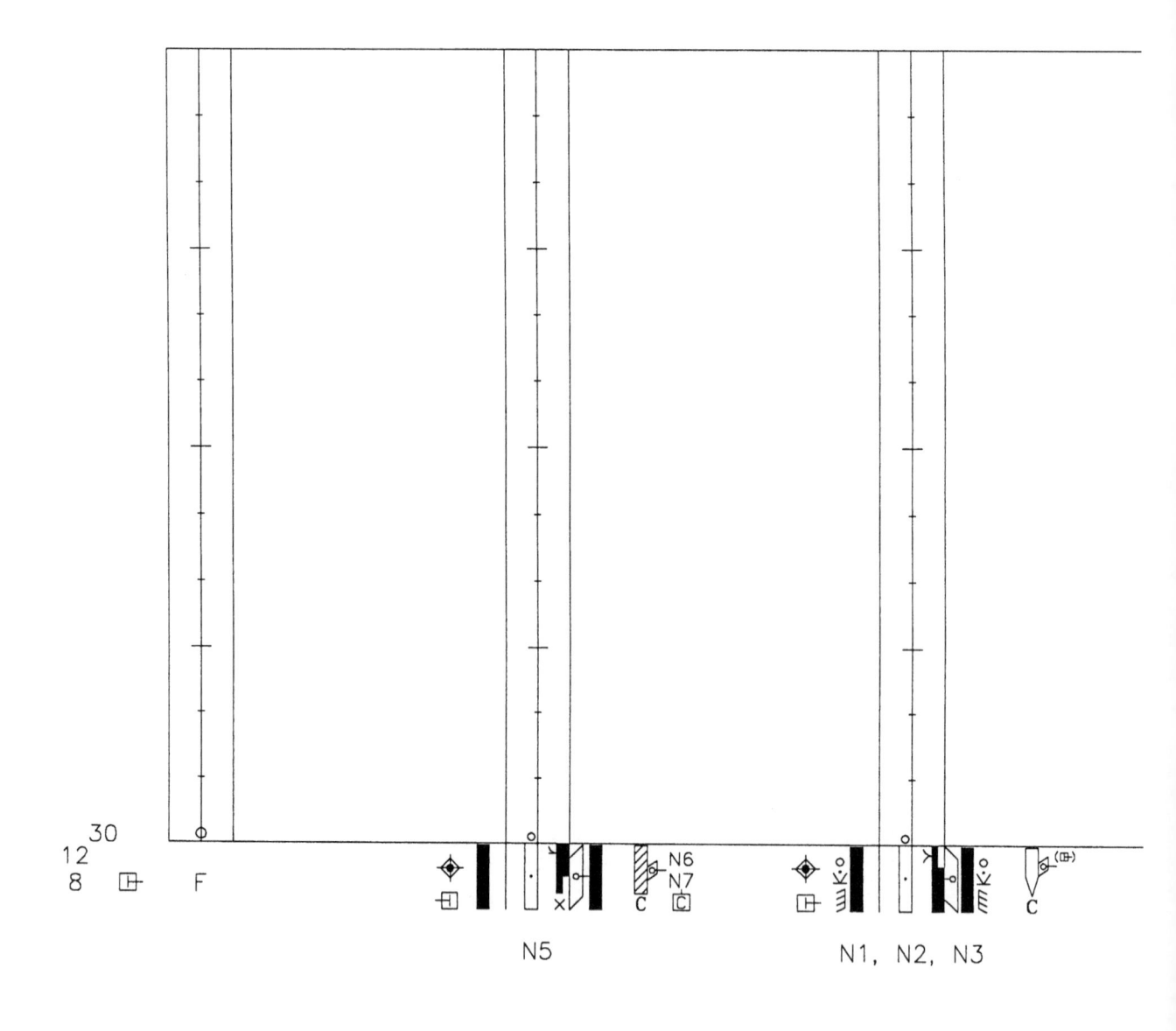

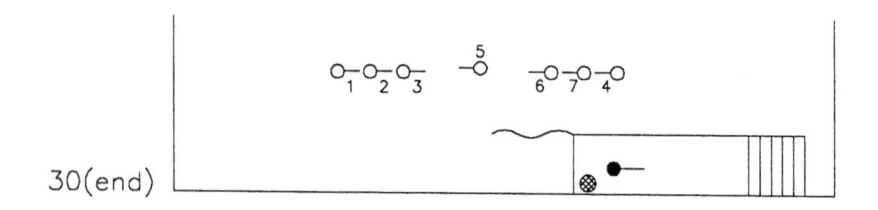

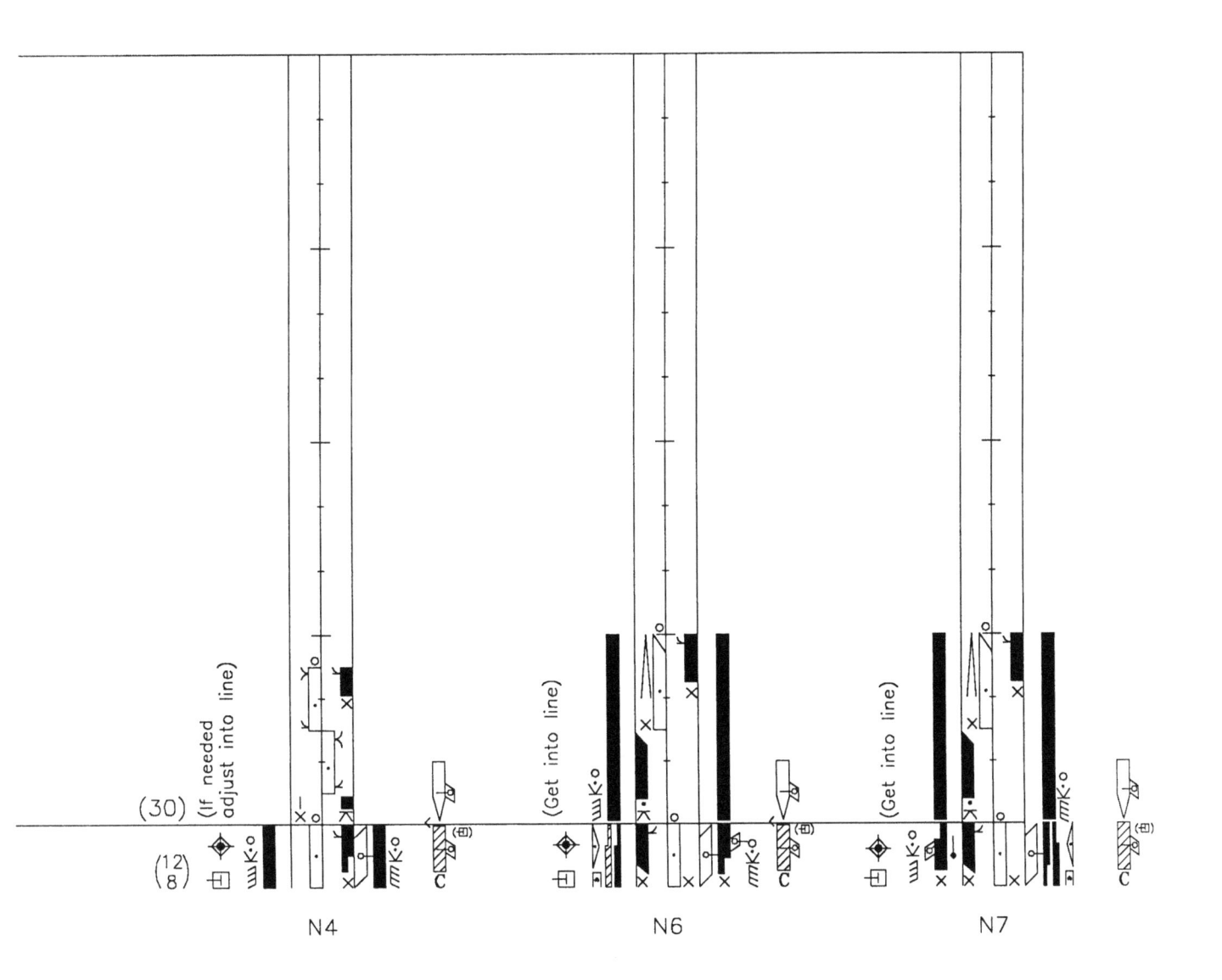

THE CHOREOGRAPHIC SCORE 87

(30) (If needed adjust into line)

(12)
(8)

(Get into line)

(Get into line)

N4

N6

N7

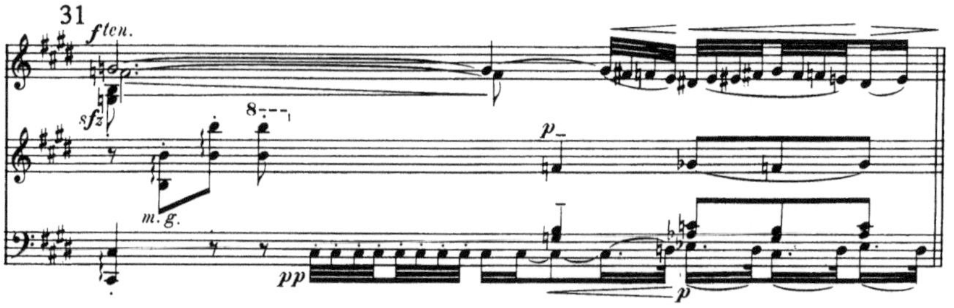
31
f ten.
sfz
m.g.
p
pp
p

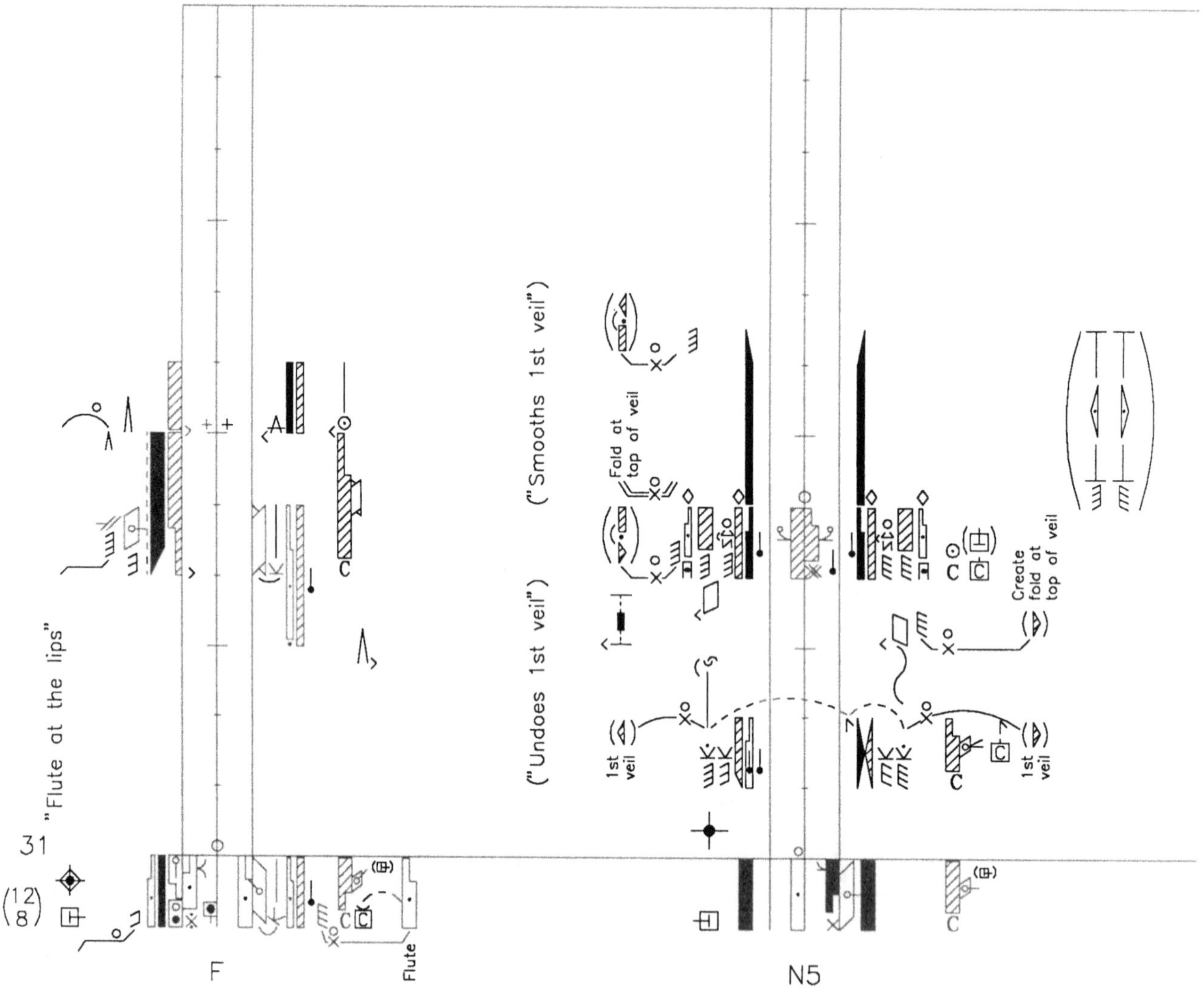
31
(12/8)
"Flute at the lips"
("Undoes 1st veil")
("Smooths 1st veil")
Fold at top of veil
1st veil
Create fold at top of veil
Flute
F
N5

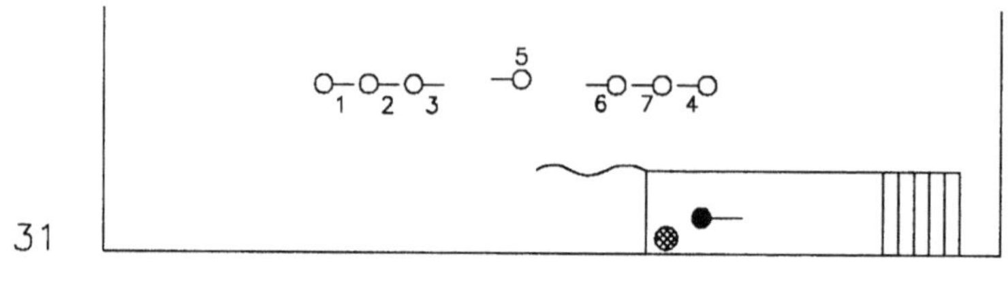
31
1 2 3 5 6 7 4

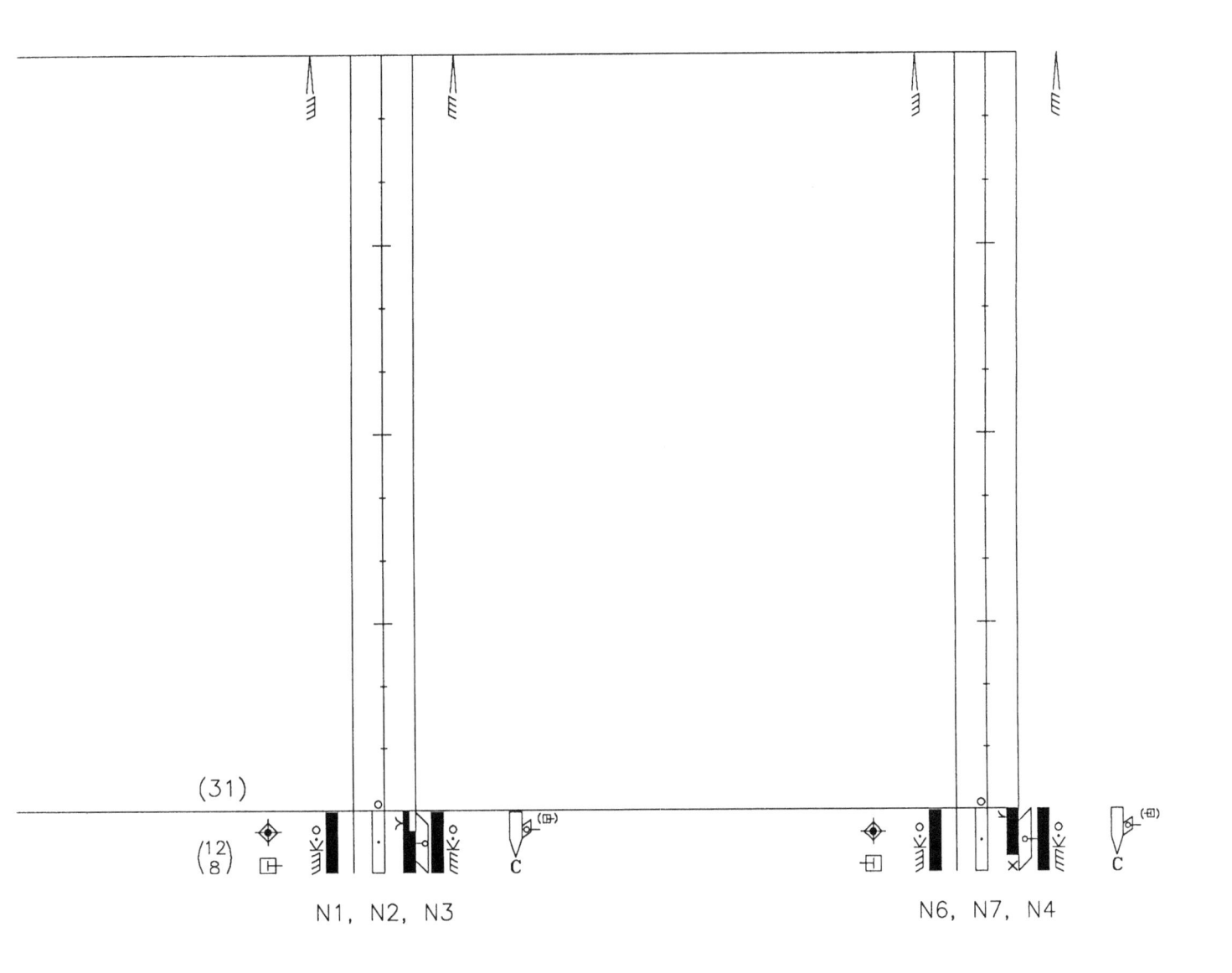

THE CHOREOGRAPHIC SCORE

(31)

(12)
(8)

N1, N2, N3   N6, N7, N4

32
33
sfz

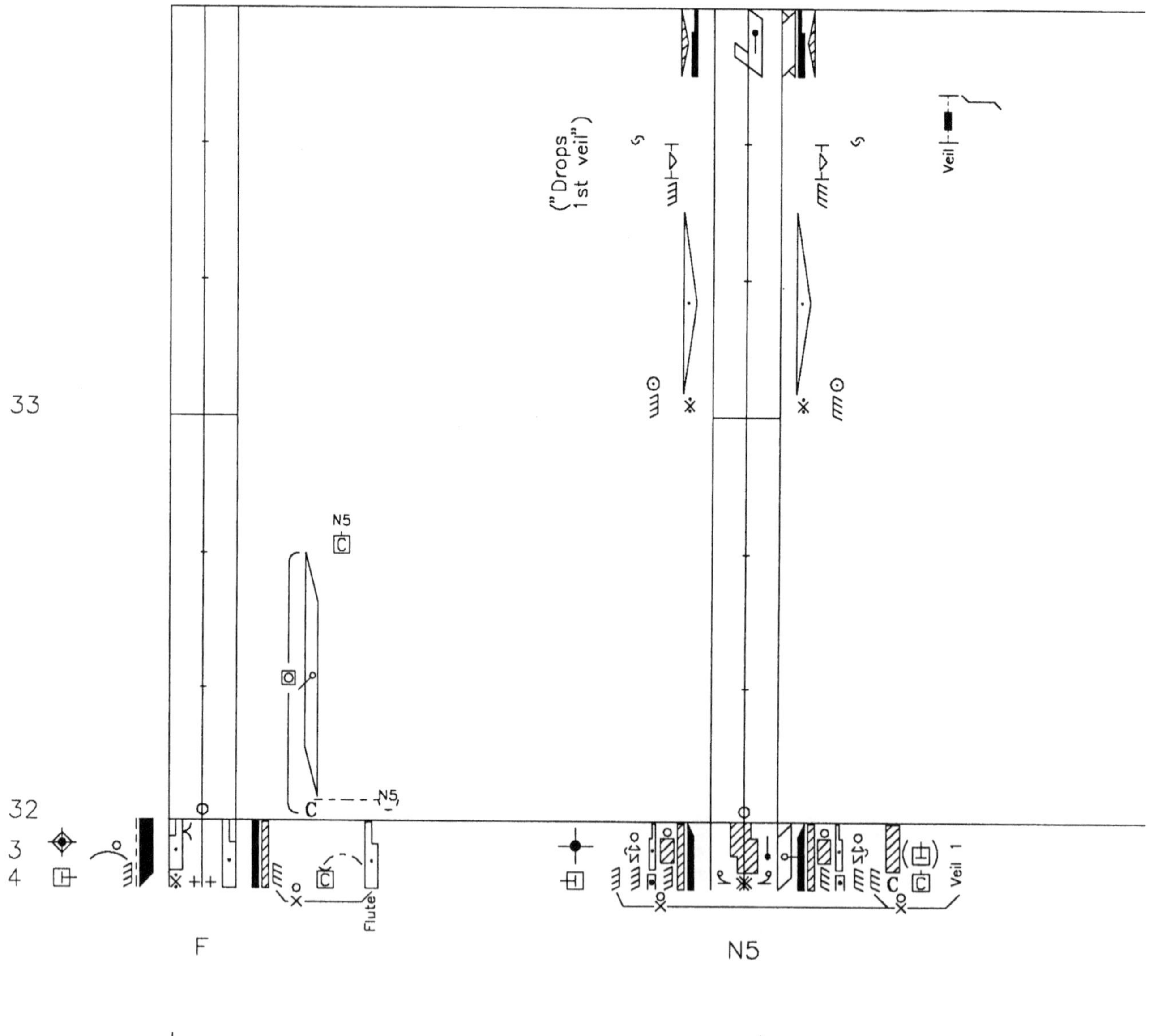
33
32
3
4
("Drops 1st veil")
Veil
N5
N5
Flute
Veil 1
F
N5

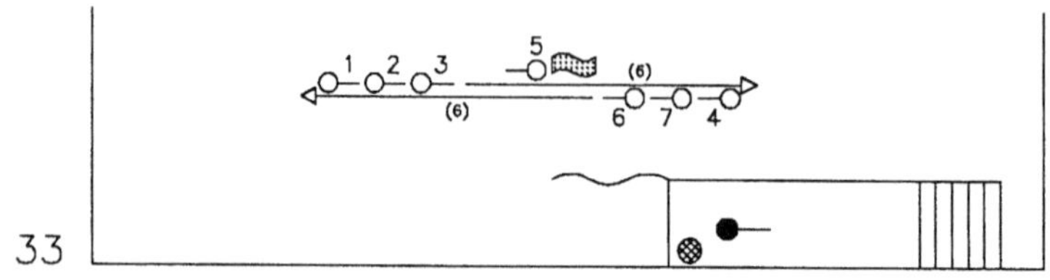
1
2
3
5
(6)
(6)
6
7
4
33

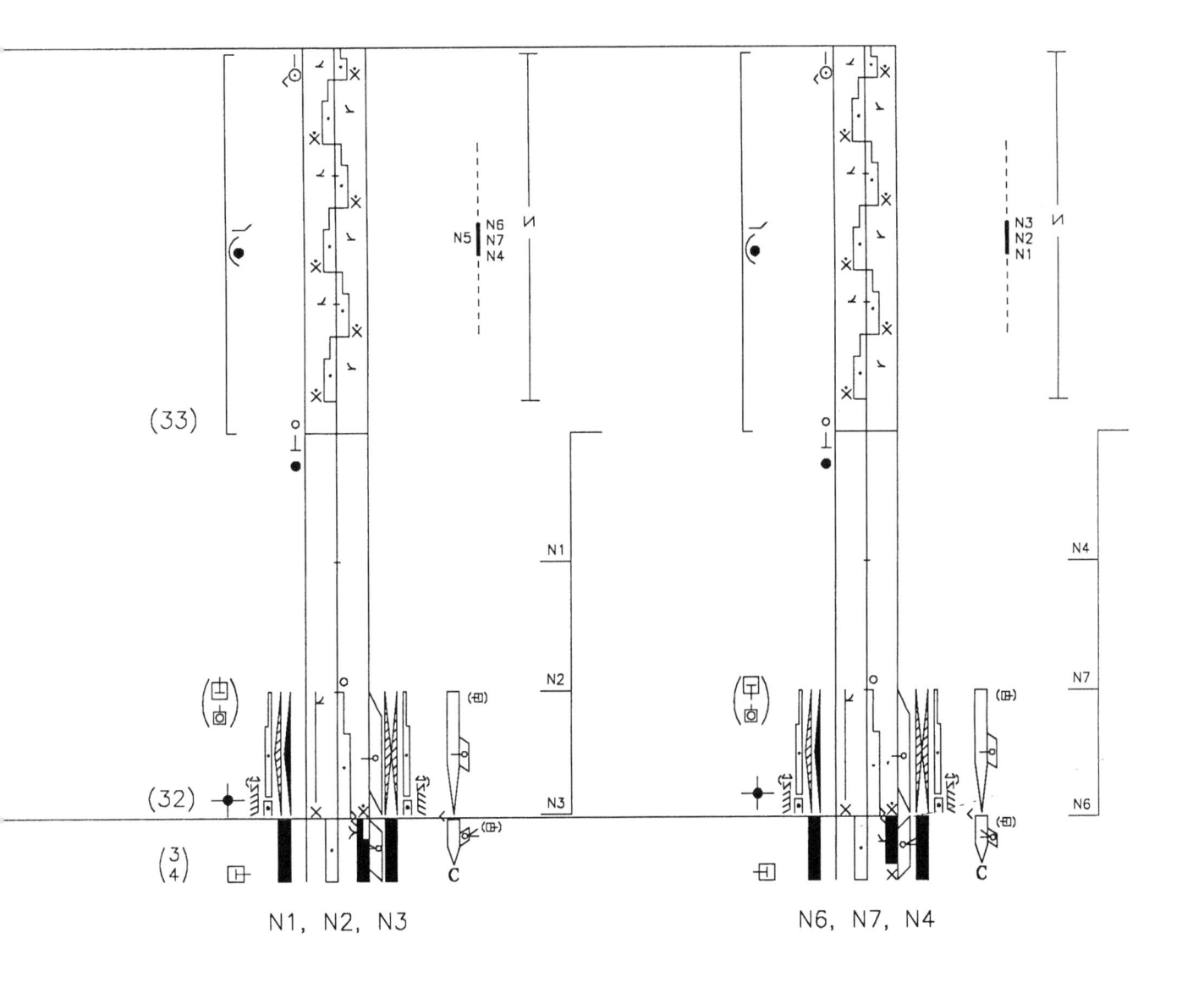

THE CHOREOGRAPHIC SCORE

(33)

N5 N6
N7
N4

N3
N2
N1

N1

N2

(32)

N3

(3)
(4)

N1, N2, N3

N4

N7

N6

N6, N7, N4

92 NIJINSKY'S *FAUNE* RESTORED

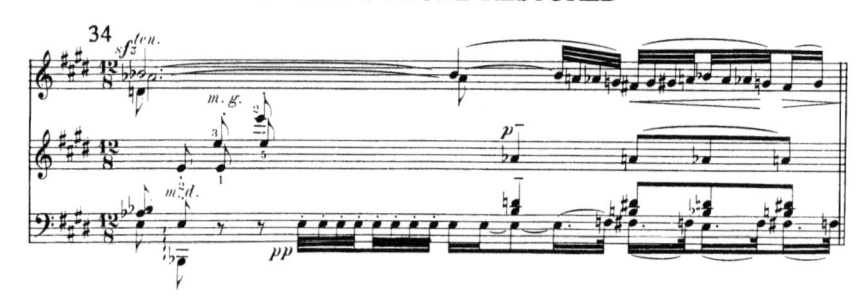

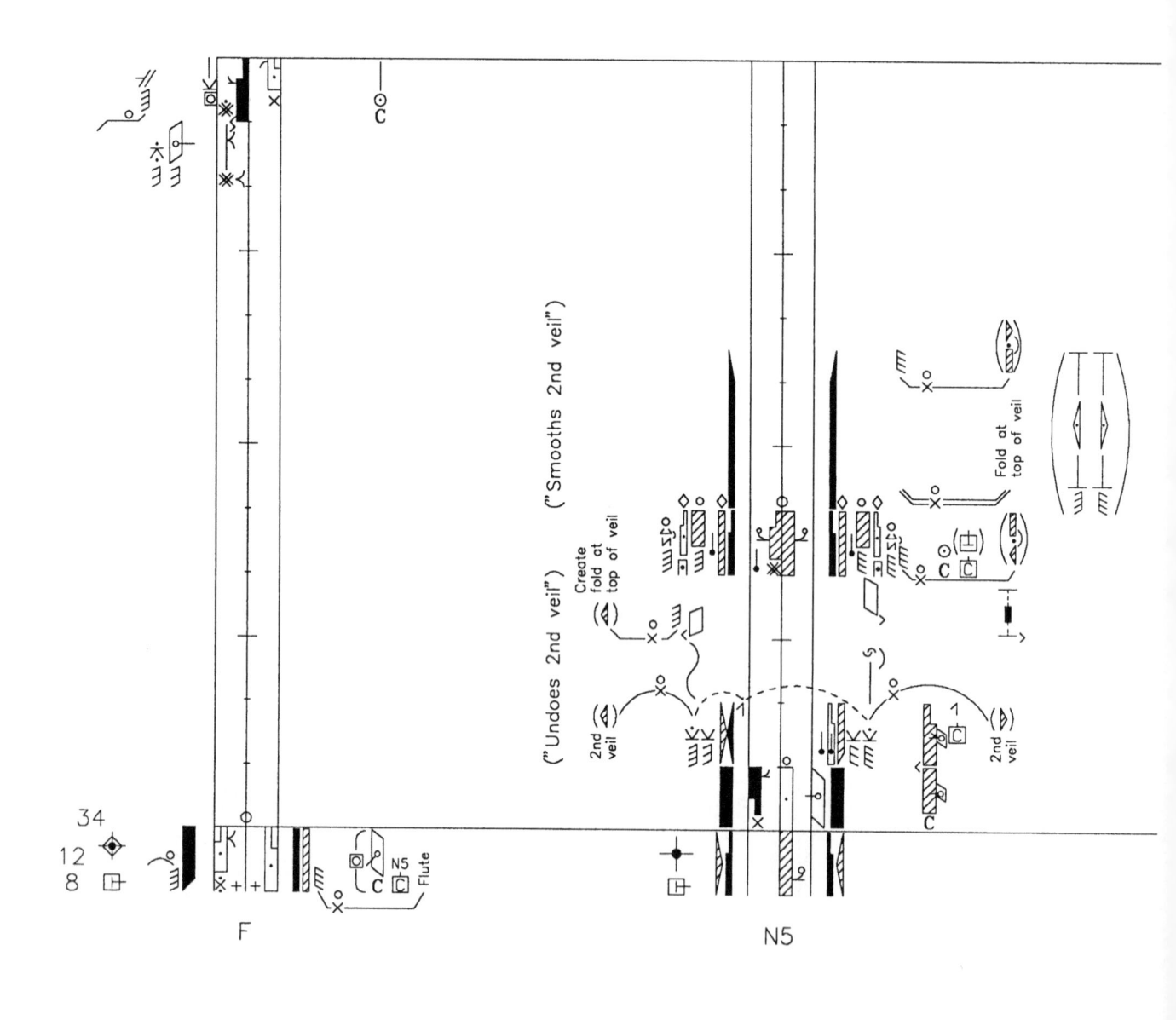

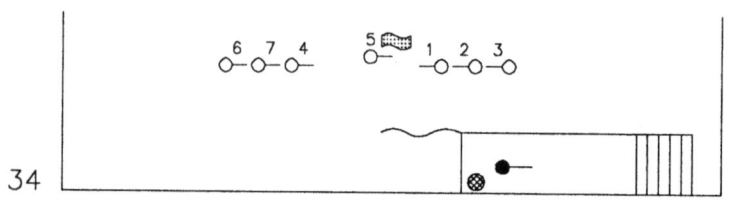

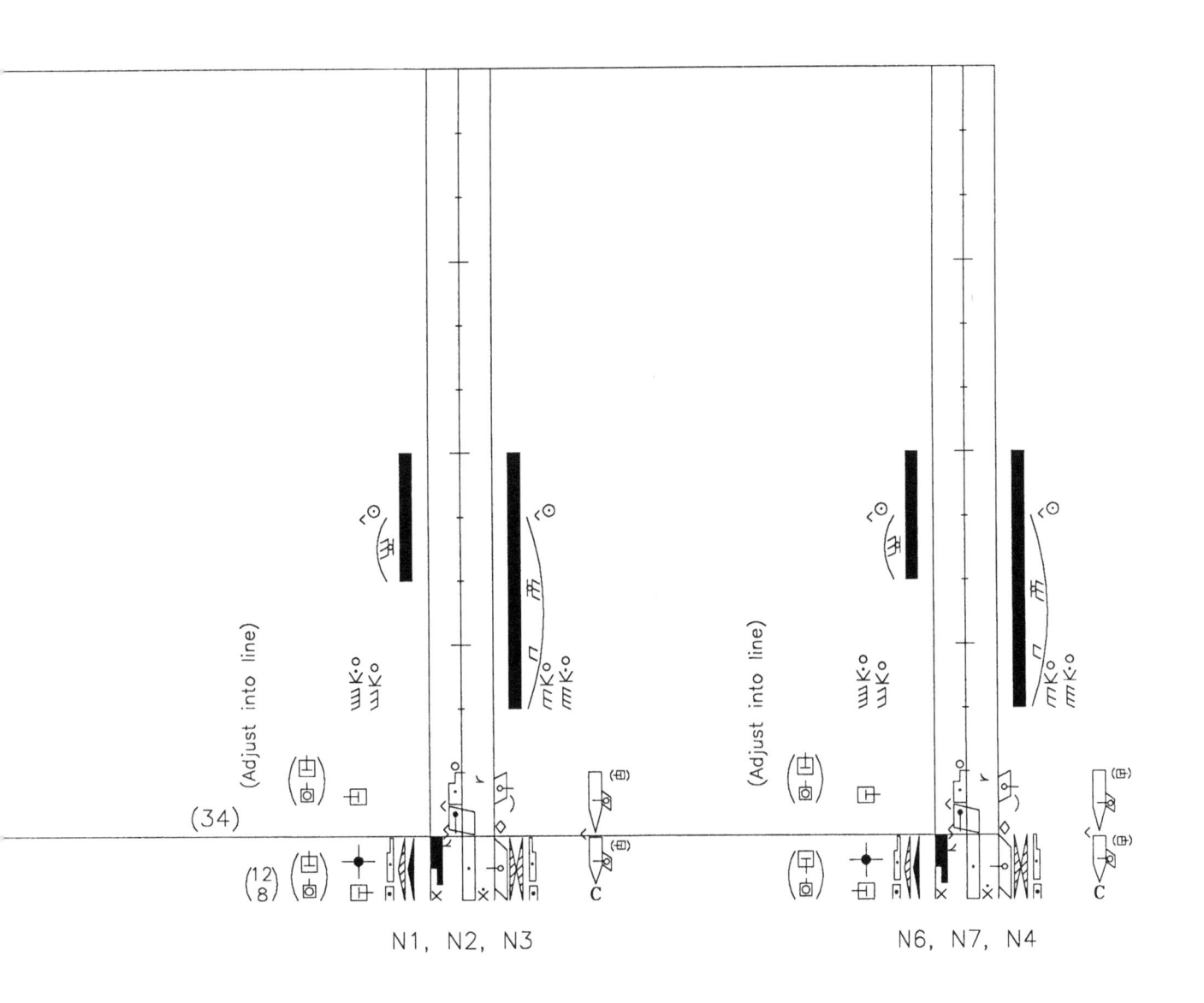

THE CHOREOGRAPHIC SCORE

(Adjust into line)

(34)

(12)
(8)

N1, N2, N3   N6, N7, N4

94 NIJINSKY'S *FAUNE* RESTORED

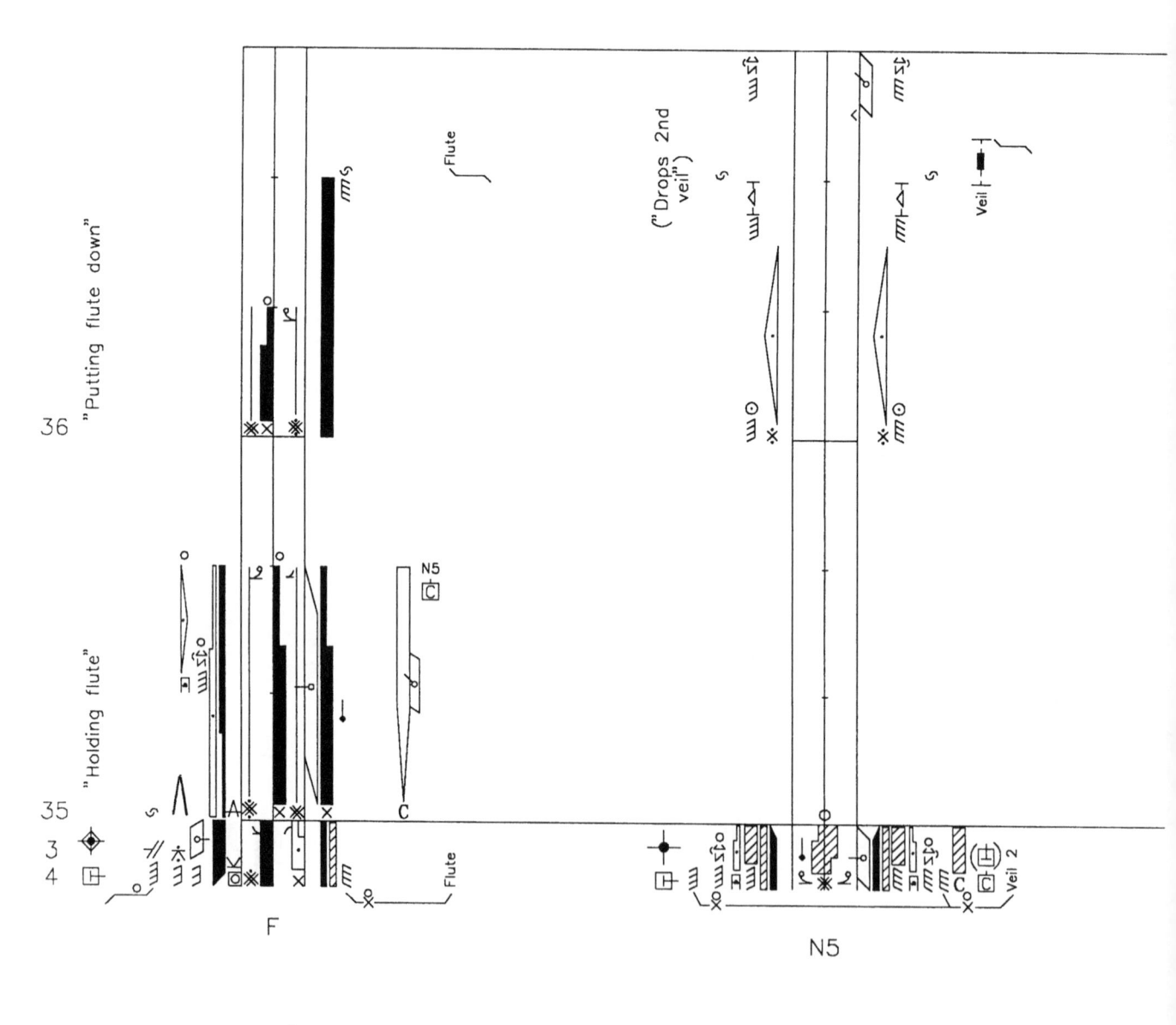

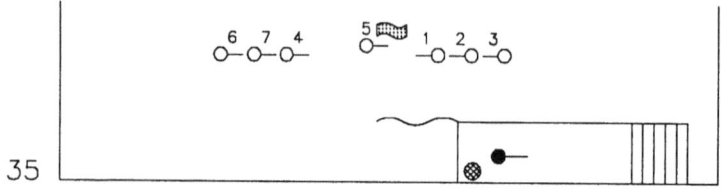

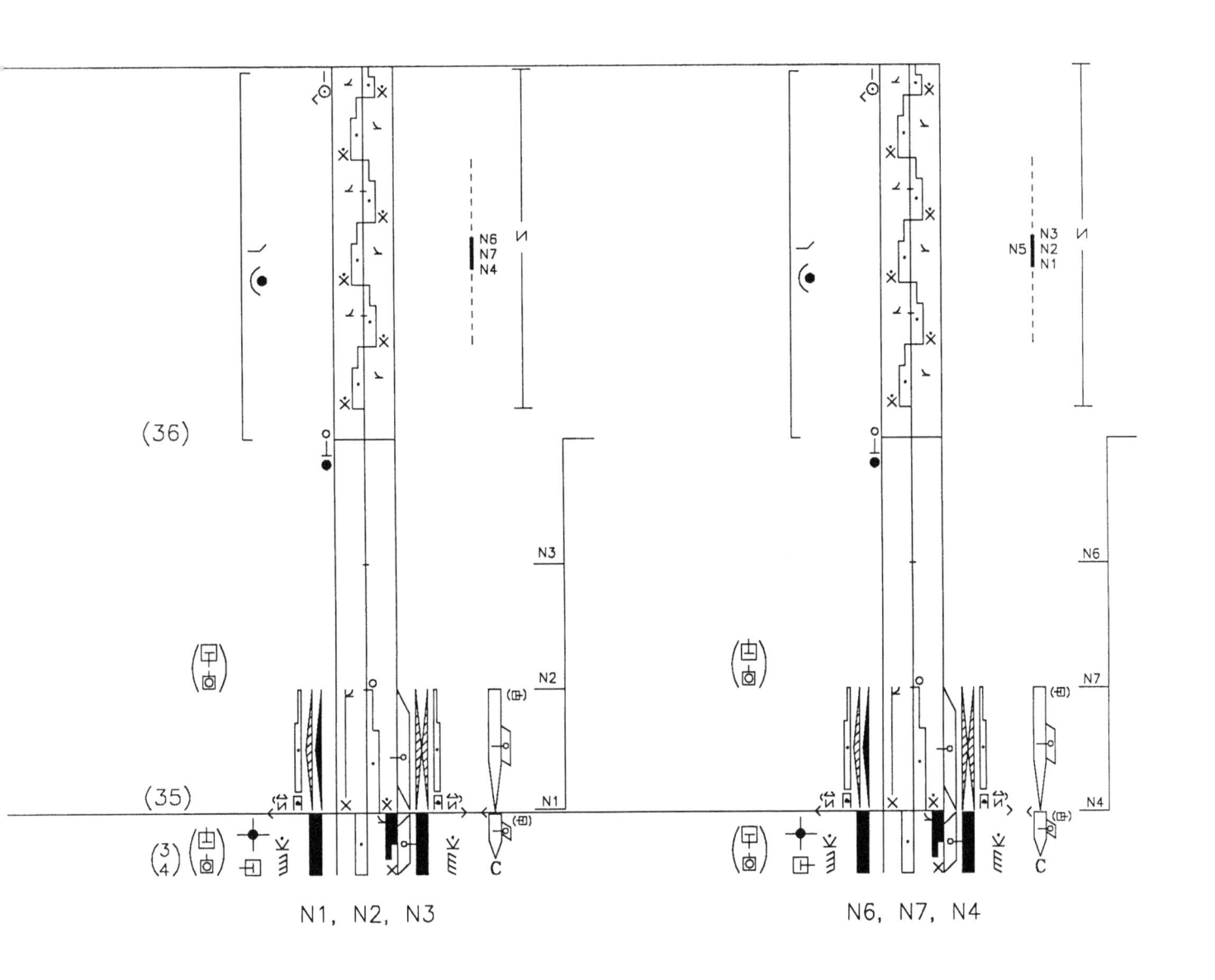

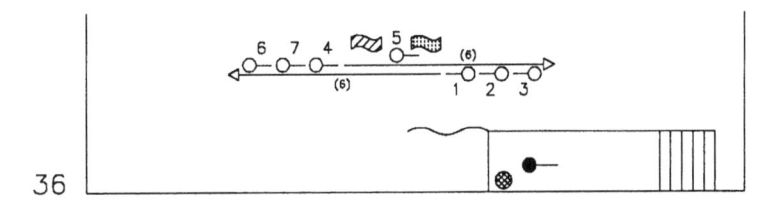

THE CHOREOGRAPHIC SCORE 95

N1, N2, N3   N6, N7, N4

37 En animant
38
Htb.
doux et expressif
p
Cordes
m. d.

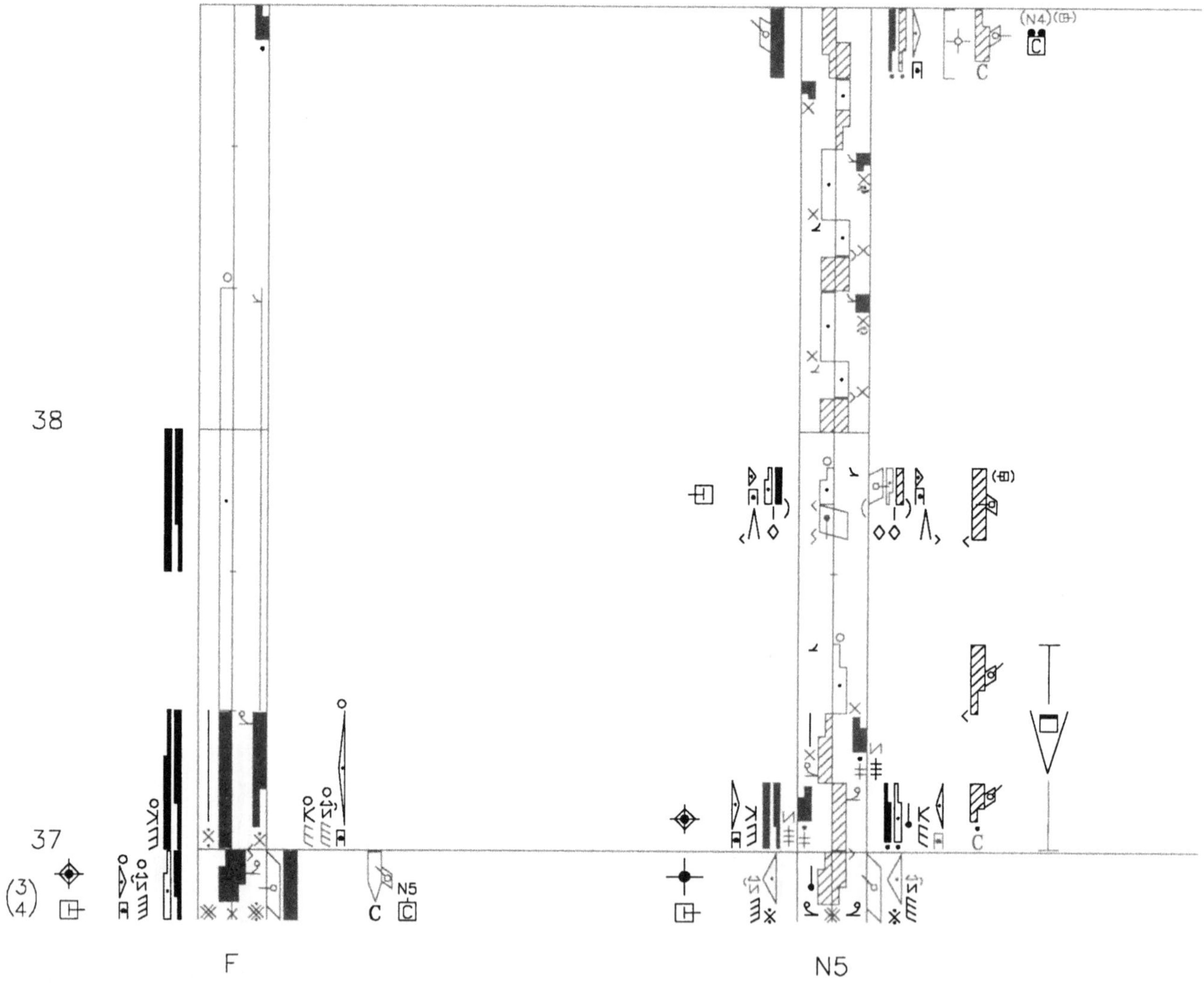
38
37
F
N5
C
(N4)

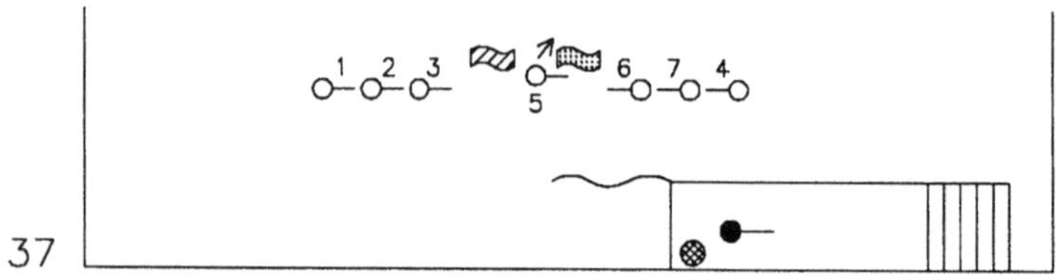
37

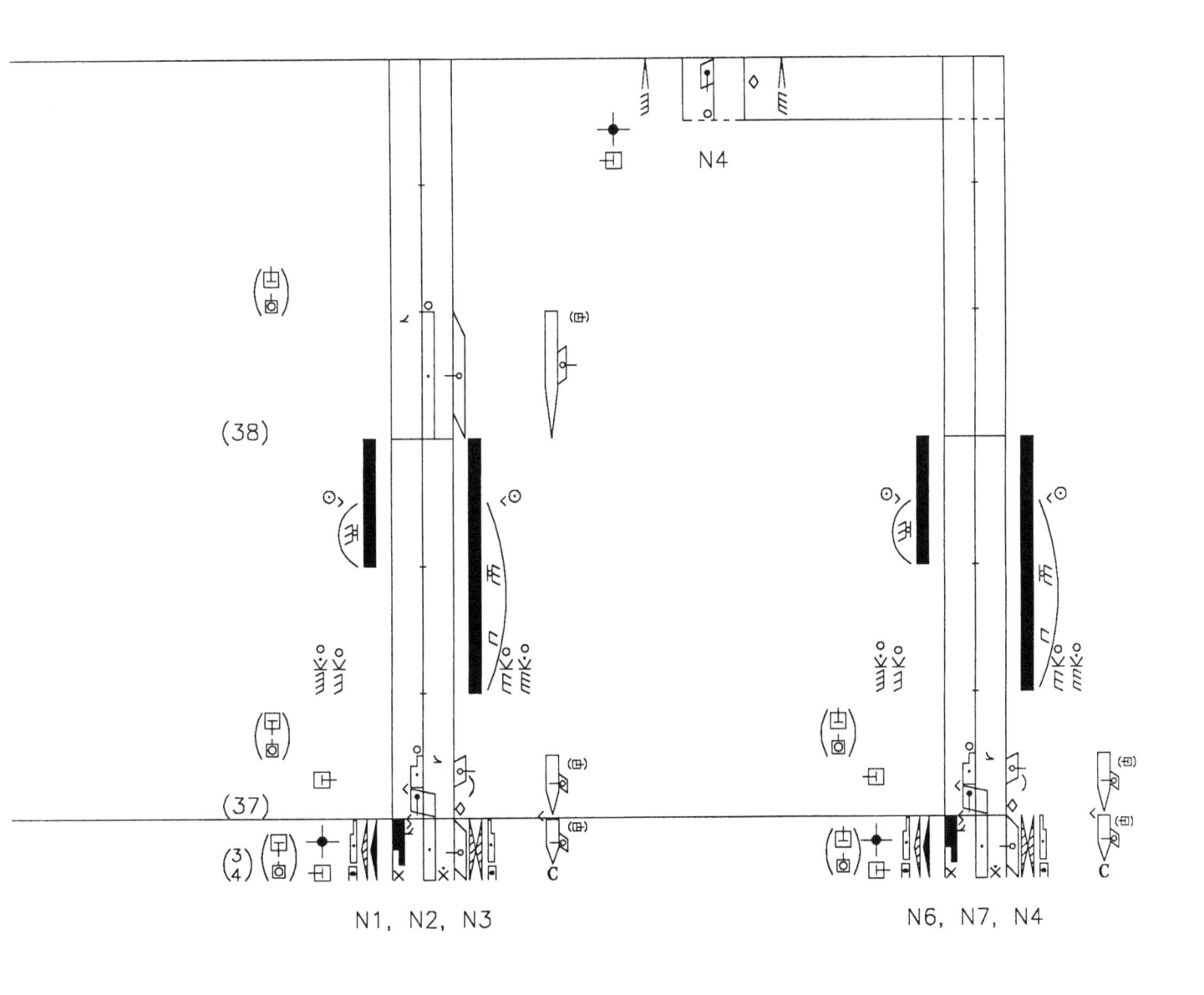

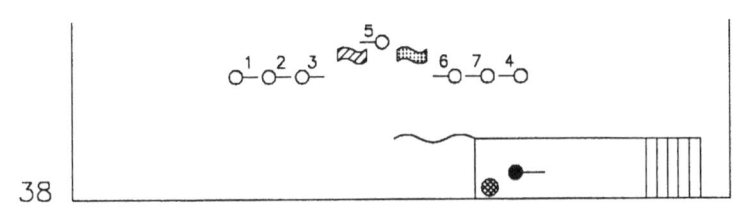

… THE CHOREOGRAPHIC SCORE 97

N1, N2, N3   N6, N7, N4

98 NIJINSKY'S *FAUNE* RESTORED

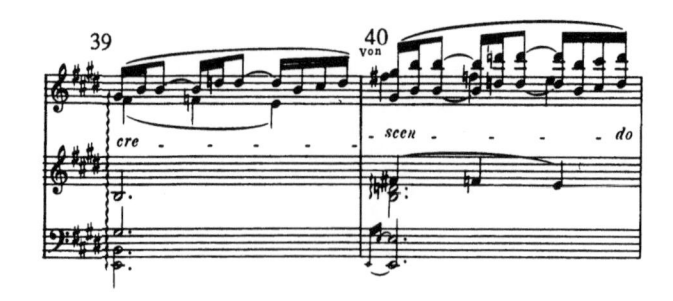

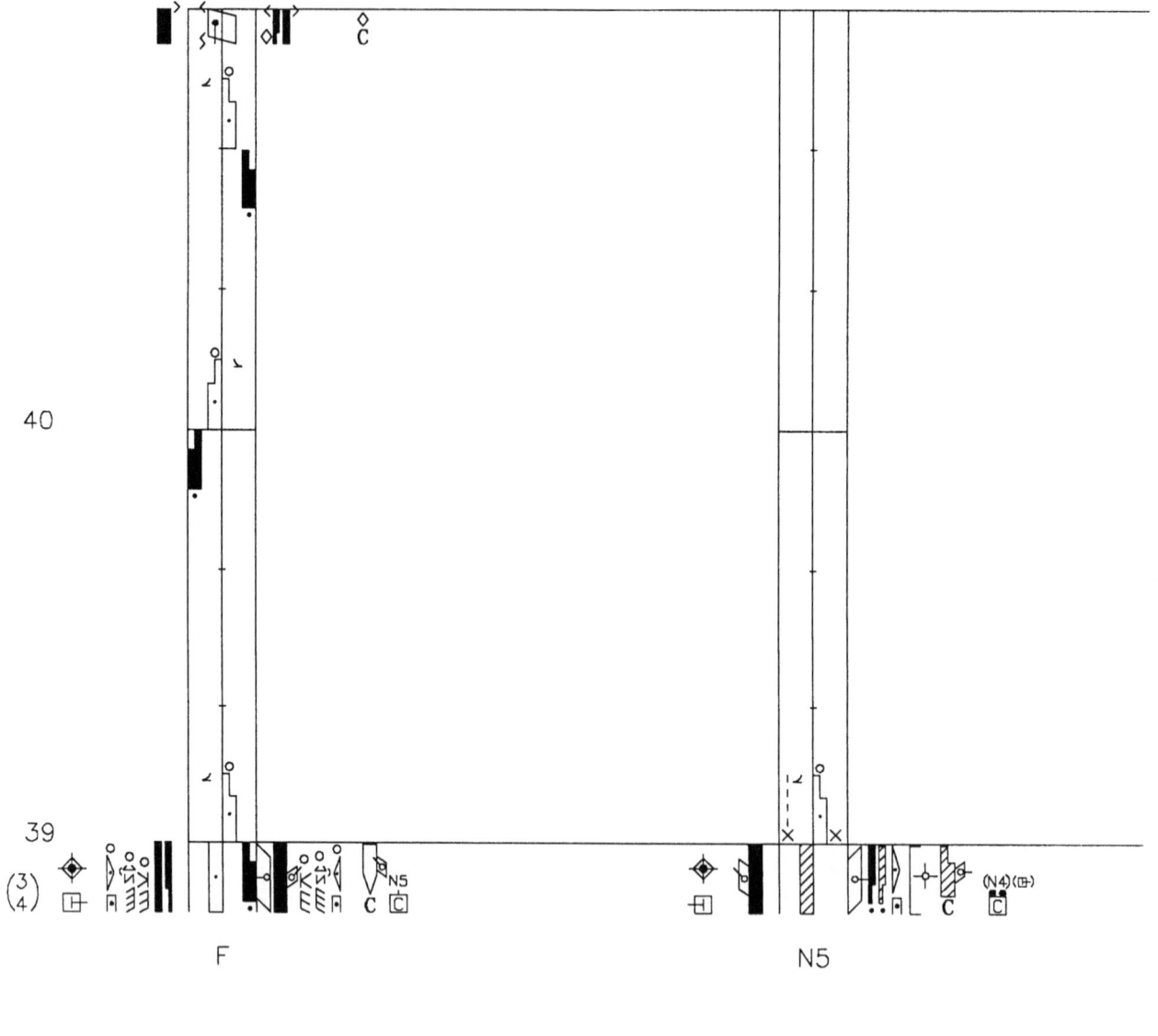

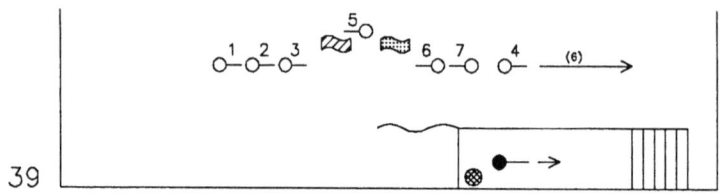

THE CHOREOGRAPHIC SCORE 99

Style of walk
for nymphs,
meas. 39, 40

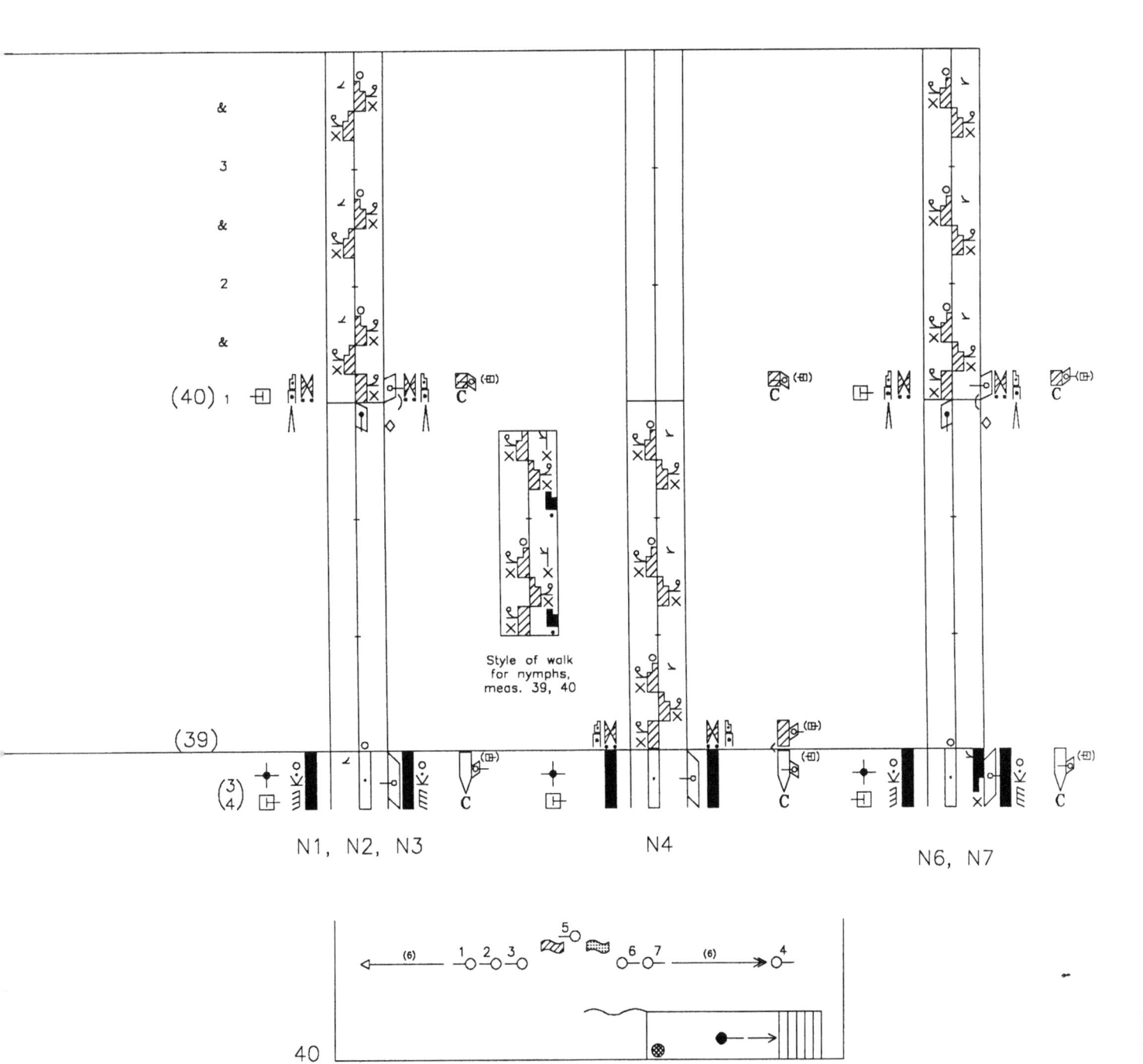

N1, N2, N3   N4   N6, N7

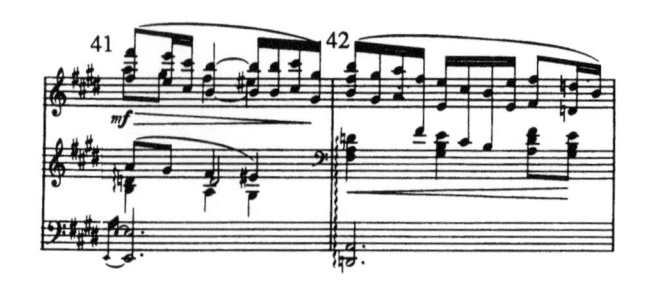

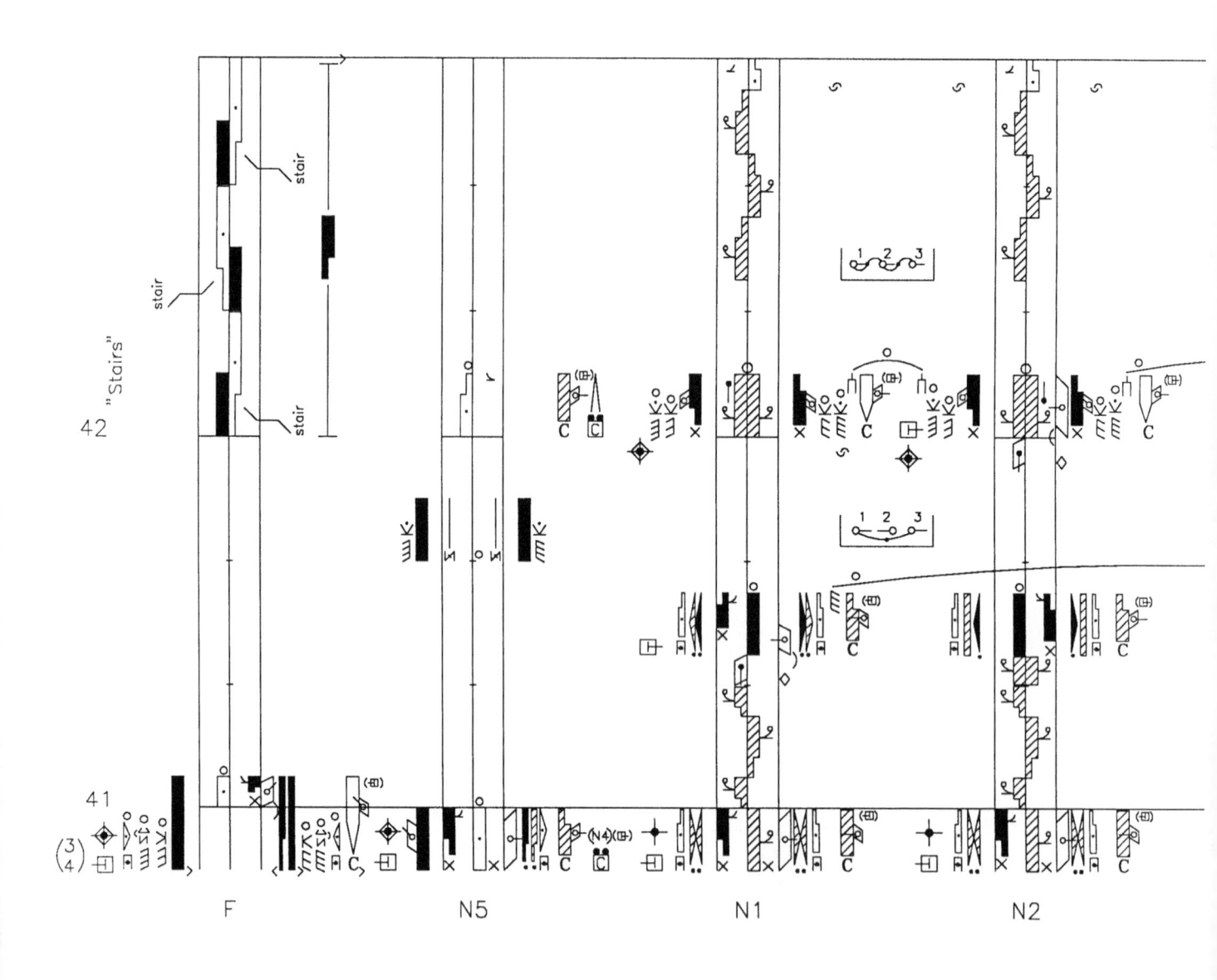

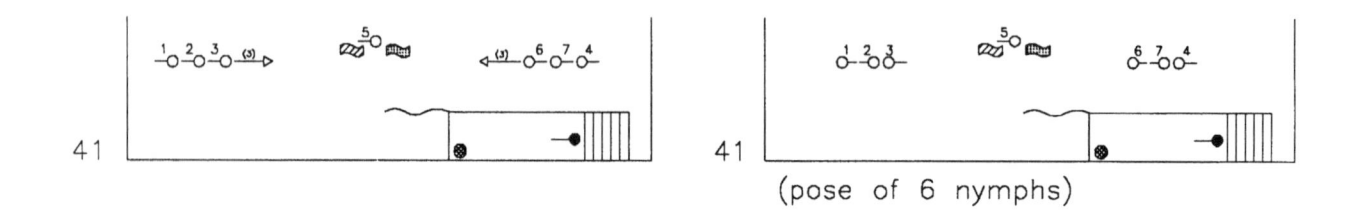

"Stairs"

42

41

F   N5   N1   N2

41 (pose of 6 nymphs)

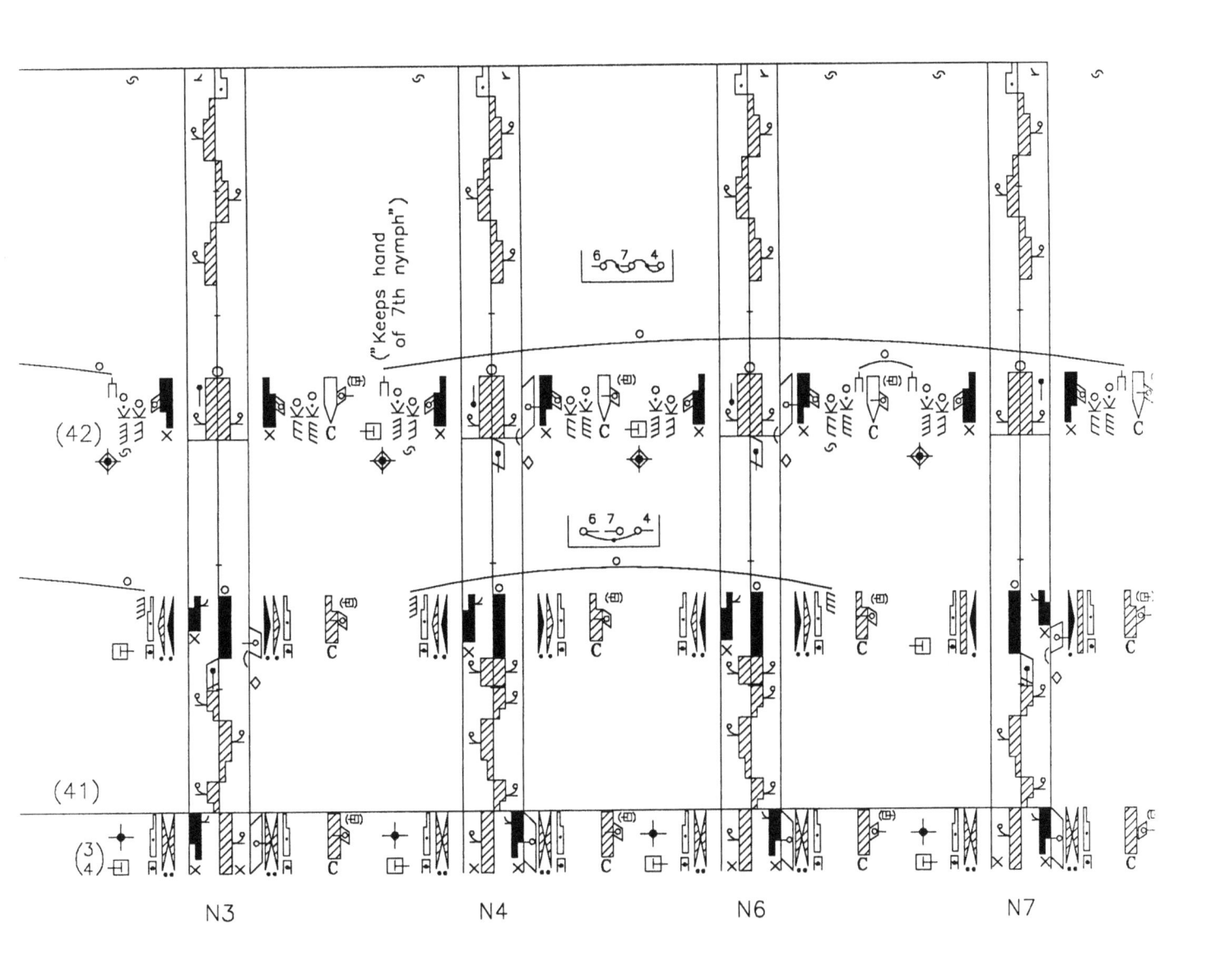

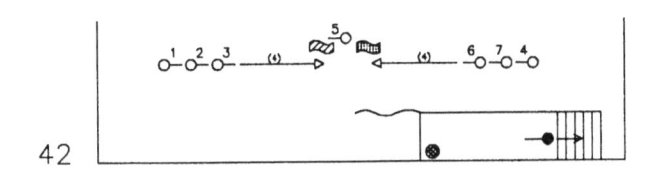

THE CHOREOGRAPHIC SCORE 101

("Keeps hand of 7th nymph")

(42)

(41)

(3/4)

N3   N4   N6   N7

42

102 NIJINSKY'S *FAUNE* RESTORED

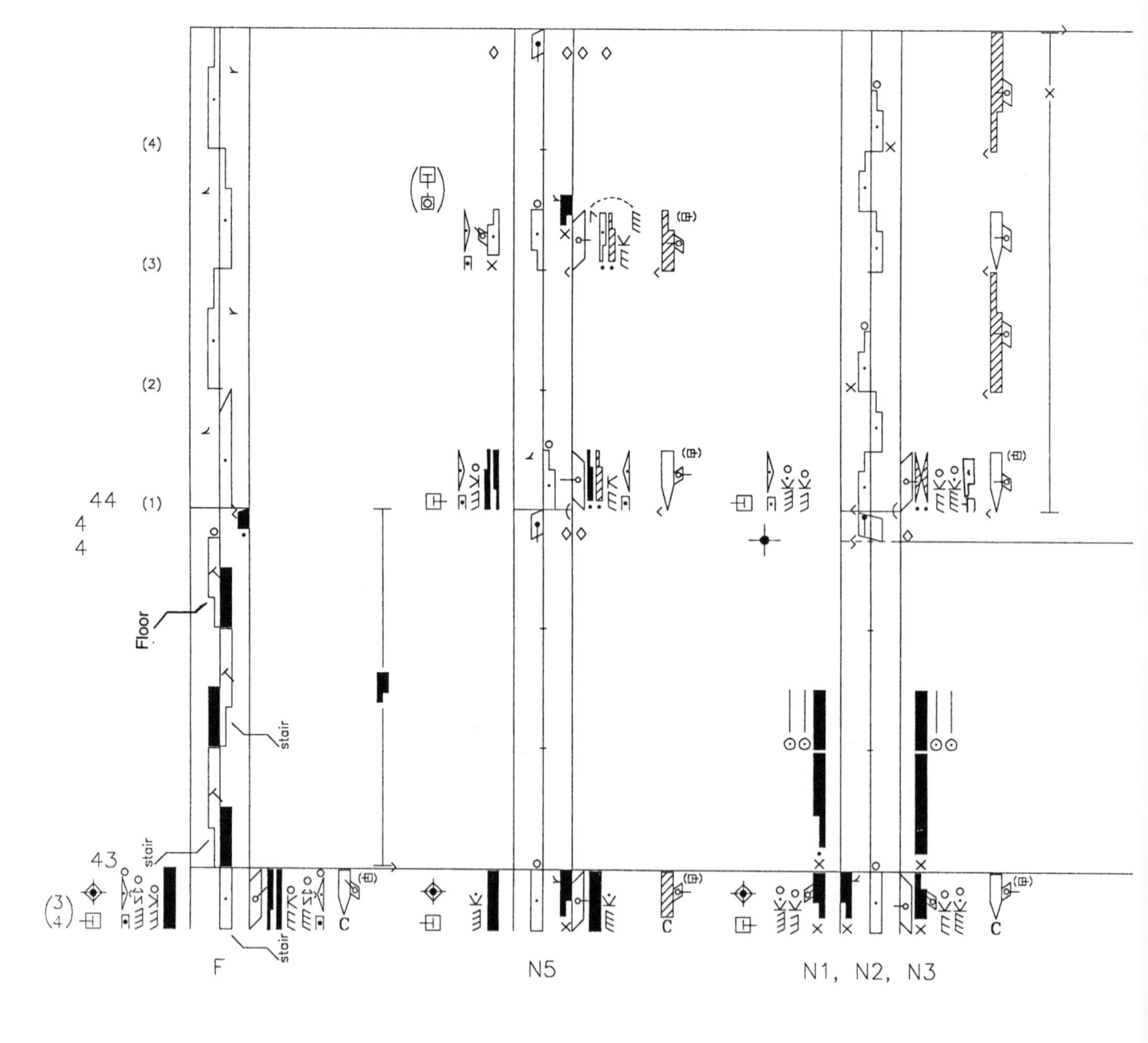

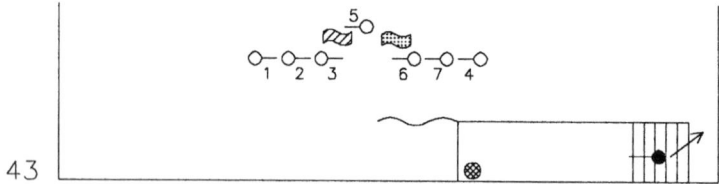

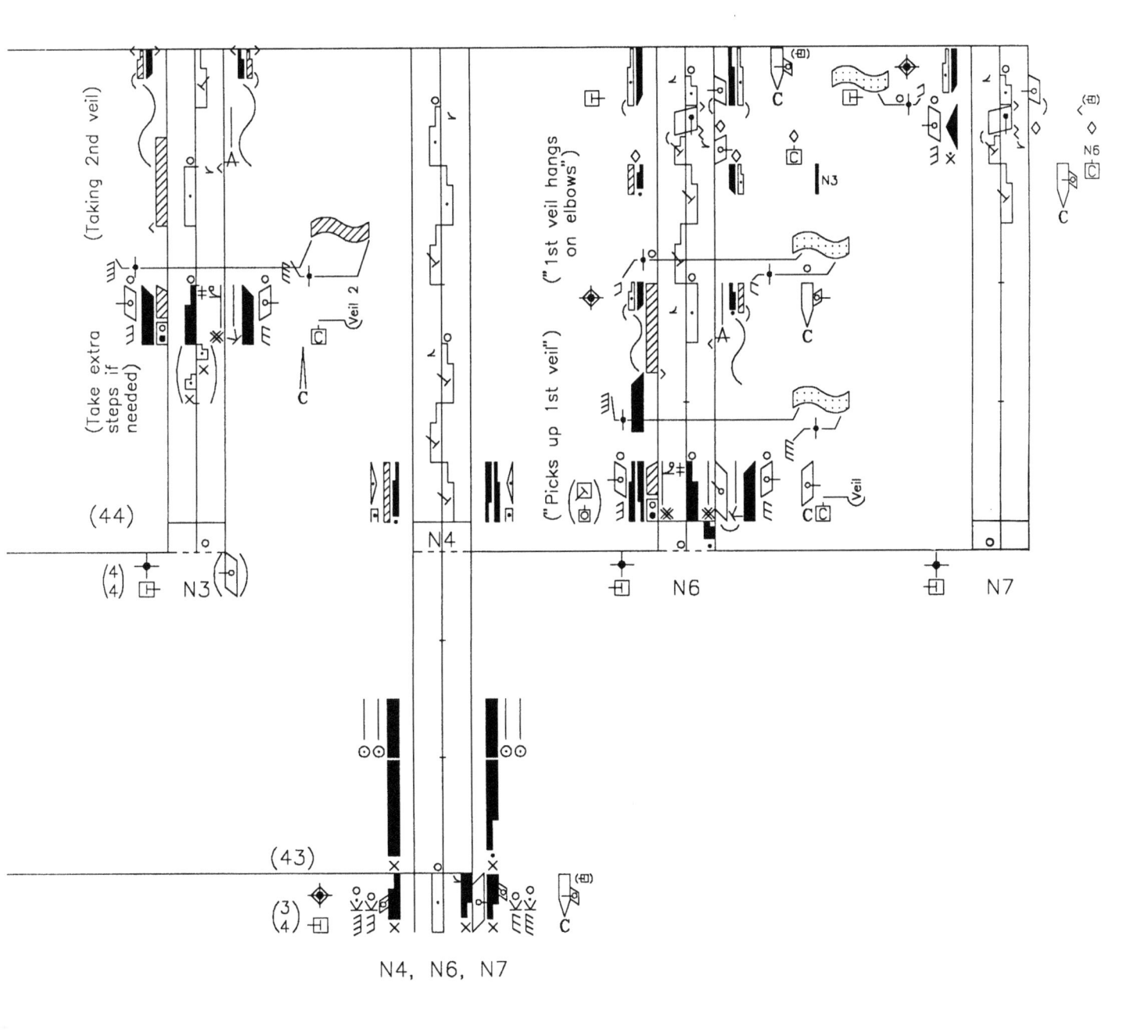

THE CHOREOGRAPHIC SCORE

103

N4, N6, N7

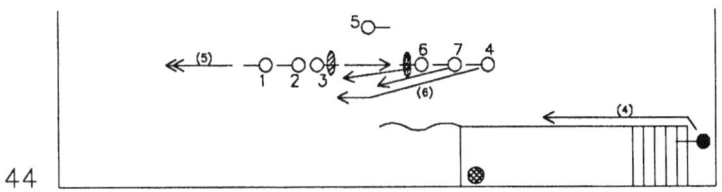

44

45
46
mf
Cor A.
m.g.

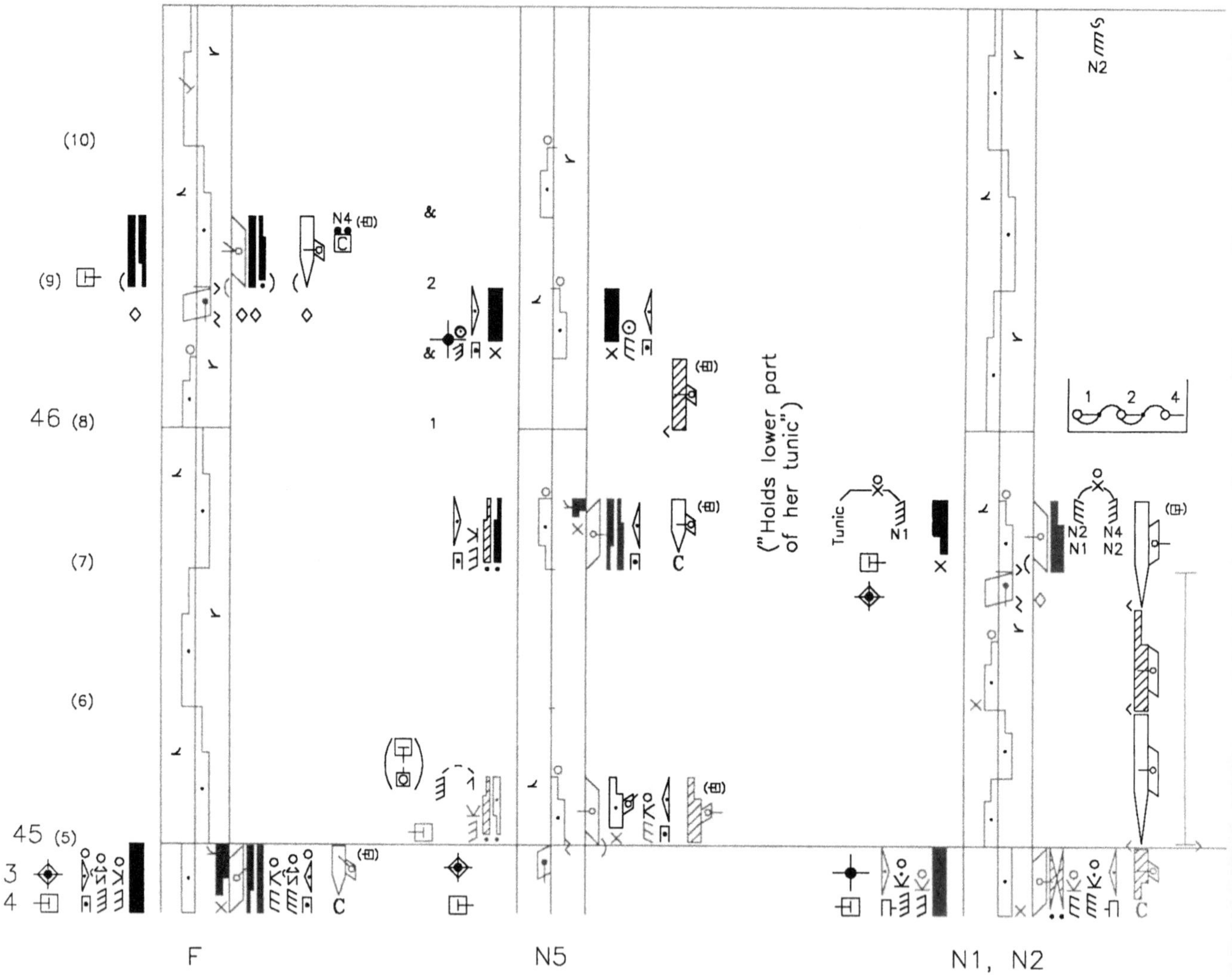
(10)
(9)
46 (8)
(7)
(6)
45 (5)
3
4
N4
("Holds lower part of her tunic")
Tunic
N1
N2
N4
F
N5
N1, N2

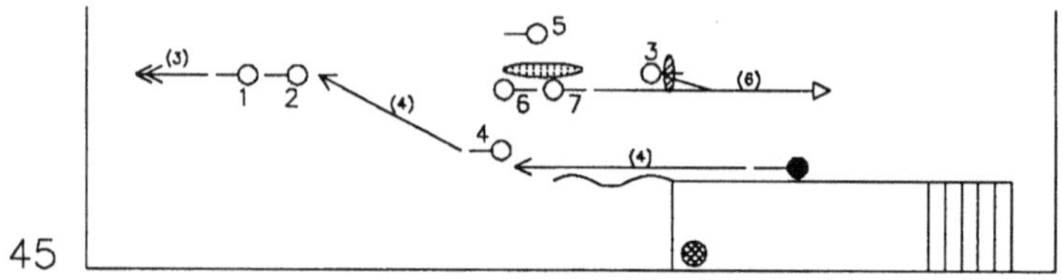
45

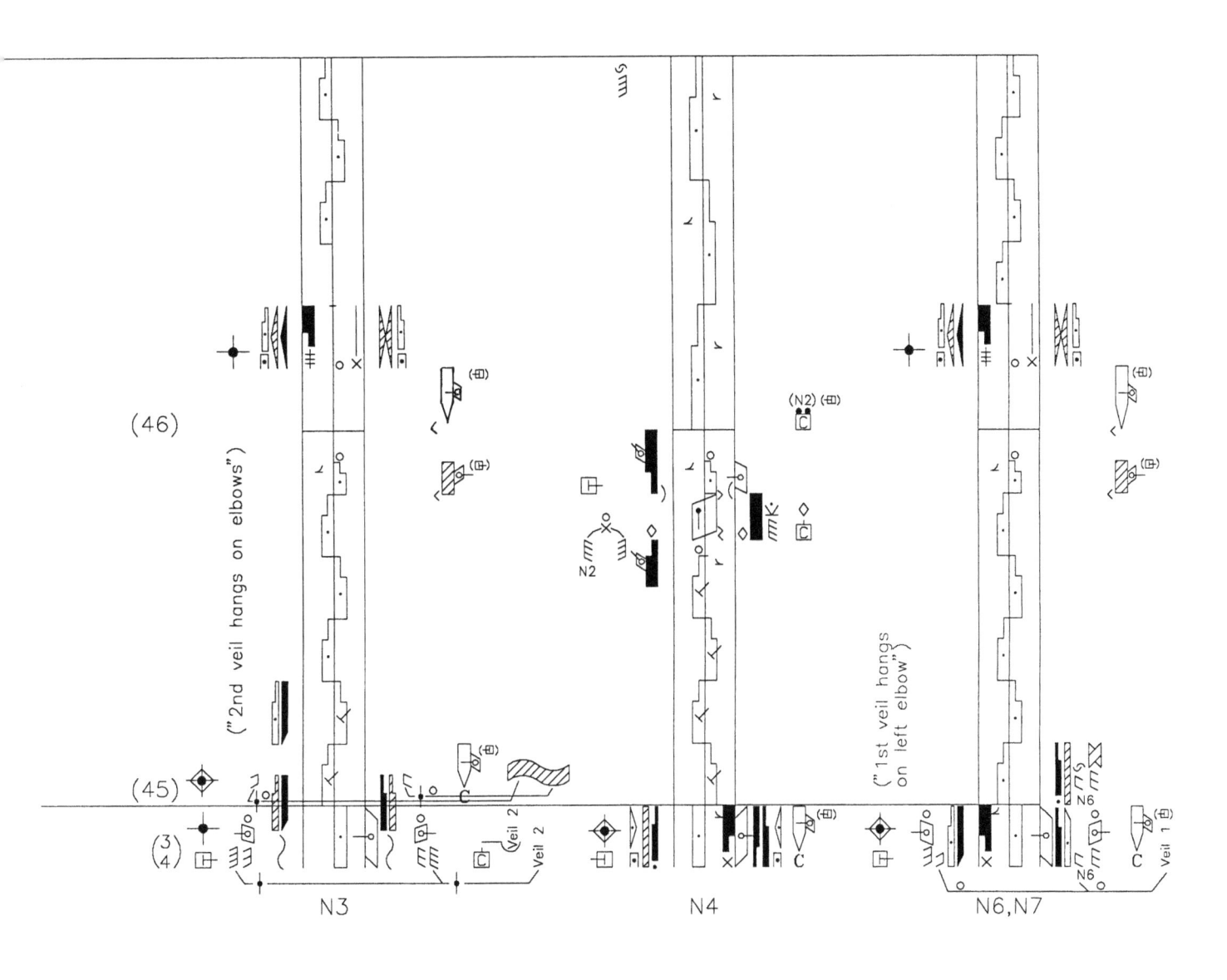

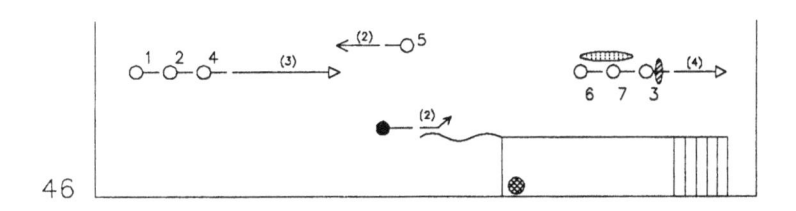

THE CHOREOGRAPHIC SCORE

47

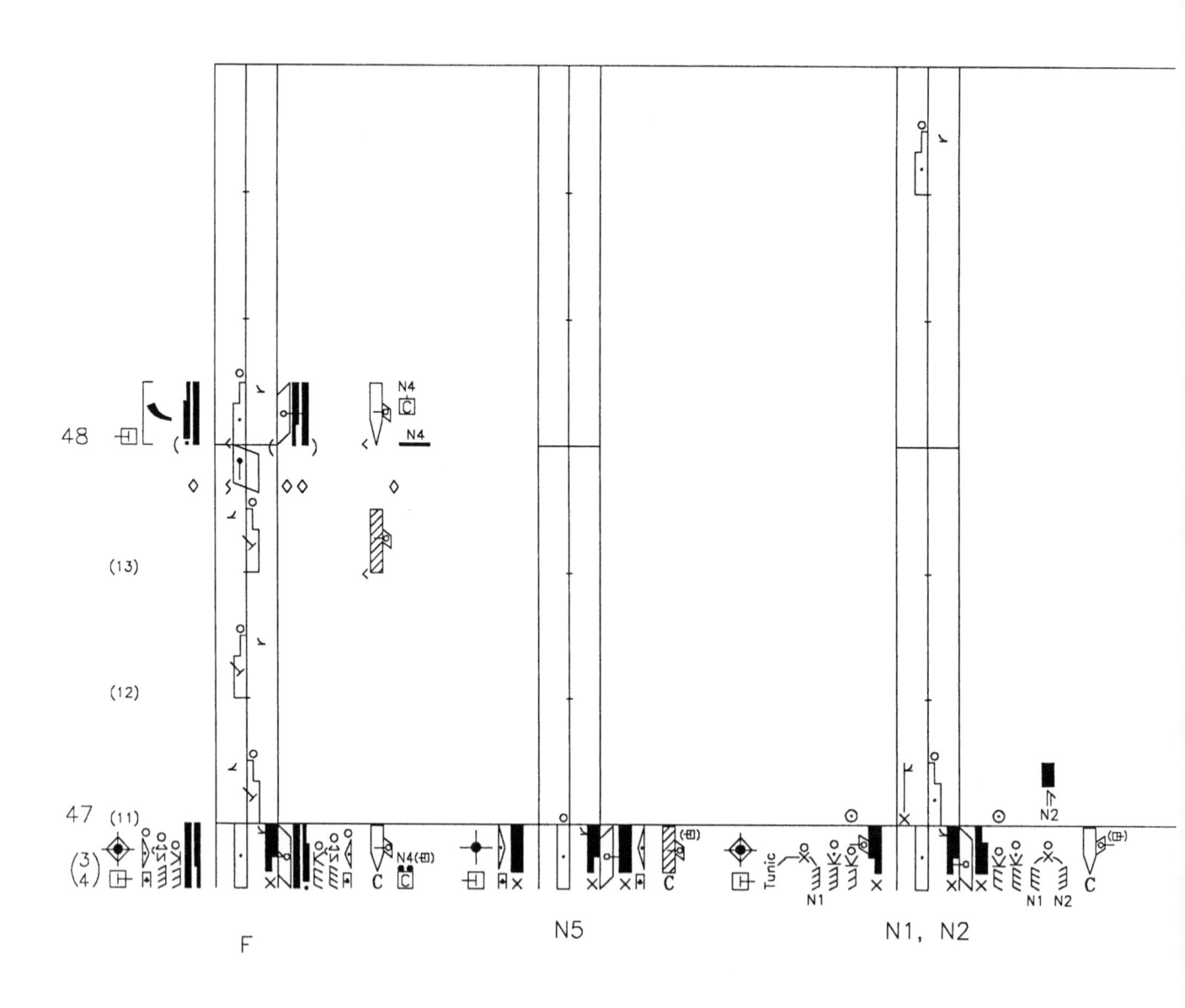

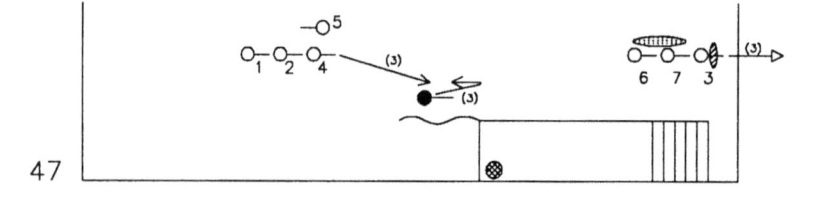

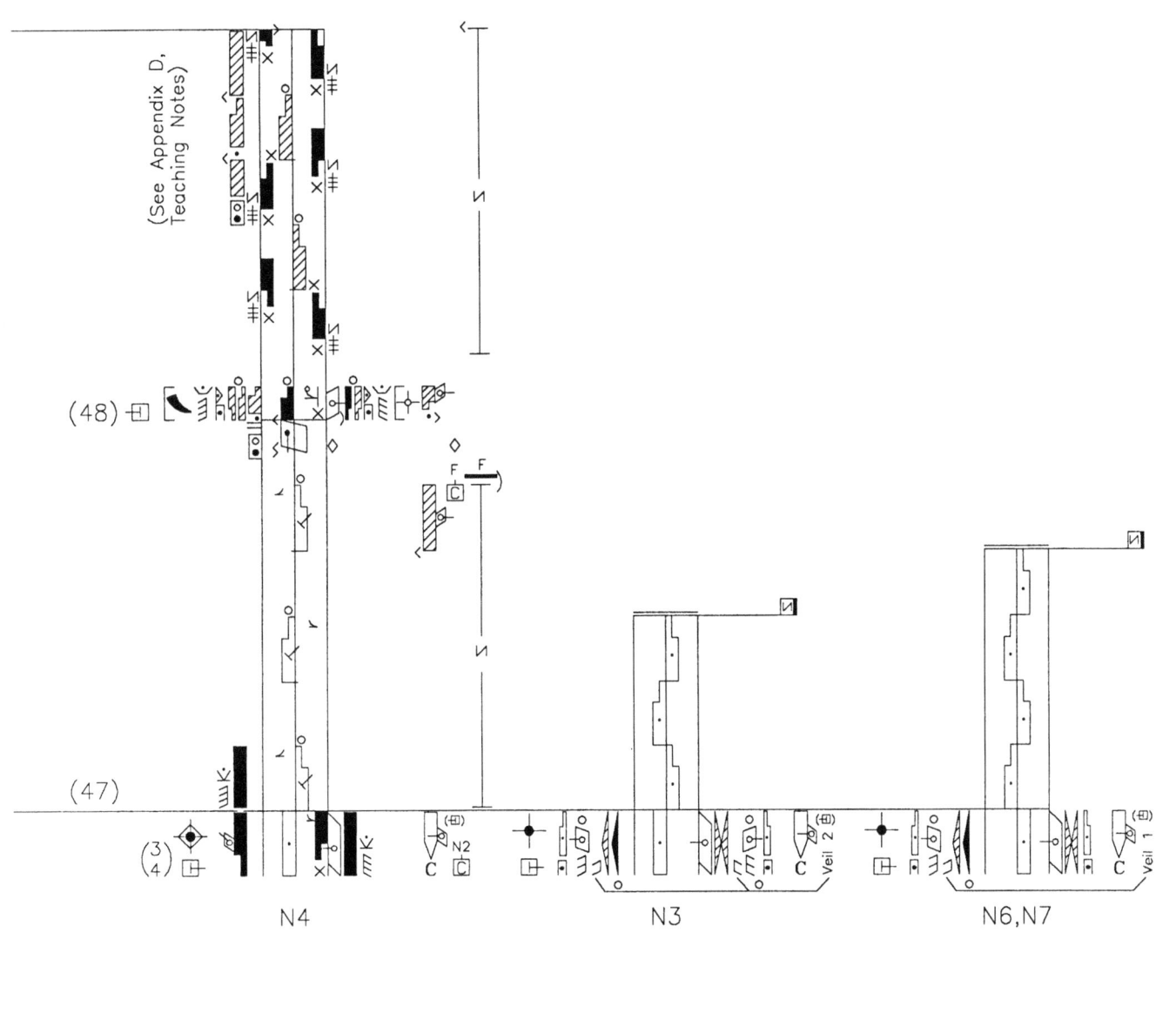

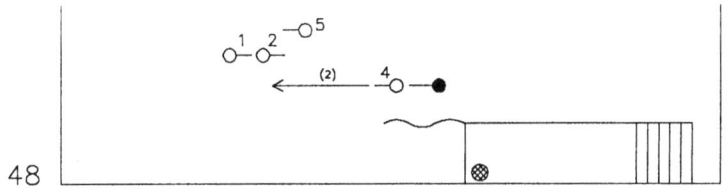

THE CHOREOGRAPHIC SCORE

107

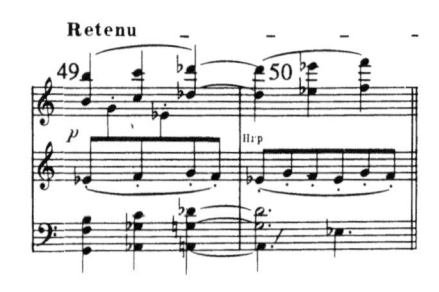

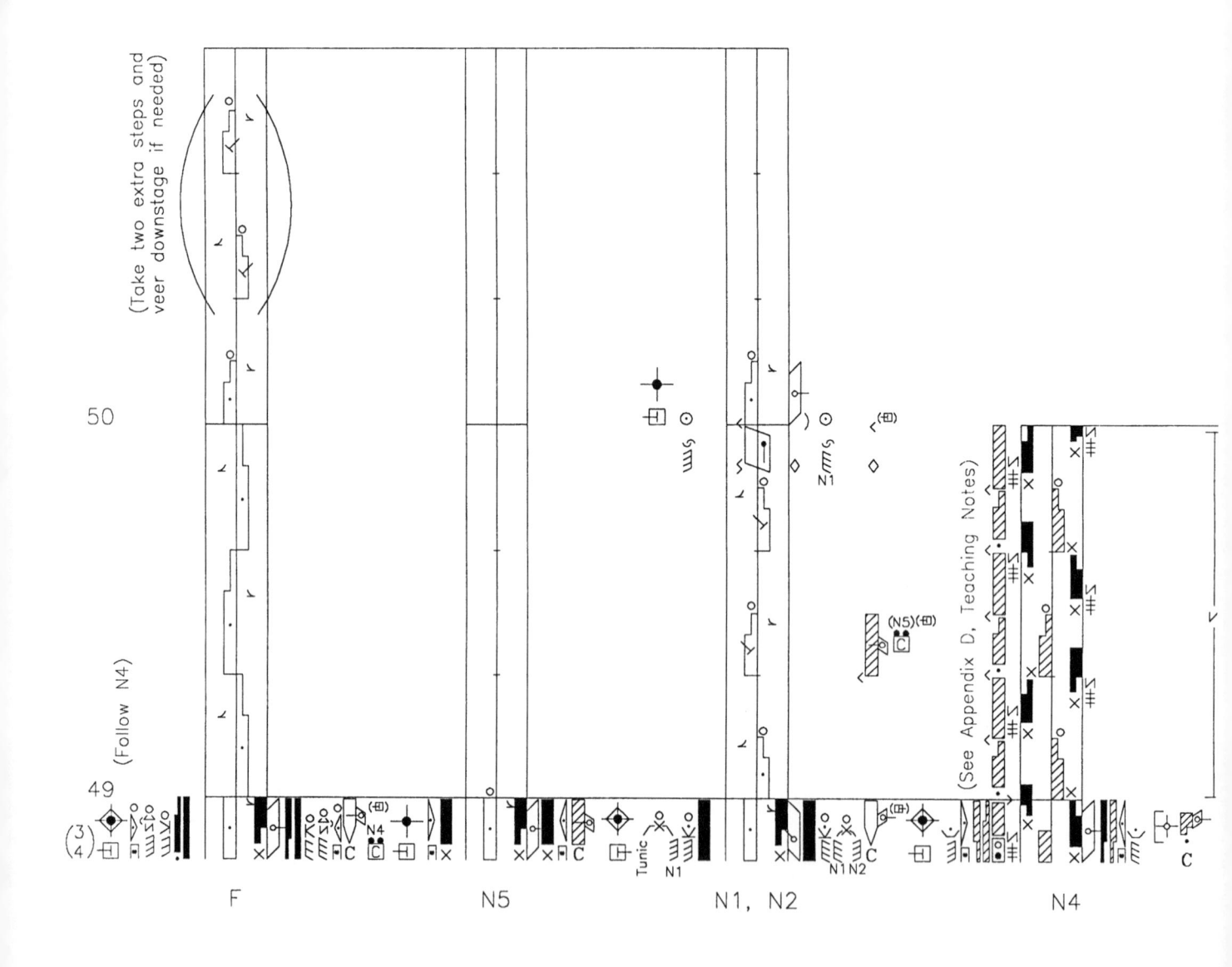

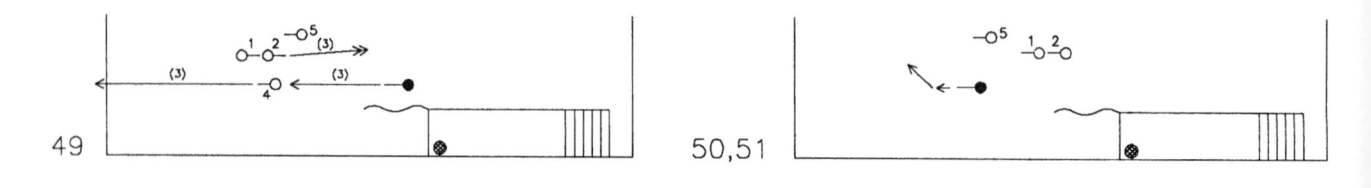

NIJINSKY'S *FAUNE* RESTORED

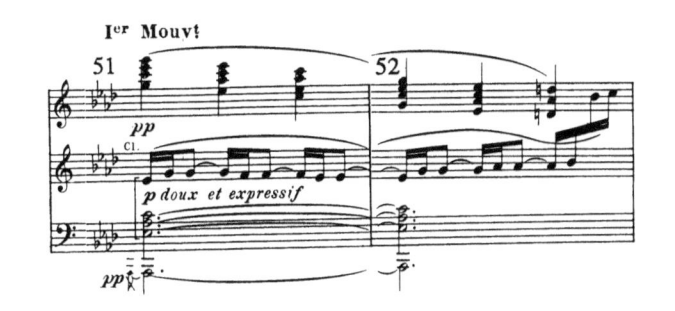

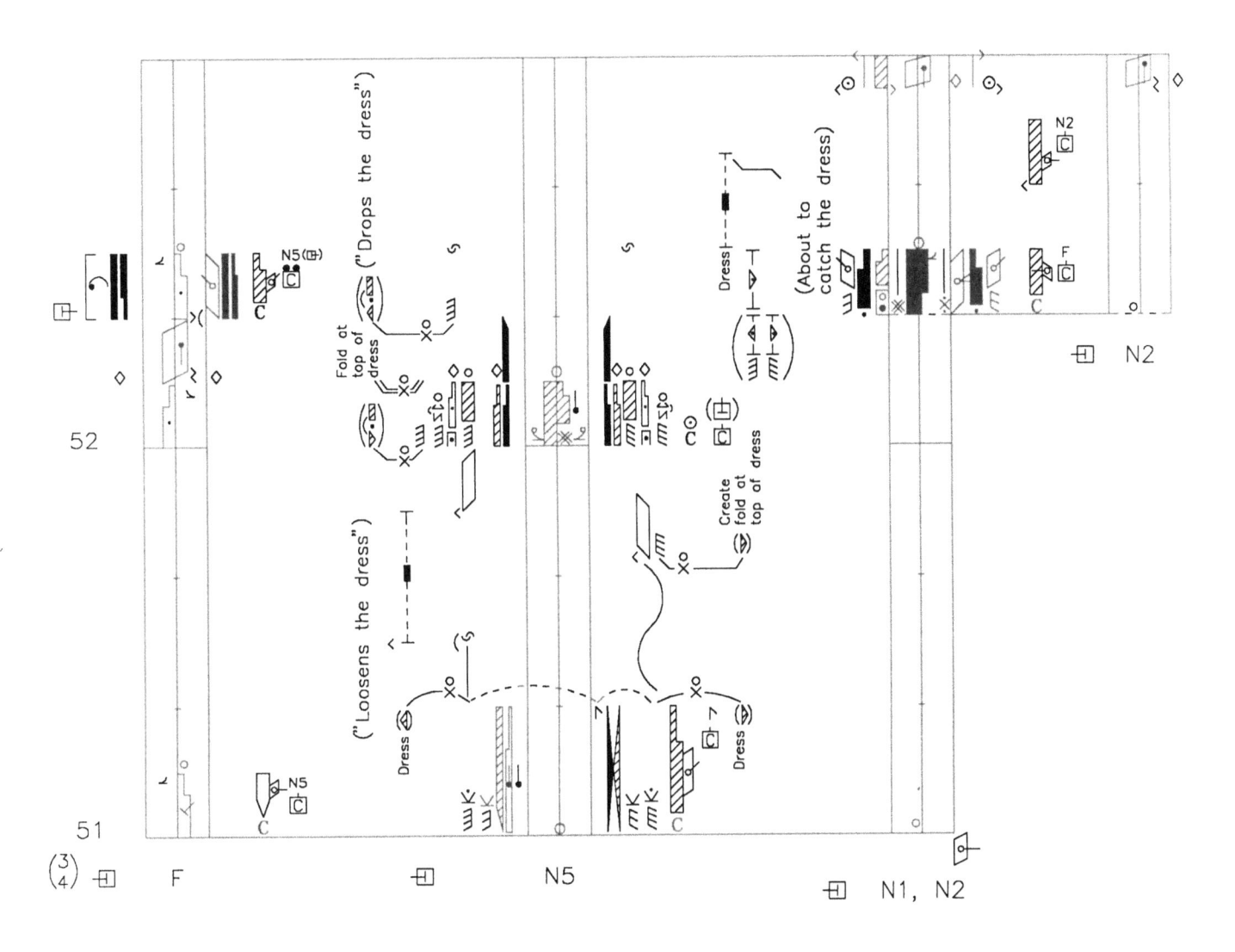

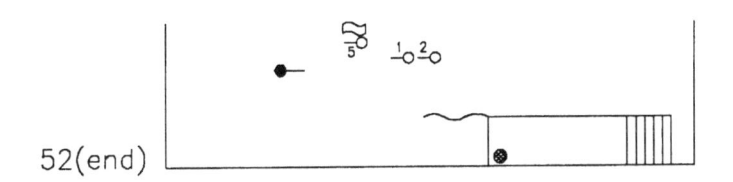

THE CHOREOGRAPHIC SCORE

110 NIJINSKY'S *FAUNE* RESTORED

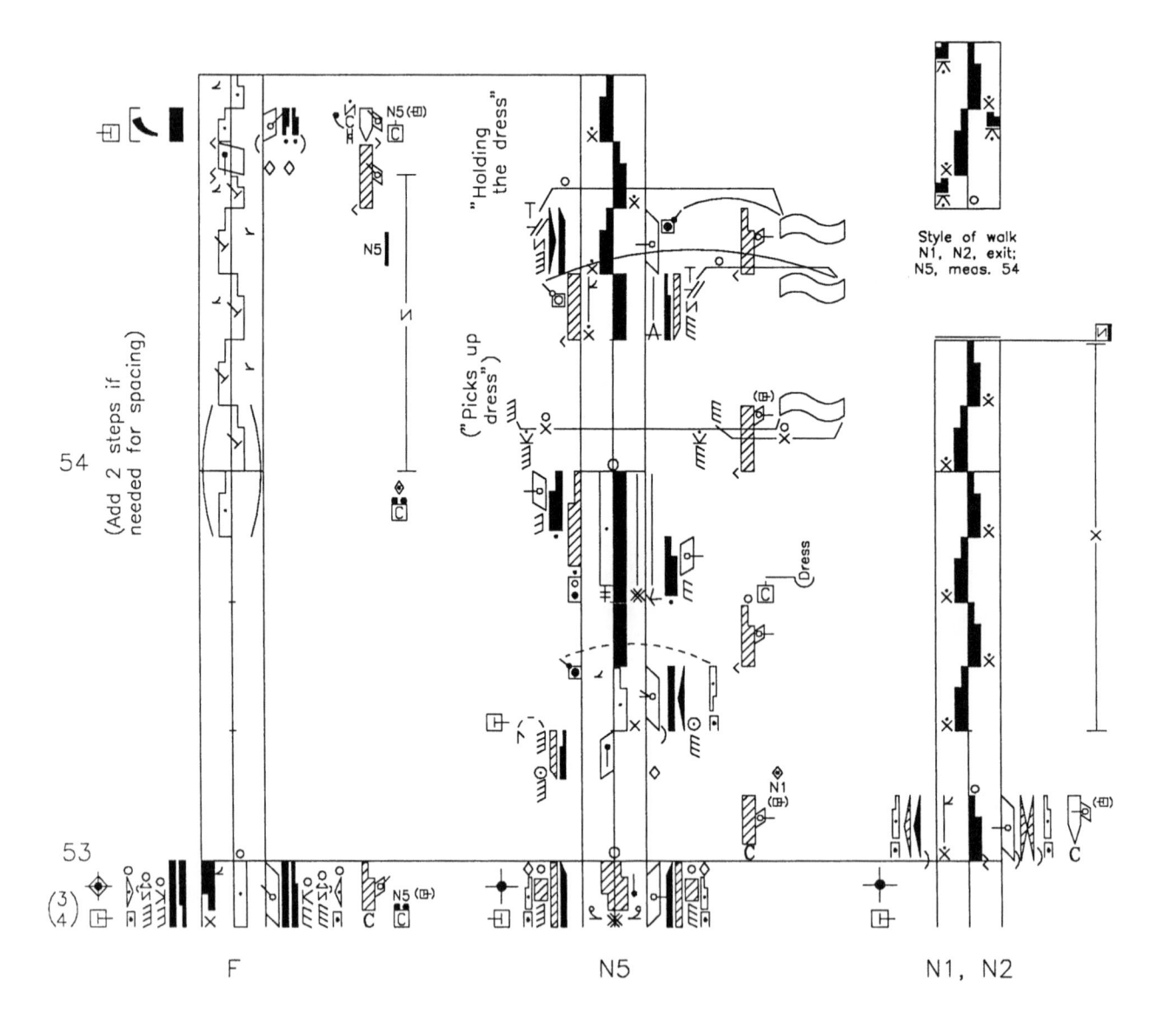

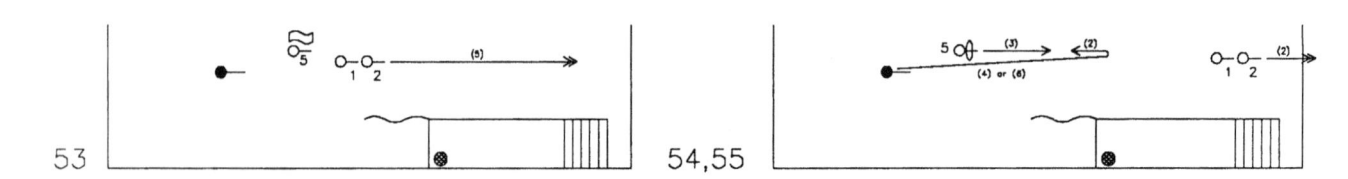

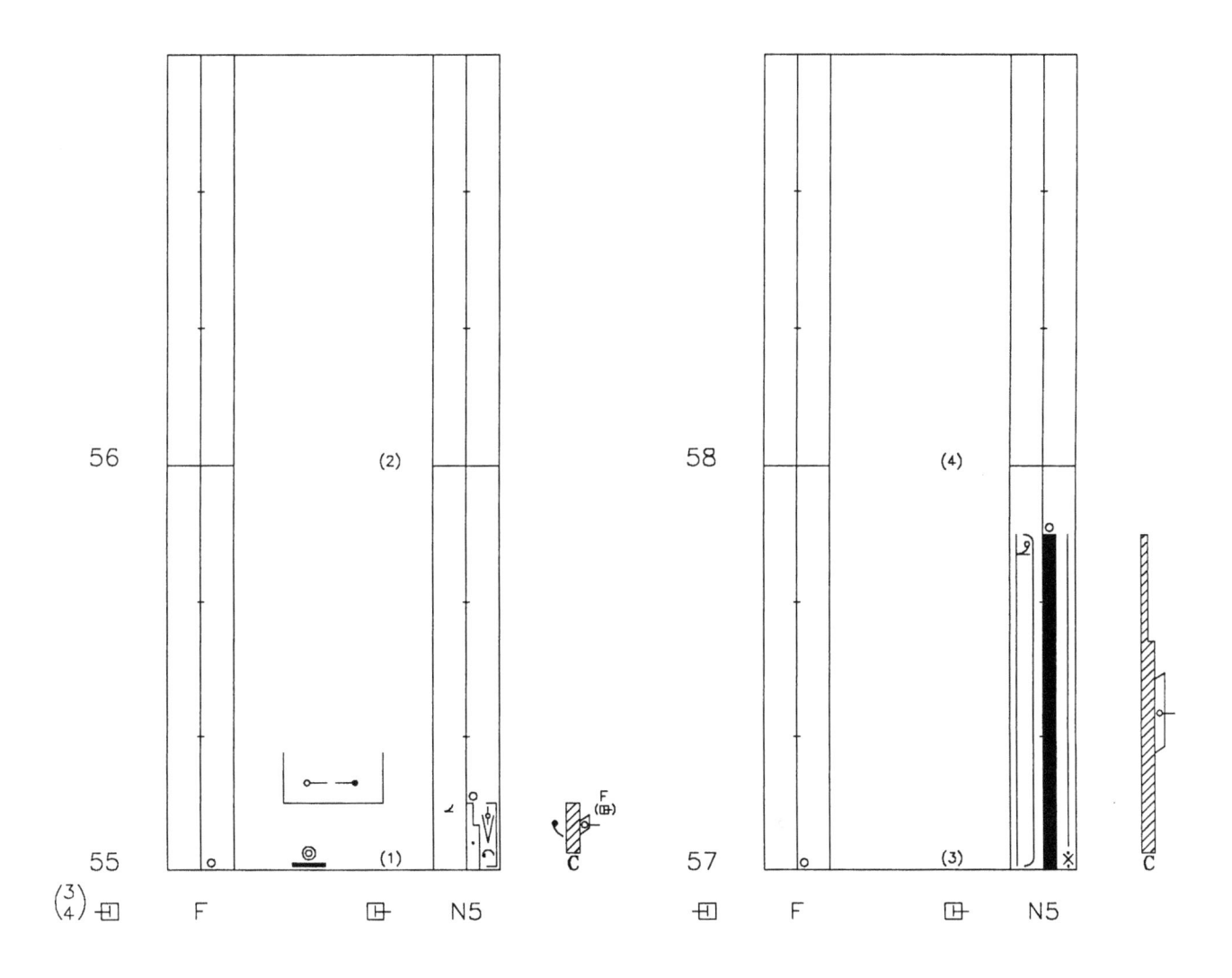

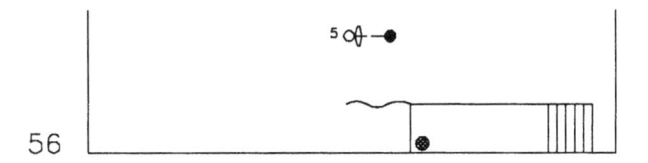

THE CHOREOGRAPHIC SCORE

112 NIJINSKY'S *FAUNE* RESTORED

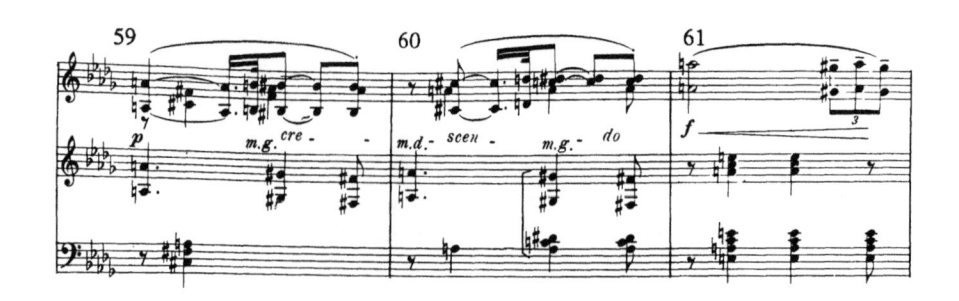

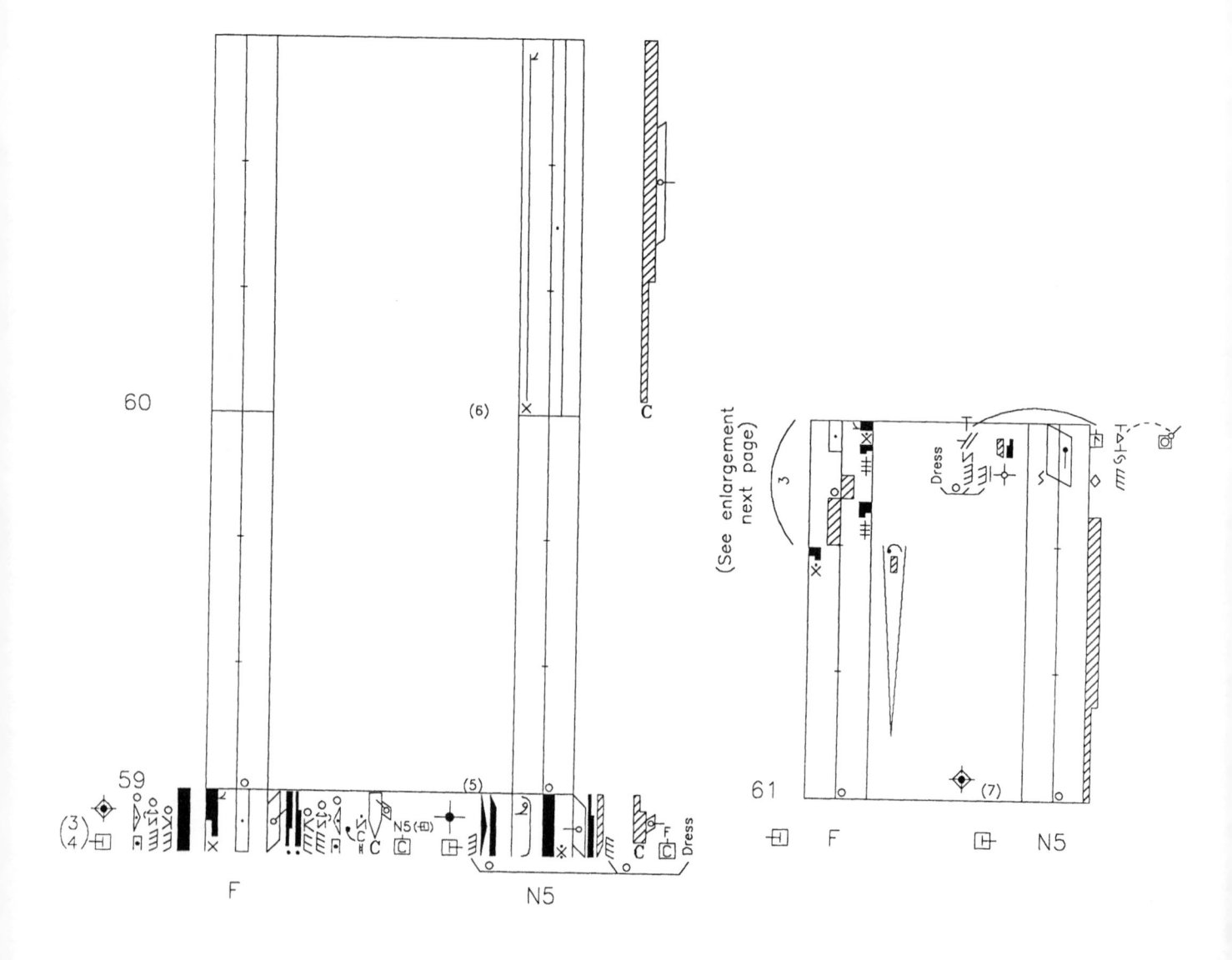

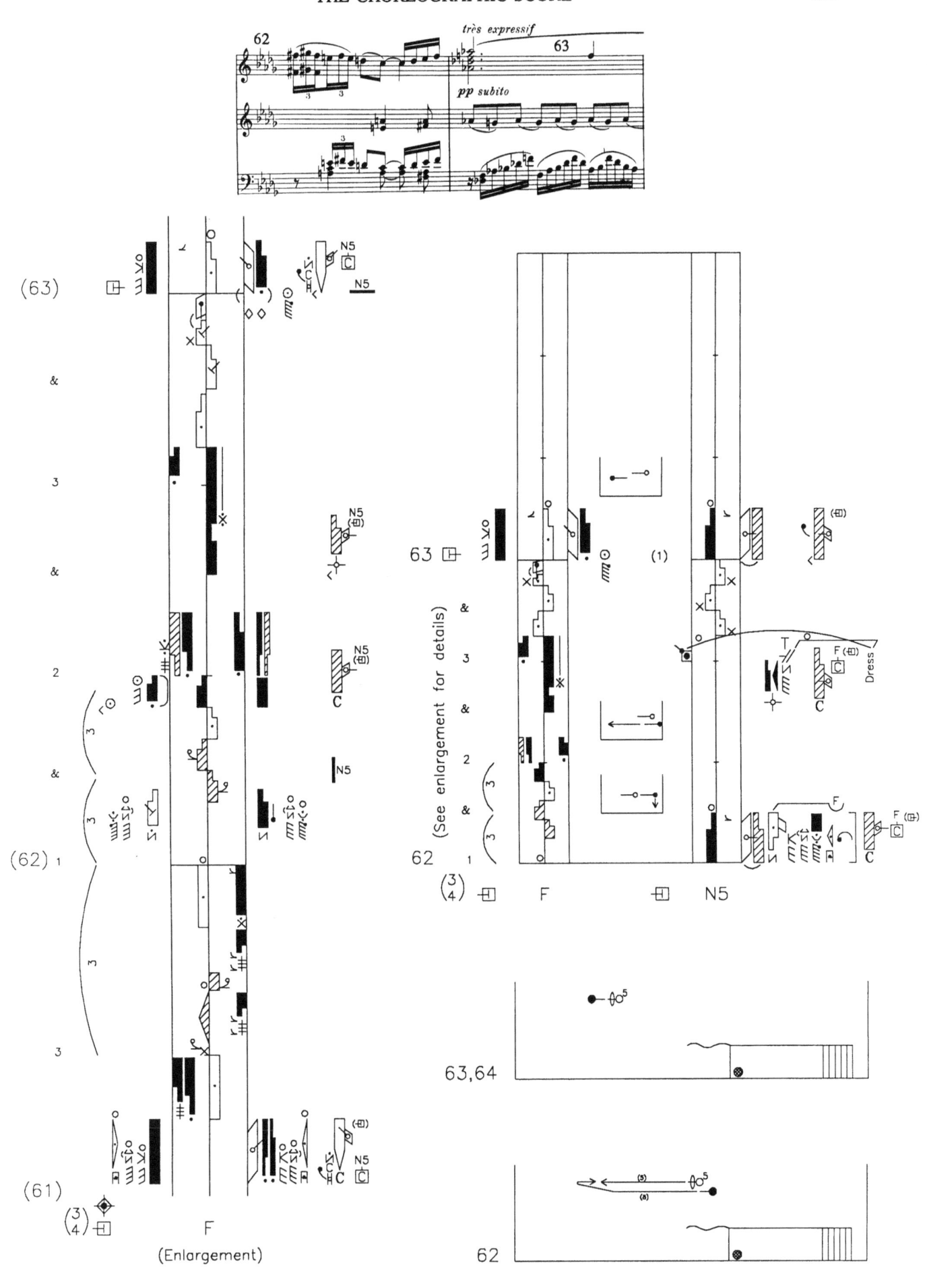

THE CHOREOGRAPHIC SCORE

113

64–66

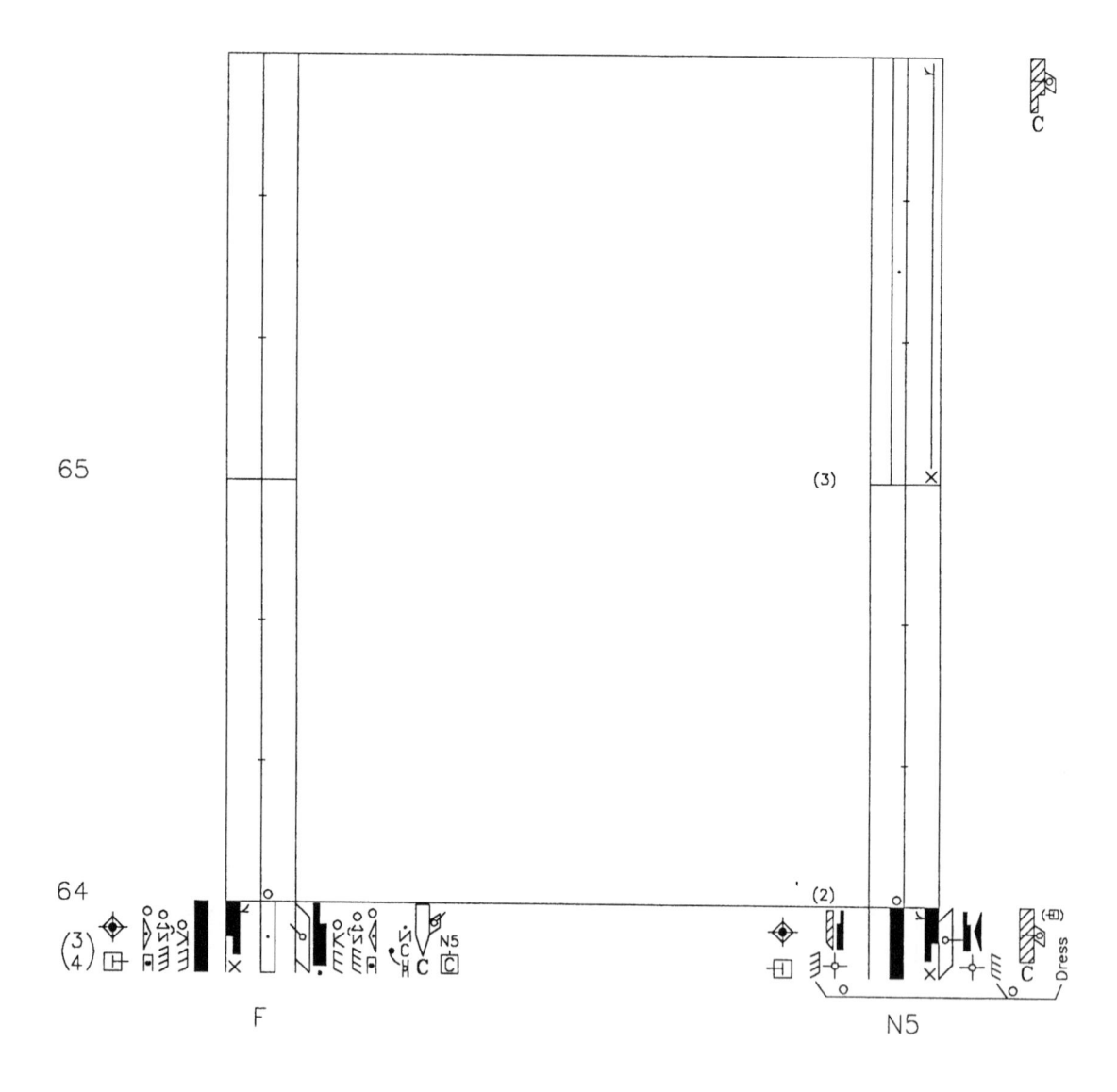

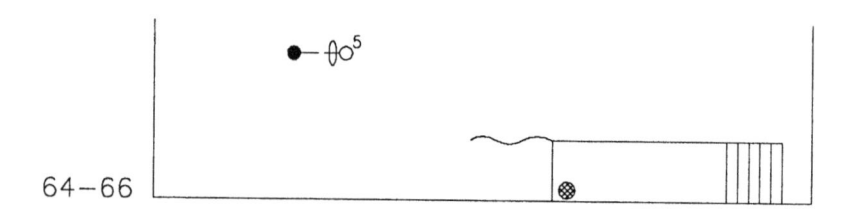

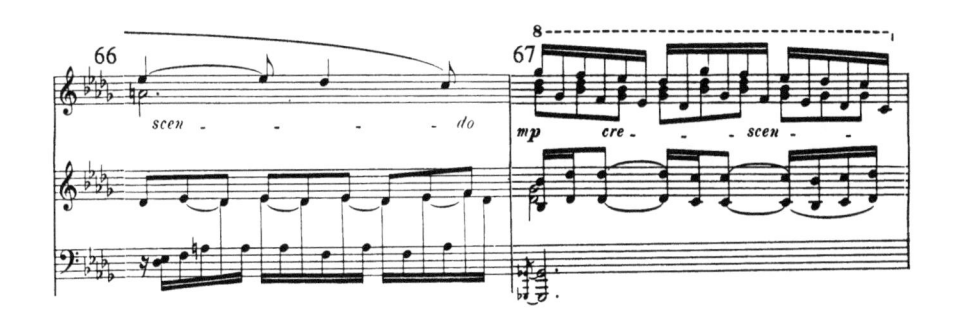

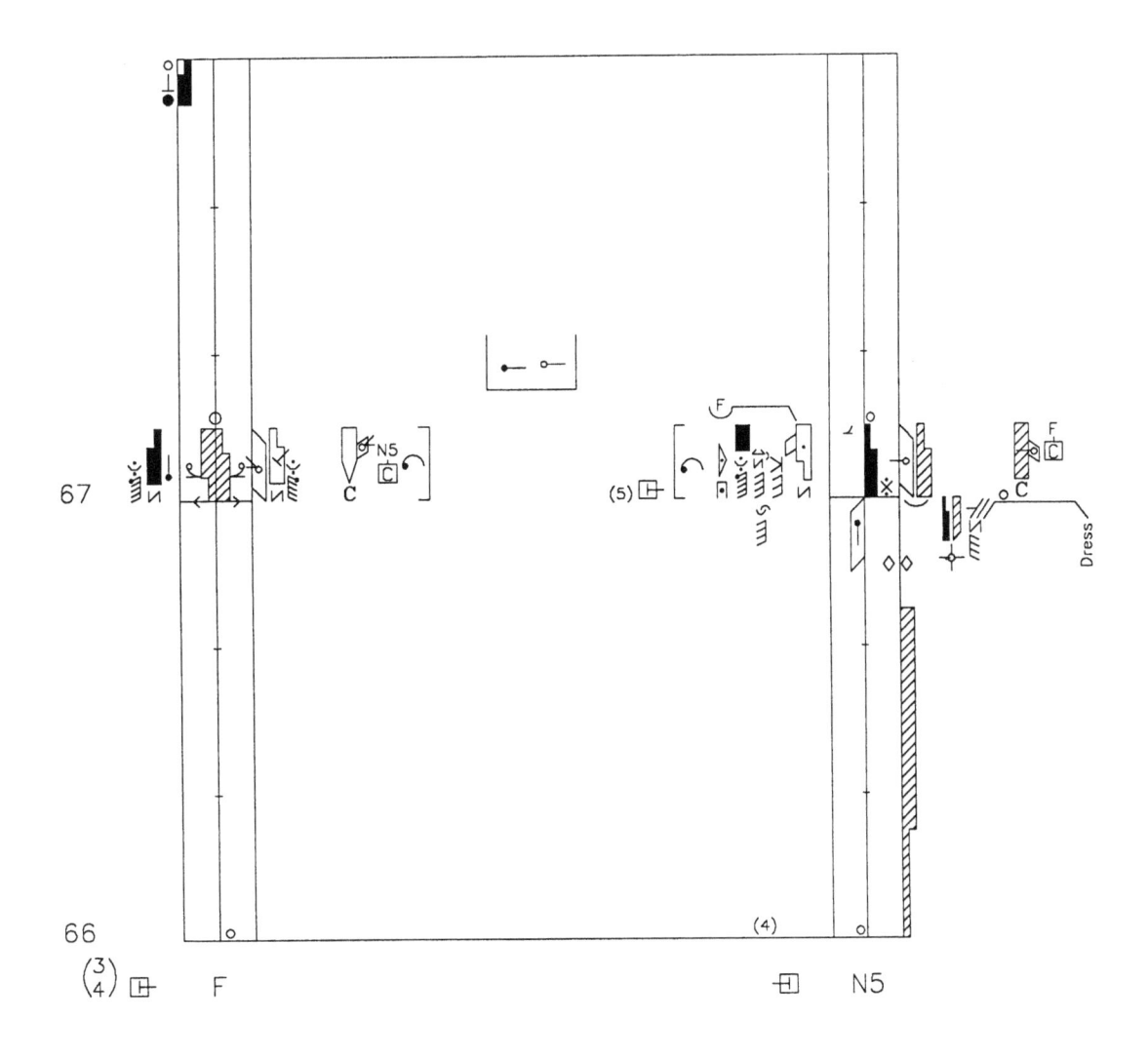

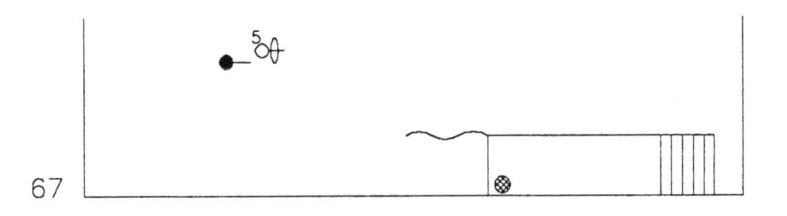

THE CHOREOGRAPHIC SCORE

Style of walk
N5, meas. 68, 70
(Enlarged)

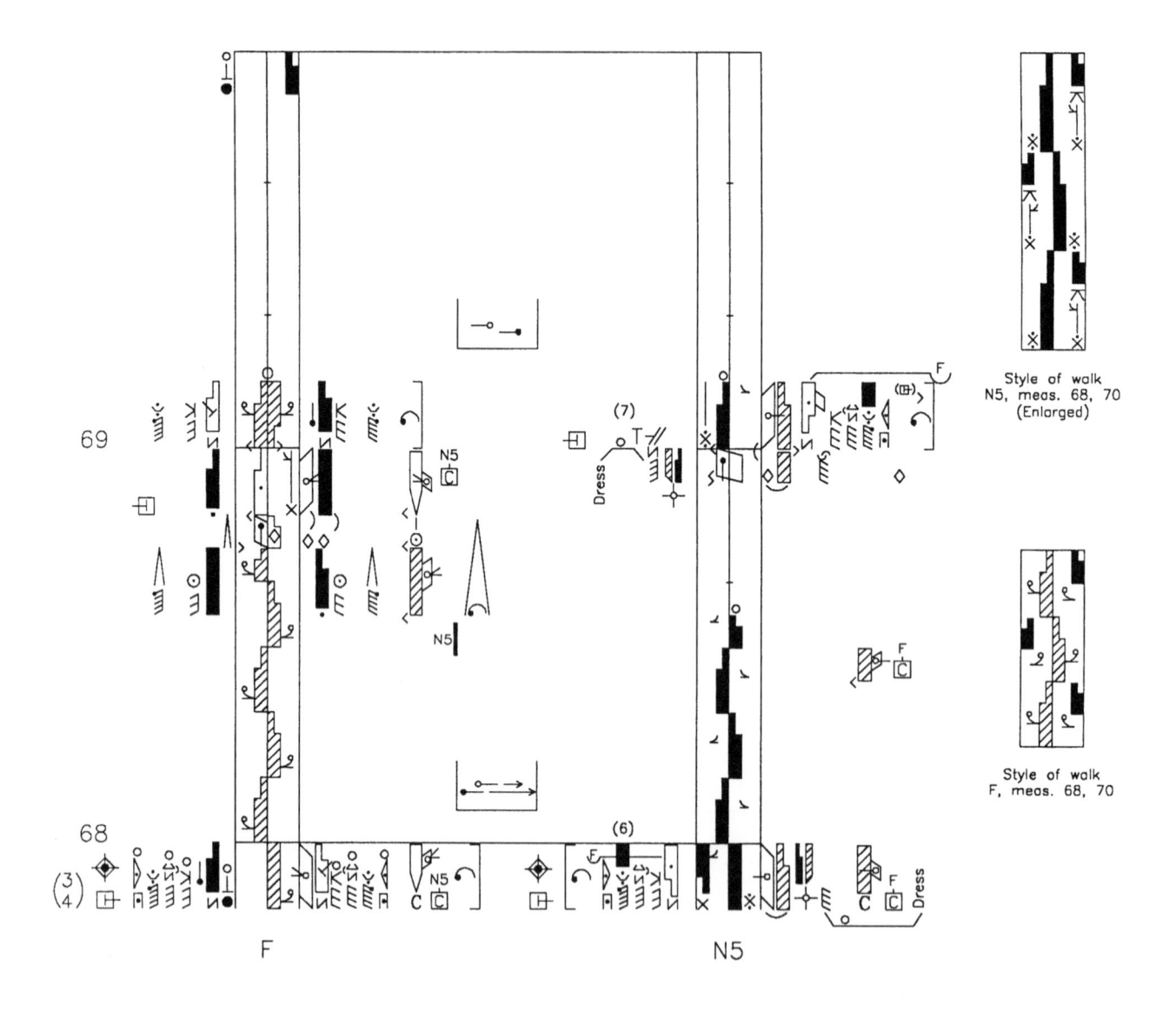

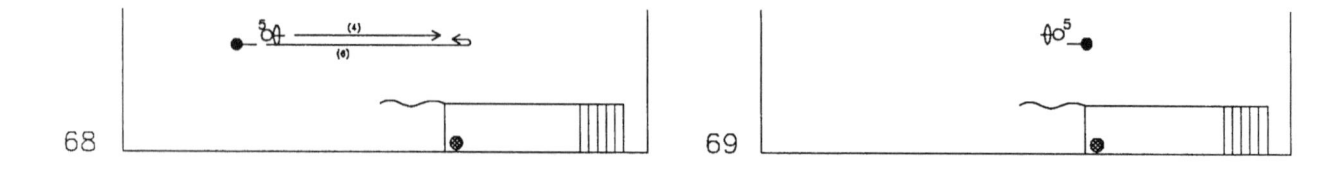

Style of walk
F, meas. 68, 70

THE CHOREOGRAPHIC SCORE 117

Style of walk
F, N5, meas. 71–73
N5, meas. 76

Style of walk
N6, N2, N1, N7, N3
meas. 71–73

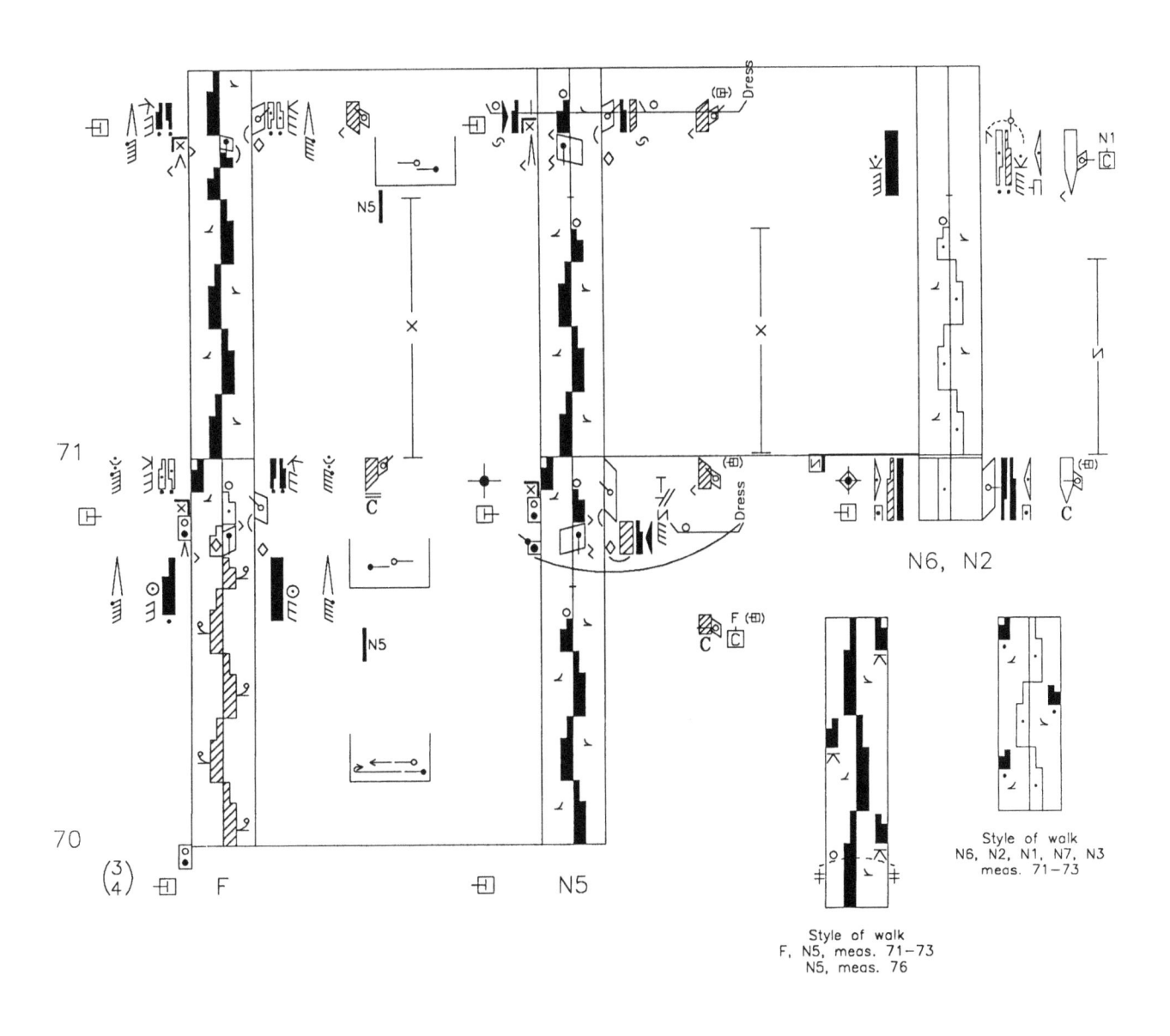

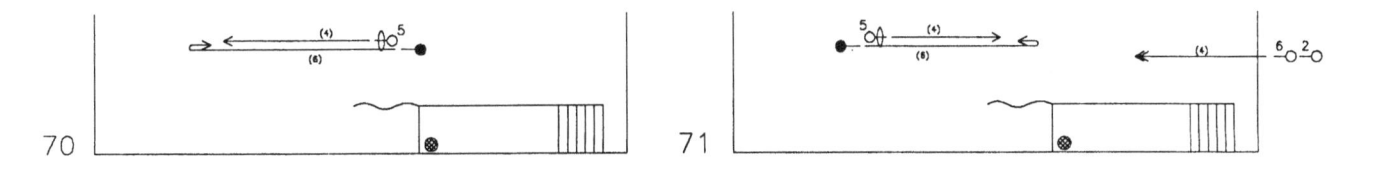

72
73
mf
p

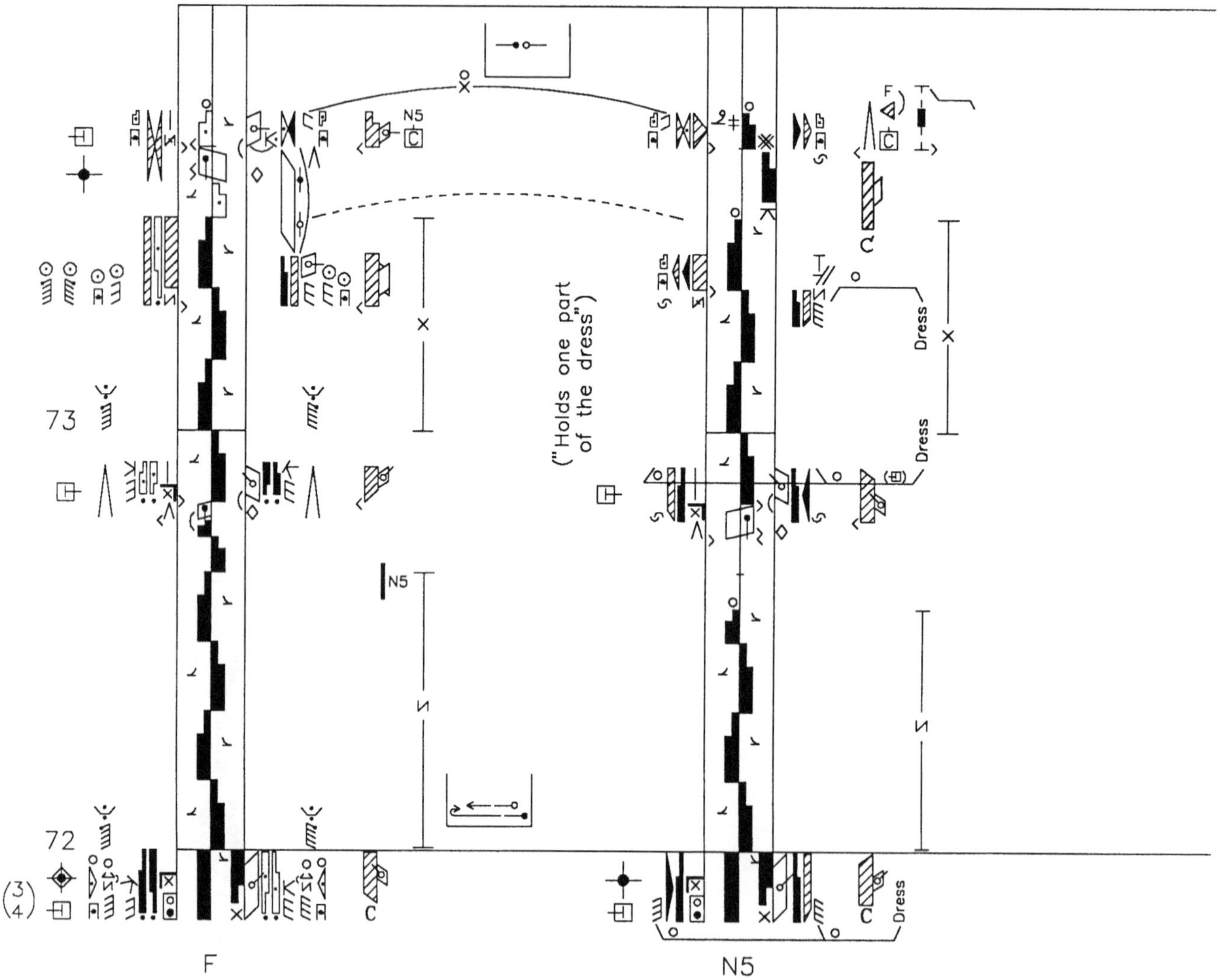
73
72
(3
4)
N5
("Holds one part of the dress")
Dress
Dress
Dress
F
N5

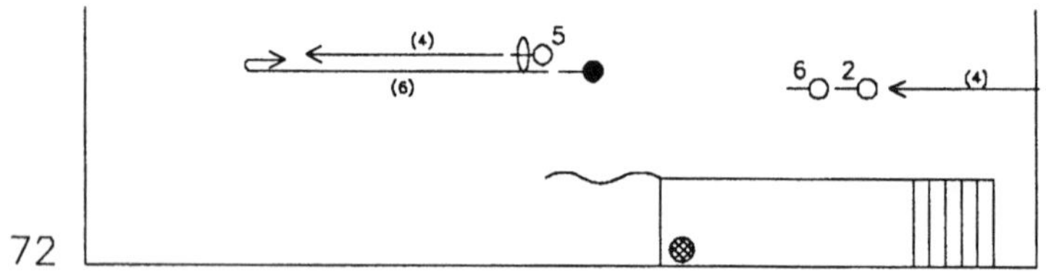
(4)
(6)
5
6
2
(4)
1
72

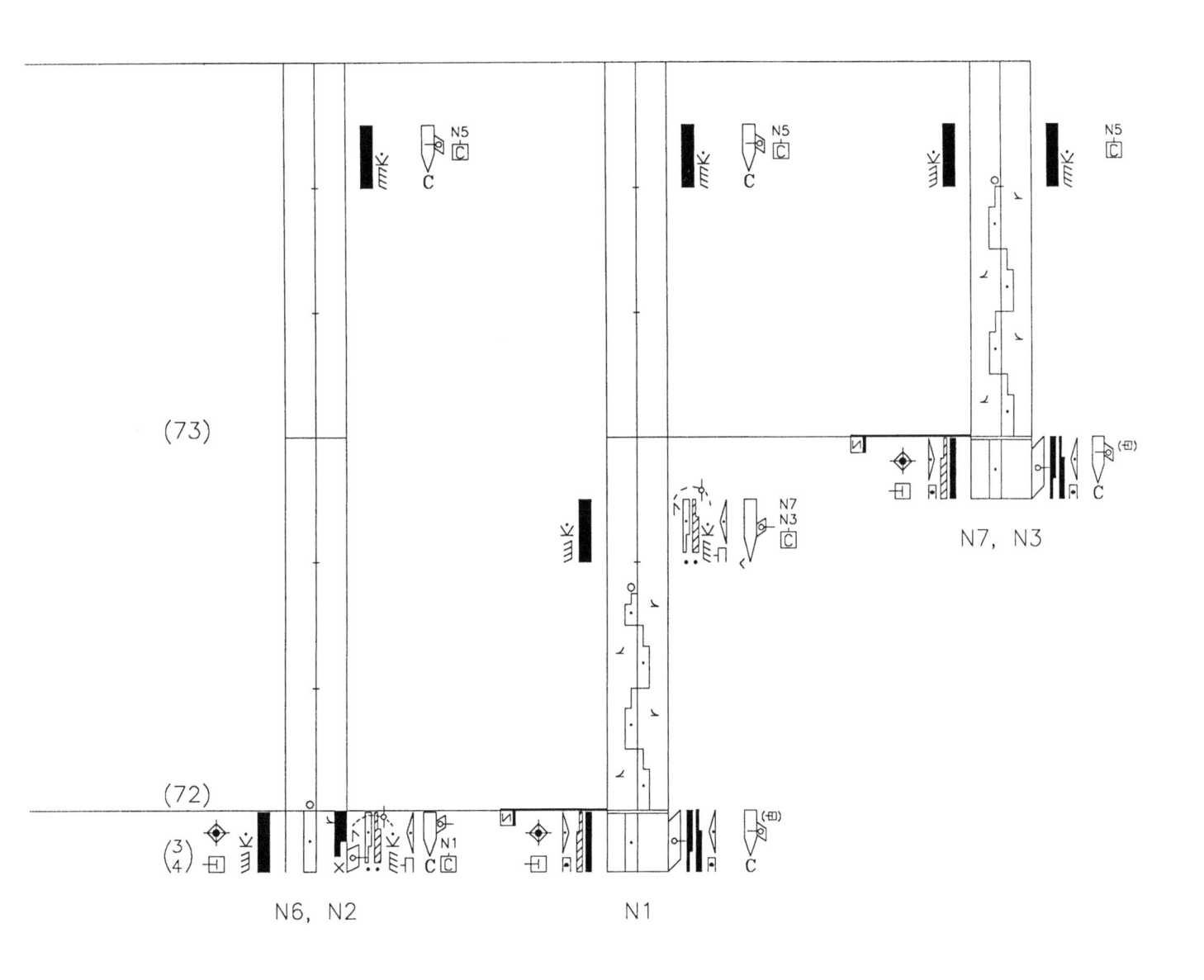

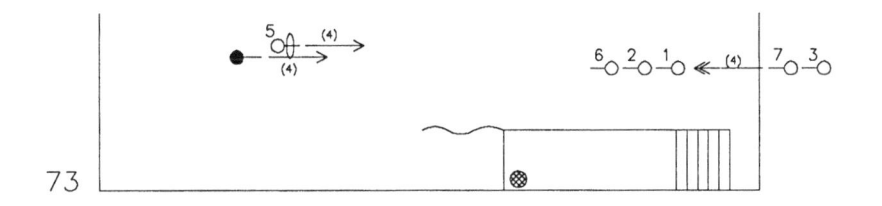

THE CHOREOGRAPHIC SCORE

(73)

(72)

(3)
(4)

N6, N2

N1

N7, N3

73

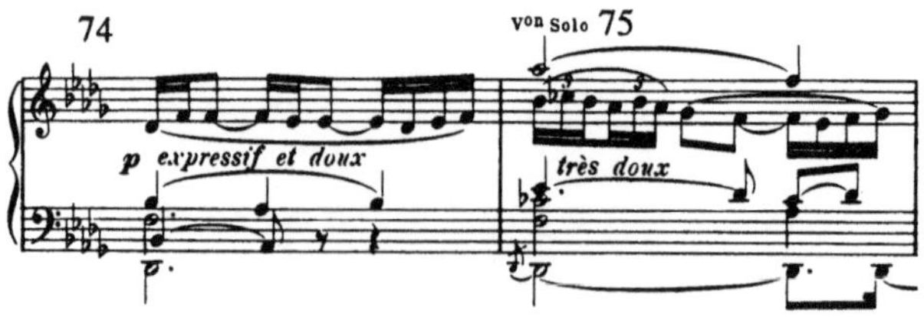
74
von Solo 75
p expressif et doux
très doux

75
74
"Pointing with his thumb like a horn"
("Takes the dress")
(As though wrapping)
Dress
N5
N6
F
N5

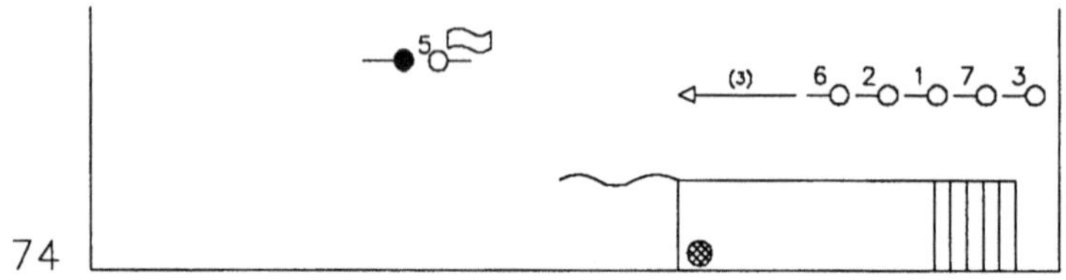
74

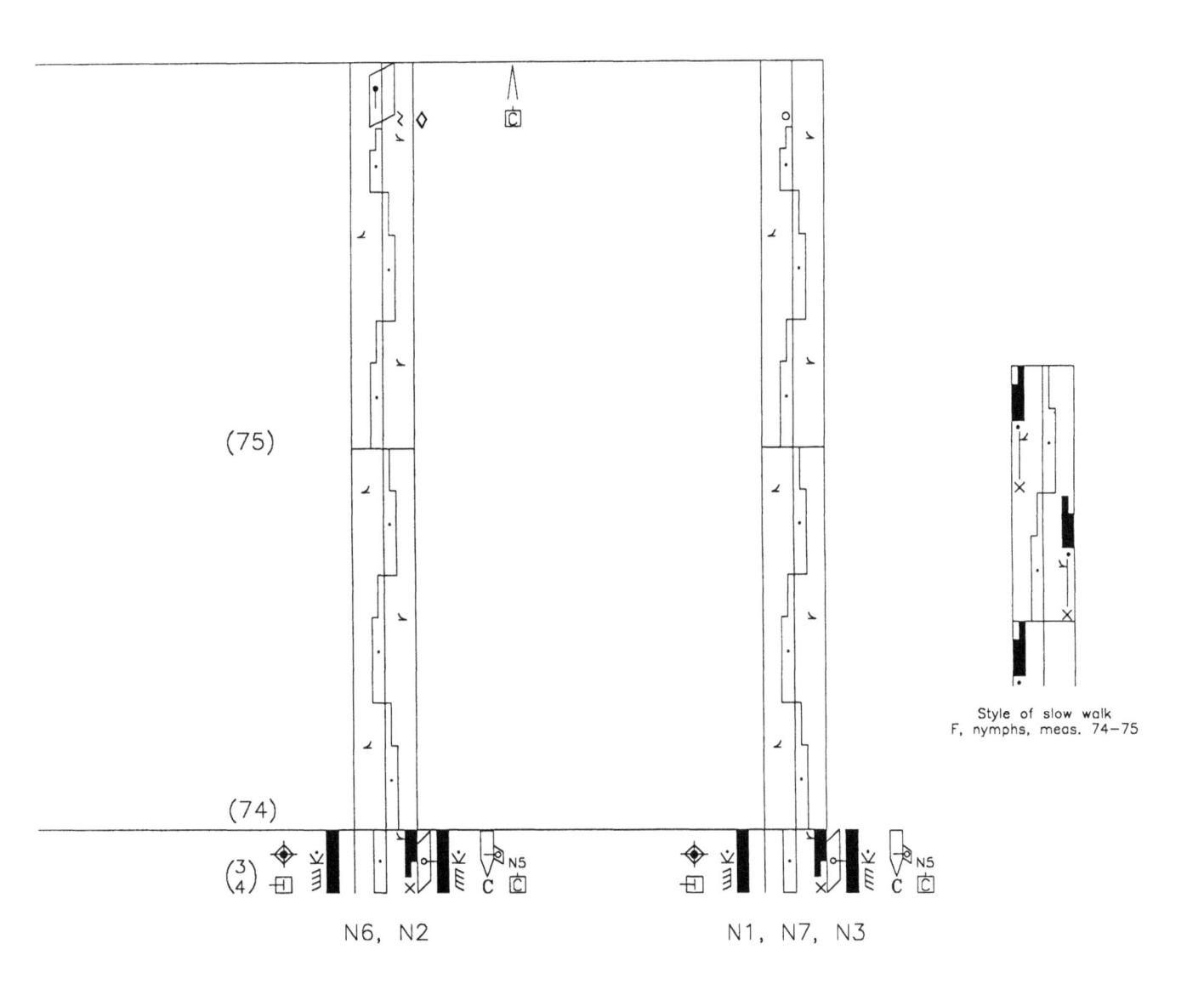

THE CHOREOGRAPHIC SCORE

(75)

(74)

(3)
(4)

N6, N2   N1, N7, N3

Style of slow walk
F, nymphs, meas. 74–75

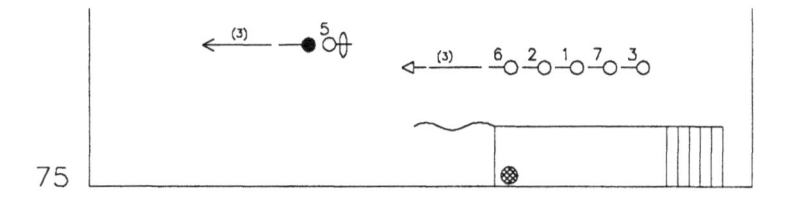

75

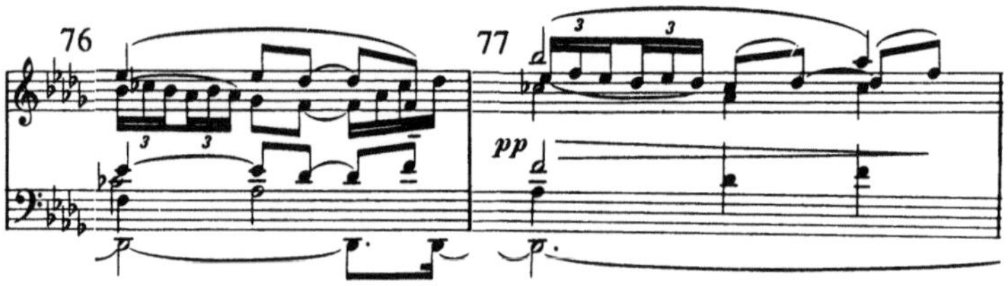
76
77
pp

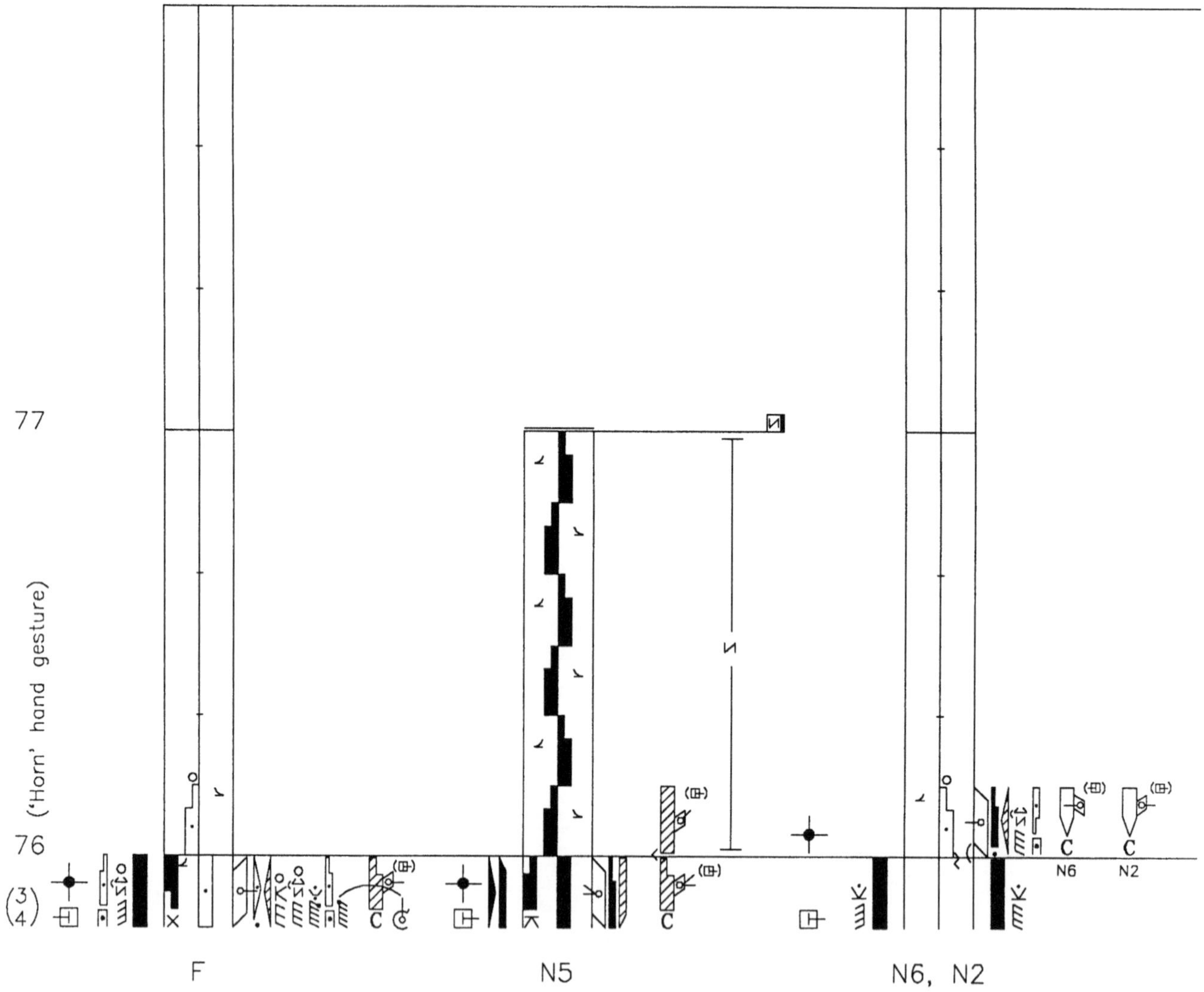
77
76
('Horn' hand gesture)
F
N5
N6, N2
N6
N2

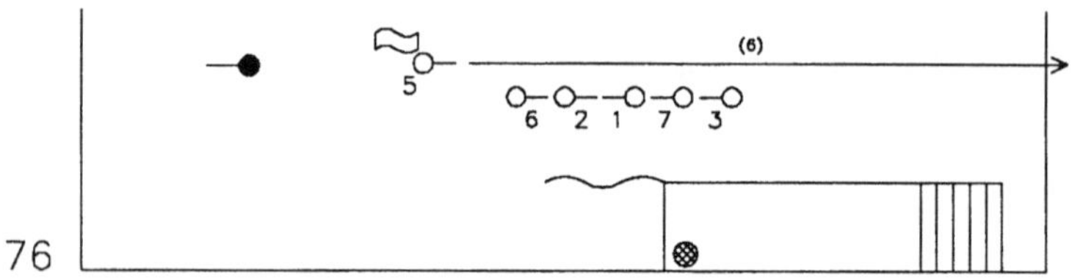
(6)
5
6 2 1 7 3
76

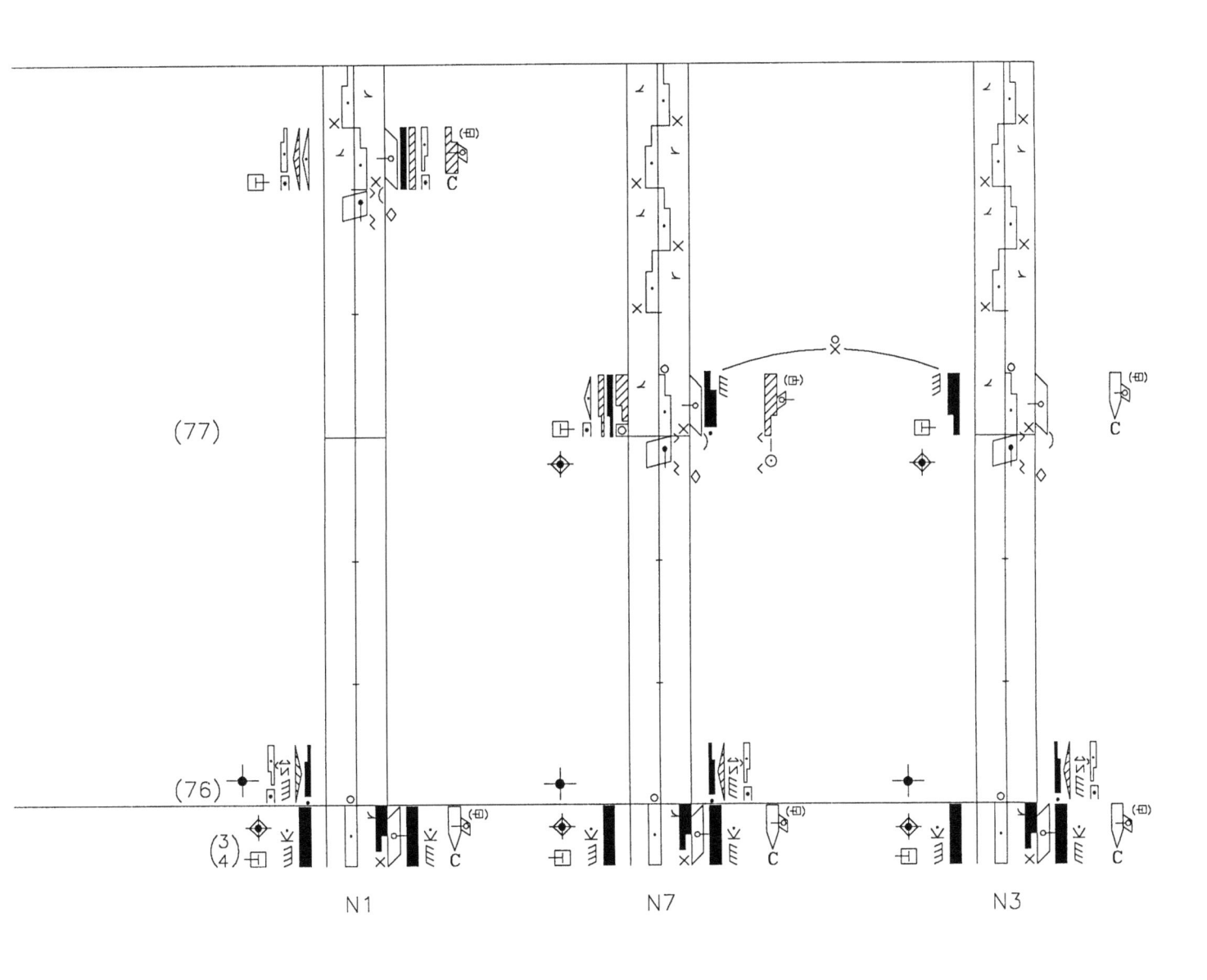

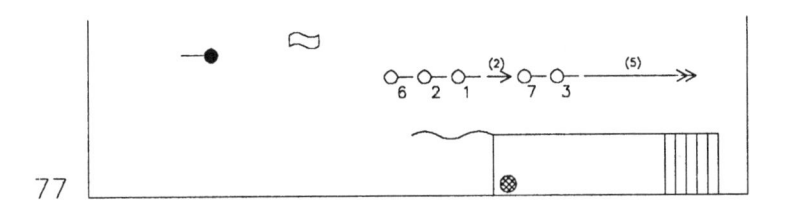

THE CHOREOGRAPHIC SCORE

(77)

(76)

(3)
(4)

N1   N7   N3

77

124 NIJINSKY'S *FAUNE* RESTORED

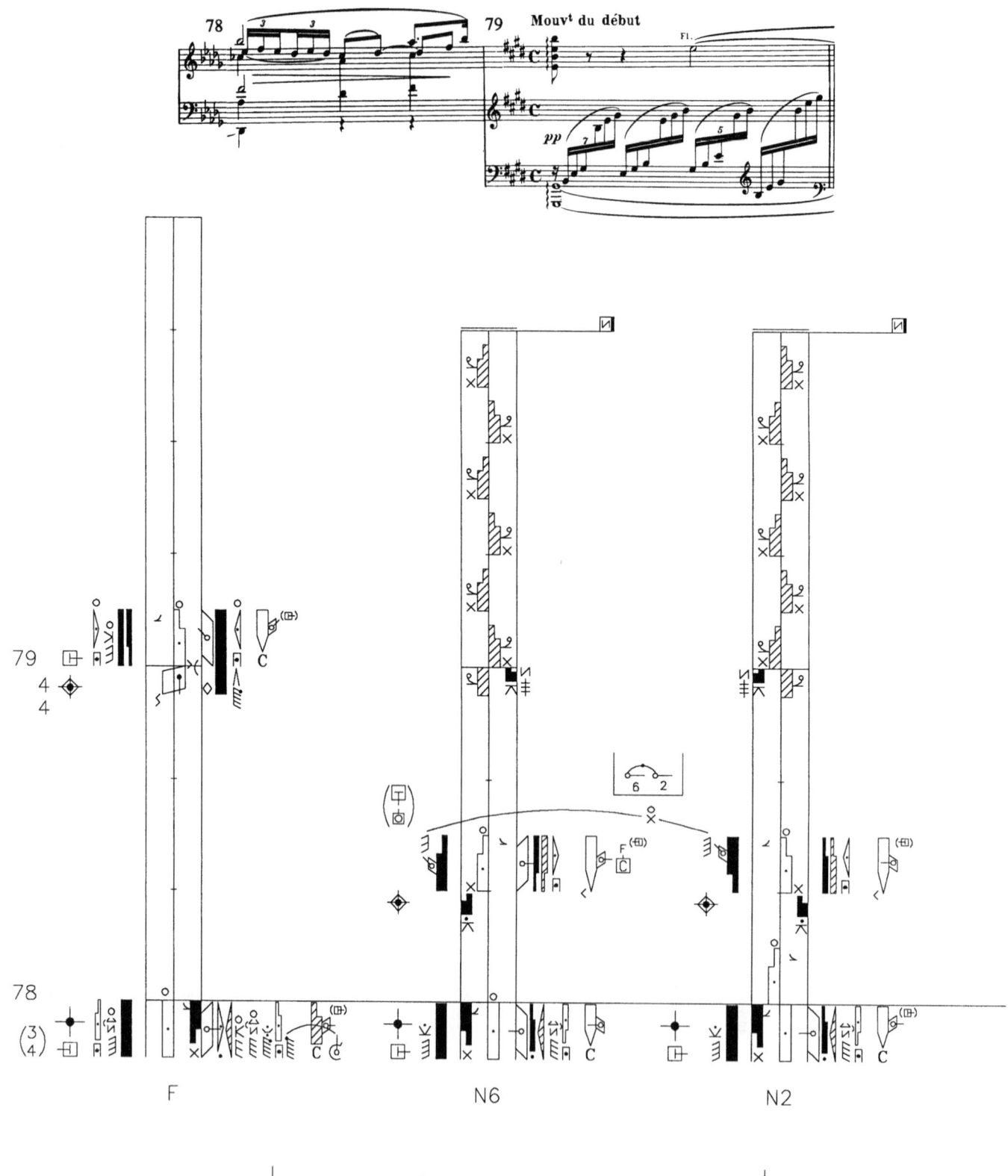

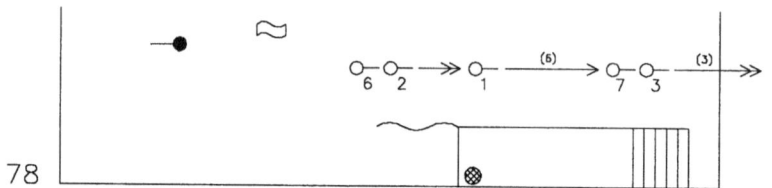

THE CHOREOGRAPHIC SCORE

125

Style of walk
N6, N2, exit

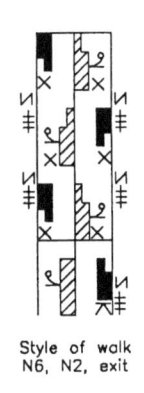

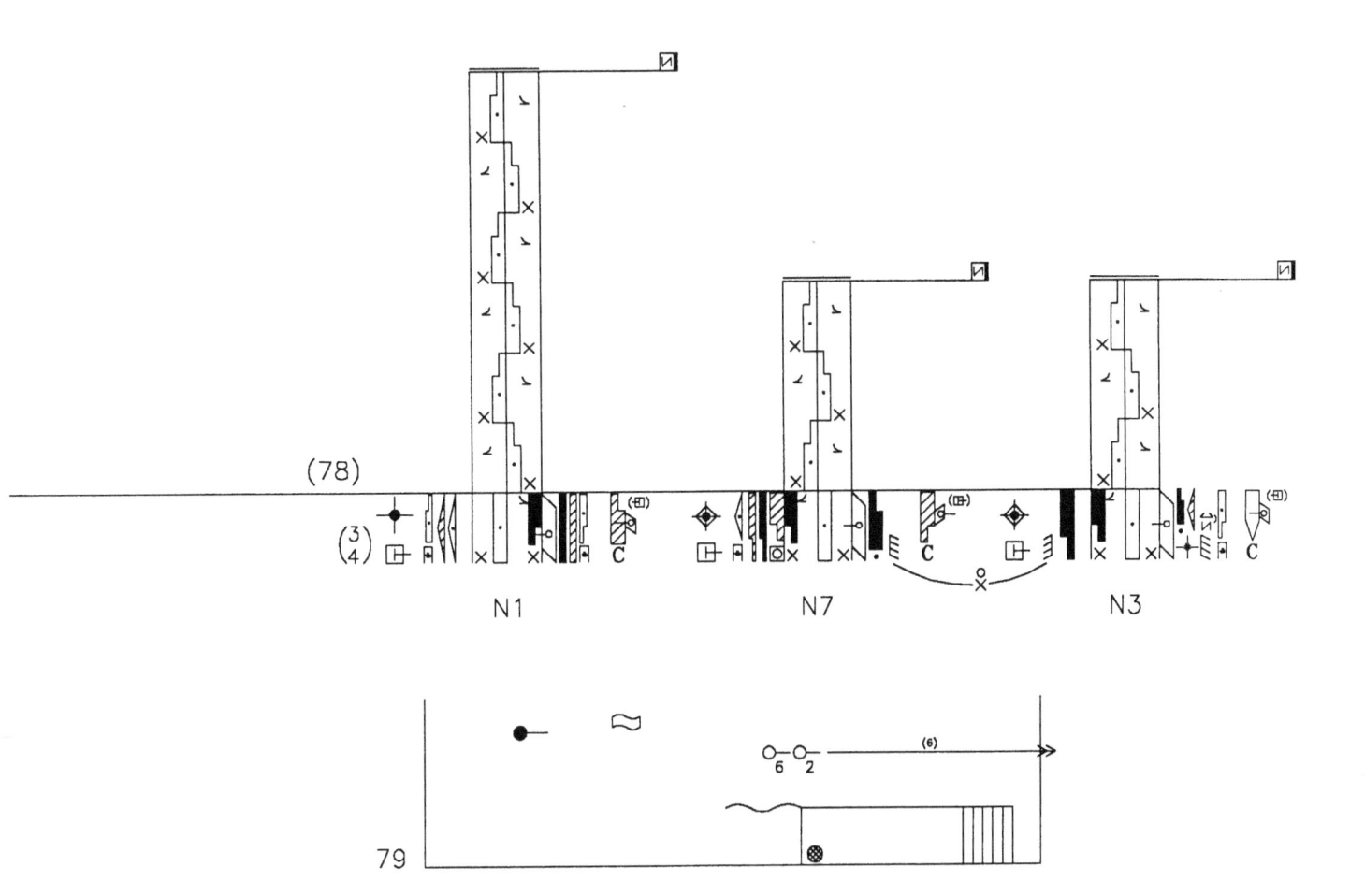

(78)

(3)
(4)

N1　　　　　　N7　　　　　　N3

79

126 NIJINSKY'S *FAUNE* RESTORED

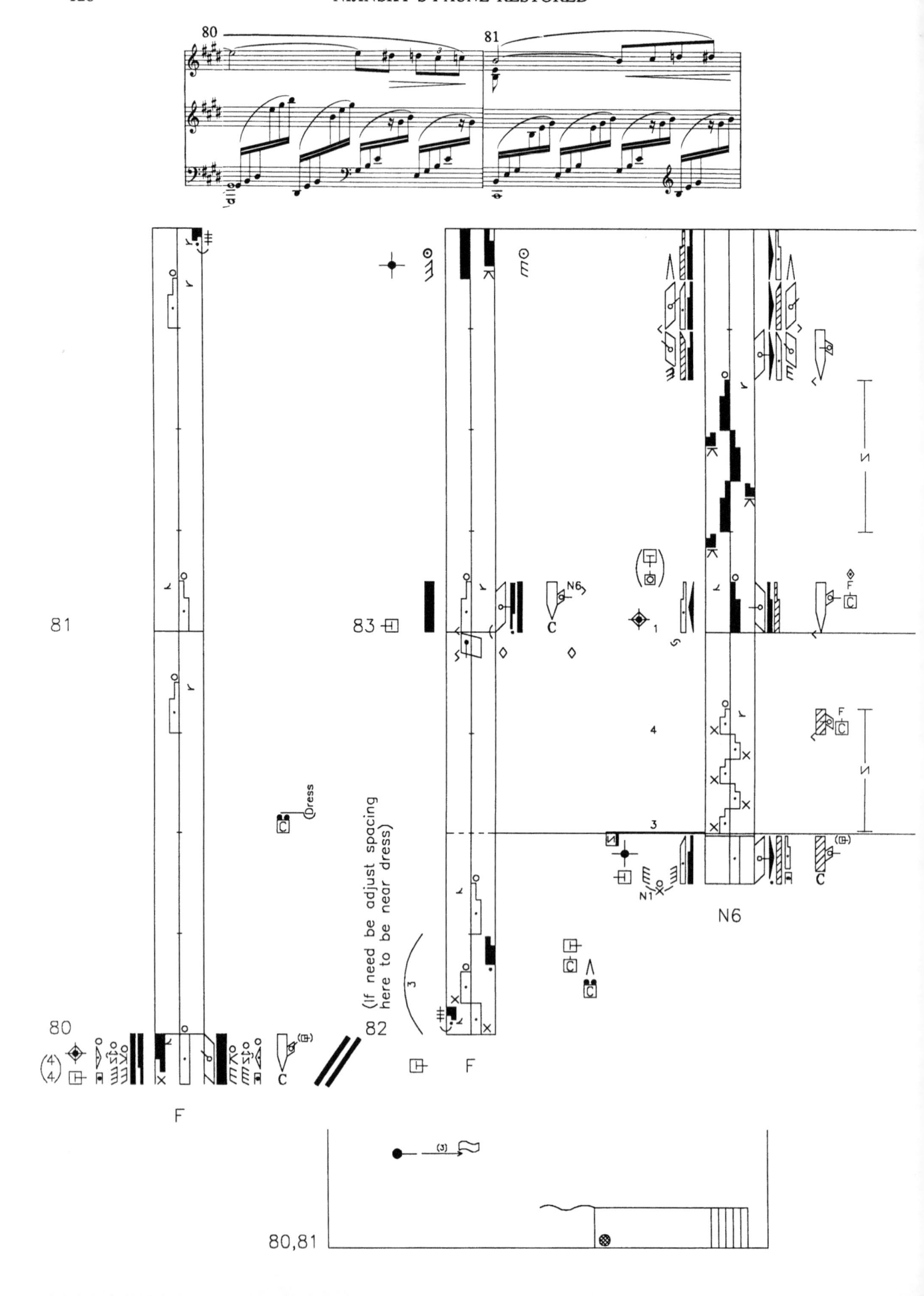

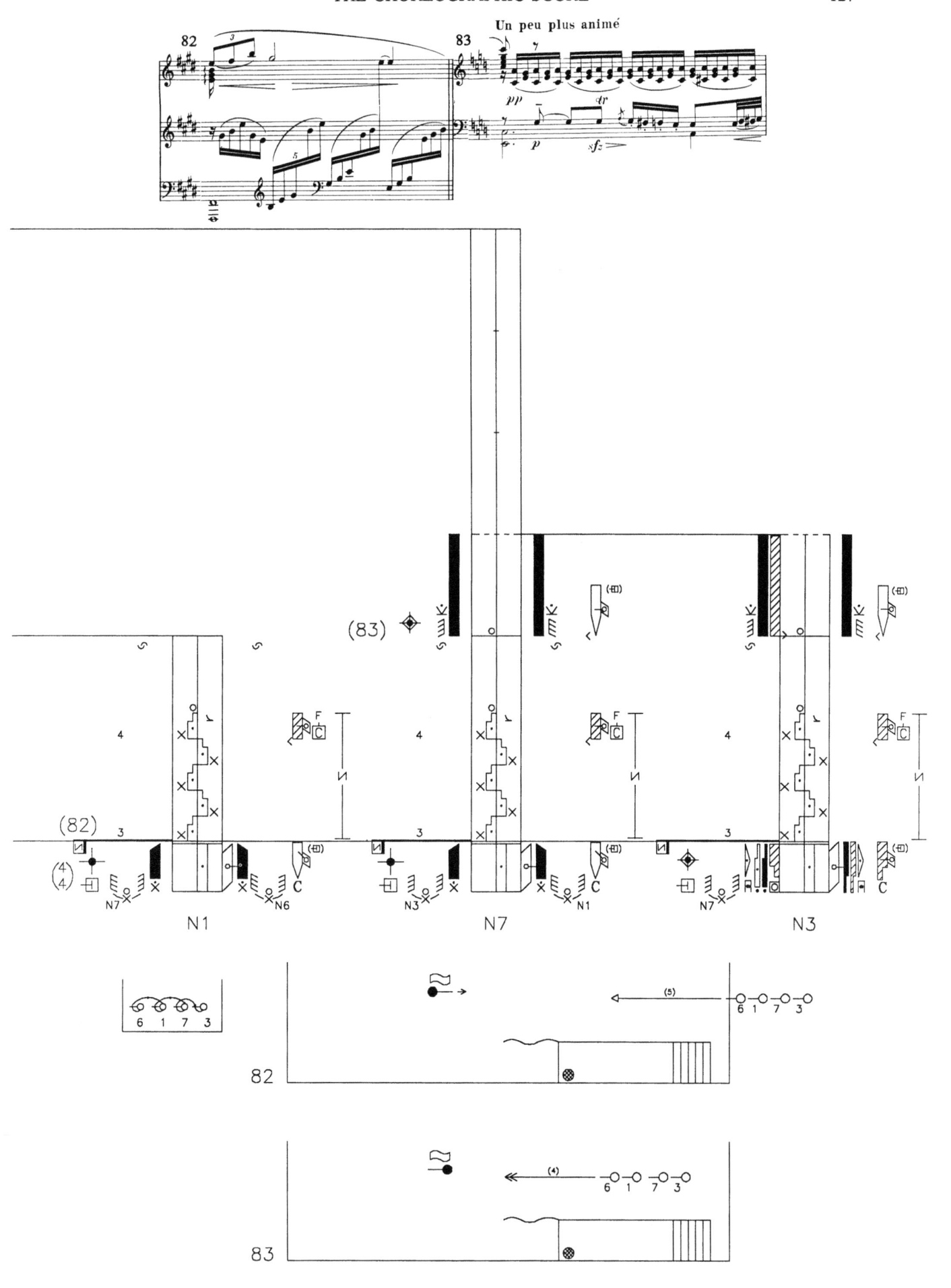

THE CHOREOGRAPHIC SCORE
127

128   NIJINSKY'S *FAUNE* RESTORED

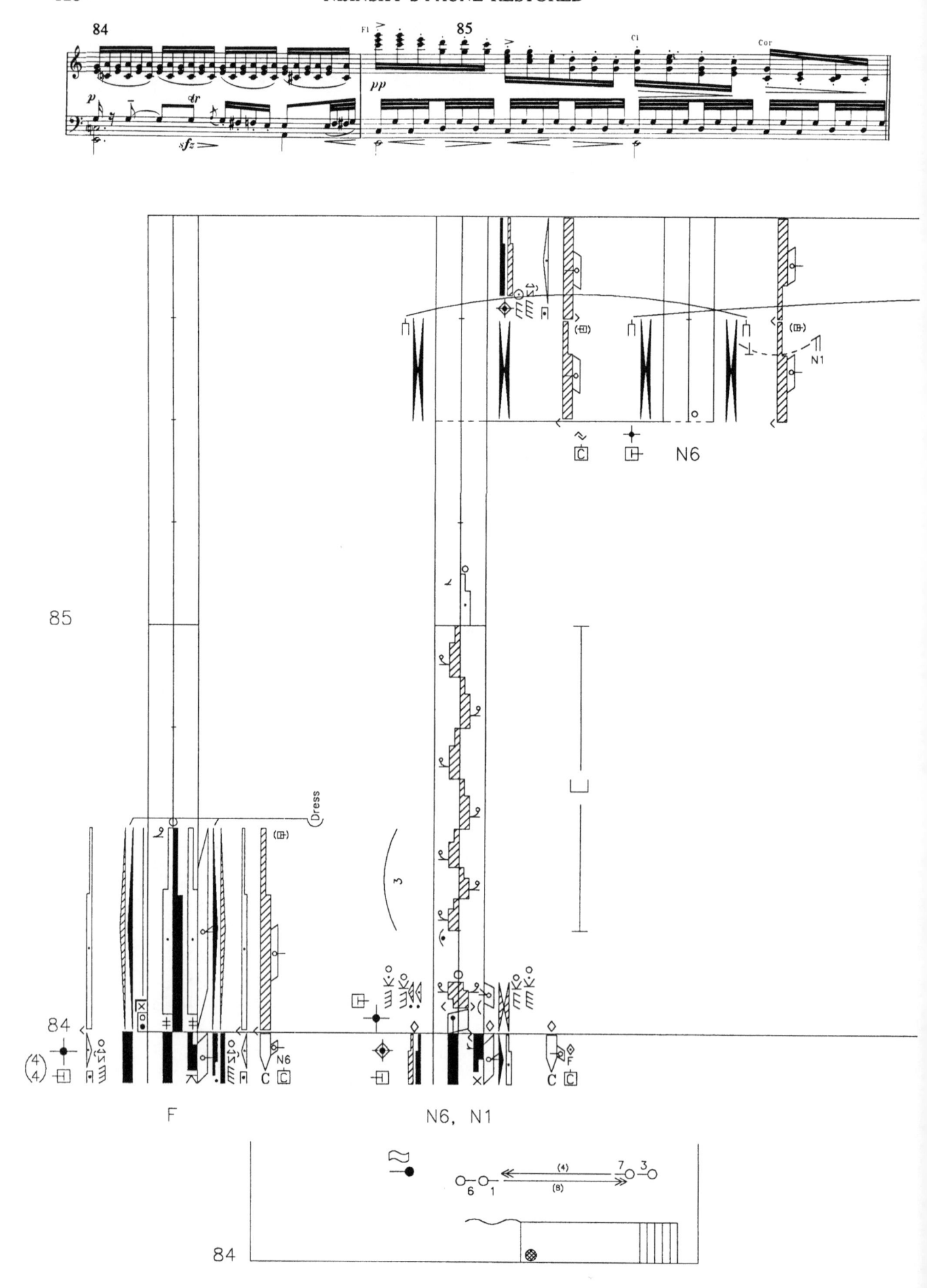

THE CHOREOGRAPHIC SCORE 129

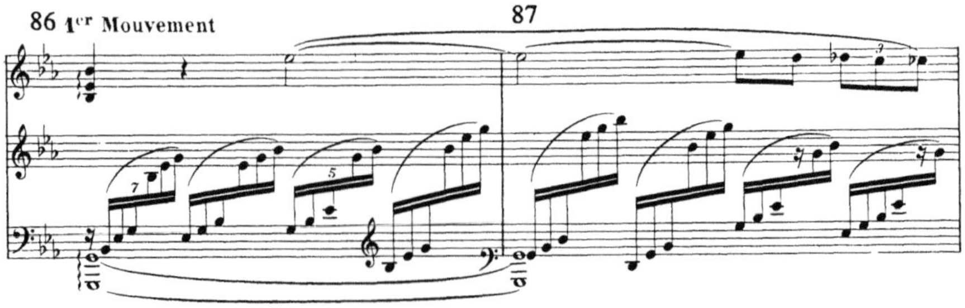
86 1er Mouvement
87

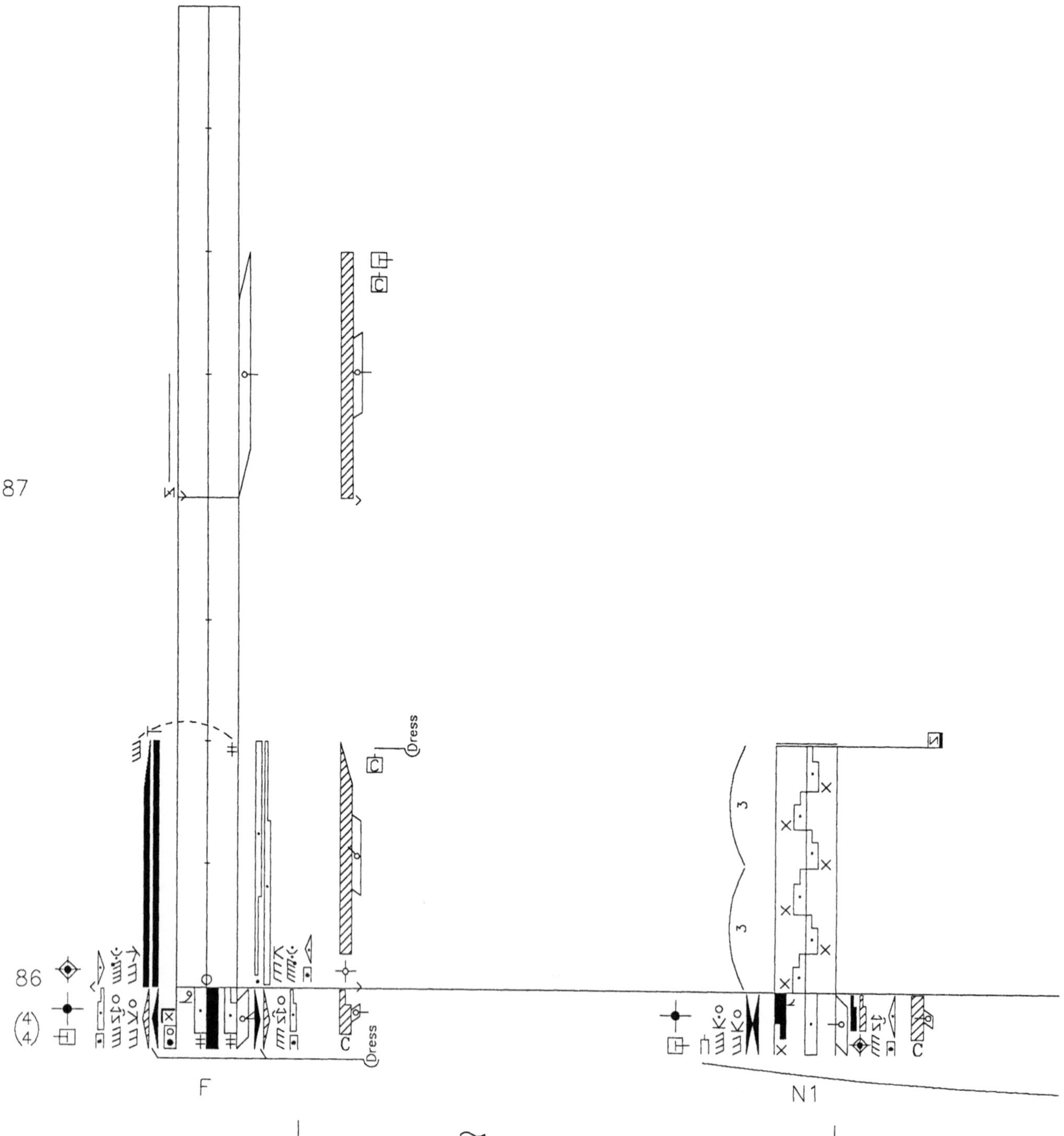
87
86
(4)
(4)
Dress
Dress
C
C
C
F
N1

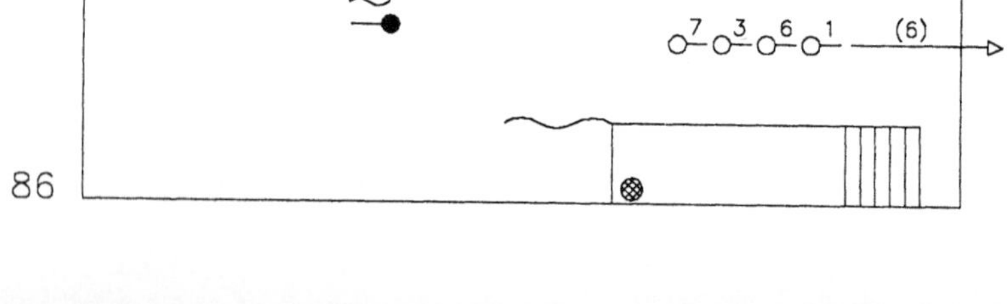
86
7
3
6
1
(6)

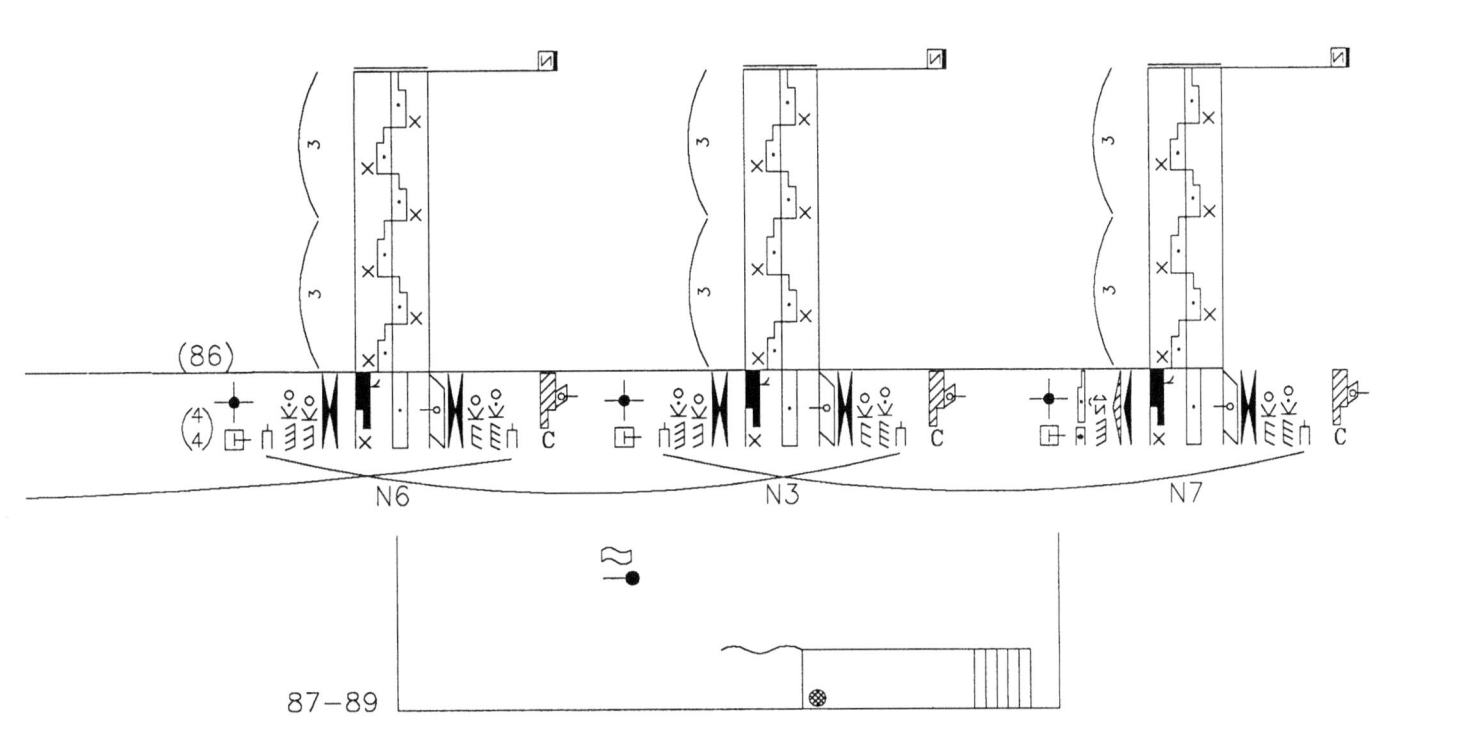

THE CHOREOGRAPHIC SCORE

131

132 NIJINSKY'S *FAUNE* RESTORED

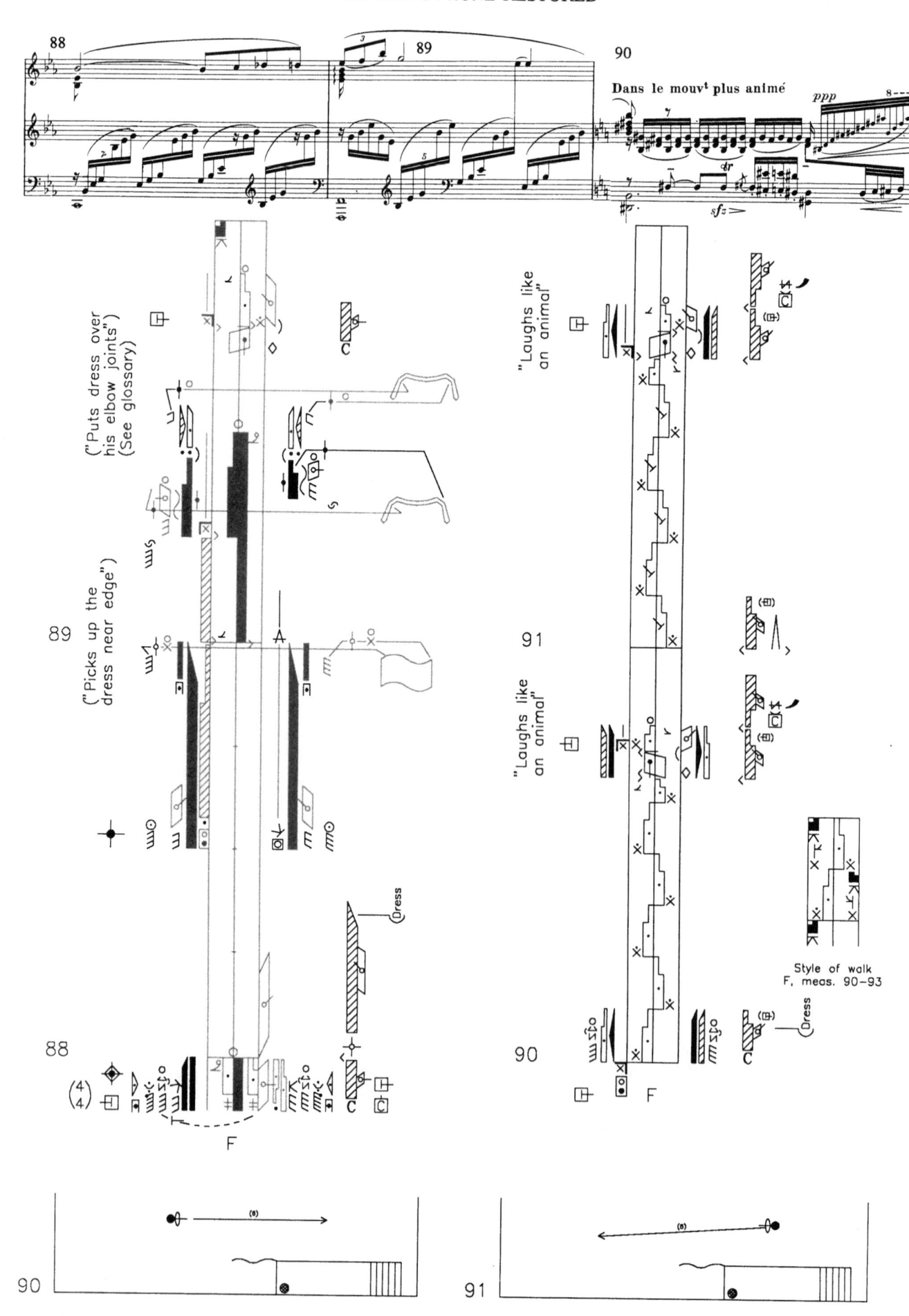

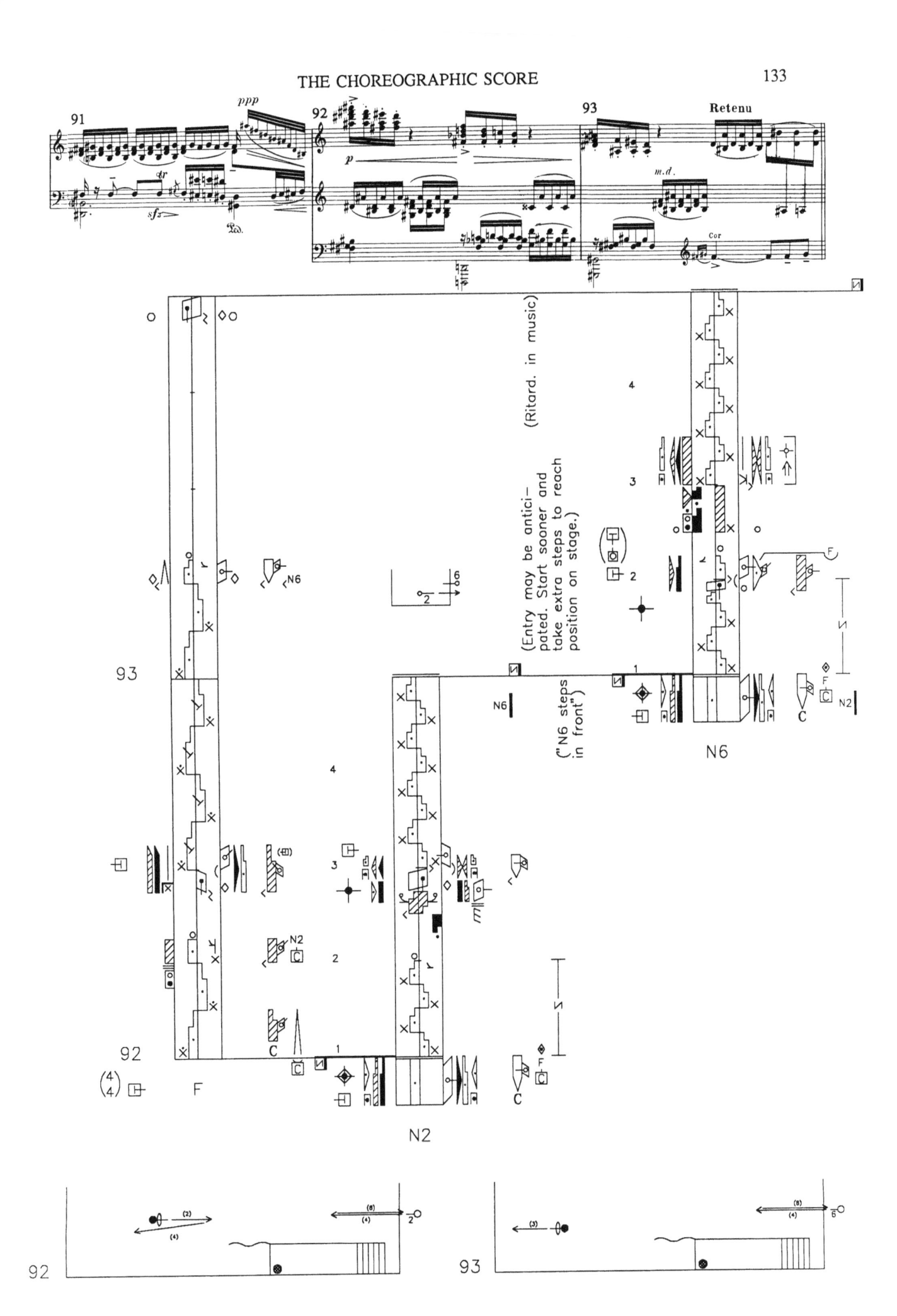

THE CHOREOGRAPHIC SCORE

94 Dans le 1ᵉʳ Mouvᵗ avec plus de langueur

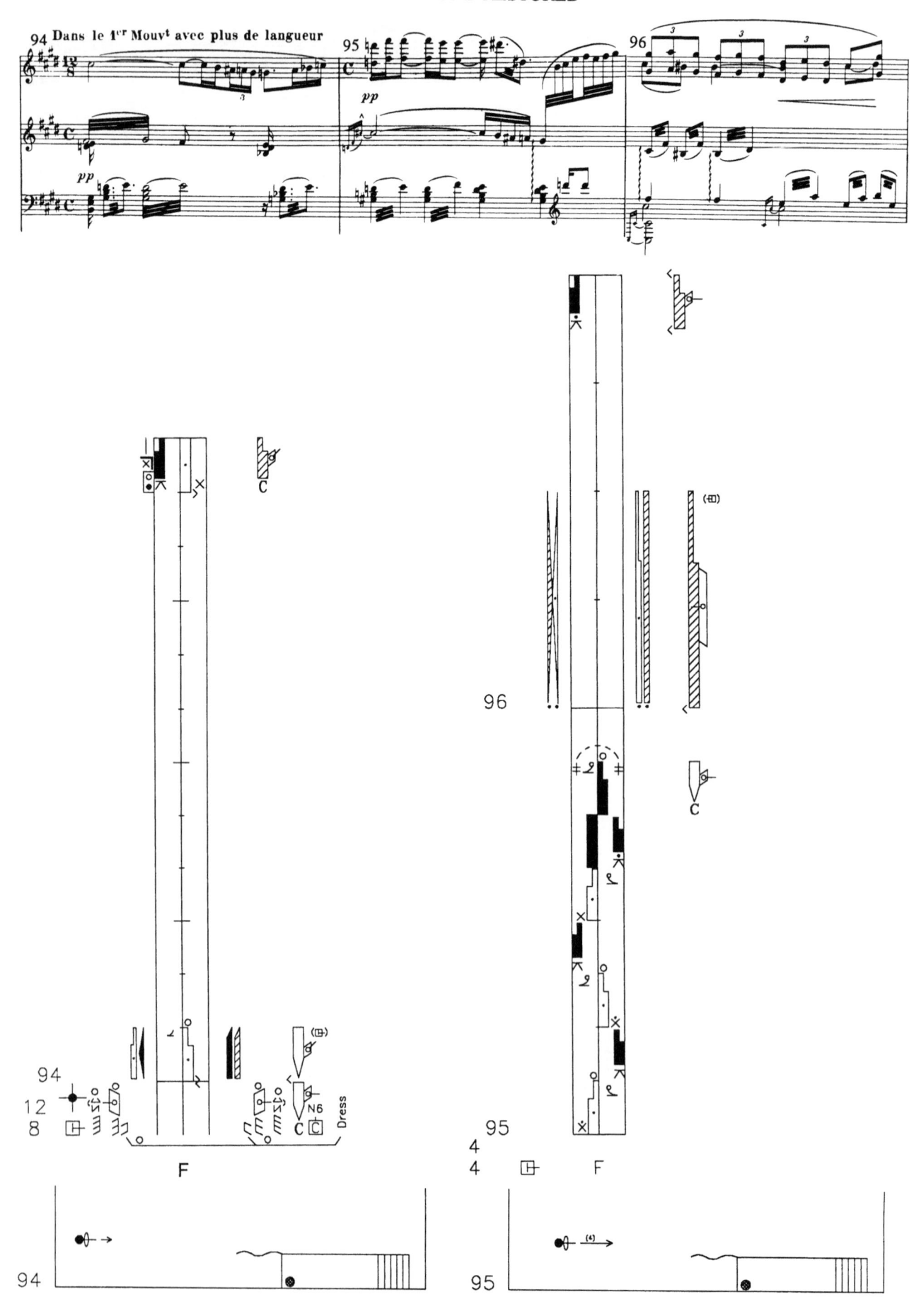

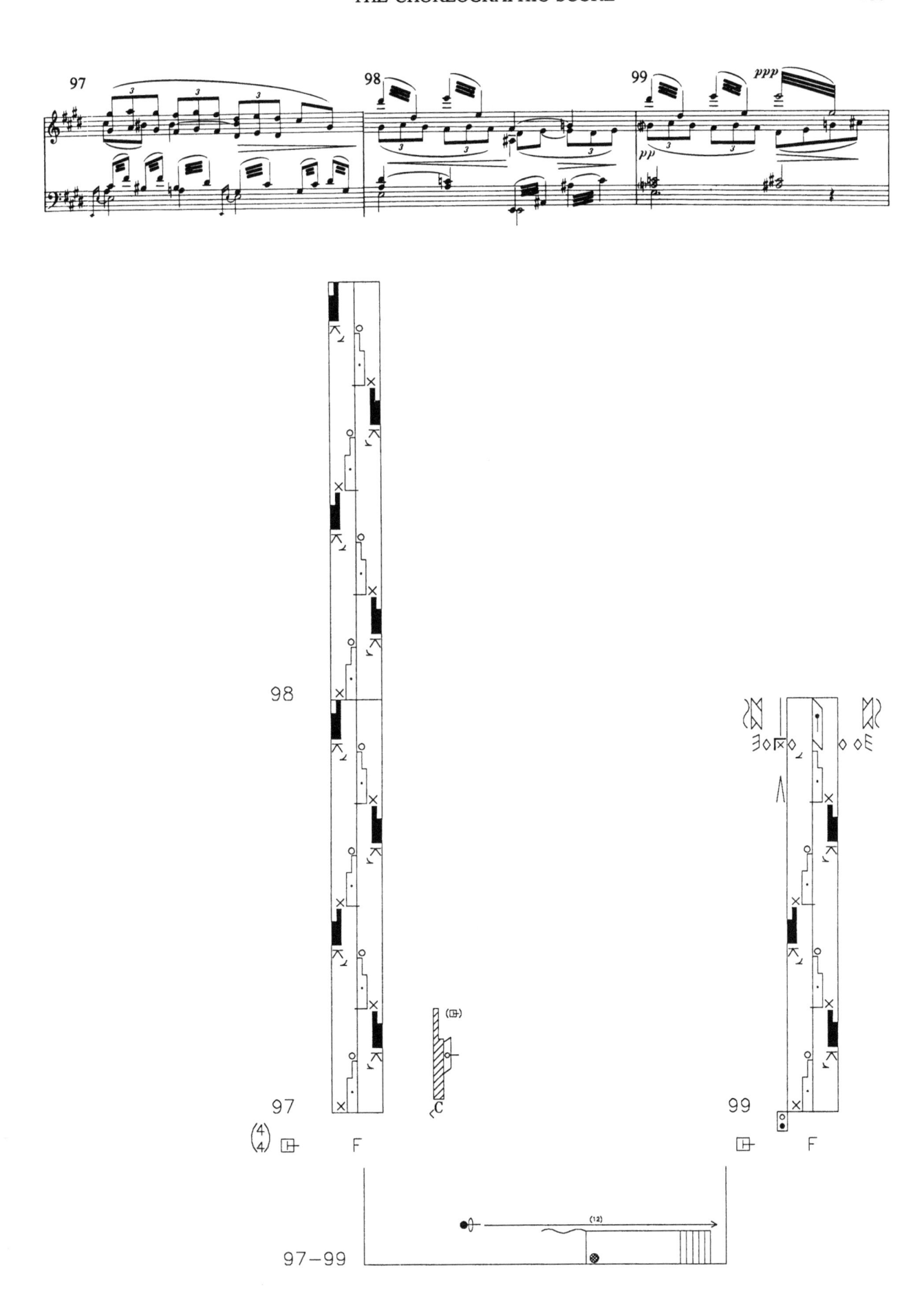

THE CHOREOGRAPHIC SCORE

100
m.g.
m.d.
ten.
Harpe
101
102 Retenu

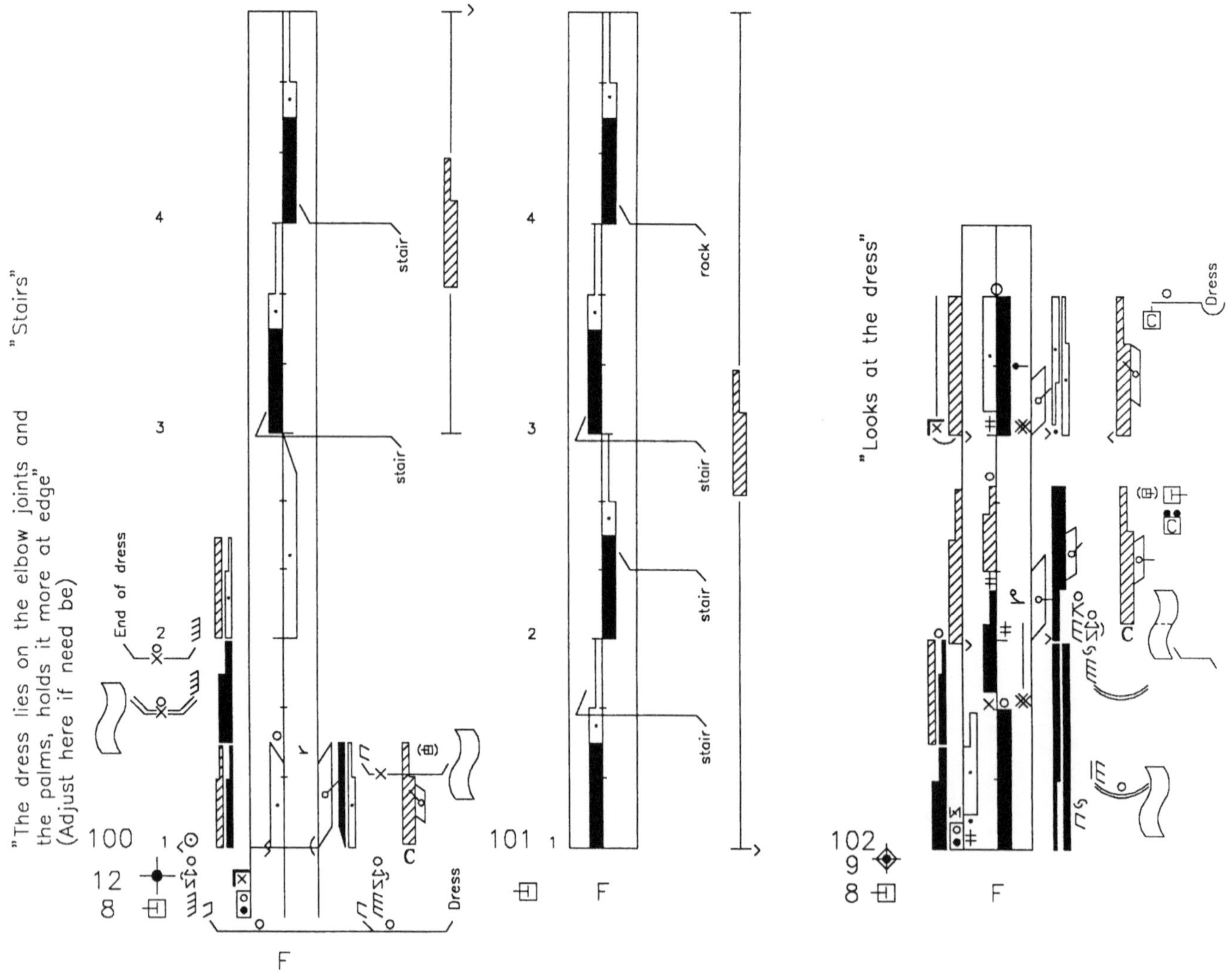
"The dress lies on the elbow joints and the palms, holds it more at edge"
(Adjust here if need be)
"Stairs"
"Looks at the dress"
End of dress
stair
rock
Dress
100
101
102
F

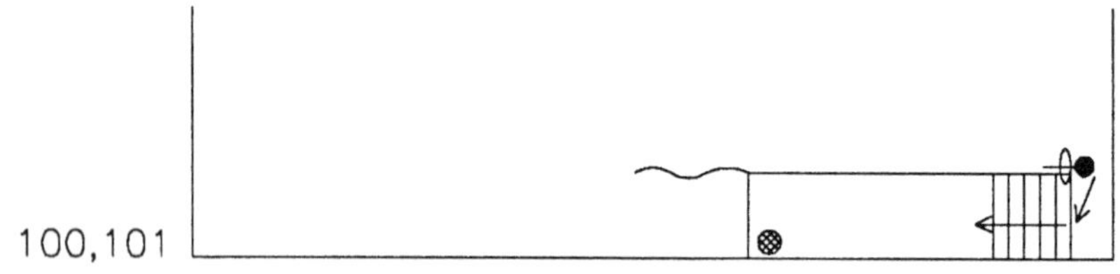
100,101

THE CHOREOGRAPHIC SCORE

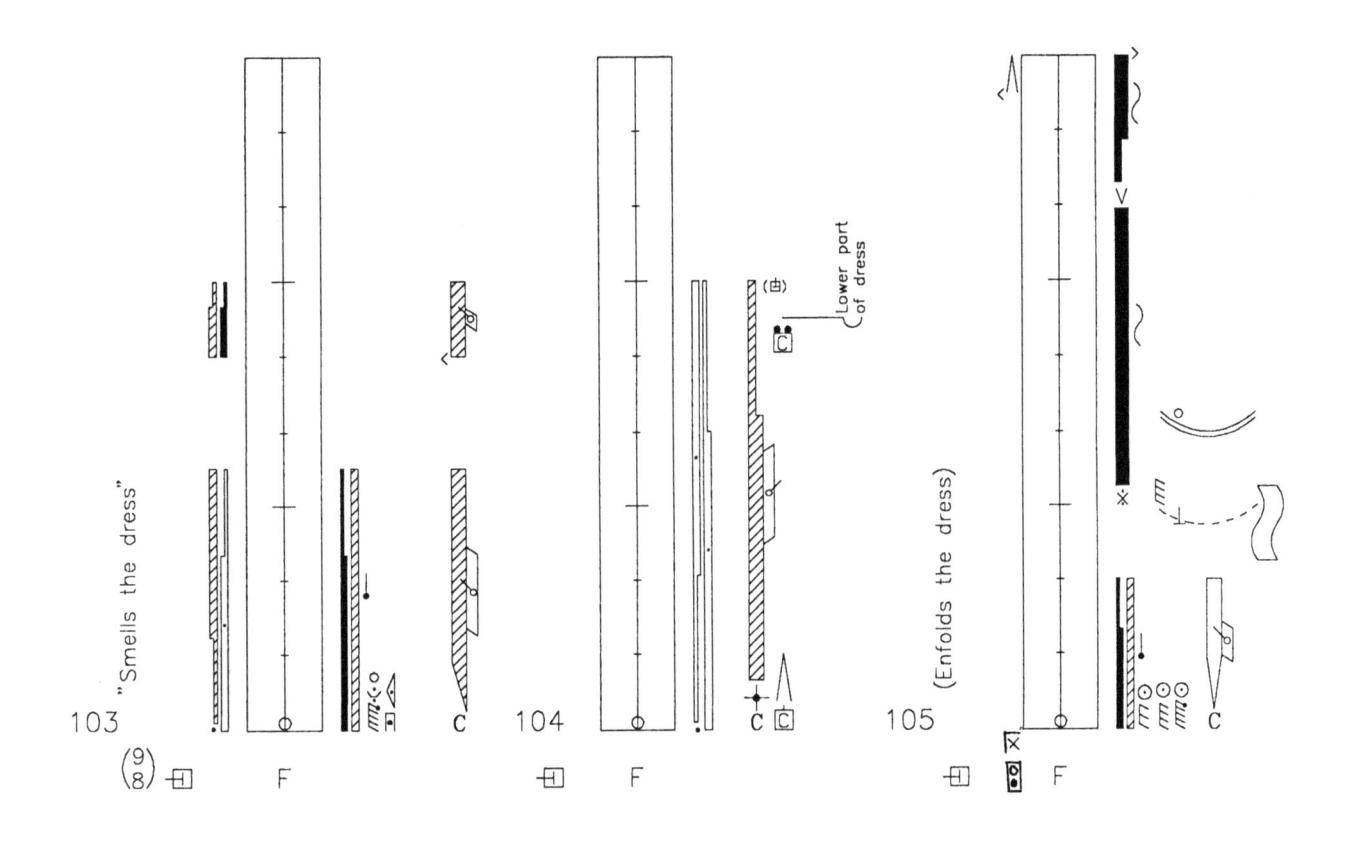

103 — 105

138 NIJINSKY'S *FAUNE* RESTORED

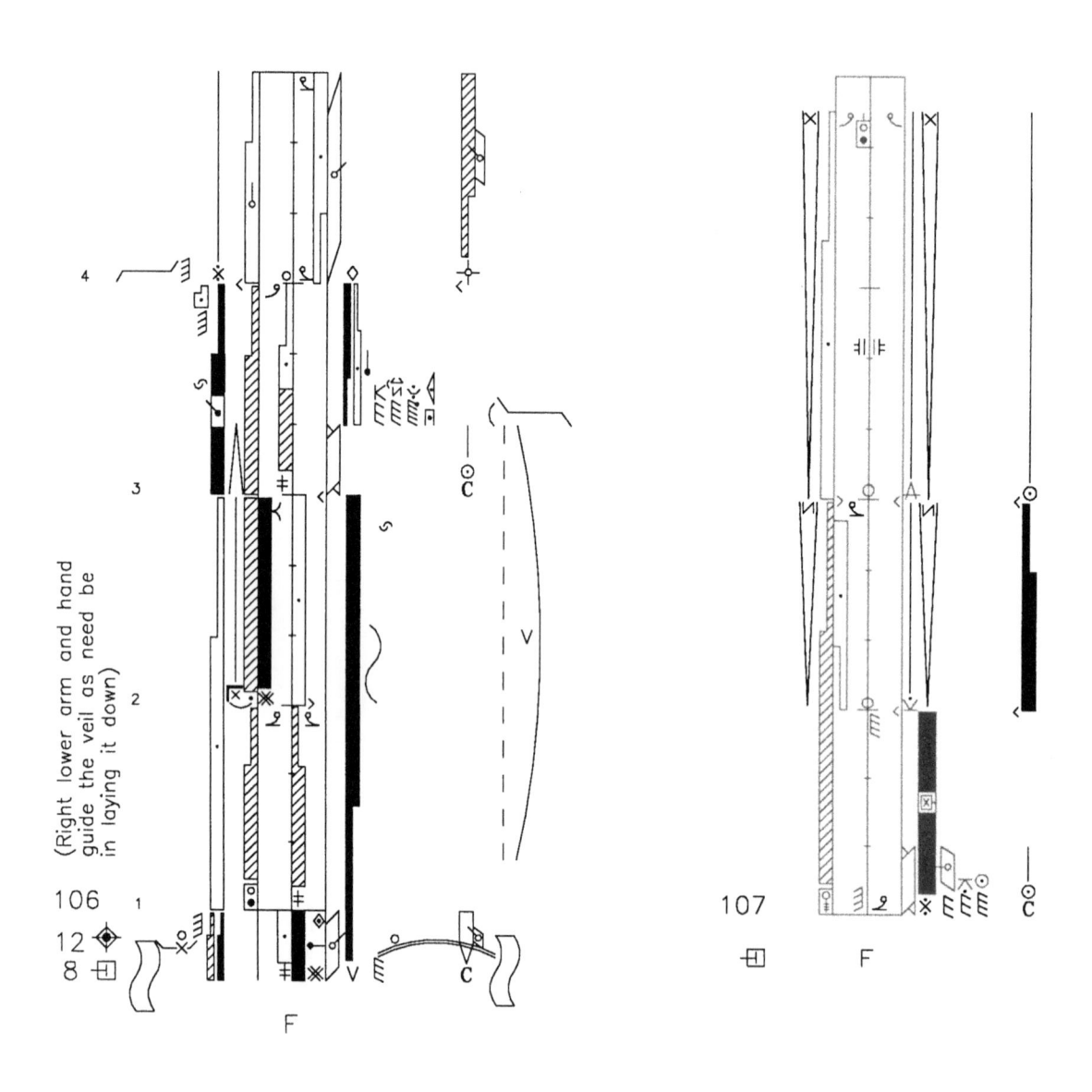

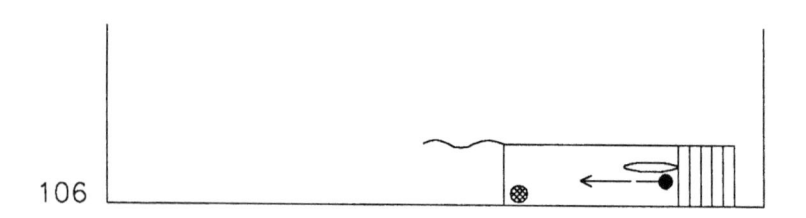

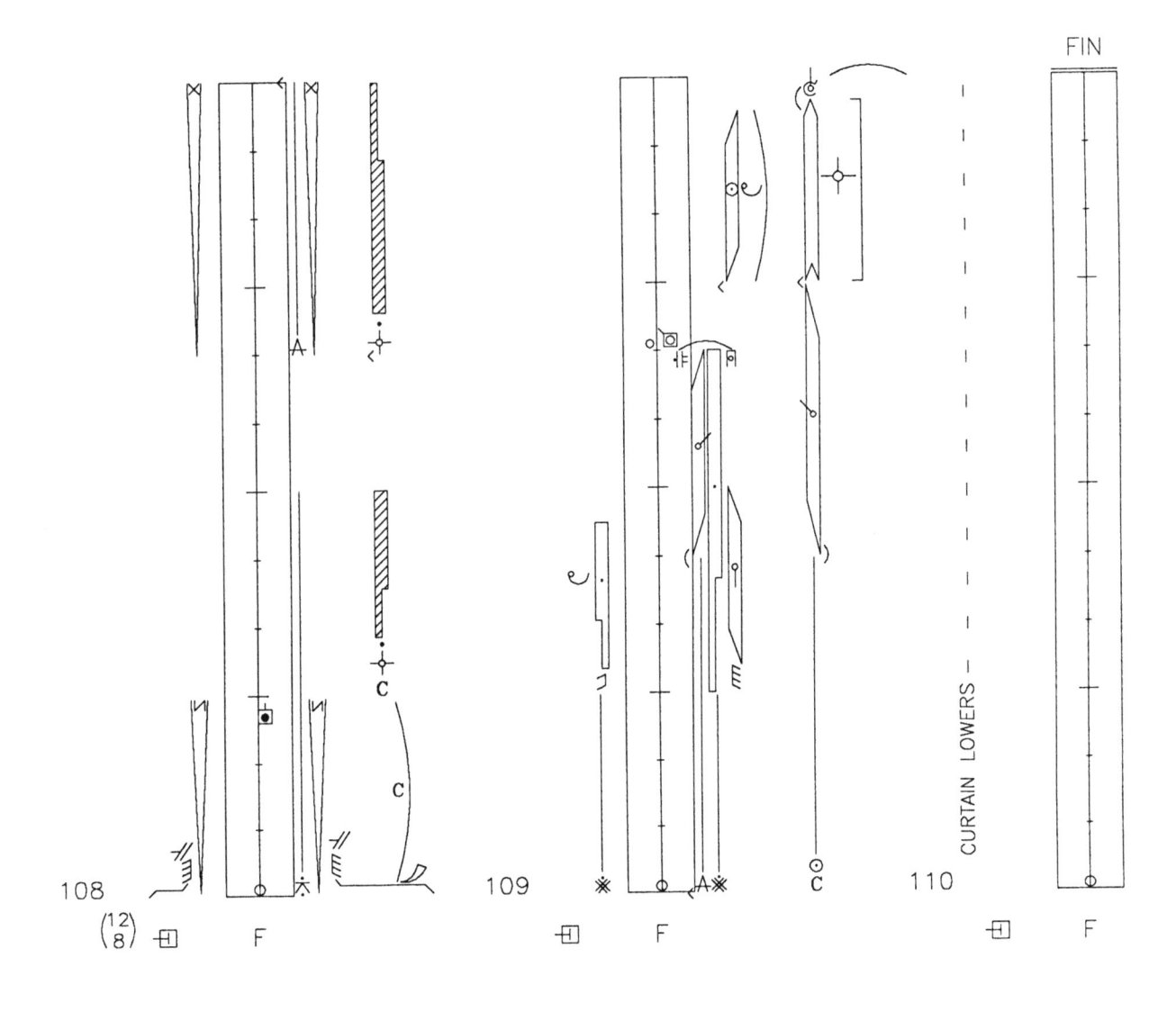

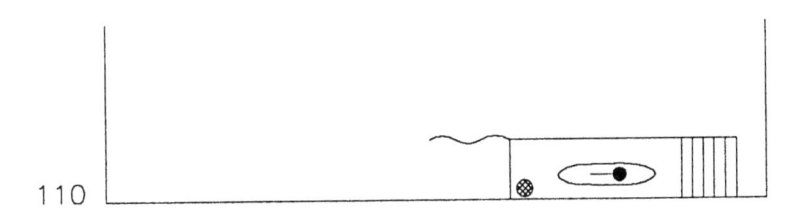

THE CHOREOGRAPHIC SCORE

139

Vaslav Nijinsky studying the music score of *Till Eulenspiegel*, 1916

AN EXPLANATION OF VASLAV NIJINSKY'S SYSTEM OF DANCE NOTATION

Measures 29, 30 and 31 from Nijinsky's score. The sixth and seventh nymphs are easing into place. Then, as the chief nymph loosens and holds up the first veil, the faun sits up and begins to take notice.

TABLE OF CONTENTS

Foreword to Nijinsky's System 145

Explanation of the System 147

A. Timing
    1. Use of Music Notes 147

B. Indication of the Body
    2. The Principal Divisions 148
    3. Right and Left Limbs 148
    4. Major and Minor Parts of the Body 148

C. Spatial Indications
    5. The Seven Levels for 1st Degree Parts 149
    6. The Progression of Directions 150

D. Articulations
    7. Flexion of Arms and Legs 151
    8. Flexion of the Torso 153
    9. Flexion of the Wrist 153
    10. Flexion of the Ankle 154
    11. Bending ('Flexion') for the Head 154
    12. Flexion of the Fingers 155
    13. Rotation 155
    14. Shoulder Movements 157

E. Standing
    15. Positions of the Feet 157
    16. Use of Parts of the Foot 158
    17. Crouch Position 161

F. Stage Orientation
    18. Stage Directions 161

G. Locomotion
    19. Walking 162
    20. Turning 165
    21. Jumping, Springing 166

H. Contact
    22. Touching 167

I. Miscellaneous
    23. Entrances, Exits 168
    24. Timing; Use of Music Notation 169
    25. Use of Repeat Signs 171
    26. Systems of Reference for Direction 172
    27. Statement of Key 172

J. Rules
    28. Validity 173

K. Movement Details Not Covered
    29. Length of Step 175
    30. Looking, Gazing 176
    31. Palm Facing 176
    32. Indications for Relating 176

FOREWORD TO NIJINSKY'S SYSTEM

Surely the rarest individual in the world of dance is the dancer-choreographer who is also a notator, recording a ballet in his own dance notation system. Before Nijinsky, only Arthur Saint-Léon held this distinction. Nijinsky's concern with notation is well known, yet few realize the extent of his vision, so clearly expressed in his letter to Reynaldo Hahn, written in 1918 while Nijinsky was in St. Moritz. Nijinsky writes:

".....I am perfecting the system of dance notation, which I have invented in these last years. I am very happy to have found this notation, which for centuries has been searched for, because I believe, and I am sure, my dear friend, you will agree, that this notation is indispensable for the development of the art of dance. It is a simple and logical means to note down movements. In a word, this system will provide the same service for the artists of the dance that musical notes give to musicians."

Although it is not through use of *his* system that Nijinsky's dream is gradually being realized, his contribution is not to be overlooked. What he achieved is at last coming fully to light, revealing a side of Nijinsky previously unknown and unappreciated - that of theorist, movement analyst, and painstaking scribe.

On looking at Nijinsky's score of *L'Après-midi d'un Faune* one might at first glance take it to be music notation. The five-line staff is used, the symbols are music notes, but wait - there is something odd about them, some are oblong, many have markings on the note-stem, and there are non-musical signs placed between the notes. If this is dance notation, then how do these signs represent the information needed to indicate movement? Parts of the body must be indicated, so how and when are these used? And directions for the dancer's limbs must be shown as well as the direction on stage in which he or she faces, and the direction of traveling. Any dance notation system must cope with these factors and many more. Above all, timing must be indicated. Here the method of showing the beats and the subdivisions of beats for particular actions is obviously borrowed from music notation, the movement symbols having the same time value as in music.

Nijinsky's system did not emerge entirely out of the void. As a student at the Maryinsky Theatre School he had learned the movement notation system invented by Vladimir Stepanov, and first published in 1892. Stepanov was the first in history to base such a system on an anatomical analysis of movement and to use music notes for timing. A Russian manual on the system (the first book was published in French in Paris) was produced by Alexander Gorsky who continued with the system after Stepanov's early death. The question that comes immediately to mind is "How different is Nijinsky's system from Stepanov's? If there is a close link, why, since Stepanov's book has been available all these years, has it taken until 1987 for Nijinsky's system to be deciphered and the score of *Faune* translated?" Briefly, Nijinsky used the modifications which Gorsky had made in Stepanov's system, modifications which were not known until comparatively recently when an English translation of Gorsky's book became available. In addition, Nijinsky changed the numbering for the directions on stage and departed radically from Stepanov's method of indicating spatial directions for the main parts of the body. A small but important point - he reversed left and right for the signs showing rotation of the head and torso. Only when ballet materials and notated poses of *bas relief* pictures recorded by Nijinsky came to light could the key to his system be discovered. With the deciphering of these materials and translation of the score of *Faune* it was possible to ascertain the extent to which Nijinsky had departed from Stepanov in establishing his own system.

Were the changes Nijinsky made an improvement? The reversal in direction of rotation for torso and head is of no consequence. However, for the stage directions his addition of intermediate points, providing a total of 16 divisions, was a useful development. His method of showing degrees in direction and level for limbs and torso is far more practical and easy to remember than Stepanov's. For each section of the staff - the torso, the arms, the legs - Stepanov had a different method of indicating directions; Nijinsky made each section of the staff the same.

Another question frequently asked is how conversant was Nijinsky with music. One has only to work with the score of *Faune* for a short time to realize the extent of his understanding, certainly of music notation. He keeps careful track of the time value of each part of a movement, particularly in the stepping patterns where he indicates precise timing for each gesture of the free leg prior to its taking weight. An interesting point is Nijinsky's use of the music signs for rests. Because remaining still is shown by repetition of the same note tied with horizontal bows, he was able to reserve the rest signs to indicate exits, i.e., the dancer off stage, his visually-based reasoning obviously being that since rests in music mean absence of sound, in dance they should mean visible absence of the performer.

This presentation of Nijinsky's system relates to that used for the score of *Faune*, recorded in 1914-1915. Much has been written about his later concentration on notation during 1917-1918. It has since been discovered that the note books he wrote then contain quite new ideas regarding analysis and description of movement, ideas that remained inconclusive with no indication of practical application, and bear no relation to his earlier usages in the *Faune* score.

The following explanation of Nijinsky's system as used in the score of *Faune* is designed to provide a key to those who may wish to delve into the score in the British Library in London and work out for themselves what is written. For clarity each item is illustrated in Labanotation. In order to link this explanation to Nijinsky's score, wherever possible examples from the score itself are given, or redrawings of these have been made where Nijinsky's symbols are not sufficiently clear for reproduction. Identification of the excerpts is given thus: F - faun; N1 - first nymph; N2 - second nymph; and so on. The number which follows is the measure number in Nijinsky's score. These measure numbers were not provided by Nijinsky but were added to facilitate reference.

EXPLANATION OF THE SYSTEM

In every system of dance notation the means must be found to record on paper the following aspects of movement: the part of the body moving; the kind of movement (direction, rotation, flexion) and the amount of such movement; locomotion; stage orientation; contact with the floor; and timing.

Following Stepanov's lead Nijinsky's view of movement was based on an anatomical analysis, the torso and limb segments being moved through flexion of the joints and /or rotation of the limbs.

A. TIMING

1. Use of Music Notes

To indicate timing, Nijinsky adopted Stepanov's use of music notes as movement symbols, the same time values being given to these notes as in music notation. Both Stepanov and Nijinsky explained carefully the established music note values. Ex. 1a is taken from the Gorsky book.

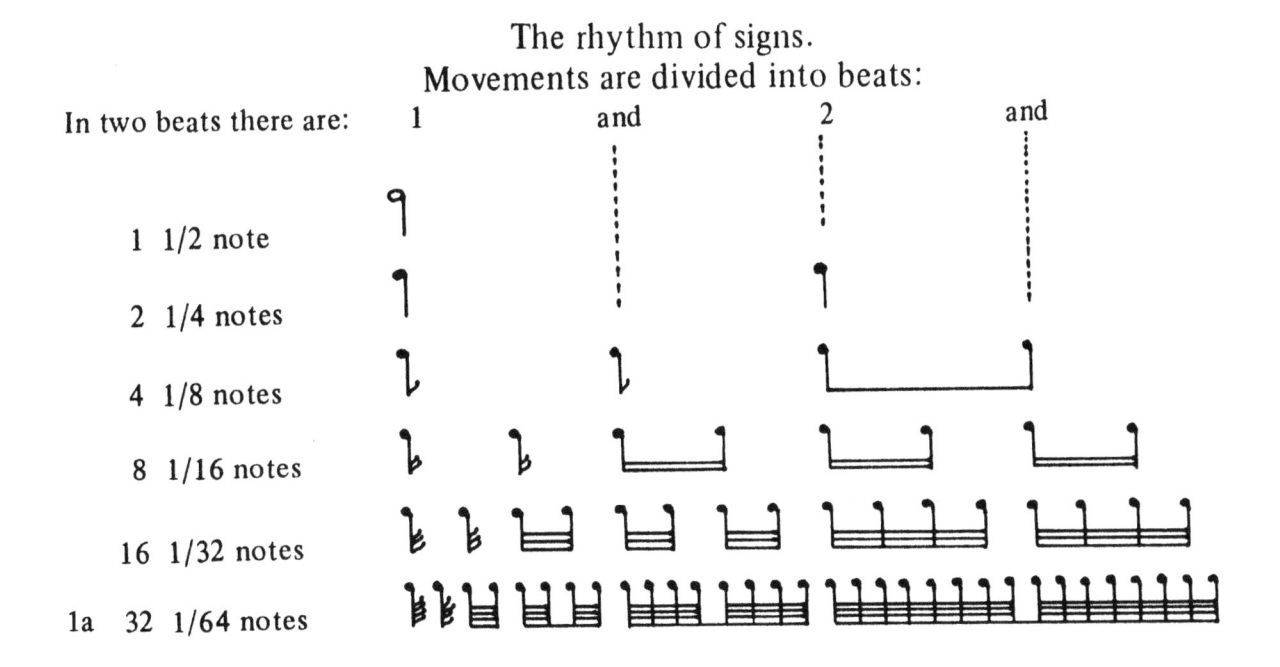

The rhythm of signs.
Movements are divided into beats:

	1	and	2	and
In two beats there are:				
1 1/2 note				
2 1/4 notes				
4 1/8 notes				
8 1/16 notes				
16 1/32 notes				
1a 32 1/64 notes				

Both Stepanov and Nijinsky followed the music rules concerning dotted notes, i.e., the addition of a dot after the note augments the duration by half its value. They also adopted the validity rule that a stated accidental (additional minor indication) is in effect for that particular note for the rest of the measure.

B. INDICATION OF THE BODY

2. The Principal Divisions

The staff, composed of three sets of five lines, represents the principal divisions of the body. The top section is for the torso and head; the middle section for the arms; the lowest section for the legs, Ex. 2a.

Torso & Head

Arms

2a Legs

A key is used for each part of the staff. The key consists of two dots placed either side of one, two or three vertical lines centered on the middle horizontal line. For the torso one vertical line is used; for the arms two lines, and for the legs three lines.

3. Right and Left Limbs

The stem of the music note which indicates the movement is drawn downward for the right limb and upward for the left.

Limbs of the right side: (stem downward)   or   3a

Limbs of the left side: (stem upward)   or   3b

For torso and head movements the stem usually points downward.

4. Major and Minor Parts of the Body

The torso is divided into three parts, the limbs into four.

1st degree parts:
For the torso this is the **pelvis** which, hingeing at the hip joint, carries with it the chest and head.
For the arms it is the **upper arm** which, moving from the shoulder joint, carries with it the lower arm and hand.
For the legs it is the **upper leg** which, moving from the hip joint, carries with it the lower leg and foot.

2nd degree parts:
For the torso this is the **chest**; moving from the waist, it carries with it the head.
For the arms it is the **lower arm**; hingeing at the elbow, it carries with it the hand.
For the legs it is the **lower leg**; hingeing at the knee, it carries with it the foot.

3rd degree parts:
For the torso this is the **head** moving from the neck.
For the arms it is the **hand** moving from the wrist.
For the legs it is the **foot** moving from the ankle.

4th degree parts:
For the arms these are the **fingers** bending from the base knuckles.
For the legs they are the **toes**.

Note: How movement of these specific parts of the body is written is explained in sections 5-12.

C. SPATIAL INDICATIONS

Spatial placement of any part of a limb or of the torso is described as the direction and degree of articulation in the joint from which that limb or torso segment moves.

5. The Seven Levels for 1st Degree Parts

Nijinsky gives the degrees of Ex. 5a for the directional scale of notes. For each direction the rise of level is by $22\frac{1}{2}°$, as illustrated here.

For arms and legs the 'zero' point is straight down, i.e., their normal placement, Exs. 5b and 5d.

For the torso this same note placement represents straight up, its normal position, Ex. 5f.

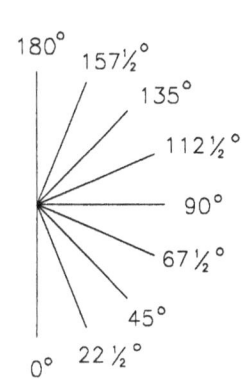

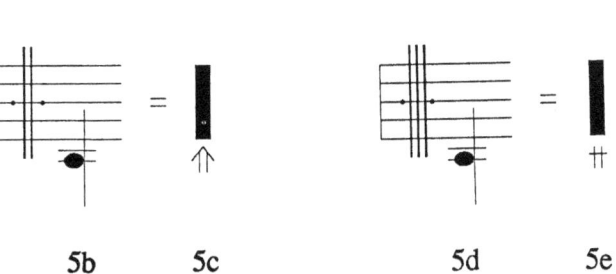

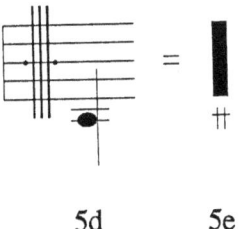

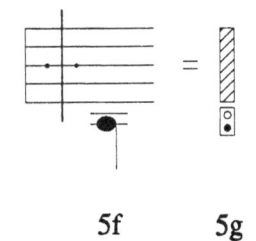

5a

| 5b | 5c | 5d | 5e | 5f | 5g |

Arms down   Legs down   Torso up

6. The Progression of Directions

The directions forward, sideward and backward are shown by placement of the music note on the lines or spaces of the five-line staff. The higher the note, the higher the level, as shown in the following chart:

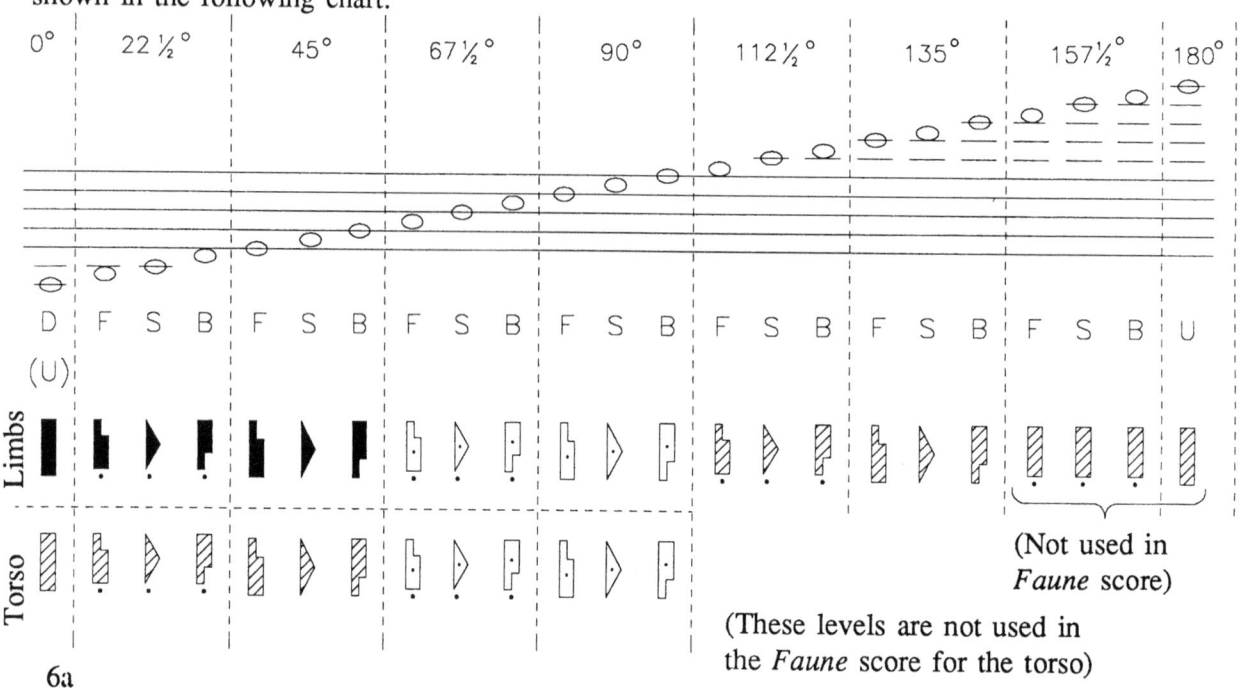

6a

In the diagram above, D = down; F = forward; S = sideward; B = backward; and U = up. Notes placed on the staff show direction and level for 1st degree parts of the body (pelvis, upper arm, thigh), the rest of the torso or limb being carried along in the same line, unless otherwise indicated. Note that sideward is always to the open side; crossing is described as adduction.

Ex. 6b below shows the left arm down and the right arm to the front at a 90° level (i.e., forward horizontal). Ex. 6d shows the torso inclined slightly backwards (22½°).

Diagonal Directions

Diagonal directions are shown by combining the two appropriate notes:

6f, 6g: Right forward diagonal for the right leg, low level (45°)

6h, 6i: Right backward diagonal for the right leg, low level (45°)

Directions of Minor Parts of the Body

Direction and level are not directly stated for 2nd, 3rd and 4th degree parts, placement results from degree of flexion of the joint together with the rotational state of the limb above. For example, spatial placement of the lower arm depends on the degree of flexion in the elbow joint and any inward or outward rotation of the upper arm. For 2nd degree parts indications for flexion and for rotation are placed on the stem of the music notes, as in 6j (for flexion see **D - Articulations**, sections 7-11, pp. 151-155; for rotation see **Rotation**, pp. 155-157).

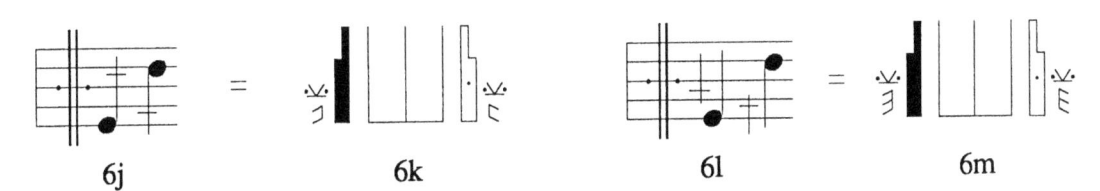

6j   6k   6l   6m

For 3rd degree parts, the appropriate indication is placed on a vertical line to the left of the music note, as in Ex. 6l (see sections 9-11, pp. 153-155).

Note: The Labanotation 8/8 scale is used here for folding to provide degrees comparable to those used in Nijinsky's system.

Direction and level for 4th degree parts (fingers and toes) are indicated by grace notes (small auxiliary notes). A single grace note is used for indication of all the fingers, Ex. 6n being for the right hand, 6o for the left, 6p for both. Directions for the fingers are related to the base of the hand. Thus 'down' is in line with the lower arm when the wrist is not bent, sideward (for the thumb) is to the open side, away from the palm, and so on (see **Flexion of the Fingers**, p. 155).

Five grace notes are used to show individual fingers, the one on the left being the thumb, the others following in sequence. Ex. 6q shows the familiar hand position used by the faun. The thumb is pointing to the side of the hand (90° from 'down'), the fingers are in line with the base of the hand, the right arm is forward low and the wrist is abducted (see **Flexion of the Wrist**, pp. 153-154).

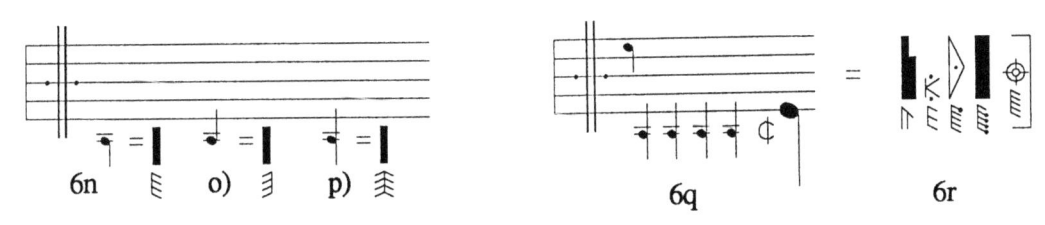

6n   o)   p)   6q   6r

D. ARTICULATIONS

7. Flexion of Arms and Legs

Flexion of the 'mid-joint' of the arm or leg (i.e., elbow or knee) is shown as mentioned above, by one or more horizontal strokes on the stem of the note; the more strokes, the greater the degree of bend.

7a 7b 7c 7d 7e 7f

$\quad = 45°\quad\quad\quad = 90°\quad\quad\quad = 135°$

The above degrees of flexion are augmented or diminished by use of the signs for 'greater than' and 'less than' written on the stem of the note.

> = greater than   7g

< = less than   7h

7i   7j

In Ex. 7i the right arm is sideward at a 45° level and bent a little more than 45° at the elbow, shown in 7j.

Note: When these signs are placed on an unmodified note, such as 7k, they modify an indication already given in the Key (see **Statement of Key**, p. 172).

Through comparison of Nijinsky's usage of these signs in his score of *Faune* and photographs of the same positions, the following scale is that which he used for the angles at elbow or knee. Ex. 7k represents the normally held limb. Note that two of the degrees possible in this progression, those of ● and ● , were not used by Nijinsky in the score of *Faune*.

Left

Right

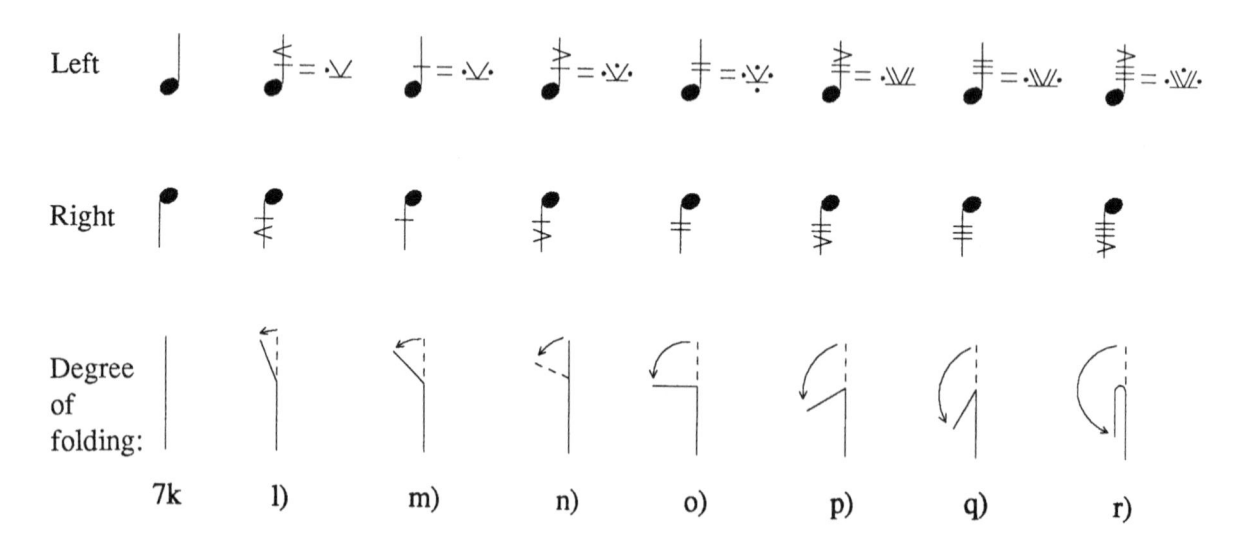

Degree of folding:

7k   l)   m)   n)   o)   p)   q)   r)

The above indications (Exs. 7l-r) for forward folding (∨) are for the elbow; Nijinsky also used the same signs for 'backward' folding (∧) of the knee joint. Anatomically elbow and knee joints are not normally capable of bending in the reverse direction, nor in either sideward direction, thus such indications do not appear on the note stems for arms and legs.

8. Flexion of the Torso

Flexion for the torso means bending the 'mid-joint', i.e., the waist, thereby spatially displacing the chest (the 2nd degree part of the torso). For the waist, direction of flexion can be forward, backward, to the left or to the right side with the intermediate diagonal directions shown by combining the appropriate forward and sideward or backward and sideward signs.

| forward | backward | to right side | to left side | right forward diagonal | right backward diagonal |

8a   b)   c)   d)   e)   f)   g)   h)   i)   j)   k)   l)

In the score of *Faune* only one degree of torso flexion is used, providing approximately 45° flexion from the upright position. In Ex. 8m the torso is upright with the chest inclined backward.

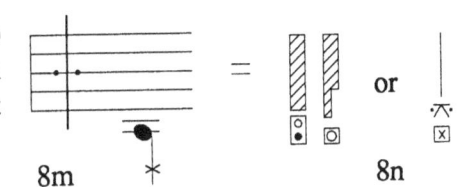

8m   8n

9. Flexion of the Wrist

Direction of wrist flexion can be forward, backward, toward the thumb side (adduction) or toward the little finger side (abduction). In forward wrist flexion the palm of the hand approaches the lower arm. In the *Faune* score only one degree of such flexion is used, the amount being 45° or slightly less. Stepanov and Gorsky used the term 'adduction' for wrist flexion toward the little finger and 'abduction' for flexion toward the thumb edge. To avoid confusion the Labanotation analysis and terms are being used here.

Left wrist

Right wrist

| forward flexion | backward flexion | abduction (toward little finger) | adduction (toward thumb) |
| 9a | 9b | 9c | 9d |

Note: Wrist adduction is not used in the *Faune* score. However, backward wrist flexion with wrist abduction are sometimes used for the faun and occasionally wrist abduction for the leading nymph.

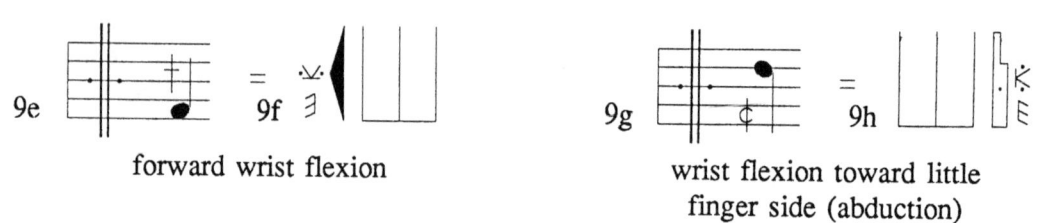

forward wrist flexion

wrist flexion toward little finger side (abduction)

In Ex. 9i, taken from Nijinsky's score, the right wrist is abducted while the left wrist is both abducted and flexed backward, producing a diagonal direction for that wrist. This occurs in measure 90 for the faun.

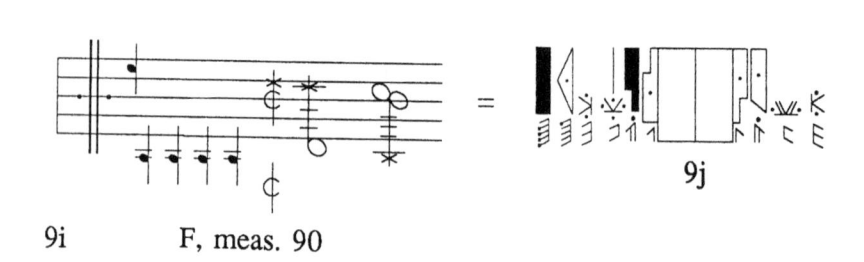

9i   F, meas. 90

10. Flexion of the Ankle

Because of his background in anatomical analysis and terminology, Nijinsky used the sign for 'forward' flexion for what in ordinary, everyday terms is called stretching the ankle. In the *Faune* score he shows two degrees of such flexion (foot and ankle stretched), Exs. 10a and 10d. Conversely, the sign for 'backward' flexion, Ex. 10g, produces a bent 'forward folded' ankle.

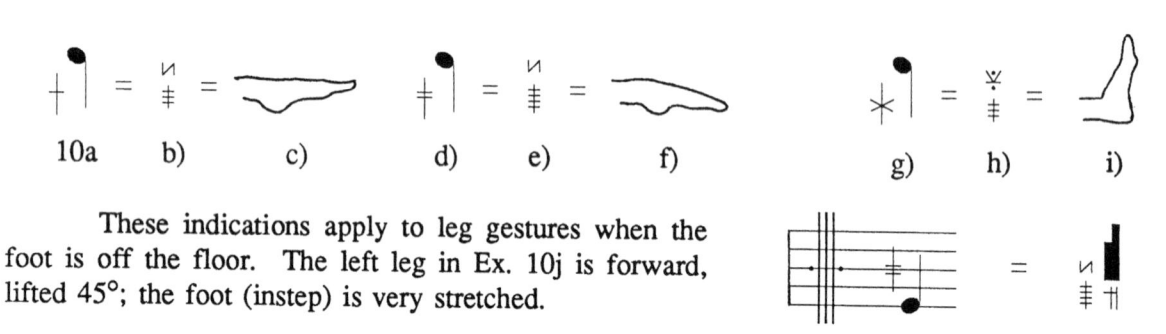

10a   b)   c)   d)   e)   f)   g)   h)   i)

These indications apply to leg gestures when the foot is off the floor. The left leg in Ex. 10j is forward, lifted 45°; the foot (instep) is very stretched.

10j   10k

11. Bending ('Flexion') for the Head

Inclining the head, written on the top section of the staff, is indicated as flexion in the neck, the full range of eight directions being possible.

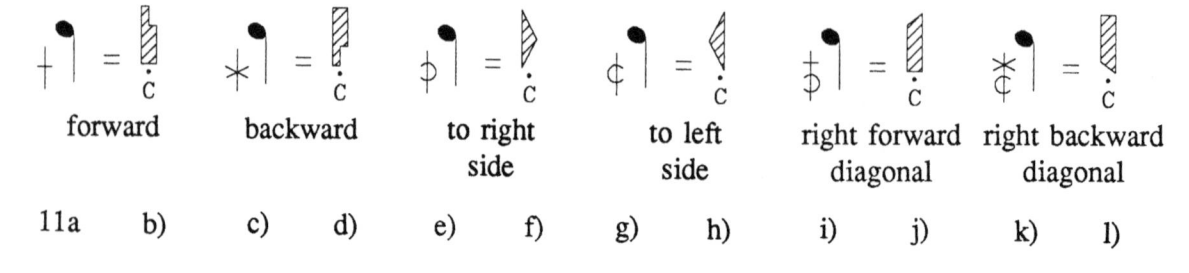

forward   backward   to right side   to left side   right forward diagonal   right backward diagonal

11a   b)   c)   d)   e)   f)   g)   h)   i)   j)   k)   l)

In 11m, the torso is upright and the head is inclined toward right forward diagonal.

In the forward direction two degrees of bending are used in the *Faune* score. From comparison with the de Meyer photographs it appears that for the ballet the degrees should be interpreted as in 11o and 11q.

The first degree, Ex. 11o, produces a slight tilt forward resulting from a pulling in of the chin and lengthening of the back of the neck; however, the eye-line is not changed. The second degree, Ex. 11q, is a forward inclination of the head in which the eye-line follows the head tilt in the normal way.

12. Flexion of the Fingers

Direction for the fingers is shown by placement of a grace note on the staff. This direction in the *Faune* score relates specifically to the four fingers. For Nijinsky 12a indicates 45° away from normal. In Labanotation this would be forward high from ⊕ , 12d.

Flexion of the fingers is indicated by strokes placed on the stem of the grace note. Nijinsky uses two degrees of forward flexion for the fingers. In Ex. 12e the fingers are shown to have 45° of forward flexion. Because they have more than one joint this flexion produces a curve, the fingertips being at a 45° angle in relation to their base. Ex. 12g shows 90° bend, the degree used when holding hands, (hands 'grasping').

For individual fingers five grace notes are used, the first one being the thumb, the last one the little finger. In Ex. 12i the thumb and four fingers are given specific directions and are flexed forward to a 'right angle', producing a greater degree of curve for holding the flute. (F, starting position in Nijinsky's score).

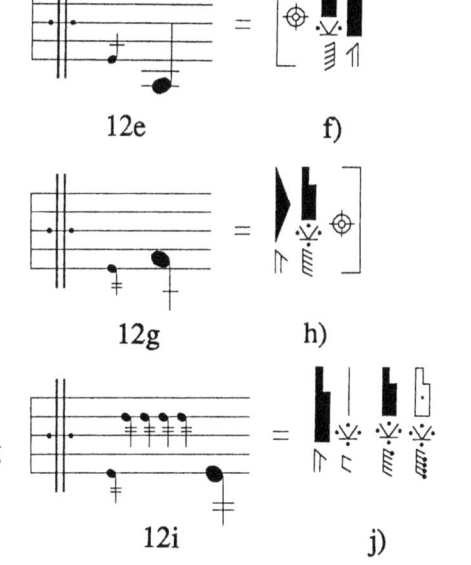

13. Rotation

Angular shaped signs for rotation are placed on the note stem to indicate rotation of the chest, upper arm or upper leg (thigh). Degree is shown by a single 'angle' for 45° and a double angle for 90°. For chest and head, rotation is to the right or left; for the limbs the description is in terms of inward and outward, the angle of the sign pointing in toward the note-head for inward rotation and away from it for outward rotation.

Chest Rotation

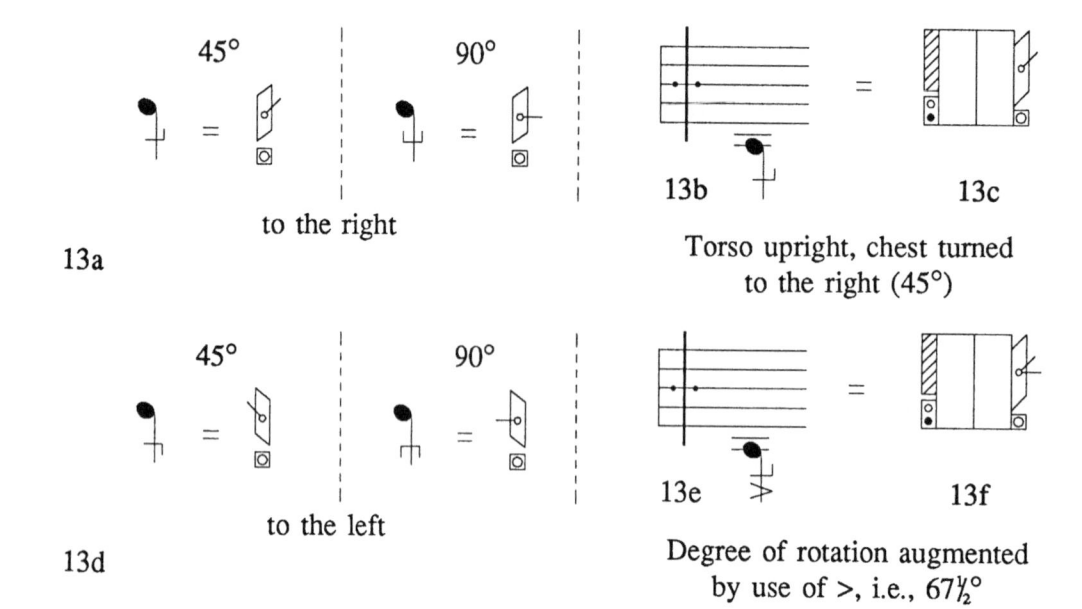

13a to the right
13b 13c Torso upright, chest turned to the right (45°)

13d to the left
13e 13f Degree of rotation augmented by use of >, i.e., 67½°

Upper Limb Rotation

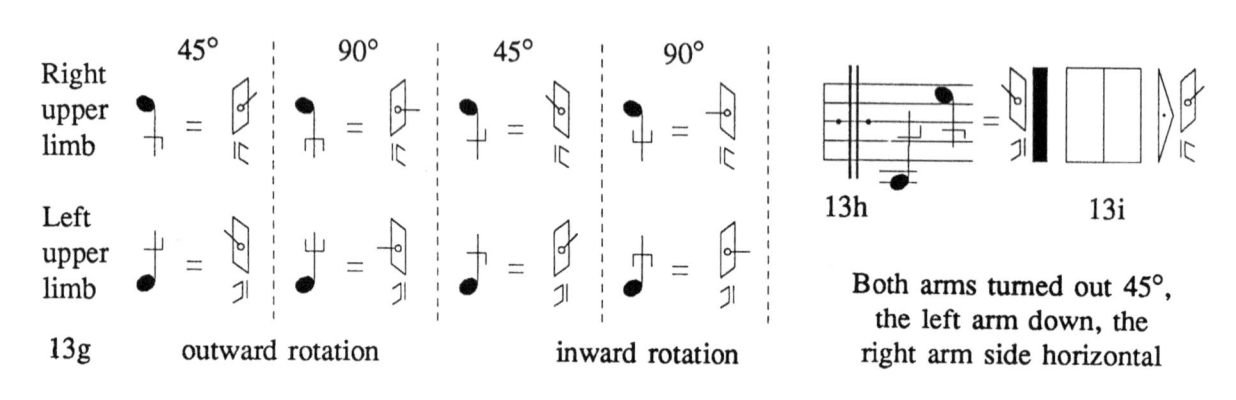

Right upper limb

Left upper limb

13g outward rotation   inward rotation

13h 13i Both arms turned out 45°, the left arm down, the right arm side horizontal

For 3rd degree parts (head, lower arm, lower leg) the appropriate indication is placed on a vertical line to the left of the music note. When elbow or knee is bent, the resulting spatial placement of the lower limb depends on the rotational state of the upper limb. Hand directions and palm facing depend on the rotational state of the upper arm as well as of the lower arm.

Head Rotation

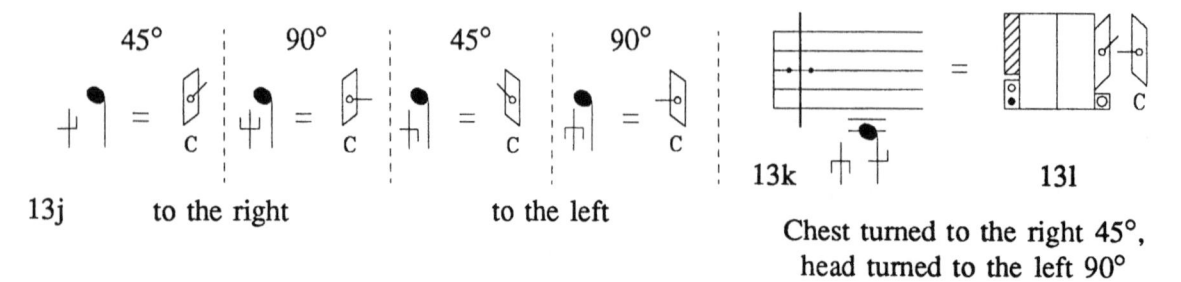

13j to the right   to the left

13k 13l Chest turned to the right 45°, head turned to the left 90°

Lower Limb Rotation

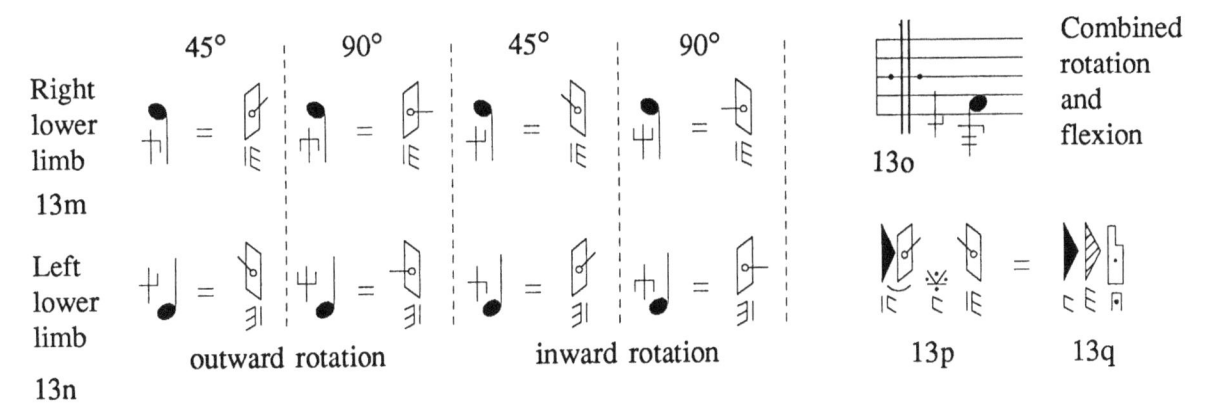

Right lower limb
13m

Left lower limb
13n

45°	90°	45°	90°
outward rotation		inward rotation	

13o — Combined rotation and flexion

13p   13q

In Ex. 13o Nijinsky's description is: right upper arm side low, rotated outward 45°, elbow bent 90°, lower arm rotated inward 45°; this position is written as 13q in the standard Labanotation directional description.

14. Shoulder Movements

In the *Faune* score Nijinsky frequently used the indication of one shoulder forward and the other back to show an augmentation of the accompanying chest rotation, i.e., an added *épaulement*. A shoulder forward is shown by an 'x' placed on a horizontal stroke at the end of the stem of the music note, Ex. 14a. For a backward shoulder movement the 'x' is placed outside the line at the end of the note stem, Ex. 14b.

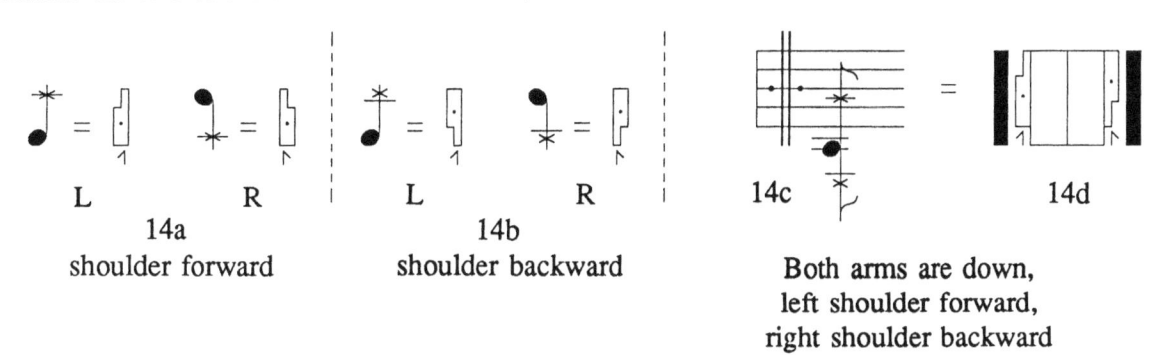

L   R   L   R
14a   14b
shoulder forward   shoulder backward

14c   14d

Both arms are down,
left shoulder forward,
right shoulder backward

E. STANDING

15. Positions of the Feet

1st and 2nd positions are indicated below. The oblong note states whole foot contact.

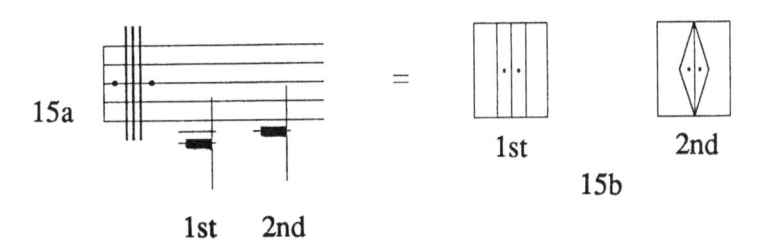

15a

1st   2nd

         1st   2nd
         15b

The 4th and 5th positions are shown here with the right foot front.

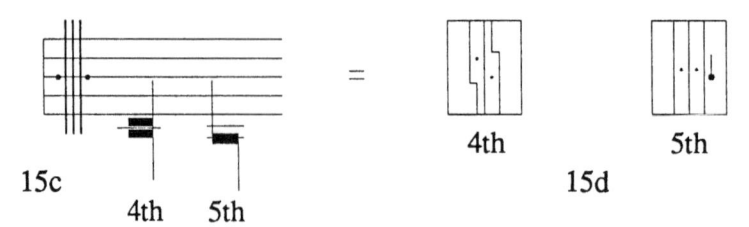

15c 4th 5th   15d 4th 5th

Third position was not used in the ballet notations nor in the score of *Faune*.

In the *Faune* score positions with weight on both feet rarely occur; usually weight is on one foot, the other merely touching the floor.

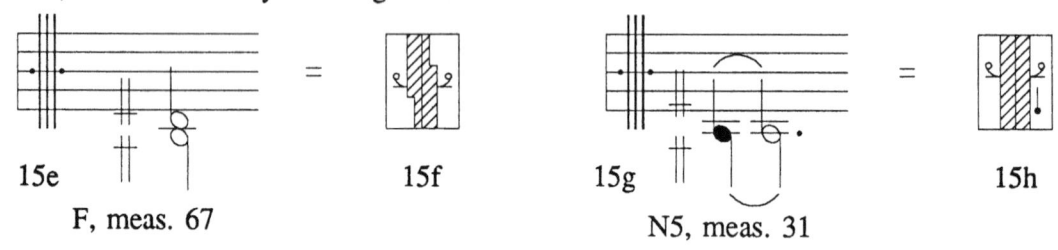

15e   15f
F, meas. 67

15g   15h
N5, meas. 31

In 15e the faun is standing on high half-toe in 4th position, right foot forward, left foot backward. In 15g the fifth nymph is also on high half-toe but in 5th position, right foot front.

Weight-bearing

Nijinsky had no specific means of stating placement of weight. While he used oblong notes to indicate the whole foot contacting the ground (as in the positions of the feet) and round notes for gestures, he also used a round note for supporting on the half-toe, Ex. 15i, and on *pointe*, Ex. 15k. The appropriate modifier being placed at the left of the note.

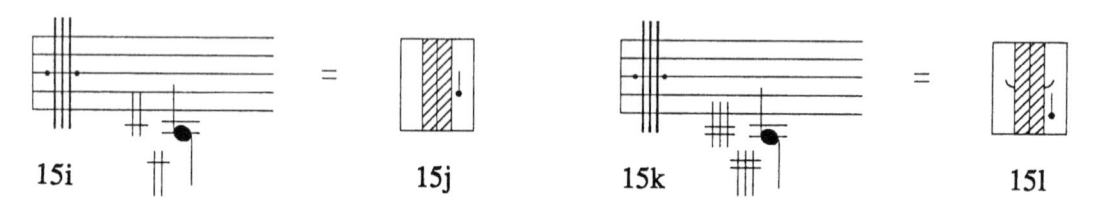

15i   15j   15k   15l

In the score of *Faune*, Nijinsky also used oblong notes for supporting on the arms (elbow, hand) and the body. In such cases the meaning must be 'the flat surface' of that part. From the configuration of the body and limbs, written through degrees of flexion in the various joints, one arrives at a crouching, kneeling or lying position.

16. Use of Parts of the Foot

The following examples include use of these details for supports and gestures taken from the score of *Faune* or from his ballet notations. The literal translation of Nijinsky's description is marked VN; the standard Labanotation description is marked LN.

Whole Foot

As mentioned before, for whole foot contact with the floor an oblong note-head is used, Ex. 16a. Whole foot contact as a gesture in place does not occur in *Faune* or in Nijinsky's ballet notation.

Ex. 16c shows a *grand plié* in 2nd position in 2nd position as in Nijinsky's ballet notations.

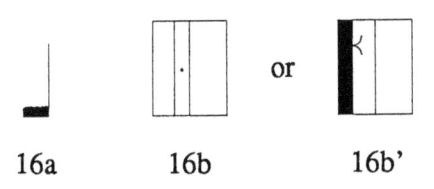

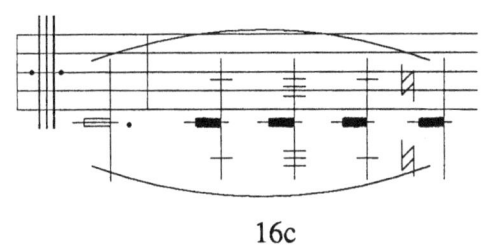

16a   16b   or   16b'

16c

Ball of Foot

The double vertical lines for 'ball of foot' are modified by adding the appropriate indication for ankle and instep extension (see **Flexion of the Ankle**, p. 154).

Exs. 16d and 16f show simple ball of foot contact without weight; exact use of the foot depends on the direction of the leg and how much it is bent. Such contact often occurs as a resultant touch.

16d   16e   16e'   16f   16g

In Ex. 16h the right foot is shown as a gesture touching at the back on the ball of the foot (the result of a previous step forward), the leg slightly bent.

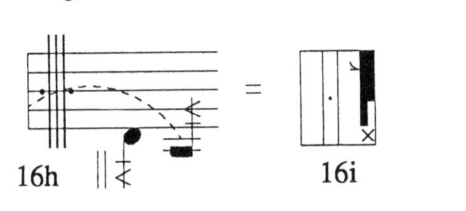

16h   16i

N3, meas. 22

High Half-toe

Exs. 16j and 16l indicate ball of foot support with somewhat stretched foot and ankle, i.e., between normal half-toe and 3/4 *pointe* (high arch).

16j   16k   16k'   16l   16m

Ex. 16n shows walking forward, stepping on the high half-toe, the preparatory gesture having a stretched ankle.

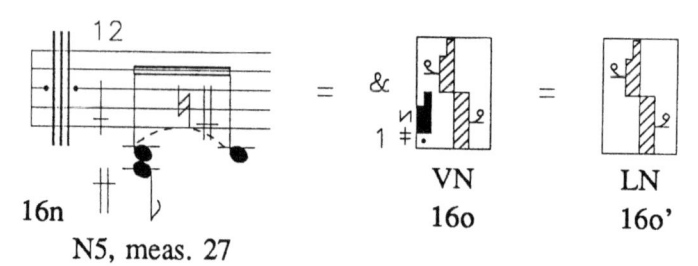

16n
N5, meas. 27

16o
VN

16o'
LN

Instep

Stretched instep, as in 16p, is used in measure 106 as the faun kneels. In the score the resulting contact of the instep is written as 16r (see **Glossary**, p. 48).

16p 16q 16r

The extended instep is also used for the faun's final position when he is lying prone, his legs being 'down', i.e., in line with his torso, 16s.

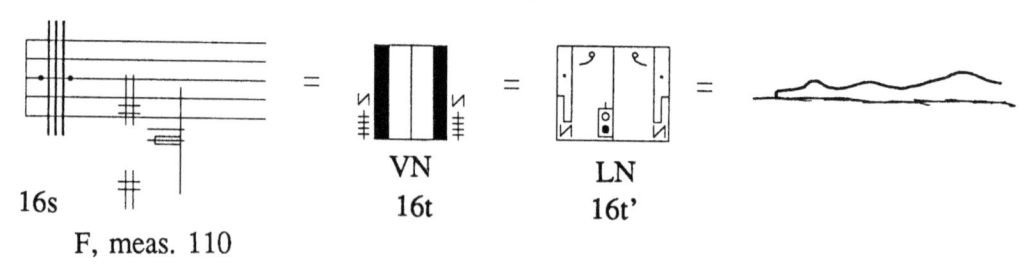

16s
F, meas. 110

16t
VN

16t'
LN

Pointe

Heel

16u 16v 16v'   16w 16x 16x'

Supporting on *pointe*, Ex. 16u, appears in the ballet notations; it does not appear in the score of *Faune*. The sign of 16w states the degree of ankle flexion which produces a heel contact as in 16x. This indication is used in his ballet notation for a minor turn on the heel to change front. Such flexion of the ankle is used in *Faune* only in the context of crouching.

For gestures Nijinsky used the following: Ex 16y shows ankle extended (not forced); in 16z foot and ankle are fully stretched.

16y 16z

Ex. 16aa shows the *pointe* contacting the floor; this sign was previously used to indicate *en pointe* in Ex. 16u. In 16cc the ankle is stretched and abducted, i.e., a wrapped foot as in *petits battements sur le cou-de-pied*. Abduction for the ankle is the same term and movement for both Nijinsky and Labanotation.

17. Crouch Position

Ex. 17a shows the bent ankle, used when crouching. In this position the weight is on the ball of the foot. The exact use of the foot depends on the level of the thigh of the supporting leg, thus the notation of 17b may have the thigh in any of the levels of 17d. Nijinsky's way of showing such details in a crouch is by giving the direction for the thigh and the degree of knee flexion.

Ex. 17e shows a crouch with weight on the ball of the right leg, the knee pointing forward between forward low and forward horizontal. The left knee is forward horizontal, less bent, and the foot contact is on the ball of the foot.

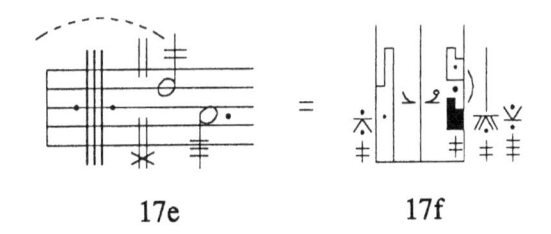

F. STAGE ORIENTATION

18. Stage Directions

Nijinsky used numbers to indicate the directions faced on stage, towards the audience being 0, stage right - 4, upstage - 8, stage left - 12, with the corners and intermediate directions indicated as in Ex. 18a.

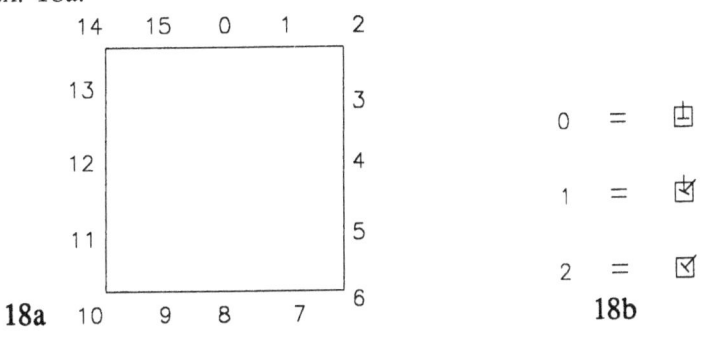

The direction faced on stage is written just above the staff for the legs. In Ex. 18c, taken from Nijinsky's original score, the performer is shown to be facing 4 (stage right), then facing 12 (stage left).

N4, meas. 25

18c

G. LOCOMOTION

19. Walking

As in the Stepanov system, a step, a transference of weight is written in Nijinsky's notation by first showing the free leg moving as a gesture into the desired direction and then indicating the same leg to be in the downward direction with whole foot contact, shown by the oblong note. The preparation and the support are linked by a dotted bow.

Ex. 19a shows a step forward on the left leg, next to which is the literal translation into Labanotation (marked VN) and then the standard Labanotation statement (marked LN) for a step forward.

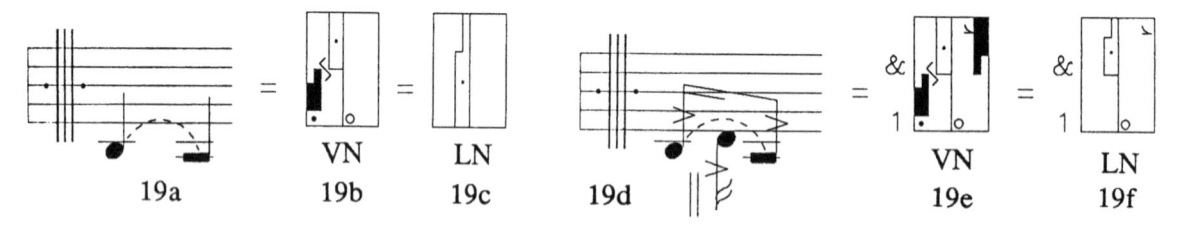

19a 19b VN 19c LN 19d 19e VN 19f LN

At the end of each forward step the resultant contact with the floor for the other leg is also indicated. In Ex. 19d the right leg has a resultant backward contact on the ball of the foot at the end of the step forward on the left foot. Note the off-beat timing of this step. The literal translation and the standard Labanotation for 19d are given in 19e and 19f.

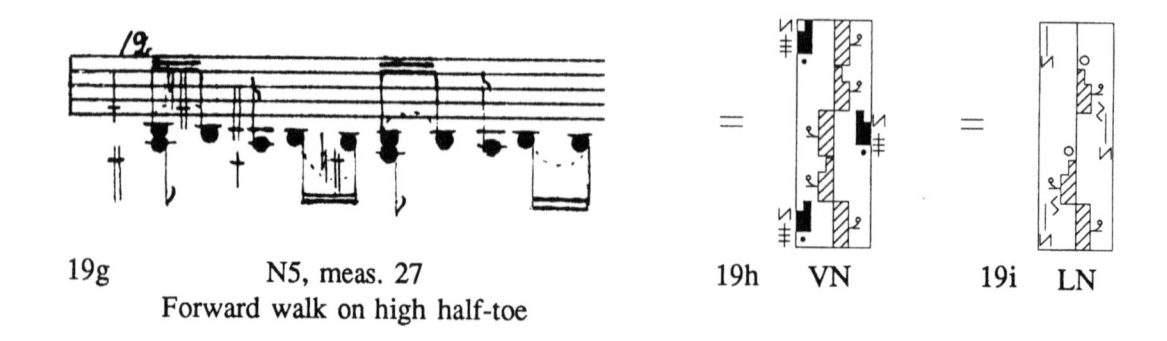

19g   N5, meas. 27   19h VN   19i LN
Forward walk on high half-toe

Ex. 19g shows the forward walk on high half-toe of the chief nymph's entrance. The sign ⊺ states that the foot is pointed as she prepares to take each step. This is then cancelled by the natural sign ♮ (see **Validity**, pp. 173-174) and weight is taken on the high half-toe. For half-toe steps the music note for taking weight shows the same direction as the preceding gesture, i.e., not in 'place' (the leg straight down) as with steps onto the whole foot, as in Ex. 19a.

In Ex. 19j, after the forward step on the left foot, the leg slightly bent, the nymphs take quick backward steps on high half-toe. This pattern is similar to the forward steps of 19g, but preparation and support are shown to be backward instead of forward. The foot is pointed for the preparatory gesture and this point is cancelled before weight is taken on high half-toe. Placement of the various supplementary indications sometimes caused problems (see **Timing; Use of Music Notation**, pp. 169-171). In the LN example a 'zed caret' links the stretched gesture to the following step for which it is a preparation.

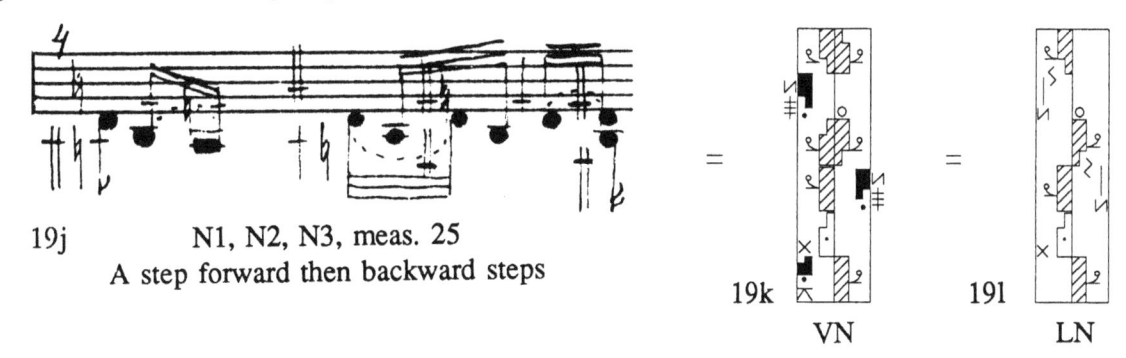

19j   N1, N2, N3, meas. 25
A step forward then backward steps

19k   VN   19l   LN

Indication of Direction of Travel

Traveling in the *Faune* ballet is usually forward into the direction the feet face; thus the direction faced on stage and the direction of travel are usually the same. As noted, the facing direction is written just above the leg section of the staff. The direction of traveling is written at the top of the whole staff, just above the torso section. Ex. 19m shows the entrance of the sixth nymph on measure 28, the facing direction and the traveling both being toward 12.

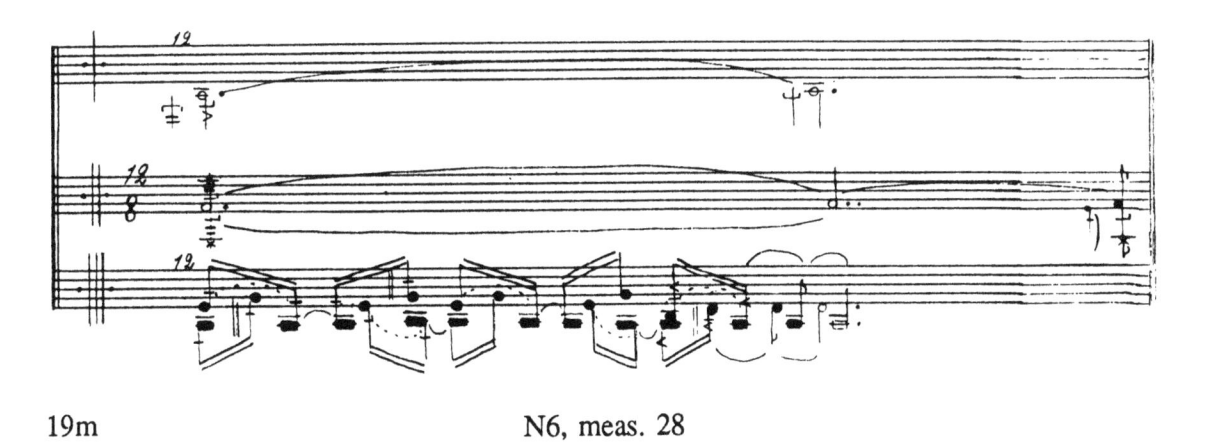

19m   N6, meas. 28

Ex. 19n shows measure 25, in which the first three nymphs start with a step forward toward stage direction 4. Then, still facing 4, they travel backwards toward 12, as shown at the top of the staff. This is a rare instance of backward steps being used in the *Faune* score.

19n   N1, N2, N3 meas. 25

Modification of Traveling

At times, however, the dancers need to veer slightly upstage or downstage. The faun also briefly moves slightly downstage after coming down from the rock, and later upstage to return to the rock. Such modifications from the flat path between 12 and 4 are shown by the appropriate numbers being placed at the top of the whole staff, as in Ex. 19o.

19o   N7, meas. 44-46

In Ex. 19o, as the 6th nymph picks up a veil, the 7th nymph, facing 12, takes a step in that direction then walks toward 11 (moving slightly upstage), turns to face 4 and travels slightly upstage towards 5. In measure 46 she travels straight to 4, exiting on measure 47. These deviations occur to avoid the 3rd nymph who passes downstage of N7. The deviation toward 5 was found not to be needed for spacing and so was omitted from the Labanotation score.

20. Turning

A change of front is shown by use of stage numbers placed above the section of the staff for the legs. A gradual change of front is indicated by a series of numbers which reveal the direction of turning. For continuous turning a dotted line connects the numbers. The indication (+) means turn clockwise, while (-) shows turning counterclockwise.

For full turns, *pirouettes*, the plus or minus sign is placed in parentheses and a number is added to show the number of turns.

Ex. 20c shows a *pirouette en dehors* from 5th right foot behind to 5th right foot front with the legs straightening at the end. Note the use of the natural ♮ to cancel the leg flexion at the end.

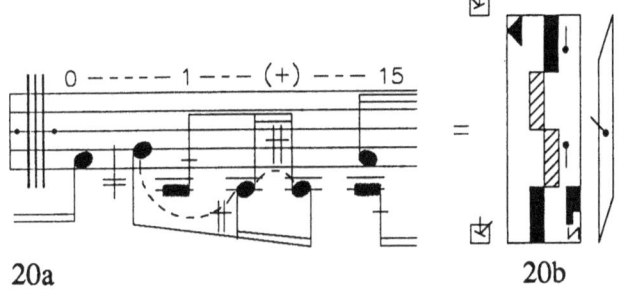

20a 20b

Pas de bourrée under, turning clockwise, ending facing 15

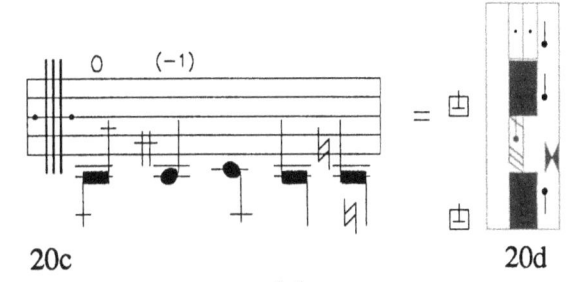

20c 20d

Pirouette en dehors, starting right foot behind

In the score of *Faune*, Nijinsky did not use turn signs to indicate change of front; instead he wrote the new stage direction to be faced, the turning always being to the open side, toward the audience.

Ex. 20e, taken directly from Nijinsky's score, shows a change from facing 12 to facing 4, ending with weight on the right leg, the left touching backward on the ball of the foot. The swivel turn is achieved as simply as possible. In this example the first three nymphs finish walking with weight on the left foot, the right touching behind, they then swivel to the right (the open side for this placement of the feet).

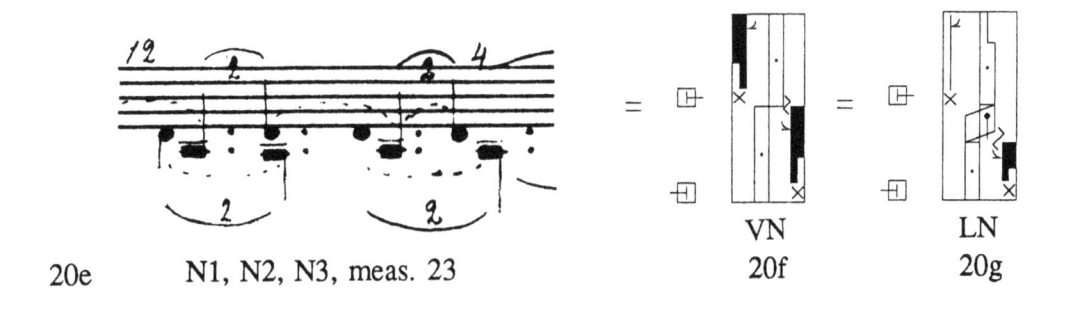

20e N1, N2, N3, meas. 23   VN 20f   LN 20g

21. Jumping, Springing

A spring into the air (jumping) is shown by simultaneous leg gestures for both legs and the absence of the dotted bow for a subsequent step. Ex. 21a shows an *assemblé* over with the right leg. Starting in 5th *demi-plié*, right foot behind, the left leg gestures straight down, the right leg extends to the side, both with stretched feet. The landing is in 5th, right foot front. As *demi-plié* was given earlier in the measure, the signs for bending need not be repeated on the landing.

21a *Assemblé* over   VN 21b   LN 21c

In 21d the *echappé sauté* in 2nd, the spring is from 5th right foot behind, to 2nd and then to 5th right foot front. The legs are shown to be down while in the air.

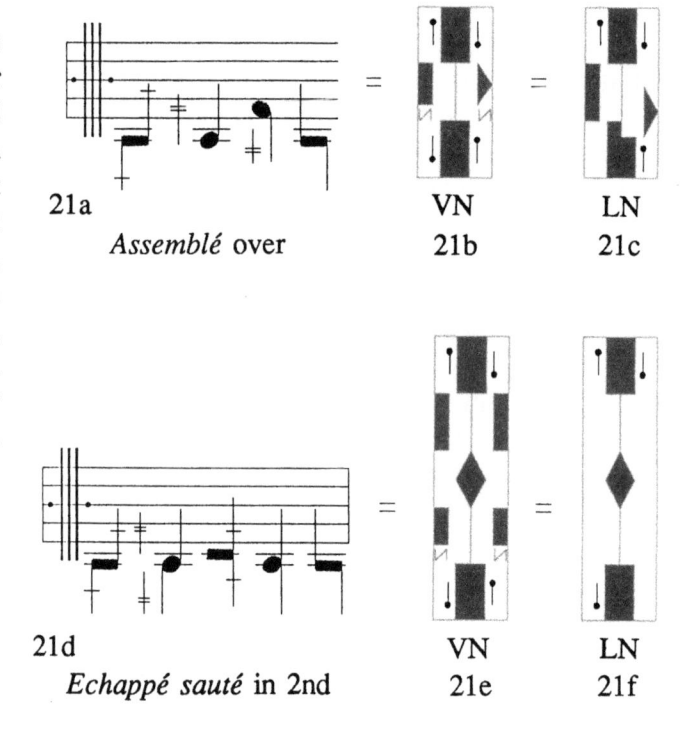

21d *Echappé sauté* in 2nd   VN 21e   LN 21f

Note Nijinsky's inaccurate movement description for the *assemblé* which should leave the floor from one foot, not two. Such analysis was found also in the ballet notations written in Stepanov's notation and showed lack of careful analysis in writing ballet.

Two springing movements occur in the *Faune* score, the first done by N4 (the 'Joyful Nymph') and the other by the faun.

In Ex. 21g, from Nijinsky's score, counts have been added for clarification. After walking forward on the left foot, N4 takes a high 4th position, right foot front, knees slightly bent, (count 7). While in the air, (count 8) the toes are pointed, the left leg is down while the right lower leg lifts swiftly backward (the knee very bent). Landing is on the left foot on count 9. Note the use of the naturals ♮ to cancel the previous indications for ankle 'flexion'.

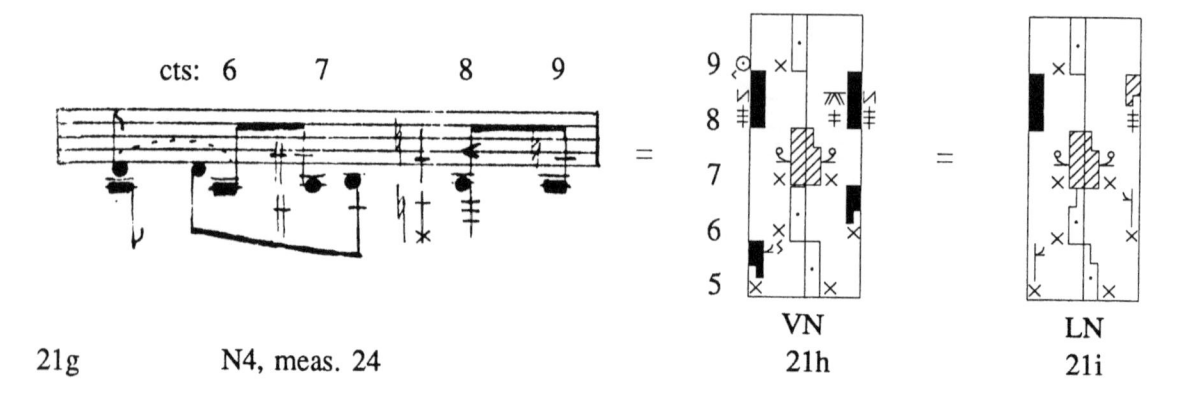

cts: 6   7   8   9

21g   N4, meas. 24   VN 21h   LN 21i

In 21j below, the faun, has just stepped onto the left foot at (a), he then gestures with both legs (the right leg forward, the left backward with the knee very flexed and also the ankle flexed, (b). This takes him into the air, which continues during (c). He then lands forward on the right leg on count 'and' of 2 (d). The direction for landing is not 'down' but forward which suggests that more than normal distance forward is covered during the jump. On count 3 he is preparing for the step forward on the left foot, (e).

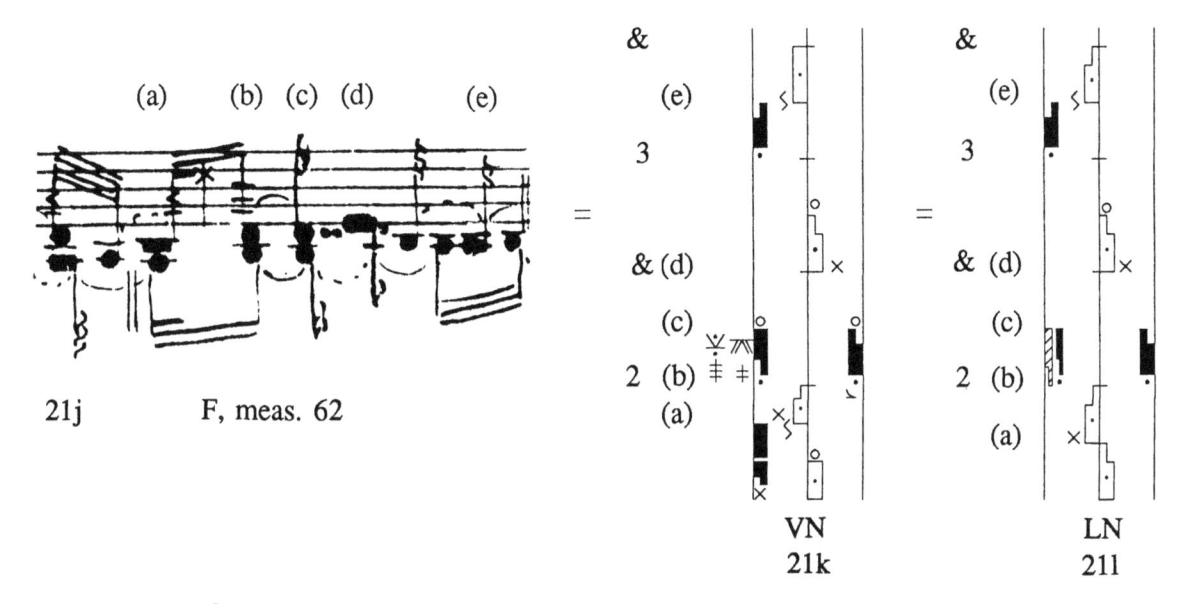

21j F, meas. 62

21k VN

21l LN

H. CONTACT

22. Touching

Nijinsky gives word-notes in the score for holding the flute, picking up the grapes, etc., and on measure 41 for the 4th nymph he includes the instructions "Keeps hand of seventh nymph". However, in most instances, he indicates contact between the nymphs' hands through small thick vertical bows in the score, Ex. 22a.

22a   signs for contact placed next to hand indications

In 22b the 2nd nymph is shown to be holding the hands of those on either side of her; a contact bow swings upward from her left hand, and another downward from her right hand. The accompanying nymphs (not shown here) have only one bow, that for the 1st nymph swinging downward (towards the 2nd nymph's staff) and that for the 3rd nymph swinging upward, thus it is clear which hands are in contact.

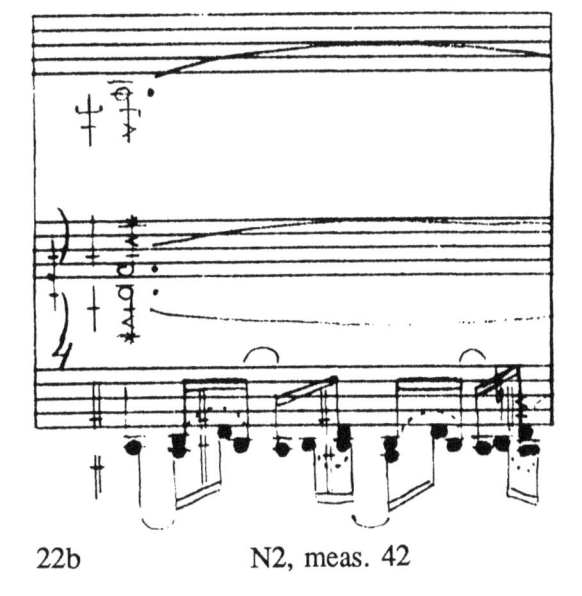

22b N2, meas. 42

In addition to the specific placement of the arms, Nijinsky showed that the arms crossed in taking hands by overlapping the bows, as in 22c.

Ex. 22d shows the entrance in measure 82 of the 1st and 7th nymphs who have crossed arms as they hold hands. This is shown in the crossing of the vertical bows. Note that the rests at the start of the measure indicate they are still off stage (see **Entrances, Exits**, p. 168).

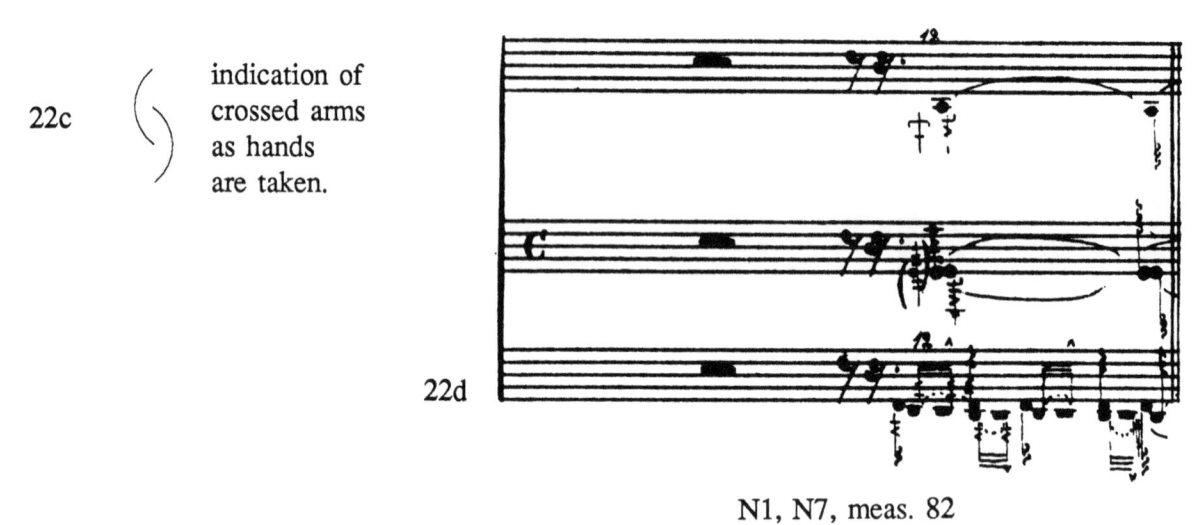

22c indication of crossed arms as hands are taken.

22d

N1, N7, meas. 82

I. MISCELLANEOUS

23. Entrances, Exits

As just mentioned, Nijinsky uses music rest signs to indicate off stage, i.e., before entrances and after exits. In Ex. 23a the 1st nymph comes in from stage right (facing and traveling toward 12) halfway through measure 21. In Ex. 23b the 3rd nymph exits stage right on measure 47 as she and the two others carry off the two veils.

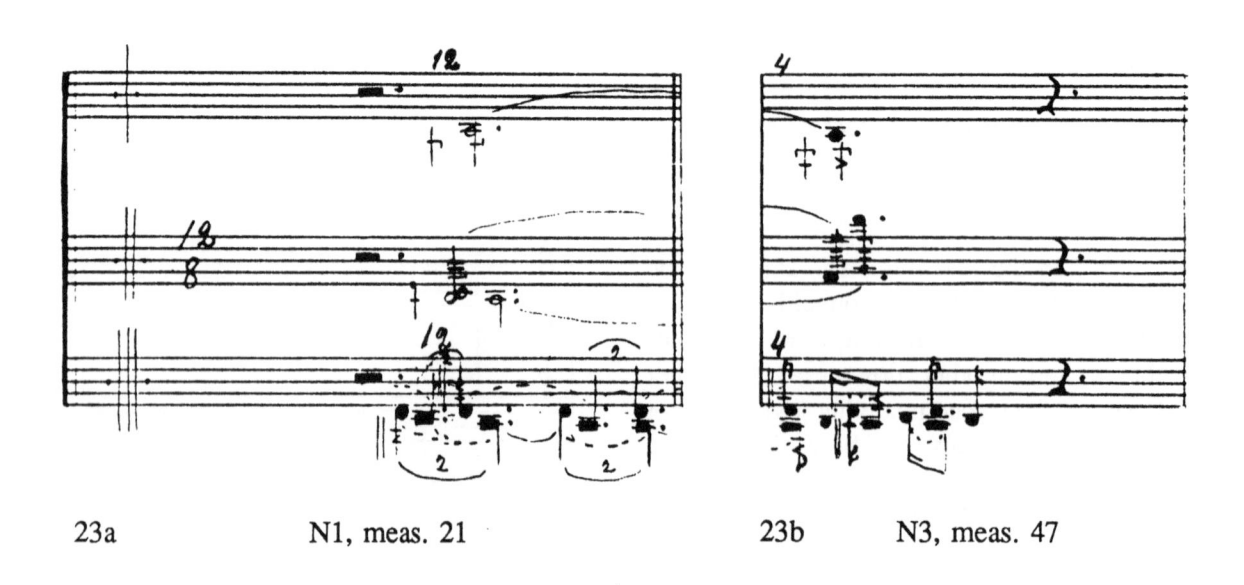

23a   N1, meas. 21   23b   N3, meas. 47

24. Timing; Use of Music Notation

As in Stepanov's system, Nijinsky uses music notes with the same time value durations as in standard Western music notation. The time value is also applicable to use of oblong notes for contact of the whole foot on the floor. In each measure the notes add up to the meter indicated. Placement of the movement indications sometimes causes a problem, 24a. Because of signs adjacent to the music note, simultaneous actions cannot always be lined up one above the other as in a chord in music. Therefore the timing for each limb - this is particularly true for the legs - must be worked out individually to ascertain on which beat or subdivision of a beat the gesture or support occurs. Approached in this way, the movements made sense and every beat was found to be accounted for.

Note: Counts have been added to Exs. 24a and 24b to indicate the main beats, those for the left leg being placed above and those for the right leg below.

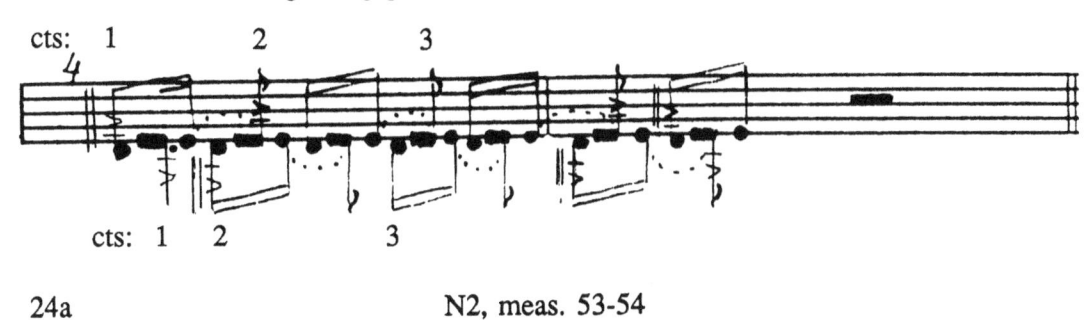

24a   N2, meas. 53-54

In Ex. 24b we see an even greater separation between placement of the right and left legs on count 5, yet the note values within the whole measure add up correctly.

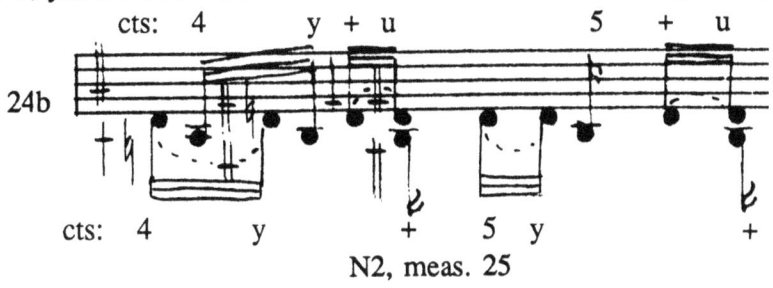

24b   N2, meas. 25

Precise Timing

In Ex. 24c, the most complex sequence in the ballet, Nijinsky spelled out in great detail the exact timing for each leg gesture and support. In actual practice, when the music is played at its normal speed, it is very difficult to count each movement and perform it on the beat specifically designated for it. In analyzing the movements so carefully, probably in slow motion, Nijinsky became aware of details which do not appear fully, or cannot be given specific attention, when the sequence is performed at speed. In reconstructing the sequence, the movement pattern is placed on the music, the key counts are adhered to, with the rest falling into place as the movement naturally dictates.

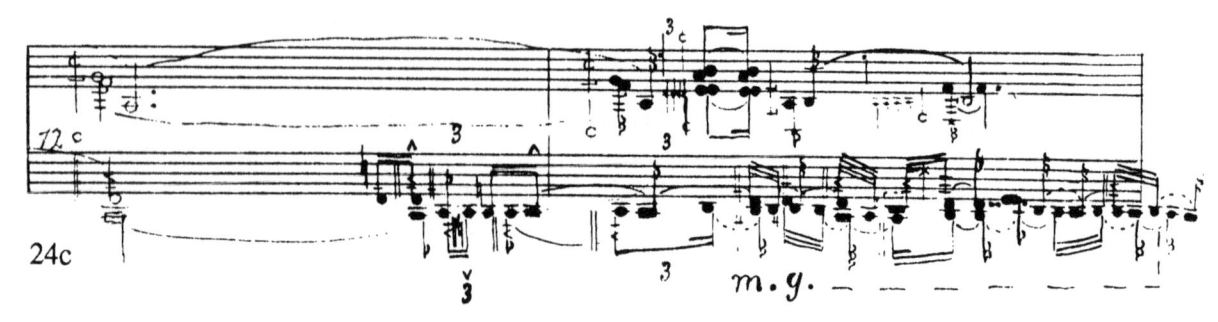

F, meas. 61-62

On-beat, Off-beat Steps

In several places in the score of *Faune* Nijinsky has written the walking patterns as being performed off the main beat, as in Ex. 24d, where the preparatory gesture before the step is written on the first beat after the bar line, the step following a sixteenth note (semi-quaver) later. In contrast Ex. 24e clearly shows the preparatory gesture as happening before the bar line, the step occurring on count 1.

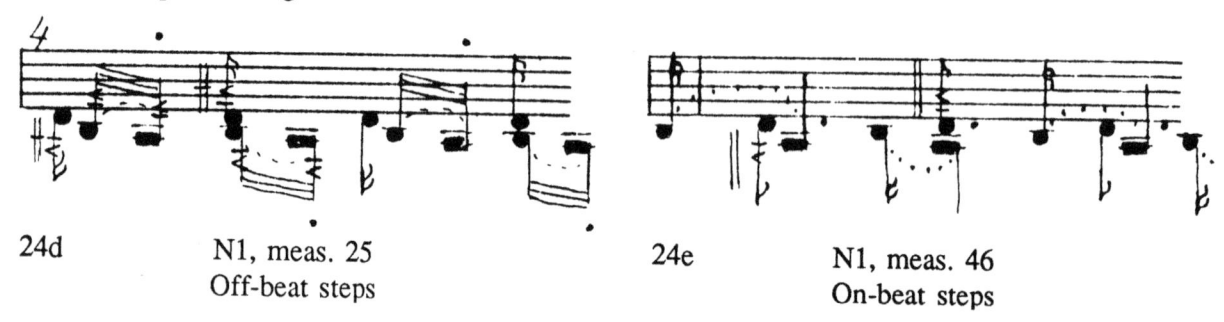

24d N1, meas. 25
Off-beat steps

24e N1, meas. 46
On-beat steps

Performing such off-beat steps appears not to be easy; in actual practice the music pulls the steps onto its own rhythm. From interviews with people who had learned the ballet in 1931, the movements had been shown without any counting. With the fluidity of the music in mind and the lack for the most part of an obvious recurring pulse, the movement phrases were placed on the appropriate time span, the steps falling into place. In working from Nijinsky's score his meticulous spelling out of duplets or triplets in 12/8 meter has to be carefully rehearsed to produce the desired effect.

Placement of Dot for Dotted Notes

Using adapted music notes sometimes posed problems. In keeping track of the exact time values for each movement, Nijinsky did not always place the dot for dotted notes right after the note it modified.

In Ex. 24f the dot for the right leg gesture is placed after the note for supporting on the left leg. For the comparable gesture for the left leg the dot is placed correctly next to the note.

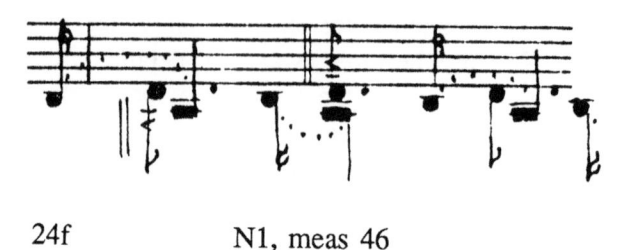

24f N1, meas 46

In Ex. 24g the dot for the first note appears to belong to the second note.

Ex. 24h shows a similar misplacement for an arm indication, both dots being placed after the note for the right arm. Other spacing problems were also met.

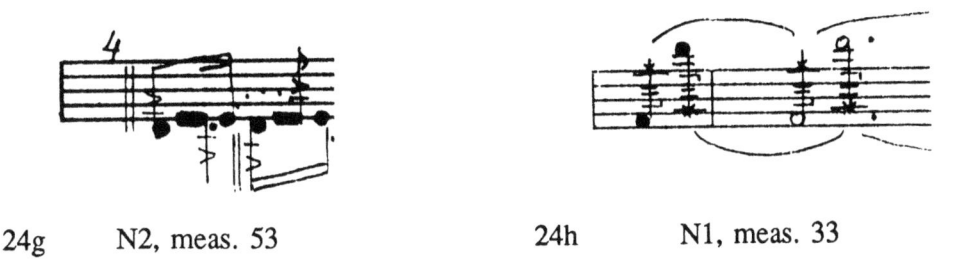

24g   N2, meas. 53   24h   N1, meas. 33

25. Use of Repeat Signs

Nijinsky applied adapted music notation signs for repeats for two distinctly different usages. In Ex. 25a the sign ⁄⁄ is used in measure 2 to mean hold the position; it appears again in measure 4 with the same meaning.

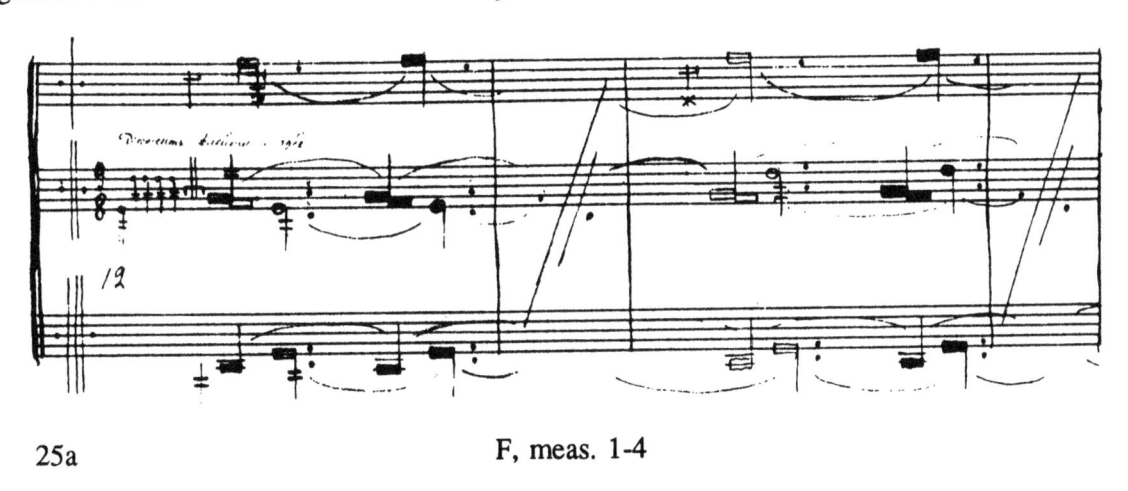

25a   F, meas. 1-4

In a similar usage in Ex. 25b the sign is accompanied by a number 9 which indicates that the position is to be held for 9 measures.

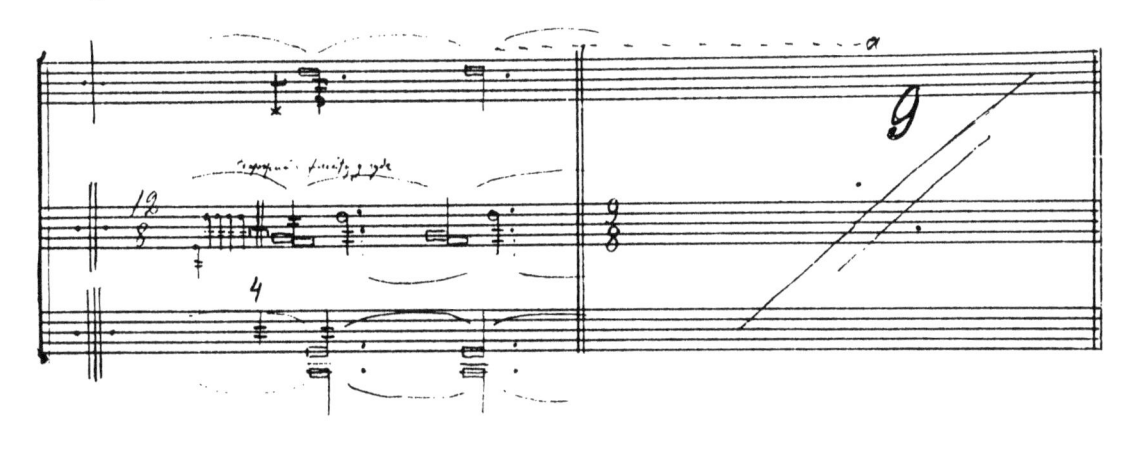

25b   F, meas. 21-22

In contrast to the above, Ex. 25c shows measure 18 (our numbers), in which the sign is used as an instruction to repeat the movement of measure 17; this is clear from the word notes within these two measures which state "Puts down one bunch and takes another".

25c   F, meas. 17-19

Ex, 25d shows an example from Nijinsky's ballet notations. A *grand battement* to the side with the right leg is to be repeated three times and then repeated four times to the other side.

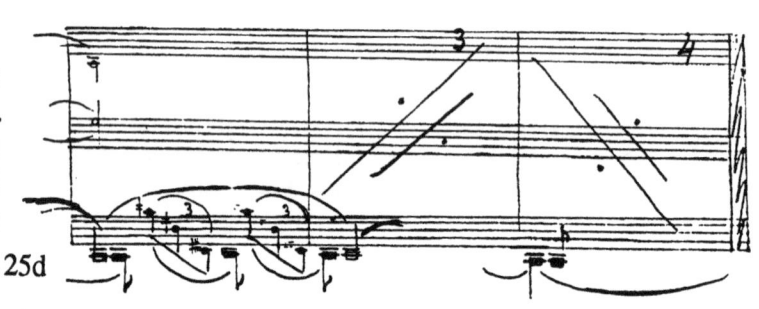

25d

26. Systems of Reference for Direction

Nijinsky related directions for the upper arms and thighs to the system of directions based on the build of the body, i.e., the Body Key. As we have seen, directions as such were not given for the lower arms and lower legs, their movements resulted from flexion in the elbow and knee joints together with the degree of rotation of the upper limb.

Direction of steps is taken from Stance, i.e., the direction in which the hips (feet) are facing. Additional indication of travelling is stated in terms of the room directions, i.e., towards 12, 4 or the intermediate directions 3, 11, etc.

27. Statement of Key

Stepanov gave a key with the full 90° turn-out of the legs, 27a. In his Cecchetti notations Nijinsky indicated a little less leg rotation, 27b. He also indicated a very slight bend for the arms, 27c.

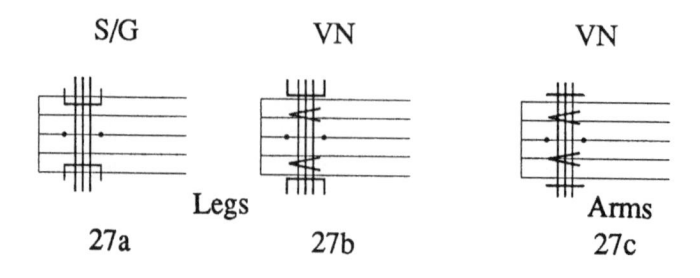

S/G	VN	VN
	Legs	Arms
27a	27b	27c

However, in the score of *Faune* he indicated a key for legs slightly bent for all the nymphs in measures 32 to 34, Ex. 27d. This did not appear again (perhaps overlooked in the copying process?).

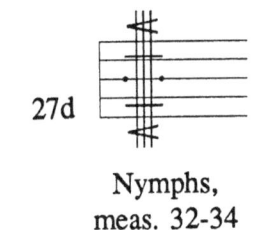

27d

Nymphs, meas. 32-34

J. RULES

28. Validity

Nijinsky followed the rules established in music notation regarding:

Accidentals

There is an automatically understood application throughout the measure of an accidental (modification) given earlier for a particular 'note'. The modification is not repeated but is understood to be in effect for each subsequent identical note. The accidental must be repeated in the next measure. This is also true of head indications which, if held, must be repeated in the next measure.

In Ex. 28a, the head tilted forward and turned to the left remains in effect on count 3, but must be repeated in the next measure, as must the indication of chest rotation.

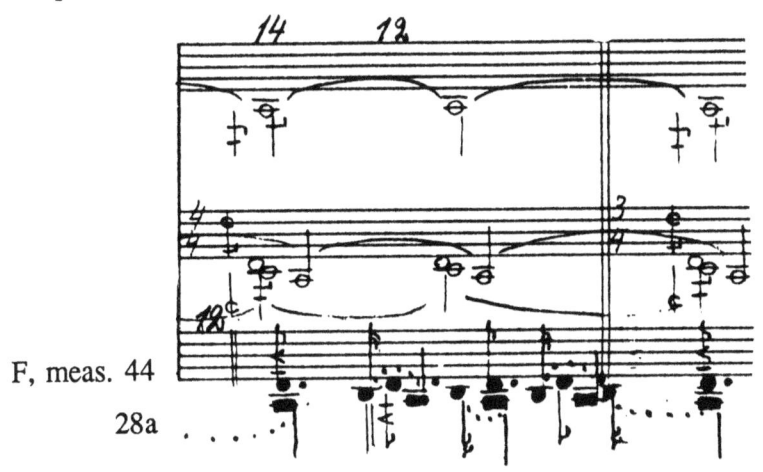

F, meas. 44

28a

For the feet the signs ‖ for the half-toe contact are stated for the first left and right backward leg gestures and then need not be restated within the rest of the measure.

Cancelling Accidentals

As mentioned, accidentals are in effect for the remainder of the measure. Cancellation of accidentals is achieved by use of the natural sign ♮. This natural sign is also used to cancel indications given in the key (e.g., degree of flexion to be used throughout) or, occasionally, indications placed on the stem of a note.

In Ex. 28b before the step backward on the right foot, the initial stretching of the ankle is cancelled so that the step is on the high ball of the foot. The result of a natural indication carries through for the rest of the measure.

28b   N2, meas. 25

Tied Notes

The tying of the same note indicates holding that note. For dance such holding means retaining that position.

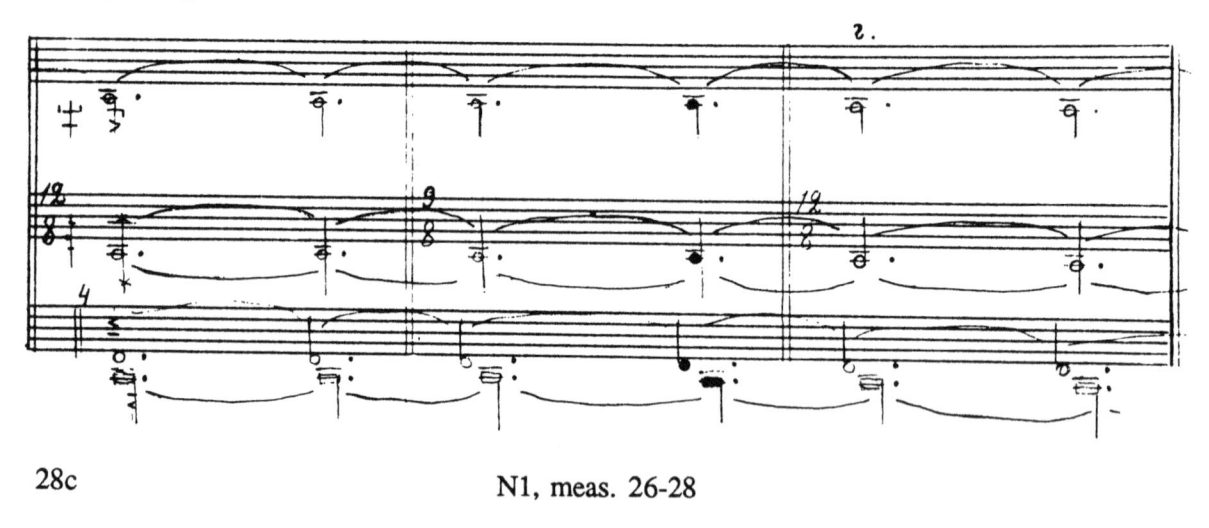

28c   N1, meas. 26-28

In Ex. 28c N1 holds still for measures 26 to 28. In the notation the positions for torso, arms and legs are repeated and each indication is bowed to the next.

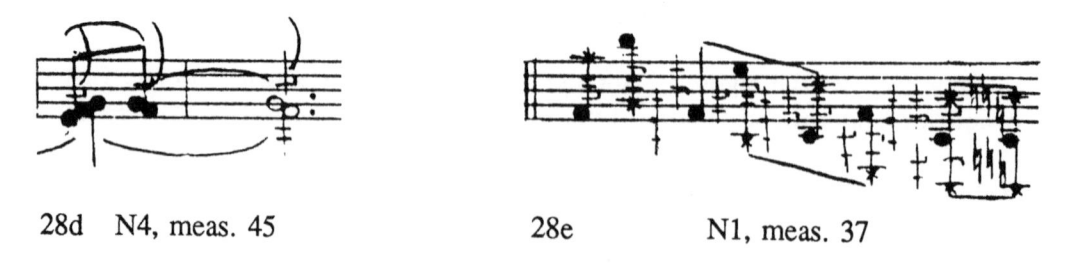

28d   N4, meas. 45   28e   N1, meas. 37

In Ex. 28d, upper arm rotations are repeated so as not to be cancelled. Specific cancellation is shown in Ex. 28e for arm details. At the end of the measure, hand flexion, wrist and upper arm rotation need to be cancelled for the last place low indication of the arms.

K. MOVEMENT DETAILS NOT COVERED

As judged from his ballet notations and the text of *Faune*, Nijinsky's system lacks certain information much needed in reconstructing a choreographic work. These are:

29. Length of Step

No indication exists for length of step. While high steps tend to be shorter and low steps longer, much variation can exist with little effort, variations which change the effect of a stepping pattern. Steps in which the legs remain constantly bent suggest less traveling. It is possible that a longer step was intended in places where a higher preparatory leg gesture is shown before a step taken with a bent knee, as in the following examples.

29a   N1, N2, N3, meas. 33   29b
LN

The fact that in Ex. 29a a bent knee is stated as the leg is raised $22\frac{1}{2}°$ forward in preparation for the step and that the leg is shown as bent for the subsequent taking of weight suggests that a small step will result.

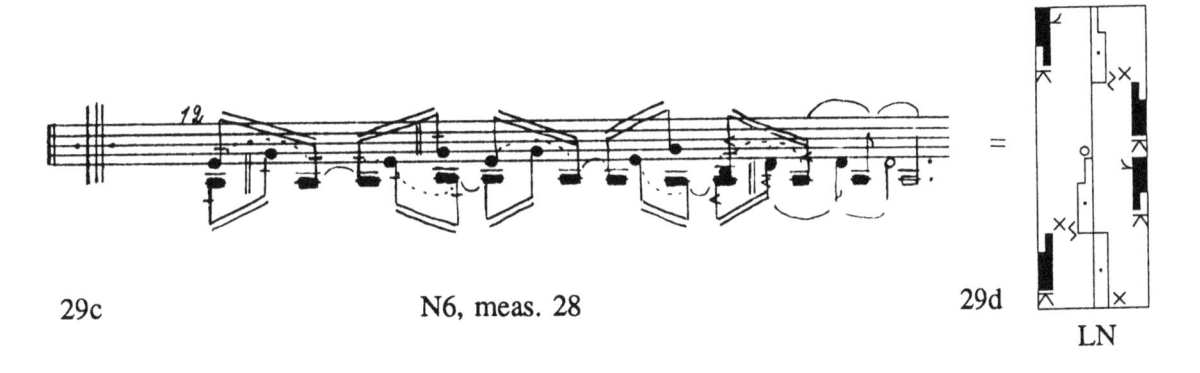

29c   N6, meas. 28   29d
LN

In Ex. 29c the legs are also slightly bent all the time. However there is a significant difference. Whereas in 29a the thigh is raised $22\frac{1}{2}°$, in 29c it is raised $45°$. This difference may have been intended to indicate that a longer step is to be taken in 29c. Certainly N6 has to cover a considerable distance in five steps.

30. Looking, Gazing

The direction into which the face looks is not given in Nijinsky's system. While rotation for the head will change where the face is directed, it is not the same message as looking at a person or into a direction. Also missing is indication of eye movement. In the photographs of Nijinsky in *Faune* there is one instance of the faun giving a sideward glance.

31. Palm Facing

The direction into which the palm faces is important as the palm is very expressive. Nijinsky gave no direct statement concerning that detail. Rotation of the upper and/or lower arm produces a change in direction for the palm, but such description provides no certainty that an exact palm facing result will be achieved. Verification of palm facing in *Faune* came from the photographs.

32. Indications for Relating

How performers relate to each other, specifically addressing someone with a look or gesture, closeness, etc., are not provided; only the sign for contact, touch, is given. Grasping, carrying, etc., are recorded in words.

APPENDIX A

Chronology of Nijinsky's Performances in the Rôle of *Faune*

DATE	THEATER	CAST
29 May 1912 31 May 1912 1/3/5/7/8/10 June 1912	Théâtre du Châtelet	Vaslav Nijinsky/Lydia Nelidova Leocadia Klementovich, Henriette Maicherska, Kopetzinska, Tcherepanova, Olga Khokhlova, Nadia Baranovitch, Bronislava Nijinska, Dirigent: Pierre Monteux
11/12/12/17/18/19/20 December 1912	Neues Königliches Opernthéater (Kroll), Berlin	V.Nijinsky/L.Nelidova, B.Nijinska, Lubov Tchernicheva, Stachko, H.Maicherska, L.Klementovitch, Kopentzinska, Dirigent: P.Monteux
30 December 1912 2/3/4/6 January 1913	Magyar Allami Operahàz, Budapest	V.Nijinsky/L.Nelidova, B.Nijinska, Stachko, H.Maicherska, L.Klementovitch, Kopentzinska, Dirigent: P.Monteux
10/11 January 1913	K. K. Hofoperntheater, Wien	V.Nijinsky/L.Nelidova, B.Nijinska, L.Tchernicheva, Kopetzinska, H.Maicherska, L.Klementovitch, Olga Khokhlova, Dirigent: P.Monteux
26 January 1913	Königliches Opernhaus, Dresden	V.Nijinsky/L.Nelidova, B.Nijinska, L.Tchernicheva, O.Khokhlova, H.Maicherska, L.Klementovitch, Kopetzinska, Dirigent: P.Monteux
17 February 1913	Royal Opera House, Covent Garden, London	V.Nijinsky/L.Nelidova, Bonietska, N.Baranovitch, Tcherepanova, H.Maicherska, L.Klementovitch, Kopetzinska, Dirigent: P.Monteux
15 April 1913	Opéra de Monte Carlo	V.Nijinsky/L.Nelidova, B.Nijinska, L.Tchernicheva, O.Khokhlova, H.Maicherska, Kopetzinska, Janina Bonietska, Dirigent: P.Monteux
18 April 1913	Opéra de Monte Carlo	V.Nijinsky/L.Nelidova, B.Nijinska, L.Tchernicheva, Maria Piltz, O.Khokhlova, H.Maicherska, Kopetzinska, Dirigent: P.Monteux
17/23 May 1913 12/17/23 June 1913	Théâtre des Champs-Elysées	V.Nijinsky/L.Nelidova, B.Nijinska, L.Tchernicheva, O.Khokhlova, H.Maicherska, Kopetzinska, J.Bonietska, Dirigent: P.Monteux

DATE	THEATER	CAST
27 June 1913 2/9/16/22 July 1913	Theatre Royal, Drury Lane, London	V.Nijinsky Cast replacement for one of the nymphs: Sokolova
25 September 1913 1/2/4 October 1913	Teatro Colon, Buenos Aires	V.Nijinsky/L.Tchernicheva, H.Maicherska, Hilda Bewicke, Kopetzinska, O.Khokhlova, J.Bonietska, Romola de Pulszky Dirigent: Rhenè-Baton
29/30 October 1913	Rio de Janeiro	V.Nijinsky
(10 June 1914)	Birmingham	
24/28 (Matinée) October 1916	Manhattan Opera House, New York City	V.Nijinsky, Flores Revalles Dirigent: P.Monteux
30 October 1916	Opera House, Providence, Rhode Island	V.Nijinsky, F.Revalles, Dirigent: P.Monteux
9/10 November 1916	Opera House, Boston	V.Nijinsky
9 December 1916	Coliseum, Fort Worth	V.Nijinsky, Dirigent: P.Monteux
(12 December 1916)	Convention Hall, Kansas City	V.Nijinsky
26 December 1916	The Auditorium, Los Angeles	V.Nijinsky
20 February 1917	Pitt Theatre, Pittsburgh	V.Nijinsky Dirigent: P.Monteux
10 June 1917	Madrid	V.Nijinsky
24 August 1917	Teatro Municipal, Rio de Janeiro	V.Nijinsky/L.Tchernicheva, Antonova, Vera Nemtchinova, Marie Chabelska, Nura & Lydia Soumarokova, Radina, Dirigent: Ernest Ansermet
1 September 1917	Teatro Municipal, Sao Paolo	V.Nijinsky/L.Tchernicheva, Antonova, V.Nemtchinova, M.Chabelska, N.&L.Soumarokova, Radina, Dirigent: E.Ansermet
14/19/20/23 September 1917	Teatro Colon, Buenos Aires	V.Nijinsky/L.Tchernicheva, Antonova, V.Nemtchinova, M.Chabelska, N.&L.Soumarokova, Radina, Dirigent: E.Ansermet

* Dates in brackets cannot be verified; they refer to reviews only.

APPENDIX B

Chronology of Nijinsky's Notation Experience

The following is a chronology of Nijinsky's interest in and development of dance notation:

1902-7: Learns the Stepanov dance notation system at the Imperial School. Develops an interest in the subject.

1912: Choreographs *L'Après-midi d'un Faune*.

1913: Starts notating *Faune* in Stepanov notation. An unfinished page is included in Bronislava Nijinska's *Early Memoirs*.

1914-15: Develops his own system, based on the Stepanov method but with significant differences. He shows direction through use of a five-line staff for each part of the body; other modifications are developed. He writes many examples of Cecchetti ballet technique in this new system as well as notating the poses of the *bas relief* figures in Luca Della Robbia's Cantoria. This period culminates in his recording the whole of the score of *Faune* in great detail. The score is complete except for most of the floor plans and specific details for the final two measures.

1917-18: Develops new ideas in notation. Uses a three-line staff and special keys comparable to treble clefs. Appears to be embarking on mathematical ideas on the lines of the Eshkol-Wachmann system which appeared in 1958. His notes repeat again and again the basic information on how direction, parts of the body and timing are shown but does not spell out any specific movements. In the absence of practical examples these later ideas do not culminate in a usable system.

APPENDIX C

Nijinsky's Word Notes

In his score Nijinsky wrote word notes indicating the action at that moment. The translation of them is given here with our interpretation. In instances where the action is obvious from the notation these word notes have not been included in the Labanotation score. Note that Nijinsky's use of the word 'tunic' is treated more specifically for our own purposes: the word 'veil' being used for the first two parts of the dress taken off by N5; '1st veil' being easier to fit into the score than '1st part of the dress'. The third part, the largest, is called 'the dress'.

MEASURE		LITERAL TRANSLATION	OUR INTERPRETATION
1	F	"Holding the flute at the lips"	Same
16	F	"Puts down the flute and takes a bunch of grapes"	Same
17	F	"Holding and looking at bunch of grapes"	Looks at bunch of grapes
17 (end)	F	"Puts down one bunch of grapes and takes another"	Same
18	F	"Holding and looking at grapes"	Looks at bunch of grapes
20 (end)	F	"Hold flute"	Same
21	F	"Hold the flute at the lips"	Same
21	N2	"Hold the tunic of the first nymph"	Holds the tunic of the 1st nymph
25	N4	"Holding the tunic"	Same
27	N5	"Hold the tunic"	Holds her tunic
31	F	"Flute at the lips"	Same
31	N5	"Opens out part of the dress"	Undoes 1st veil
31	N5	"Smooths her dress"	Smooths 1st veil
33	N5	"She throws away the first part of her dress"	Drops 1st veil
34	N5	"Opens out second part of tunic"	Undoes 2nd veil
34	N5	"Smooths her dress"	Smooths 2nd veil
35	F	"Holding flute"	Same
36	F	"Putting flute down"	Same
36	N5	"Throwing away second part of tunic"	Drops 2nd veil
41	N1	"Keeps her hands down"	Not used (meaning not clear)
41	N3	"Keeps her hands down"	Not used (meaning not clear)
41	N4	"Keeps hand of seventh nymph"	Not used
41	N6	"Keeping hand"	Not used
42	N4	"Keeping seventh nymph"	Keeps hand of 7th nymph
42	F	"Stairs"	Same
44	N6	"Having taken the tunic"	Picks up 1st veil
44	N6	"Hangs at the elbow"	1st veil hangs on elbows
45	N1	"Holding the lower part of the tunica"	Holds lower part of her tunic
45	N2	"Holding hand"	Not used
45	N3	"Tunica hangs at the elbow"	2nd veil hangs on elbows
45	N6, N7	"Tunica hangs at the elbow"	1st veil hangs on left elbow
46	N1	"Hold"	Not used

APPENDIX C

MEASURE		LITERAL TRANSLATION	OUR INTERPRETATION
46	N2	"Hold"	Not used
46	N3	"Tunica hangs at the elbow"	Not used
46	N6	"Tunica hangs at the elbow"	Not used
51	N5	"Opens out third part of tunica"	Loosens the dress
52	N5	"Throwing away third part of tunica"	Drops the dress
54	N5	"Having taken one part of the dress"	Picks up dress
54	N5	"Holding the dress"	Same
59	N5	"Holding the dress"	Not used
73	N5	"Putting on one part of the dress"	Holds one part of the dress
74	F	"Pointing with his thumb like a horn"	Same
74	N5	"Having taken the dress"	Takes the dress
75	N5	"Holding the dress" (2x)	Not used
77	N3	"Holding the hand of seventh nymph"	Not used
88	F	"Having taken the dress"	Picks up the dress near edge
89	F	"Puts the dress on his elbow joints"	Puts dress over his elbow joints
90	F	"Laughs like an animal"	Same
91	F	"Laughs like an animal"	Same
92	above the score	"N6 (makes a step forward)"	N6 steps in front
100	F	"The dress lies on the elbow joints and the palms, holds it more at the edge"	Same
100	F	Stairs	Same
102	F	"Looks at the dress"	Same
103	F	"Smells the dress"	Same

APPENDIX D

Teaching Notes

Styles of Walking Sequences

Nijinsky's choreographic score reveals several variations in walking patterns. Before learning the ballet it is important to practise these walks holding the body in the appropriate position: legs parallel (feet pointing forward); a twist in the upper body (shoulder line) with head retaining the direction of the feet; arms in the appropriate position for each variation. The sequences given here are in the order in which they appear in the ballet and contain the details given by Nijinsky. These details should be practised even though they are less obvious at performance tempo.

Ex. A shows the first simple walk toward stage left, with the left arm gesturing into the direction of travel, the right arm down with hand curved. The walk should be quite natural, fluent and simple. For the leg which has just released weight there should, however, be an awareness of contact with the ground on the ball of the foot. There is no extra 'picking up' action between steps. It should be noted that the timing of the steps on this entrance is two steps evenly covering three beats of music: thus four steps are taken in the time of six beats.

In Ex. B the forward steps toward stage right are quicker and performed with slightly bent legs. The left arm is raised sideward from the shoulder (backward from Stance), the hand curved and some distance above the shoulder.

Ex. C shows the swift backward steps which follow Ex. B. These steps are on high half-toe: the ball of the foot is supporting the lifted body. The last step lowers the body to normal standing, the right foot resting on the floor in front. In this backward walk, though each foot must of course reach backward to take a step, no specific, active gesture as such is performed.

Ex. D is the entrance step of the chief nymph (N5), who covers ground with high steps on the $3/4$ ball. Her importance is reflected by the level of these steps and by the fact that between each step her foot stretches as it advances. Her left arm indicates the direction in which she is traveling; the right is backward low, rounded, the hand holding her tunic. Once this entrance step has been practised for style it should be placed correctly on the music: the preparatory gesture for each step - while not marked or exaggerated - should take place on the beat so that the actual step occurs on the 'and' count. This slight delay in taking the steps requires practice to master. The leg gestures showing the style described by Nijinsky are included in the notation.

Ex. E is the entrance walk used by both N6 and N7. Here the timing is also off the beat (as in Ex. D), but the legs are very slightly bent and slightly bent leg gestures lead into each step. The notation for this leg gesture shows the leg to be forward low with the knee slightly bent (folded). Note the head position on this entrance. Both nymphs are late; they come in after the chief nymph, and their lowered heads suggest an apologetic air. While the

APPENDIX D 183

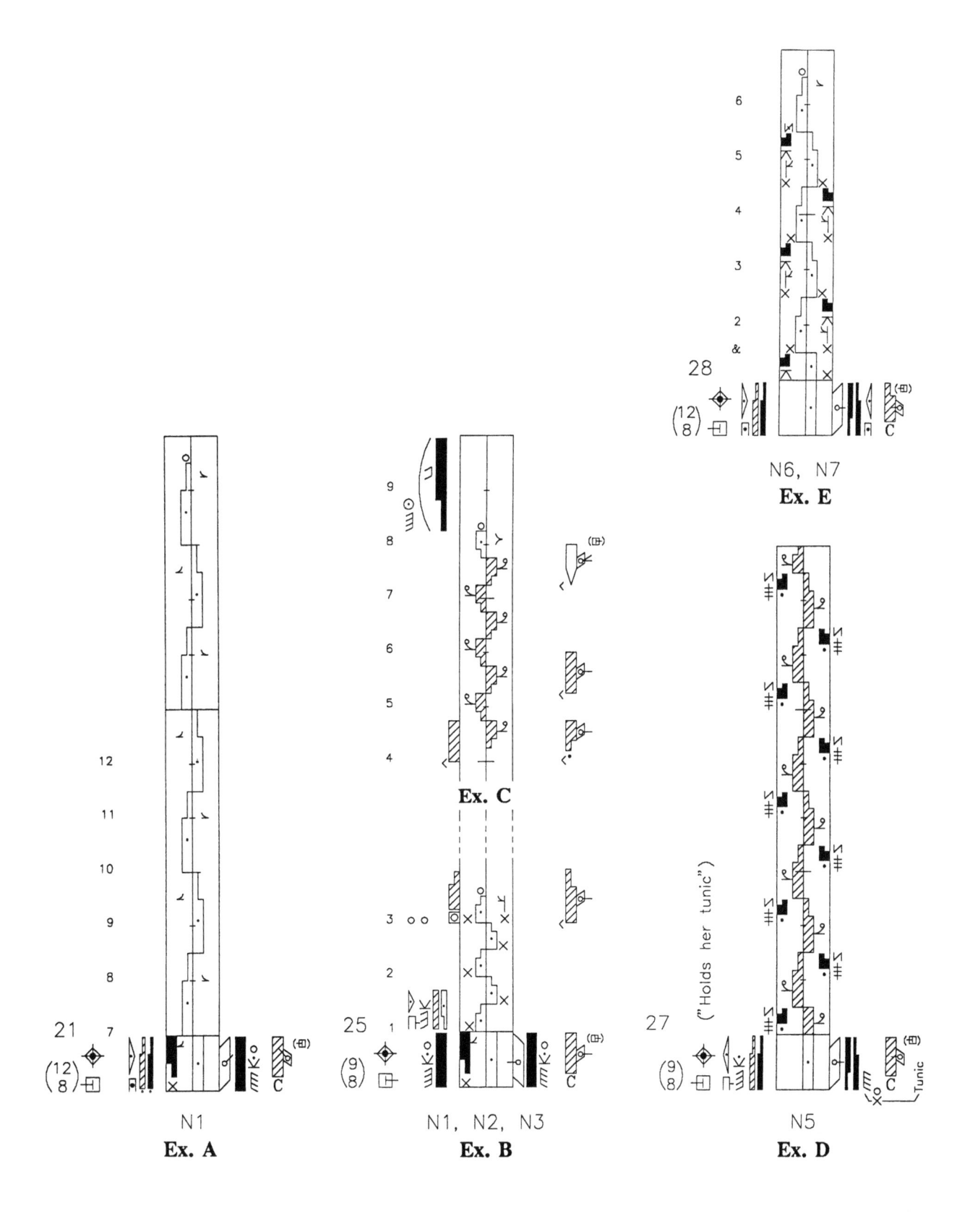

N6, N7
Ex. E

N1
Ex. A

N1, N2, N3
Ex. B

Ex. C

N5
Ex. D

first three nymphs entered with ordinary walking steps, the slight knee flexion here suggests that N6 and N7 do not wish to be observed arriving late.

Ex. F is the walking pattern which occurs when N6 and N7 ease into their places in line with the other nymphs. The slower steps with pauses between create a cross rhythm, i.e., a rhythm countering that of the music. While this 'countering' produces a much more interesting effect than would be achieved by following the rhythm of the music, it is difficult for dancers to master. Their inner rhythmic pulse must be steady in order for them to maintain their time pattern even when the music seems to urge them to move faster, i.e., to take steps without pauses between them.

Ex. G is performed only by N5. Steps in place occur rarely. This is an important moment, when the chief nymph appears to be 'bathing' and performs what can well be understood as 'paddling' steps. The foot pattern is akin to what is often called 'feathering', a soft rising and lowering in which the feet clearly articulate. After performing this 'up-down-down, up-down-down' pattern, she lifts the lower leg in preparation for each of the two backward steps, as though she is stepping out of a pool.

Ex. H shows a rhythmically uneven step pattern on high half-toe with slightly bent legs. It is performed first by N4 (the joyful nymph), who appears to be bubbling with energy and high spirits. During a quiet waiting period she becomes inattentive and 'wanders off' on her own with this rhythmic step, her arms raised in a high angled shape. For this step foot articulation is important. The leg gestures Nijinsky recorded before each step have been omitted, as they occur naturally. While these steps are light and high they should not be sprung: i.e., there is no intentional rising off the ground. The other five supporting nymphs join in this brief lapse of attention, performing the same step pattern.

Ex. I occurs when the six attending nymphs return to their duties and 'pull themselves together': their steps are on high lifted half-toe, similar in style and timing to the entrance step of the chief nymph.

Ex. J is the difficult exiting leaping sequence performed by N4 after she unexpectedly encounters the faun. She turns and exits stage left, leaping from foot to foot, her legs being slightly bent during the leap and on the landing, which is on half-toe. Nijinsky wrote this exit step with more detail than can comfortably be mastered. He indicates the torso as inclining forward slightly on each landing, as though the nymph is panting. The impression is that she may have mixed feelings. If she were really scared she would merely run off as fast as possible. But she is looking back at the faun, perhaps wondering if he is going to follow her. It is not a comfortable step pattern to perform; perhaps we can assume that she is not at ease, not sure how she feels about the encounter.

Ex. K is for N1 and N2, the last two attending nymphs to leave after all five have stood observing the faun. They exit stage right with smooth, fairly low steps. This is the first instance of such low level steps. Later N5 exits with the same steps. The leg gestures which Nijinsky indicated before each step occur naturally in such a walk and need not be stressed.

APPENDIX D 185

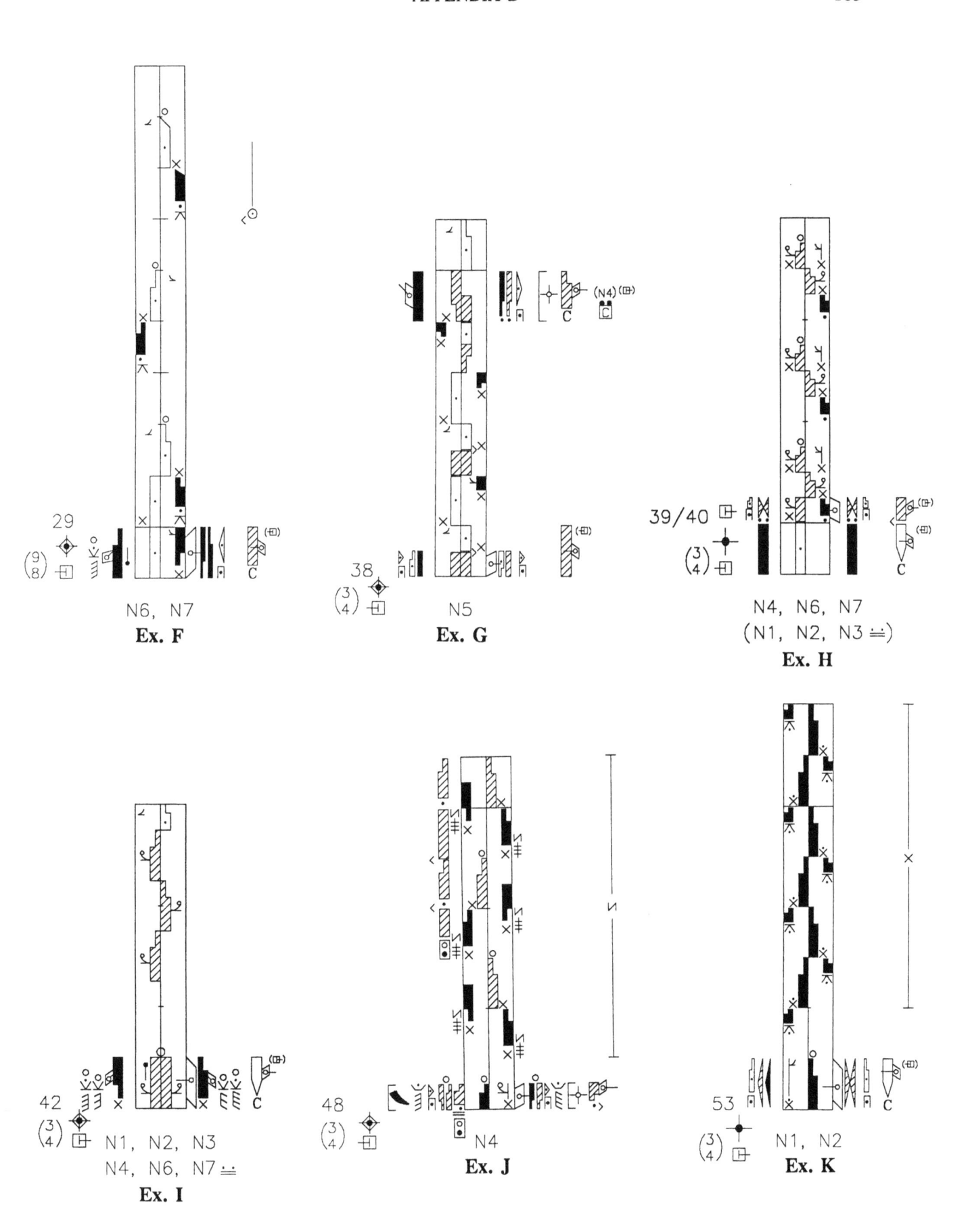

N6, N7
Ex. F

N5
Ex. G

N4, N6, N7
(N1, N2, N3 ≐)
Ex. H

N1, N2, N3
N4, N6, N7 ≐
Ex. I

N4
Ex. J

N1, N2
Ex. K

Ex. L shows the high uplifted footsteps used by the faun as he walks to and fro just behind the chief nymph. Nijinsky did not state length of step, but the indication of leg gestures before each step suggests striding out, which the faun must do to pass beyond N5. With these steps he appears to be dominating her, expressing his internal energy and feelings. Note the indication that his weight is placed forward: such forward placement helps him cover ground.

Ex. M shows N5's low steps when she is walking at the same time as the faun and in the same direction. Her left arm is backward as though repulsing him.

Ex. N illustrates N5's steps in measure 71 when both the faun and N5 walk to and fro with low steps. Because distance of traveling is reduced and steps are smaller, the knees remain close together. On this step both dancers have the torso contracted over the diagonal back surface nearest the audience. From this walk one has the impression that she is feeling 'under his shadow' or in some way dominated. She seems uncertain and hence self-protective, the latter feeling being expressed by her arm gestures, which enfold her body, covering it with the last part of her dress.

Ex. O shows the exit step for N2 and N6, who travel with high steps on slightly bent legs. The nymphs prepare for each step by stretching the foot, but with a slightly bent knee. Each foot is stretched when in the air; in performance it is difficult not to exaggerate the slight spring on this exiting step.

Placement of the Arms

In **Details on Movement Style and Usage**, p. 24, much specific information is given for the variations in placement of arms and hands. A great deal of practice is required for the dancers to be able both to reach the correct destinations and to hold their arms and hands without stiffness. Achieving the flatness of arms in relation to the body (the shoulder line) is not easy. Often the elbow is too far backward, or the wrist is angled - 'bulging out' instead of being straight. The hand must be in line with the shaft of the lower arm.

These arm positions require a special awareness of space around the body - an awareness quite different from that experienced in the familiar placement of arms in ballet. It is an awareness of design of quite another kind. Dancers should work with a mirror and should help one another by watching for incorrect movement.

Nijinsky employed subtle variations in the basic arm positions, some positions being a little higher, some a little lower. In the notation those that are a little lower are written with a dot before the direction symbol. It is better to practise the standard directions (shown by the symbols) first, **then** learn to arrive at the slightly lower position for each gesture.

Keeping the hands flat (but not stiff) requires practice: it is easy to forget the flatness and allow the hands to become three-dimensional, with articulated fingers, thus destroying the desired effect. In each change from one position to another the moment of arrival should be made clear with respect to both space and time but it should not be abrupt. A negative tension should be avoided; but 'attention', the aliveness that makes the audience notice particular gestures, should be present.

APPENDIX D 187

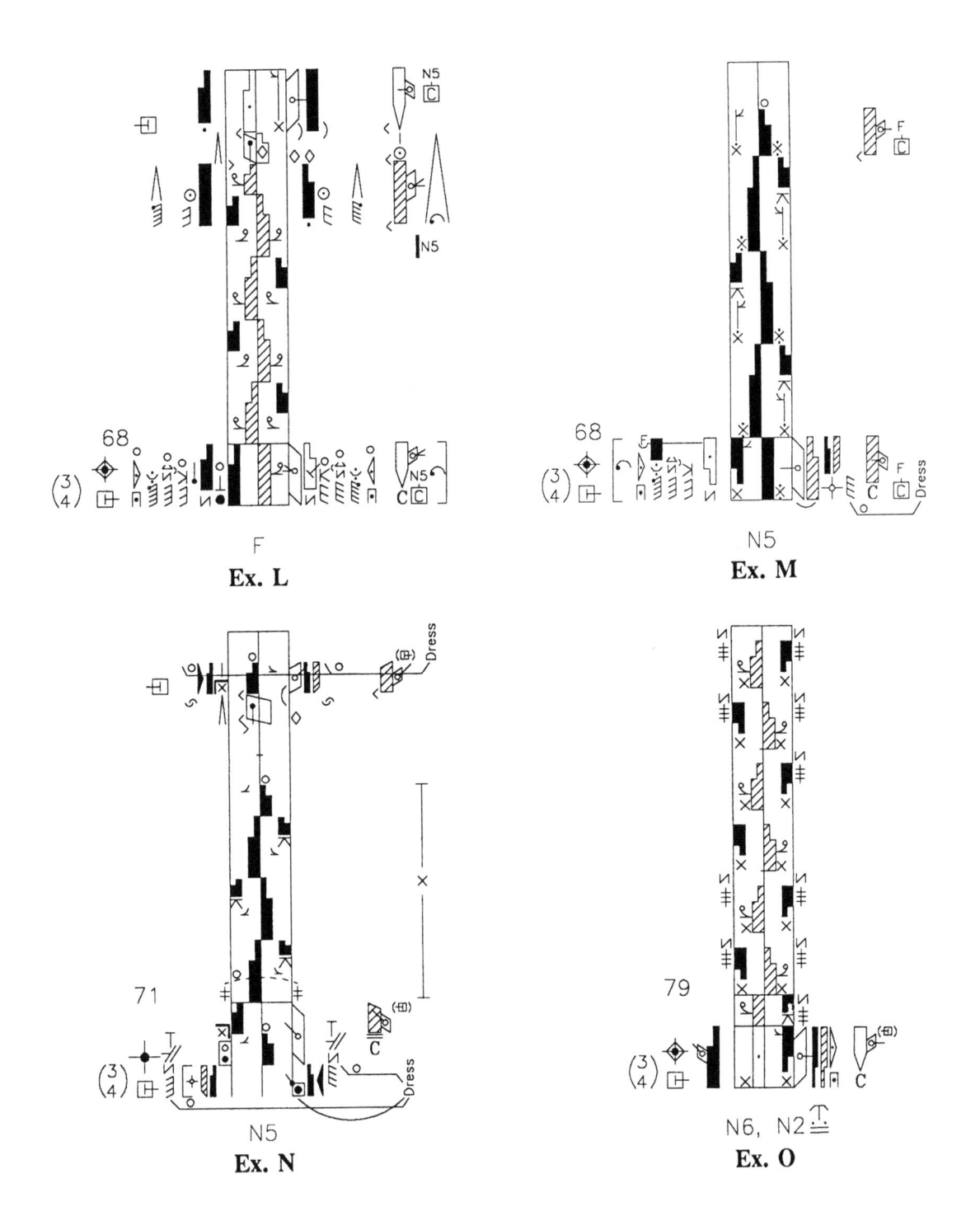

Ex. L

Ex. M

Ex. N

Ex. O

Because the choreography seems sparse and simple, mastering it appears to pose no challenge and the need for extra practice is not felt. On the contrary, the very simplicity and unfamiliarity of the movement require that the walks and arm gestures be rehearsed constantly, just as virtuoso movements (for example, quadruple pirouettes) would be assiduously practised.

The Head Alignments

Holding the head in opposition to the shoulder line can be a strain at first; it takes practice to arrive at the desired position with neck and shoulders relaxed. As can be seen from the de Meyer photographs (see **Photographs** pp. 58-70), the dancers' shoulder lines are not always square to the audience. Care should be taken, however, to achieve sufficient upper body turn for the audience to receive a distinct impression of two-dimensional flatness. We do not know, of course, how far the nymphs' performances fell short of what Nijinsky wanted. Striving for full profile in rehearsal can result in too much tension; nevertheless, practice to achieve the natural, easy effect must continue.

The tilt of the head is very important. Experience has shown that few dancers are familiar with a true forward head inclination (forward high), and find it difficult to incline the head without involving the upper body. Yet it is just this use of the head which expresses a certain **inward** focus, as in the 2nd nymph's 'shyness' on entering, N6 and N7's 'apology' for being late, and when all six take their apology pose after having wandered off and 'neglected' their duties to the chief nymph. This head inclination must be marked in such a way that it will be seen clearly. While the upper body is not included, it is also not specifically (actively) excluded - 'active' exclusion would produce inappropriate tension in the shoulder area.

It is the 'alert' head position which poses a real challenge during rehearsals. Because the build of neck and head varies greatly among dancers, what produces the right expression in one performer must be less - or more - exaggerated in another. It is important to establish clearly **when** the alert head position appears: a logical reason for its occurring will make it easier to master. Analysis of the score shows that it occurs for the attending nymphs when they are 'on duty'. The alert position produces an active, alive expression which is in contrast to the more relaxed, normal head position of the first three nymphs when they enter, when they wander off, and at certain other 'off duty' moments. The main feature, as described in **Details on Movement Style and Usage**, p. 22, is the lengthening of the back of the neck, which produces a slight upward shift of the head and a resultant very slight drawing in of the chin. In such resultant movements the body part is not energized, i.e., adjustment is allowed to happen but is not featured. During the alert head position the eye-line remains forward, i.e., there is no lowering of the gaze.

Change of System of Reference Key

Nijinsky wrote his score completely in the Body Key - he had no other choice; yet the choreography predominantly demands a Stance Key. As mentioned before, the Labanotation score makes use of the Standard Key, the Stance Key and occasionally the Body Key. When gestures relate to the body the Standard Key is used, the Stance Key being given for gestures relating to the path of travel. In a few instances decisions on choice of key were based on which key most facilitated reading; for example, symmetrical arm poses are more quickly read when written in the Standard rather than in the Stance Key (see **Details on Movement Style and Usage, pp. 25-26**).

The degree of upper body twist is not always the same. When a ¼ twist occurs, the direction for arm gestures can be read as easily from Standard as from Stance. However, when ⅛ or 7/16 twist occurs, use of the Stance Key is much clearer.

The chart below, which begins with the entrance of the nymphs, is designed to show transitions from use of the Stance Key to the Standard, with an indication of why a key change occurs. The faun's transitions are shown after he has come down the steps. Study of this chart reveals much about both the character of and the motivation for the movement phrases.

When and Why Changes Take Place

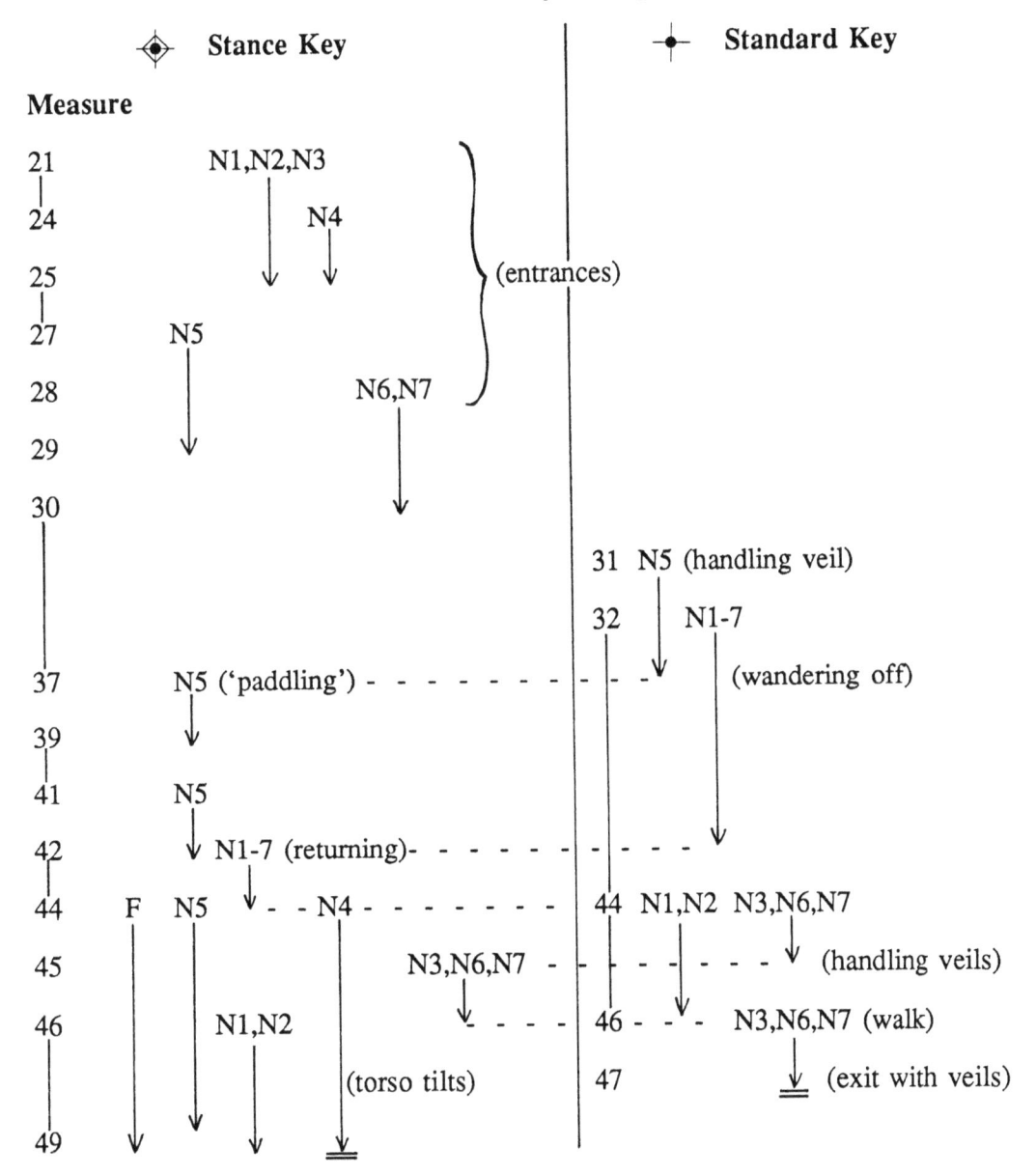

◆ **Stance Key**   ✚ **Standard Key**

Measure

Measure	Stance Key	Standard Key
21	N1,N2,N3	
24	N4	(entrances)
25	↓ ↓	
27	N5	
28	N6,N7	
29	↓	
30		
31		N5 (handling veil)
32		N1-7
37	N5 ('paddling') - - - - - - - - ↓	(wandering off)
39	↓	
41	N5	
42	↓ N1-7 (returning) - - - - - - - -	
44	F N5 ↓ - - N4 - - - - - - -	44 N1,N2 N3,N6,N7
45	N3,N6,N7 - - - - - - ↓	(handling veils)
46	N1,N2 ↓ - - -	46 - - ↓ - N3,N6,N7 (walk)
47	(torso tilts)	↓ (exit with veils)
49	↓ ↓ ↓	

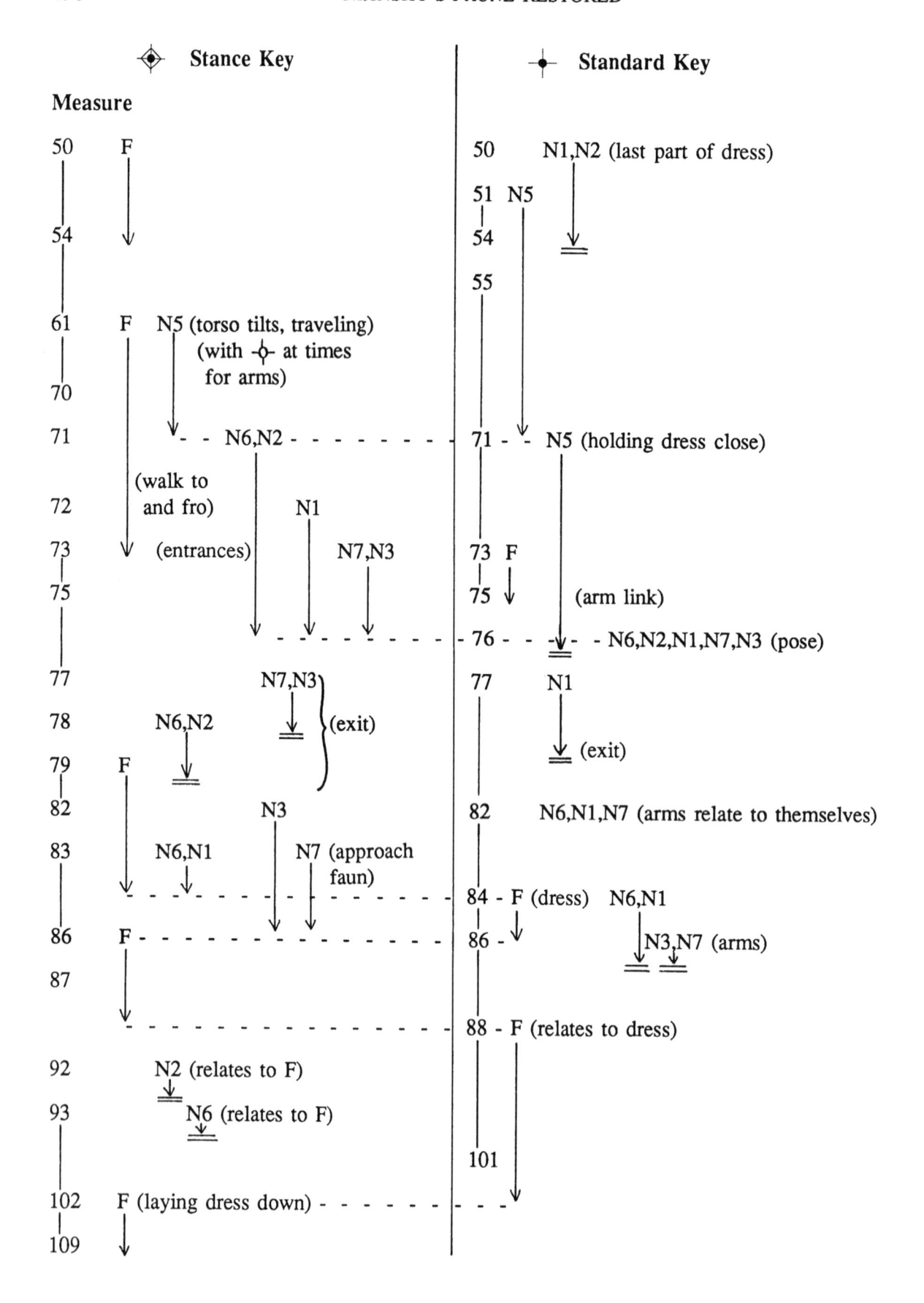

NIJINSKY'S *FAUNE* RESTORED

◆ Stance Key　　　　　　　　　　✦ Standard Key

Measure

Stance Key	Standard Key
50　F	50　　N1,N2 (last part of dress)
｜	51　N5
54　↓	｜
	54
	55
61　F　N5 (torso tilts, traveling)	
｜　　(with ◆ at times	
｜　　for arms)	
70	
71　↓- - N6,N2 - - - - - - - - -	71 - - ↓ - N5 (holding dress close)
｜　(walk to	
72　 and fro)　 N1	
73　↓ (entrances)　N7,N3	73　F
｜	｜
75	75　↓　(arm link)
｜　　　　　↓　↓　↓	
	- - - 76 - - ↓ - - N6,N2,N1,N7,N3 (pose)
77　　　　　N7,N3⎫	77　　N1
78　 N6,N2　 ↓ ⎬(exit)	
79　F　 ↓ ⎭	↓ (exit)
｜	
82　　　　　　N3	82　　N6,N1,N7 (arms relate to themselves)
83　 N6,N1　 N7 (approach	
｜　 ↓　 ↓　 faun)	
- - - - - - - - - - - - - - - - -	84 - F (dress)　N6,N1
86　F - - - - - - - - - - - - -	86 - ↓
87	↓ N3,N7 (arms)
↓	
- - - - - - - - - - - - - - - - -	88 - F (relates to dress)
92　　N2 (relates to F)	
｜　　 ↓	
93　　　 N6 (relates to F)	
｜　　　 ↓	
	101
	↓
102　F (laying dress down) - - - - - - - - - -
｜
109　↓

Floor Plans

Because floor plans are so easy to read, enlarged sheets of plans placed on the studio wall will help the dancers see their placement on stage in relation to each other and to their line of travel. Length of step does not exist in Nijinsky's system and is rarely given in the Labanotation score; performers must gauge their distances carefully in order to arrive at the right place. In rehearsing the ballet much time is spent achieving the correct spacing; therefore the floor plans must be given constant careful attention.

Music Recording

The following orchestral recording of the *Prélude à l'Après-midi d'un Faune* has been found to be the most suitable for rehearsals:

Berlin Philharmonic Orchestra
H. von Karajan - conductor
Karlheinz Zoller - solo flute

Recorded by Deutsche Grammophon Gesellschaft 1965
Reference No. 923075

APPENDIX E

Transcription - Adjustments Made

For future researchers some account of the task we faced in this Nijinsky project may be of interest. Inevitably problems arose and decisions had to be made, to a surprising degree these were minor.

The perfection of any score takes time and a trained eye is needed to proofread the final draft. Nijinsky's score of *Faune* was not proofread, as is evident from the many small mistakes to be found. Had he himself gone carefully through the score he would have discovered most of them. This he obviously did not do. In addition the score is slightly incomplete. We do not know why he dropped the project without, for example, writing in all the rest of the floor plans, plans which were greatly needed and the absence of which made mounting the work difficult. The amount of travel on stage, the proximity of the dancers, etc., had to be determined by trial and error.

In two other respects the score is unfinished. For N3 in measure 45 Nijinsky's wording states "Tunica hangs at the elbow", yet just previous to that N3's staff was left blank; no movement is indicated for such picking up of the veil as is given for N6 in measure 44. Our solution for N3 was to give her the same kind of movement in picking up the veil as was indicated for N6. At the end, when the faun carries the dress up to his rock, there is detailed notation until the very final movements, for which only a skeletal indication is given. Perhaps Nijinsky had not decided what detail to include for the faun's final lying down on the dress. Certainly the score is unfinished, for in a measure of 4/4 he has indicated movement for only three beats - the fourth beat is missing. Since Nijinsky was meticulous in accounting for every beat in every measure, no matter how intricate the rhythm, there is no question that the notation is unfinished in this measure. For the faun's final movements we decided to use only the outline, the simplicity of which has proved to be dramatically effective for the last moments of the ballet.

When we consider that Nijinsky was not a trained notator, we realize how remarkable is the careful detail in his score. That there are errors does not change the value of the score. It was easy to determine that a notation indication was an error and what it should have been, because he wrote out each dancer's part fully, including all the repeats; thus the correct notation was nearby. Movement logic also came into play: for example, at the very end he wrote that the faun lay down sideward horizontal (instead of forward horizontal). Probably a slip of the pencil placed the music note in the space instead of on the line. It could be questioned that he had decided in this score to record a different ending. Such is hardly likely to be the case, since he also gives the detail that the instep of each foot is contacting the floor, a position which is impossible when lying on the side.

Nijinsky recorded too many measures in his score. Debussy's music contains only 110 measures and research confirmed that other versions of the music do not exist. The extra measures at the end may have resulted from the pronounced *rallentando* that takes place:

Nijinsky may have lost track of the beats. Could differences between the measures point to the possibility that he had scored the choreography long before in a rough draft and that he only wrote the final score in Budapest without Debussy's score at hand? Two other measures were inserted shortly before measure 79 where the music so clearly returns to the main theme. To bring music and dance together at this point we had to telescope the previous walking patterns for the nymphs, merely allowing them less time to achieve the exiting sequences than Nijinsky had indicated.

The available photographs of Nijinsky in the ballet provided verification of the fact that he had written the ballet as originally premiered in 1912, and gave us valuable clues to details not immediately clear in the score.

In bringing to life the movements he wrote, we had to make certain adjustments. For example, it is impossible to perform up to tempo all the details he wrote for the various walking patterns. As with Saint-Léon and others who painstakingly analyzed in slow motion the movement sequences they wanted to write, Nijinsky recorded the preparatory leg gesture before each step (the natural bringing forward of the leg prior to its taking weight). At a slow pace this gesture is important and can be carefully performed, but to articulate the gesture fully during faster steps becomes impossibly artificial, even grotesque. While his details are noted and are discussed with the dancers in mounting the ballet to give them an image of what he had in mind, in practice these details cannot be fully achieved.

His use of stage facing numbers (his Front Signs) above the top line of the staff puzzled us until a complete tabulation of where they occured in relation to other movement factors revealed that they referred to the direction of travel. He stated this in addition to the stage direction faced and the direction of the steps. His need for this extra indication became apparent when the dancers pass one another or the faun must travel slightly more downstage or upstage. Such veering off the usual path occurs while the dancers are still facing the stage right or stage left direction. This subtle detail helped in determining the floor plans and also revealed how meticulously Nijinsky had recorded the sequences. In measure 84 we had to reverse his veering instructions. If N6 and N1 veer downstage as they move to stage right after chastising the faun, the next two nymphs, N7 and N3, are hidden behind them just when it is their turn to perform the chastising sequence. For the audience sight-lines it seemed important that N7 and N3 be seen for the full movement phrase.

Although Nijinsky had signs for touching (contact) which he applied to the hands, he did not attempt to indicate specifically how the veils were handled. However, the arm movements and positions he indicated provided a basis on which to experiment with suitable pieces of cloth. Logical ways were found of achieving what was needed without deviating from his recorded instructions.

The question has been raised as to how much Nijinsky, in writing down the ballet in 1915, intentionally changed the 1912 choreography. Comparisons with the de Meyer photographs show only two places where there is a slight variation in arm placement. One of these is the pose on measure 76: the photograph shows a different nymph with her head turned the other way and with the other hand raised near her shoulder. This variation does not at all change the intent of the pose and is the kind of detail that could so easily be forgotten; he may have cogitated as to which of the center nymphs was facing the other way?

Among the available photographs of the 1912 production there are some poses that are not found in Nijinsky's score. Were these poses arranged just for the camera? This is very likely to be the case: we are familiar with such composite, arranged poses of performers in a ballet, configurations which do not appear in the ballet itself. For example, there is the encounter of the faun and N4. The de Meyer photograph shows the moment as it occurs in the score but in Nijinska's *Early Memoirs* the photograph of illustration 103 shows the faun and N4 facing the opposite direction. Was this a misprint, the negative having been turned around? N4 has her left arm up, hand near shoulder, a pose she never takes in the score; the photograph may well have been posed to show brother and sister together.

At each point in the reconstruction process we resisted being influenced by current performances of the ballet, or, indeed, even by details remembered from the 1912 performances by individuals such as his sister Bronislava, when these details were not found in his score. It was imperative that what we produced should be the ballet as Nijinsky wrote it. There is ample evidence that what has resulted is extremely close to the original production.

Details on which we had to make decisions were very minor compared with the ballet as a whole. From the specific timing of the movements so carefully recorded by Nijinsky emerged a manner of performance often at odds with memory-based versions.

Interpretation of the score has been the result of evaluating the movement configurations and the relationships between the dancers as indicated by the context; there has been no intentional imposition of any personal ideas on the outcome.

In any production subtle changes inevitably take place when each dance artist takes on a rôle; such changes produced by individual personality and physique must always be allowed for. The dancer's personal interpretation and expression as well as body form will inevitably produce minor changes and often a different 'look'; but any personal mannerisms that enter need not become part of the choreography and the basis for future interpretations. Now that the score is written here for posterity, the work itself, its basic structure, need not change. As with the great classics in music, individual interpretations will vary, but the notes, the work itself will remain, uncorrupted by the vagaries of memory and the temptations of dancers to insert their own material. Nijinsky's *Faune* will endure as he recorded it.

APPENDIX F

Bibliography

Nijinsky's *Faune*

Acocella, Joan.	"Photo Call with Nijinsky: The Circle and the Center". *Ballet Review*, 14, No. 4, pp. 49-71, New York, 1987.
Adler, Alfred.	Preface to "The Diary of Vaslav Nijinsky". *Archives of General Psychiatry*, Vol. 38, No. 7, pp. 834-841, Chicago, 1981.
Beaumont, C. W.	*Complete Book of Ballets*, rev. ed., London, 1951.
Beaumont, C. W.	*Diaghilev*, London, 1933.
Beaumont, C. W.	*The Diaghilev Ballet in London*, London, 1940.
Beaumont, C. W.	*Vaslav Nijinsky*, London, 1932.
Benois, A.	*Reminiscences of the Russian Ballet*, London, 1941.
Benois, A.	*Memoirs*, Vol. II, London, 1964.
Bowlt, J. E.	"Die Ballets Russes". *Die Maler und die Theater im 20.Jahrhundert*, Schirn, Kunsthalle, Frankfurt. Exhibition, 1 March - 19 May, 1986.
Buckle, Richard.	*Diaghilev*, London, 1979.
Buckle, Richard.	*Nijinsky*, 2nd Edition, London, 1980.
Fokine, M.	*Fokine. Memoirs of a Ballet Master*, London, 1961.
Garafola, Lynn.	*Diaghilev's Ballets Russes*, New York, 1989.
Garafola, Lynn.	"Vaslav Nijinsky". *Raritan*, Vol. 8, No. 1, pp. 1-27, New Brunswick, 1988.
Gold, A., Fizdale, R.	*Misia. The Life of Misia Sert*, New York, 1980.
Grigoriev, S. L.	*The Diaghilev Ballet 1909-1929*, London, 1953.
Gross, Valentine.	*Nijinsky on Stage*, London 1971.

Haskell, A.	*Diaghileff*, London, 1935.
Hutchinson Guest, A., Jeschke, C., Nectoux, J-M., Nèagu, P.	*Nijinsky. Prélude à l'Après-midi d'un Faune*, Paris, 1989.
Karsavina, T.	*Theatre Street*, rev. ed. London, 1981.
Kirstein, Lincoln.	*Nijinsky Dancing*, New York, 1975.
Kochno, Boris.	*Diaghilev et les Ballets Russes*, Paris, 1973.
Krasovskaya, Vera.	*Nijinsky*, New York, 1979.
Lieven, Prince Peter.	*The Birth of the Ballets Russes*, New York, 1973.
Lifar, S.	*Diaghilev*, London, 1940.
Lifar, S.	*A History of Russian Ballet*, London, 1954.
Lockspeiser, E.	*Debussy, His Life and Mind*, Vol. II, London, 1965.
MacDonald, Nesta.	*Diaghilev Observed by Critics in England and in the United States, 1911-1929*, New York/London, 1975.
Magriel, Paul. (ed.)	*Nijinsky - An Illustrated Monograph*, New York, 1946
Magriel, Paul. (ed.)	*Nijinsky, Pavlova, Duncan: Three Lives in Dance*, New York, 1977.
Massine, L.	*My Life in Ballet*, London, 1968.
Mayer, C. S.	"The Influence of Leon Bakst on Choreography". *Dance Chronicle*, Vol. 1, No. 2, pp. 127-142, New York, 1977/78.
Meyer, Adolf de.	*L'Après-midi d'un Faune. Vaslav Nijinsky 1912*, New York/London, 1983.
Niehaus, M. (ed.)	*Nijinsky. Gast aus einer anderen Welt*, Munich, 1961.
Nijinska, Bronislava.	*Early Memoirs*, New York, 1981.
Nijinsky, Romola.	*Nijinsky*, London, 1933.
Nijinsky, Vaslav.	*The Diary of Vaslav Nijinsky*, ed. by Romola Nijinsky, New York, 1936.
Propert, N.	*The Russian Ballet*, London, 1921.

Rambert, Marie. *Quicksilver*, London 1972.

Reiss, Françoise. *Nijinsky ou la Grâce. Esthétique et Psychologie*, Paris, 1957.

Sokolova, Lydia. *Dancing for Diaghilev*, ed. by Richard Buckle, London, 1960.

Whitworth, Geoffrey. *The Art of Nijinsky*, New York, 1914.

Nijinsky's Notation System

Gorsky, A. *Table of Signs for writing movements of the human body according to the system of the Artist of the Imperial Theatres of St. Petersburg, V. I. Stepanov*, The Imperial St. Petersburg Theatre School, 1899 (in Russian).

Nijinska, B. *Early Memoirs*, New York, 1981.

Stepanow, W. J. *Alphabet des Mouvements du Corps Humain*, Paris, 1892.

Stepanow, W. J. *Alphabet of Movements of the Human Body*, Cambridge, England, 1958 (English translation).

Wiley, R. J. *Two Essays on Stepanov Dance Notation by Alexander Gorsky*, New York, 1958 (English translation).

INDEX

Entries of technical notation terms are followed by (LN) when referring to Labanotation and (VN) when referring to Nijinsky's system of notation. Other entries of technical terms refer to the style of the choreography rather than to notation. '(ill.)' means the item is illustrated by a drawing or photograph.

Abduction of ankle, 161
   - thumb, 34, 40, 42, 44
   - wrist, 27, 34, 40, 50 (LN), 151 (VN), 153-154 (VN)
Accelerando, 20
Accents, 2, 54 (LN)
Accidentals, 147 (LN),
   - cancelling 163 (VN), 165-166 (VN), 173 (VN)
Adduction, 150 (VN)
   - of wrist, 153 (VN)
'Alert' attention, 20
   - head position, 2, 21-22 (LN), 35-39, 42, 51-53 (LN), 188
   - torso, 17
Alignment of head, 188
Amalgamated turn, 49 (LN)
Angled thumb, 27, 34, 40-42, 44, 46, 50 (LN), 66 (ill.), 151 (VN/LN)
   - wrist, 37-39, 41, 50 (LN), 186
Ankle abduction, 161
   - extension, 159
   - flexion, 19, 40, 50 (LN), 151 (VN), 154 (VN), 160, 166
'Apology', 1, 38, 182, 188
Après-midi d'un Faune, L', xi, 1, 3-5, 11, 17-18, 145, 179, 196
   - abbreviation: *Faune*, xi, 1-8, 11-12, 17-18, 21, 25, 55, 145-146, 152-155, 157-160, 163-166, 170, 173, 175-177, 179, 192, 194-195
   - cast, 12, 14, 177-178
   - deciphering, 7-11
   - film, 7
   - music, xi, 2, 4-5, 19-20, 32, 147 (VN), 191-193
   - productions, 11
   - production notes, 12-15
   - revival of, 8-11
   - score, 5, 13, 28, 71-139 (LN), 142 (ill.), 145
   - teaching notes, 182-191
   - transcription of score, 11, 25, 146,
   - - adjustments made, 192-194
   - wording, 180-181
Archer, Kenneth, 3
Arm(s), 24, 49 (LN)
   - crossed, 168 (VN)
   - curved, 28
   - directional description for, 26
   - flexion, 151 (VN)
   - gestures, line of, 17
   - - timing for, 20

Arm(s), intermediate directions, 49 (LN)
   - key for, 172 (VN)
   - placement of, 186
   - positions, 'crooked', 24, 38-39, 41, 46
   - - frequently used, 24
   - - lower, 149 (VN), 151 (VN), 156 (VN), 186
   - - practising, 37-38, 56 (LN), 182, 184, 186, 188, 193
   - - upper, 148 (VN), 150 (VN), 155 (VN)
   - shape of, 24, 184
   - supporting on, 158 (VN)
   - system of reference for, 25-26, 172 (VN)
Articulations, 151 (VN), 184
Assemblé, 166 (VN)
Auditorium, Los Angeles, 178
Augmented chest, column for, 51 (LN)
Autography, 54 (LN)
Awareness, 52 (LN)

Bach, Johann Sebastian, 8
Bakst, Léon, 4
Ball of foot, 48 (LN), 159 (VN), 182
Ballet exercises (Cecchetti), 8, 9 (ill.), 172, 179
Ballets Inachevés, Les, 8
Ballets Russes, 4, 6, 18
bas relief, 8, 18, 145, 179
Basket, 14, 16, 29, 34
Bathing, 36-37, 43, 184
Battement, grand, 172 (VN)
   - *petits sur le cou-de-pied*, 161 (VN)
Beck, Jill, 11
Bending for the head, 154 (VN)
   - motion of, 49 (VN)
Bereda, Eleonora Nicolaevna, 3
Bert, 1, 69 (ill.)
Body, 23, 148 (VN)
   - flat, 2, 17, 186, 188
   - Key (Cross of Axes), 25, 172, 188
   - indication of (principal divisions), 148 (VN)
   - part(s), direction from, 51 (LN)
   - - major, 148 (VN)
   - - minor, 148 (VN)
   - - minor directions of, 150 (VN)
   - - supporting on, 158
   - - 1st degree part, 148 (VN), 150 (VN)
   - - 2nd degree part, 149 (VN), 151, 153
   - - 3rd degree part, 149 (VN), 151, 155

INDEX

Body part(s), 4th degree part, 149 (VN), 151
  - twist, 189
  - - change of direction, 51 (LN)
Bortoluzzi, Paolo, 1
Bournonville, August, 6
Bourrée, pas de, 165 (VN)
British Dance and Movement Notation Society, 7
British Library, xi, 3, 7, 146

Cancellation, *see* Validity
Cancelling accidentals, 163 (VN), 165-166 (VN), 173 (VN)
Canon, 20, 36-37
Cantoria, 8, 10 (ill.), 179
Career, early of Nijinsky, 3-6
Carrying the dress, 192
  - veil, 29, 38, 192
Cast, 12, 14, 177-178
Casting, 32
Catching the dress, 39-40
Cecchetti, Enrico, 5,
  - classroom exercises, 8, 9 (ill.), 172, 179
Champs-Elysées, Théâtre des, 5, 177
Change of direction for body with twist, 51 (LN)
  - system of reference key, 188
Chastising, 33, 44, 67 (ill.)
Châtelet, Théâtre du, 4-5, 177
Chemise, 30
Chest, 153
  - (augmented), column for, 51 (LN)
  - indication for, 149 (VN)
  - rotation, 155-156 (VN)
  - symbol in parentheses, 53 (LN)
  - system of reference for, 25
  - tilts, 51 (LN)
  - twist, 23, 52
Chief nymph, 5, 32, 35, 59-65 (ill.), 153, 158, 163, 182, 184, 186, 188
  - with angled thumb, 27
Chopiniana, 4
Choreographer, Nijinsky as, 4-5
Chronology, of Nijinsky's notation experience, 179
  - of performances, 177-178
Cléopâtre, 4
Coliseum, Fort Worth, 178
Colon, Teatro, Buenos Aires, 178
Comparison of definitive and memory-based versions, 19-21, 43, 194
Contact, 167 (VN), 182, 193
  - heel, 18-19, 48 (LN), 160 (VN)
  - in standing, 157 (VN)
  - resultant, 48 (LN)
  - whole foot, 162
Contraction of torso, 23 (LN), 41, 46, 51 (LN)
Convention Hall, Kansas City, 178
Cook, Ray, 11
Costumes, 14, 55 (LN), 58-69 (ill.)

Costumes, size of, 30
Crescendo, 34
Croisé leap, 40
'Crooked' position for arms, 24, 38-39, 41, 46
Crossed arms, 168 (VN)
Crouch position, 34, 37, 161 (VN)
Crouching step, 37
Curved arm, 28
  - hand, 28, 35, 39, 42, 182

Dance, description of, 24, 26, 33-46
DBP, *see* Direction from Body Part
Debussy, Claude, xi, 4, 19, 192-193
Deciphering Nijinsky's *Faune,* 7-11, 192-194
Decline, Nijinsky's, 6
Definitive version vs. memory-based, 19-21, 43, 46, 194
Demi-plié, 48 (LN), 166 (VN)
Description of the dance, 24, 26, 33-46
Deviation in step direction, 49 (LN), 193
Devouring the grapes, 2, 34
Diagonal directions, 150 (VN)
Diaghilev program, 11
Diaghilev, Serge, 4-5, 18
Diary, Nijinsky's, 6
Dionysus, 21
Direction(s), from Body Part, 51 (LN)
  - change of, with body twist, 51 (LN)
  - diagonal, 150 (VN)
  - description for arms, 26
  - deviation in step, 49 (LN)
  - of fingers, 151 (VN)
  - of hand, 156
  - intermediate, arms, 49 (LN)
  - of minor parts of body, 151 (VN)
  - progression of, 150 (VN)
  - stage, 25-26, 161, 172, 193
  - of travel, indication of 163 (VN), 193
Directional description for arms, 26
Dot, placement, (dotted notes), 170 (VN)
Dotted notes, 147 (VN), 170 (VN)
Drawings, 57
Dress, *see also* veil, 29-30, 182
  - carrying, 192
  - catching, 39-40
  - dropping, 39-40, 42, 181
  - holding up against body, 31, 39-42, 186
  - - and relating to, x (ill.)
  - laying down, 46, 70 (ill.)
  - picking up, 40, 42, 44, 68-69 (ill.), 181
  - smelling, 46, 69 (ill.), 181
  - undoing, 39, 181
Drinking the grapes, 2, 34
Dropping the dress, 39-40, 42, 181
  - the veil, 37
Dynamics, 54 (LN)

INDEX

Ear, 'listening', 52 (LN)
Early Memoirs, 2, 4, 179, 194
Echappé sauté, 166 (VN)
Emphasis, 54 (LN)
Encounter, 63 (ill.), 184, 194
Entrances, 47 (LN), 168 (VN)
Epaulement, 157 (VN)
Eshkol, Noa, 7-8
Eshkol-Wachmann system of notation, 179
Exits, 47 (LN), 168 (VN), 184, 186, 193
Expression, 2, 19, 23, 34-35, 40-41, 43, 182, 184, 186, 188, 194
  - 'off duty', 2, 188
  - 'on duty', 2, 36, 188
Extension, ankle, 159
  - foot, 160, 182, 186
  - instep, 159
  - three-dimensional of mouth, 52 (LN)
Eyes, 52 (LN), 188

Faun, 21, 32, 189, 192-194
  - angled thumb, 27
  - description of actions, 33-46
  - expression, 19
  - illustrations, 58-70
  - relationship with nymphs, 21, 184, 186
Faune, see Après-midi d'un Faune, L'
'Feathering' steps, 37, 184
Feet, positions of the, *see also* Foot, 157-158 (VN)
Festin, Le, 4
Film of Nijinsky's *Faune*, 7
Finger(s), direction and level, 151 (VN)
  - flexion, 155 (VN)
  - folding, 28
  - indication of, 149 (VN)
  - validity, 53 (LN)
Flat body, 2, 17, 186, 188
  - hands, 2, 17, 26-27, 39-40, 48, 50 (LN), 155 (VN), 167 (VN), 186
Flexion of ankle, 19, 40, 50 (LN), 151 (VN), 154 (VN), 160, 166
  - arms, 151 (VN)
  - fingers, 155 (VN)
  - head, (term), 154 (VN)
  - legs, 151 (VN)
  - torso, 153 (VN)
  - wrist, 48, 50 (LN), 153 (VN)
Floor plans, 47-48 (LN), 191-193
Flow, free, 53-53 (LN)
Flute, 16
  - handling, 33-34
  - holding, 29, 155, 167, 180
  - lifting, 58 (ill.)
  - minor shift of, 49 (LN), 59 (ill.)
  - picking up, 34
  - putting down, 37, 180
Fokine, Mikhail, 4, 18

Fold, wrist, 27, 50 (LN)
  - - combined with curved hand, 28
Folding of fingers, 28
  - timing of, 50 (LN)
Foot, ball, 48 (LN), 159 (VN), 182
  - extended, 160, 182, 186
  - heel, 18-19, 48 (LN), 160 (VN)
  - half-toe, 158, 184
  - high half-toe, 158-159 (VN), 162-163 (VN), 182, 184
  - indication of 149 (VN)
  - instep, 154 (VN), 159, 160 (VN), 192
  - - on floor, 48 (LN)
  - parts of, use, 158 (VN)
  - *pointe*, 158, 160-161 (VN)
  - pointed, sign for, 163 (VN)
  - positions of, 157-158 (VN)
  - toe, 149 (VN), 157 (VN)
  - - nail of, 48 (LN)
  - whole, 157 (VN), 159 (VN), 162
Forehead, sign for, 50, 52 (LN)
Frieze, 2, 35

Gazing, 176 (VN)
Glassman, William, 11
Gliding steps, 37
Gorsky, Alexander, 145, 147
Grace notes, 151 (VN), 155 (VN)
Grand battement, 172 (VN)
  - *jeté en tournant*, 1
  - *plié*, 159 (VN)
Grands Ballets Canadiens, Les, 11
Grapes, 16
  - devouring, 2, 34
  - drinking, 2, 34
  - handling, 34
  - holding, 29
  - looking at, 2, 58 (ill.), 180
  - picking up, 29, 167, 180
  - putting down, 29, 172 (VN), 180
  - smelling, 34
Gravity, *see* Weight
Gross Hugo, Valentine, 57

Hahn, Reynaldo, 6, 145
Half-toe, 158, 184
  - high, 158-159 (VN), 162-163 (VN), 182, 184
Hand(s) curved, 28, 35, 39, 42, 182
  - - combined with wrist fold, 28
  - directions for, 156
  - flat, 2, 17, 26-27, 39-40, 48, 50 (LN), 155 (VN), 167 (VN), 186
  - 'holding', 28, 39, 48, 50 (LN), 155 (VN), 193
  - indication of, 149 (VN)
  - 'linked', 28, 34, 38, 44, 50 (LN)
  - palms facing, 28, 176 (VN)

Hand(s), pointing, 42, 66 (ill.)
- positions, 26
- spread, 27, 39
- validity, 53 (LN)
Handling of flute, 33-34
- of grapes, 34
- of veil, 25, 30, 42, 54, 192-193
Head, 173 (VN)
- 'alert', 2, 21-22 (LN), 35-39, 42, 51-53 (LN), 188
- alignment, 188
- bending ('flexion'), 154 (VN)
- direction, 156
- forehead, sign for, 50, 52 (LN)
- inclining, 19, 21, 39-46, 154 (VN), 173 (VN), 188
- - combined with turn, 22
- indication of, 149 (VN)
- 'listening', 33, 52 (LN)
- minor tilt, 51 (LN)
- position(s), 22, 182
- rotation, 155-156 (VN)
- systems of reference for, 25
- validity, 53 (LN)
Heel, contact, 18-19, 48 (LN), 160 (VN)
Hodson, Millicent, 3
Hofoperntheater, K. K., Wein, 177
Holding the dress, 40, 42, 180-181, 182
- - and relating to, x (ill.)
- - up against the body, 31, 39-42, 186
- the flute, 29, 155, 167, 180
- the grapes, 29, 180
- hands, 28, 39, 48, 50 (LN), 155 (VN), 181, 193
- positions, 171
- up the veil, 60 (ill.)
- the veil against the body, 31, 155
Hutchinson Guest, Ann, x, 7-11

Imperial Schools (St. Petersburg & Moscow), 7, 179
Imperial Theatres (St. Petersburg), 3
Inclining the head, 19, 21, 39-41, 43-46, 154 (VN), 173 (VN), 188
- - combined with turn, 22
- torso, 184
Instep, 160 (VN)
- extension, 159
- on the floor, 48 (LN), 192
Intermediate directions (arms), 49 (LN)

Jeschke, Claudia, x, 7-8
Jeté en tournant (grand), 1
Jeux, 5
'Joyful' nymph, 5, 14, 33, 35, 39, 59 (ill.), 62 (ill.), 166, 184, 194
- facial expression, 19
- spread hands, 27
Juilliard Dance Ensemble, 11
Juilliard School, 11

Jumping, 166 (VN)

Key(s), 54 (LN), 188-191
- for arms, 25-26, 172 (VN)
- Body, 25, 172, 188
- change of system of reference, 188
- for chest, 25
- for direction, 172 (VN)
- for head, 25
- for staff, 148 (VN)
- Stance, 25, 54 (LN), 172, 182, 188-191
- Standard, 25, 54 (LN), 188-191
- used in VN System, 152, 172-173
Kneeling, 158
Kunstanstalt Gerber catalogue, 8

Labanotation, 11, 19-31, 151, 191
- comparison with Nijinsky's notation, 149-167, 175
- glossary, 47-54
- usages, 55-56
- used in teaching notes, 183-187
- wording in score, 56
Landing from spring, 59 (ill.)
Laughing, 44, 52 (LN), 54 (LN), 68 (ill.)
Laying down the dress, 46, 70 (ill.)
Leap, *croisé*, 40
- goat-like, 40
Legat, Nicolaeva, 7
Leg(s) flexion, 151 (VN)
- key, 172 (VN)
- lower, 149 (VN), 156
- rotation, 48 (LN)
- upper, 148 (VN), 155
Length of step, 175 (VN), 186, 191
Levels for 1st degree parts, 149 (VN)
Lifting the flute, 58 (ill.)
Limb(s), right and left, 148 (VN)
- lower, 149 (VN), 151 (VN), 156 (VN), 186
- - rotation, 50 (LN), 151 (VN), 155, 157 (VN)
- upper, 148 (VN), 150 (VN), 155 (VN)
- - rotation, 50 (LN), 151 (VN), 155-156 (VN)
'Linked' hands, 28, 34, 38, 44, 50 (LN)
'Listening' (head), 33, 52 (LN)
Locomotion, 162 (VN)
Looking, 52 (LN), 176 (VN), 188
- at grapes, 2, 58 (ill.)
Lying, 158, 160, 192

Major parts of body, 148 (VN)
'Marking the ground', 43
Markus, Emilia, 5
Maryinsky Theatre, 3-4
Maryinsky Theatre School, 145
Massine, Leonide, 8, 18
Maturity of Nijinsky, 5

Measure numbers, 47 (LN)
Meeting line, 47 (LN)
Memory-based vs. definitive version, 19-21, 43, 46, 194
Menegatti, Beppe, 11
Meter, 47 (LN)
Meyer, Adolf de, 1-2, 7-8, 17, 19, 23, 30, 34, 36, 55, 57, 155, 188, 193-194
Minor parts of the body, 148 (VN)
 - - directions of, 151 (VN)
 - shift (flute), 49 (LN), 59 (ill.)
 - tilt (head), 51 (LN)
Miscellaneous indications, 169 (VN)
Modification of traveling, 164 (VN)
Mood, 21, 32, 36-40, 44, 46, 182, 184, 186, 188, 194
Mouth, sign for, (extension), 52 (LN)
Movement notation, Nijinsky's, 6, 141-176, 179, 182, 186, 188, 191, 192
Municipal, Teatro, Rio de Janeiro, 178
Municipal, Teatro, Sao Paolo, 178
Music, xi, 2, 4-5, 19-20, 36, 38-39, 41-43, 182, 184, 191-193
 - notation , use of, 169-172 (VN)
 - notes, use of, 145, 147 (VN)
 - recording, 20, 191
 - tape (rehearsal aid), 32
 - theme, 34, 193
Mythology, 21

National Endowment for the Humanities, 8
Naturals 163 (VN), 165- 166 (VN), 173 (VN)
Nelidova, Lydia, 5, 32
New York Times, 18
Nijinska, Bronislava, 2-5, 33, 179, 194
Nijinsky Centenary Program, 11
 - Kyra, 5
 - Romola (de Pulsky), 5, 8, 11, 13
 - Stanislav, 3
 - Thomas Lavrientievitch, 3
 - Vaslav, xi, xii, 1-13, 17-21, 23-25, 27-29, 31-33, 35, 38, 46, 55-56, 59, 140 (ill.), 141, 145-147, 149, 151, 154, 157-161, 165-173, 175, 177-180, 182-188, 192-194
Notation, Nijinsky's system of, xii, 1-7, 9 (ill.), 10 (ill.), 18, 20, 28, 35, 142 (ill.), 141-176, 179, 182, 186, 188, 191, 192
Note(s), dotted, 147 (VN), 170 (VN)
 - grace, 151 (VN), 155 (VN)
 - music, use of, 147 (VN)
 - tied, 174 (VN)
Notebooks, 6-8
Nymph(s), 32-33, 59-67 (ill.), 188-189, 192, 194
 - chief, 5, 32, 35, 59-65 (ill.), 153, 158, 163, 182, 184, 186, 188, 193
 - - with angled thumb, 27
 - description of dance, 34-46, 59-60 (ill.)

Nymph(s), 'joyful', 5, 14, 33, 35, 39, 59 (ill.), 62 (ill.), 166, 184, 194
 - - facial expression, 19
 - - spread hands, 27
 - key for, 173 (VN)
 - relationship with faun, 21

Off-beat steps, 20, 38-39, 162 (VN), 170, 182
'Off duty' expression, 2, 188
On-beat steps, 38-39, 170 (VN)
'On duty' expression, 2, 36, 188
Opening pose, 58 (ill.)
Opera House, Boston, 178
Opera House, Manhattan, 6, 178
Opera House, Providence, Rhode Island, 178
Opera House, Royal, London, 177
Opéra de Monte Carlo, 177
Operahàz, Magyar Allami, Budapest, 177
Opernhaus, Königliches, Dresden, 177
Operntheater, Neues Königliches, Berlin, 177
Orientation, 37, 51-52 (LN), 161 (VN)
 - stage, 61, 193

'Paddling' steps, 37, 184, 189
Palace Theatre, 5
Palm facing, 26, 176 (VN)
Pan, 21
Panpipe, 14, 16
Paris Opéra, 7
Paris Opéra Library, 8
Park, Dame Merle, 11
Pas de bourrée, 165 (VN)
Pavillon d'Armide, Le, 4
'Pawing' steps, 40, 43
Performances of *Faune*, 177-178
Pelvis, indication of, 148 (VN), 150 (VN)
Petipa, Marius, 4
Petits battements sur le cou-de-pied, 161 (VN)
Petrouchka, 4
Photographs, xi, 28, 34, 55 (LN), 57-70, 140, 152-153, 188, 193-194
Picking up the dress, 40, 42, 44, 68-69 (ill.), 181
 - the flute, 34, 180
 - the grapes, 29, 34, 167, 180
 - the veil, 29, 31, 38, 50 (LN), 61 (ill.), 180-181, 192
Pirouettes, 165 (VN), 188
Pitt Theatre, Pittsburgh, 178
Plié, demi-, 48 (LN), 166 (VN)
 - *grand*, 159 (VN)
Pointe, 158 (VN), 160-161
Pointing thumb/hand, 42, 66 (ill.)
Position(s), of arms, 37-38
 - - 'crooked', 24, 38-39, 41, 46
 - - crossed, 168 (VN)
 - - frequently used, 24

Position(s) of arm(s), practising, 37-38, 56 (LN), 182, 184, 186, 188, 193
- crouch, 34, 37, 161 (VN)
- of feet, 157-158 (VN)
- of hands, 26
- of head, 22, 182
- holding, 171
- reminders, 55 (LN)
Practising arm positions, 56, 182, 184, 186, 188
- walks, 56 (LN), 182, 193
'Prancing' steps, 37
Precise timing, 169 (VN), 194
Prélude à l'Après-midi d'un Faune, 4, 19, 20, 191
Press, 54 (LN)
Production(s) of Nijinsky's *Faune*, 11
- notes, 13-16
Progression of directions, 150 (VN)
Properties, 14
Props, 16, 29
Pulsky, Romola de, 5, 11, 13
Putting down the flute, 37, 180
- the grapes, 29, 172 (VN), 180

Rallentando, 192
Rambert, Marie, 7
Rehearsal aids, 32
Relating, indications for, 176 (VN)
- to the dress while holding, x (ill.), 192
Relationship between faun and nymphs, 21
Reminders of positions, 55 (LN)
Repeat signs, 171-172 (VN), 192
Resultant contact, 48 (LN)
Revival of *Faune*, 8-11
Ritardando, 20
Robbia, Luca Della, 8, 10, 179
Rock (set), 16, 33, 38-39, 45
'Rosetta Stone' materials, 8
Rotation, 151 (VN), 155 (VN)
- arms, 50 (LN)
- chest, 155-156 (VN)
- head, 155-156 (VN)
- legs, 48 (LN)
- lower limb, 50 (LN), 151 (VN), 155, 157 (VN), 186
- upper limb, 156 (VN)
Royal Academy of Dancing College, 11
Royal Ballet School, 11
Royal, Theatre, Drury Lane, London, 178
Rubato, 20
Rules, 173-174 (VN)
Ryman, Rhonda, 11

Sacre du Printemps, Le, 3, 5
Saint-Léon, Arthur, 6, 145, 193
Saison Nijinsky, 5
San Carlo Teatro, 11

Sarabande, 8-9
Satyr, 21
Schéhérazade, 4
Score, 5, 13, 28, 71-139 (LN), 142 (ill.), 145, 188, 191, 193
- adjustments made in transcription, 11, 25, 146, 192-194
- interpreting, x (ill.), 55 (LN)
- introduction to, 55 (LN)
- wording in, 56 (LN)
Scoring, 47 (LN)
Set, 13-16, 40
Shape of arm, 24
Shift, center of weight, 53 (LN)
- minor, of flute, 49 (LN), 59 (ill.)
Shoulder movements, 23, 157 (VN)
Sitting up, 60 (ill.)
Skaggs Foundation, 8
Smelling the dress, 46, 69 (ill.)
- the grapes, 34
Sokolova, Lydia, 17, 19-20
Spatial indications, 149 (VN)
Spectre de la Rose, Le, 4
Spread hands, 27, 39
Spring, 35
- landing from, 59 (ill.)
Springing, 166 (VN)
Springy steps, 37, 39, 43, 184, 186
Staff, 193
- key for, 148 (VN)
Stage area, 16
- directions, 25-26, 161 (VN), 172
- numbers, 165 (VN)
- orientation, 52 (LN), 161 (VN), 193
- set, 13-16, 40
Stance Key, 25, 54 (LN), 172, 182, 188-191
Standard Key, 25-26, 54 (LN), 188-191
Standing, contact in, 157 (VN)
Step(s), crouching, 37
- direction, deviation in, 49 (LN), 193
- 'feathering', 37, 184
- 'gliding', 37
- length of, 175 (VN), 186, 191
- off-beat, 20, 38-39, 162 (VN), 170, 182
- on-beat, 38-39, 170 (VN)
- 'paddling', 37, 184, 189
- 'pawing', 40, 43
- prancing, 37
- springy, 37, 39, 43, 186
- timing, 20, 182, 184
- walking, 28-29
Stepanov, Vladimir Ivanovitch, 6, 145-147, 162, 166, 169, 172, 179
St. Moritz, 6, 145
St. Petersburg, 3, 7
Stretching, 49 (LN)
Strong, 54 (LN)
Struss, Karl, 1, 8, 19, 62-65

Style, Details on Movement - and Usage, 21-32
  - of gestures, 17
  - introduction to overall, 17-21
  - of performance, 2
  - of walk, 18, 28, 48, 56 (LN), 182, 193
Support(s), steps, 48 (LN)
Supporting on arms, 158 (VN)
  - on parts of the body, 158 (VN)
Suvretta Hotel, 6
Sylphides, Les, 4, 18
Systems of reference, *see* Keys

Tape (rehearsal aid), 32
Teaching notes, 182-191
Thumb, abduction, 34, 40, 42, 44
  - angled, 27, 34, 40-42, 44, 46, 50 (LN), 66 (ill.), 151 (VN/LN)
  - base joint, 50 (LN)
  - pointing, 42, 66 (ill.)
  - validity, 53 (LN)
Tied notes, 174 (VN)
Till Eulenspiegel, 6, 140
Tilt, chest, 51 (LN)
  - minor of head, 51 (LN)
  - torso, 51 (LN)
Timing, 147 (VN), 192-193
  - of arm gestures, 20
  - of folding, 50 (LN)
  - music notation, use of, 147, 169 (VN), 172
  - off-beat, 162 (VN), 182
  - precise, 37, 169 (VN), 194
  - of steps, 20, 182, 184
  - uneven, 38
  - unit, 20
Toe, 157 (VN)
  - half, 158
  - - high, 158-159 (VN), 162-163 (VN), 182, 184
  - indication of direction and level, 149 (VN), 151
  - nail, 48 (LN)
Tombé, 29
Topaz, Muriel, 11
Torso, 51 (LN)
  - 'alert', 17
  - contraction, 23 (LN), 41, 46, 51 (LN)
  - flexion, 153 (VN)
  - indication of, 148 (VN)
  - tilt, 51 (LN), 184
Touching, 158 (VN), 167 (VN), 193
Transcription of score, 11, 25, 146
  - adjustments made in, 192-194
Translation of Nijinsky word notes, 12-15, 180-181
Travel, direction of, (indication of), 163 (VN), 193
Traveling, modification of, 164 (VN)
Turn, amalgamated, 49 (LN)
  - of head, combined with incline, 22
Turning, 165 (VN)

Twist of the body, 51 (LN)
  - of the chest, 23, 52

Undergarment, 30
Undoing the dress, 39, 59 (ill.)

Validity, 53 (LN), 147 (VN), 173-174 (VN)
  - fingers, 53 (LN)
  - hands, 53 (LN)
  - head, 53 (VN)
  - thumb, 53 (LN)
Veil, *see also* Dress, 29-30
  - carrying, 29, 38
  - dropping, 37, 180
  - handling of, 25, 30, 42, 54, 180, 192-193
  - holding against body, 31, 155
  - holding up, 60 (ill.)
  - on floor, 29, 37
  - picking up, 29, 31, 38, 50 (LN), 61 (ill.), 180
  - wearing, 30
Virtuoso movements, 188
'V'-shape (arms), 25-26, 34, 38-40, 44-45

Waist, 51 (LN), 153
Walking, 162 (VN), 182, 184
  - practising, 56, 182
  - steps, 28-29
  - style of, 18, 28, 48, 56 (LN), 182
Waterloo University, 11
Weight, 27-28
  - center of, (shift), 53 (LN)
Weight-bearing, 158 (VN)
Whole foot, 157 (VN), 159 (VN), 162
Woizikowski, Leon, 7
Word instructions, Nijinsky's, 1, 28-29, 31, 38-39, 45-46, 167, 180-181
  - translation of 12-15, 180-181
Wording in the Labanotation score, 56
Wrist(s) abduction, 27, 34, 40, 50 (LN), 151 (VN), 153-154 (VN)
  - adduction, 153 (VN)
  - angled, 37-39, 41, 50 (LN), 186
  - crossing, 50 (LN)
  - flexion, 48, 50 (LN), 153 (VN)
  - fold, 27, 50 (LN)
  - - combined with curved hand, 28
  - validity, 53 (LN)

'Z-caret', 163 (VN)

www.ingramcontent.com/pod-product-compliance
Ingram Content Group UK Ltd.
Pitfield, Milton Keynes, MK11 3LW, UK
UKHW010704260225
455599UK00010B/37